WORLD HISTORY

The Easy Way

VOLUME ONE

ANCIENT AND MEDIEVAL TIMES TO A.D. 1500

Charles A. Frazee
Professor of History
California State University, Fullerton

BARRON'S

All inquiries should be addressed to:
Barron's Educational Series, Inc.
250 Wireless Boulevard
Hauppauge, NY 11788
http://www.barronseduc.com

Library of Congress Catalog Card No. 97-14772

ISBN-13: 978-0-8120-9765-8
ISBN-10: 0-8120-9765-3

Library of Congress Cataloging-in-Publication Data

Frazee, Charles A.
   World history the easy way / Charles A. Frazee.
      p.   cm.— (The easy way)
   Includes index.
   Contents: v.1. Ancient and medieval times to
A.D. 1500 — v.2. A.D. 1500 to present.
   ISBN 0-8120-9765-3 (v.1). — ISBN 0-8120-9766-1 (v.2)
   1. World history.   I. Title.   II. Series
D21.F868   1997
909.07—dc21   97-14772
                                                CIP

PRINTED IN THE UNITED STATES OF AMERICA

19 18 17 16 15 14 13 12 11

Contents

Introduction   xii
Acknowledgments   xiii

UNIT ONE   BEGINNINGS—2,000,000–3500 B.C.

Chapter 1   The First Humans   3

The Search for the First People   3
Homo erectus   3
Neandertals   7
Homo sapiens   8
Cro-Magnons   9
Language and Race   10
Inventions of the Cro-Magnons   11
Cro-Magnon Artists   12
Conclusion   13
Review   14

Chapter 2   The New Stone Age   17

Town Life   17
Jericho and Çatal Hüyük   18
Invention of Farming   20
Animal Herding   22
Technology in the New Stone Age   24
Megalith Builders   25
Conclusion   26
Review   28

UNIT TWO   THE FIRST CIVILIZATIONS—3500–1200 B.C.

Chapter 3   The Fertile Crescent   33

Tigris and Euphrates Valley   34
Towns of Ancient Sumer   34
Sumerian Religion   35
Development of Writing   37
Economic Activity   38
Culture in Ancient Sumer   40
Invaders in Mesopotamia   41
Anatolian Civilization   43
Hittites   43
Building the Hittite Empire   44
Syrian Peoples   45
Conclusion   46
Review   47

Chapter 4   Ancient Egypt   51

Nile Valley   51
Earliest Egypt   52
Old Kingdom   54
Religion in Egyptian Life   56
Arts of Egypt   59
Middle Kingdom   59
Hyksos Period   60
New Kingdom   60
Religious Reform of Akhenaten   61
Egypt's Decline   62
Conclusion   63
Review   64

Chapter 5   The First Indian Civilization   67

Geography of India   67
Peoples of the Indus Valley   68
Two Great Cities of the Indus Valley   69
The Indus Valley Economy   71
Aryans Arrive   72
Conclusion   73
Review   74

Chapter 6   Prehistoric China   75

Geography of China   75
Chinese Origins   76
Chinese Religion   78
Chinese Writing   79
Shang Dynasty   79
Conclusion   80
Review   81

Chapter 7   Mediterranean Regions in the Ancient World   83

Cycladic Origins   83
Discovery of Minoan Civilization   85
Minoans   85
Indo-European Migrations   88
Mycenaeans   90
Rest of Europe   91
Conclusion   92
Review   93

Chapter 8   The First Americans   95

Hunters of the Americas   95
Developments in Mexico   96
South America   97
Conclusion   97
Review   98

UNIT THREE   CLASSICAL WORLDS—1200 B.C.–A.D. 500

Chapter 9   Southwest Asia in a Time of Empires   101

Assyrians   101
Babylonians   102
Peoples of Syria   103
Hebrews   104
The Hebrew Bible   104
Hebrew Beginnings   105
Exodus from Egypt   106
Hebrew Monarchy   107
Foreign Conquest   108
Phoenicians and Arameans   109
Persians   111
Persian Culture in Achaemenid Times   112
Anatolia   113
Conclusion   115
Review   116

Chapter 10   India's Classical Age   120

Political Life of the Aryans   120
Brahman Religion   120
Upanishads   122
Classes and Castes   123
Jains Challenge the Brahmans   124
Buddha   125
Invasions from the West   127
Mauryan Empire   127
Ashoka   129
South India   130
Gupta Empire   131
Sri Lanka   133
Conclusion   133
Review   134

Chapter 11   China and Its Neighbors   137

Later Shang Period   137
Scribes and Silk   138
Zhous Come to Power   139
Confucius   140
Laozi and Meng Ko   141
China During Qin Dynasty   142
Han China   144
Han Court   146
Arrival of Buddhism   146
Later Han Period   147
Three Kingdoms   148
China's Neighbors   149
Conclusion   150
Review   151

Chapter 12   The Rise of Greek Civilization   154

Dorian Invasion   155
Greek Renaissance   155
Colonization   156
Athens   157
On the Road to Democracy   157
Sparta   159
Persian Attack   160
Peloponnesian War   162
Architecture of Ancient Greece   163
Theater   164
The Arts   165
Philosophers   166
Science   169
Religion   170
Athletics   171
Conclusion   172
Review   173

Chapter 13   Alexander the Great and Hellenism in Southwestern Asia   177

Rise of Macedonia   177
Alexander   178
Hellenistic World   180
Conclusion   182
Review   183

Chapter 14   The Roman Republic   185

Italian Peninsula   186
Peoples of Italy   186
Early Rome   188
Formation of the Republic   189
Conflict of the Orders   190
Roman Society   190
Roman Expansion   191
Coming of the Romans to Southwestern Asia   194
Jews and Romans   194
Roman Religion   195
Political and Economic Problems of the Late Republic   196
Europe's Other Peoples   198
Conclusion   199
Review   200

Chapter 15   The Roman Empire   203

Augustan Age   203
Successors of Augustus   205
Jesus of Nazareth   206
Christians   207
Second Century   208

Roman Buildings   209
Entertainment in Rome   211
Armenians and Persians   212
Pax Romana Evaluated   212
Rome in Jeopardy   213
Diocletian and Constantine   215
Rome Under Attack   217
Progress of Christianity   217
Western Problems   219
Germans in Italy   221
Conclusion   222
Review   223

Chapter 16   African Societies   227

Invaders in Egypt   227
Kush   228
Hellenistic Egypt   230
Carthage and North Africa   231
Egypt Under the Romans   231
Roman North Africa   233
Bantu   234
Axum   235
Conclusion   235
Review   236

Chapter 17   Indian Civilizations of the Americas   238

Olmec Civilization   238
City of Teotihuacán   241
Mayan Achievements   242
Religion of the Mayans   244
Writing   244
South America's Pacific Coast   245
Chavín Culture   245
Conclusion   247
Review   248

UNIT FOUR   EXPANDING HORIZONS—A.D. 500–1100

Chapter 18   The Islamic World of Southwest Asia   253

Arabian Peninsula   253
Prophet Muhammad   255
After Muhammad   258
Byzantine–Persian Conflict   258
Arab Conquests   258
Umayyad Caliphate   259
Life Under the Caliphate   261
Abbasid Caliphs   262
Turks Enter the Muslim World   264
Conclusion   266
Review   267

Chapter 19   The Early Middle Ages in India   270

A Period of Migrations   270
Developments Within Hinduism   271
Muslim Invasions   272
Conclusion   274
Review   275

Chapter 20   East Asian Traditions   277

China Under the Sui Dynasty   277
Golden Age of the Tangs   278
Architecture and Arts   281
Literature of the Tang Period   282
Astronomy and Inventions   283
Religion   284
Later Tang Emperors   285
Song China   285
Economic Activity in Song China   287
Cultural Life   288
Chinese Influences Reach Japan   289
Introduction of Buddhism into Japan   290
The Great Reform   291
Building the Capital at Nara   292
Heian Japan, A World at Peace   292
Asian Neighbors of China   294
Conclusion   295
Review   296

Chapter 21   African Kingdoms   300

Muslims in Egypt   300
South of the Sahara   301
Ghana, The First West African Kingdom   301
Axum   304
Conclusion   305
Review   306

Chapter 22   The Early Middle Ages in Europe   308

Byzantine World   308
Justinian and Theodora   309
Struggle Over the Balkans   312
Daily Life in Byzantine Times   313
The Byzantine Church   316
Ireland   318
England   319
English Missions to the Continent   320
Merovingian France   321
Italy and the Papacy   322
Western Monasticism   323
Conclusion   324
Review   325

Chapter 23   The Age of Charlemagne   328

Charlemagne   328
Carolingian Renaissance   331
Empire Divided   331
Northmen   332
Viking Raiders   333
Feudal Order   336
Farmers and Merchants in Carolingian Europe   337
Islamic Spain   340
Byzantine Culture and the Slavs   342
Missions to the Slavs   343
Magyars   345
Orthodox and Catholics   346
Conclusion   346
Review   347

Chapter 24   Western Recovery and East European Awakening   351

Holy Roman Empire of the German Nation   351
Cluny and Church Reformation   355
Peoples of the Iberian Peninsula   358
Normans   359
Italy Turns to Commerce   361
Byzantine Empire and the First Crusade   362
Eastern Europe   365
Society in Medieval Europe   368
Work in Medieval Europe   370
Arts and Literature   372
Conclusion   374
Review   376

Chapter 25   Developments in the Americas   380

Disasters in Mexico   380
Toltecs Dominate Mexico   381
Mississippian Culture in North America   382
Events in South America   383
Nazca, Chimu, and Moche   383
Conclusion   385
Review   386

UNIT FIVE   CHANGING TRADITIONS—A.D. 1100–1500

Chapter 26   Crusaders, Turks, and Mongols   391

Latin East   391
Mongols   394
Formation of the Ottoman State   396
Conclusion   397
Review   398

Chapter 27   The Late Middle Ages in India and Southeast Asia   400

Islam and Hinduism   400
Slave Dynasty of Delhi   402
Sri Lanka and Southeast Asia   404
Conclusion   405
Review   406

Chapter 28   East Asia in an Age of Khans and Samurai   408

Last Days of Song China   408
Khubilai Khan   408
China's Brilliant Dynasty, the Ming   411
Shoguns of Japan   413
Kamakura Shogunate   415
Korea and Vietnam   417
Conclusion   418
Review   419

Chapter 29   African Empires   422

Mamluk Egypt   422
African Life Among the Blacks   423
Mali   424
Kanem-Bornu and Songhai   425
Forest Kingdoms of Guinea   426
Ethiopia   427
Eastern Africa and the Indian Ocean Trade   428
South Africa   429
Conclusion   430
Review   431

Chapter 30   Europe in the High Middle Ages   433

Revival of Towns   433
Economic Life   436
Intellectual Life and the Birth of the University   437
Cathedrals   440
The Papacy Ascendant   442
Political Events in the British Isles   443
Kingdoms of Continental Europe   445
Fredericks of the Holy Roman Empire   448
Eastern Europe Between Germans and Mongols   450
Byzantium   453
Conclusion   455
Review   456

Chapter 31   Europe's Late Middle Ages and the Early Renaissance   459

Weather and Disease   459
Warfare and Its Consequences   461
Hundred Years' War   461
British Isles   463
Ferdinand and Isabella   464
France   465
Holy Roman Empire   466
Events in Eastern Europe   466
Fall of Constantinople   467
Moscow and the Russian Lands   468
Origins of the Renaissance   470
Humanism   471
Arts and Artists of Italy   473
Printing   475
Daily Life in Renaissance Times   475
Great Western Schism   477
European Exploration and Colonization   478
Christopher Columbus   480
Conclusion   481
Review   483

Chapter 32   Aztecs and Incas   487

Early Aztec History   487
Building Tenochtitlán   487
North of the Rio Grande   489
Inca Empire of South America   489
Society Among the Incas   491
Engineering   492
Conclusion   493
Review   494

Index   496

Introduction

It may be useful for you, the reader, to know the structure of this world history text. I have followed the two dimensions of time and space, placing events of the major regions of the world within a specific period. Although there is some minor overlap, the perimeters of the centuries under consideration are respected, so that the reader may circle the globe surveying contemporary events as they happened.

This book is meant to serve as a text or to supplement a standard volume on world history, which is usually more detailed. In it you will find a blend of information and analysis of politics, economics, religion, society, and the arts. A sample review of test items is at the end of each chapter.

I want to thank my wife, Kathleen, for her inestimable contribution in the preparation of this book.

Charles A. Frazee
June 1997

Acknowledgments

Maps by Mindy Morgan

Chapter One: Homo erectus skull, J. Thompson; hunters, E. Lumba; Levallois point, J. Thompson; funeral, E. Lumba; Stone tools, J. Thompson; Siberians, E. Lumba; Lascaux paintings, French National Tourist Office

Chapter Two: Çatal Hüyük, J. Thompson; llama, K. Frazee; pottery, J. Thompson; Stonehenge, K. Frazee

Chapter Three: Standard of Ur, Courtesy of the Trustees of the British Museum; ziggurat, J. Thompson; Babylonian tablet, Courtesy of Trustees of the British Museum; cart, J. Thompson; Sumerian statues, Oriental Institute of the University of Chicago, Victor J. Boswell, National Geographic Society © 1981; Hammurabi, Nelson-Atkins Museum, Kansas City, Mo.

Chapter Four: Rosetta stone, Courtesy of the Trustees of the British Museum; Nile, Sir Bentley Travel; Egyptian wall painting, Metropolitan Museum of Art, New York; pyramids, Egyptian Authority for the Promotion of Tourism; step pyramid, pyramid, tomb, N. Woodard; Tutankhamon, photography by the Egyptian Expedition, Metropolitan Museum of Art, New York; Abu Simbel, Egyptian Authority for the Promotion of Tourism

Chapter Five: Mohenjo-Daro and baths, Pakistan Department of Archaeology and Museums

Chapter Six: Rice planting, L. Breese; oracle bone, K. Frazee; elephant vessel, Freer Gallery of Art, Smithsonian Institution

Chapter Seven: Cycladic figures, K. Frazee; Knossos, K. Frazee; bull-jumping, Iraklion Museum, Crete; Akrotiri, K. Frazee; dolmen, K. Frazee; Lion Gate, K. Frazee; shaft grave, K. Frazee

Chapter Eight: Corn, J. Thompson; mortar and pestle, J. Thompson; rain forest, W. Engstrom

Chapter Nine: Assyrian sculpture, Courtesy of the Trustees of the British Museum; Sea of Galilee, C. Frazee; priest, J. Thompson; Mt. Sinai, California Museum of Photography; Temple, Holyland Hotel, Jerusalem; Aleppo, C. Frazee; Persians, Oriental Institute of the University of Chicago; Anatolia, K. Frazee; Trojan horse, K. Frazee

Chapter Ten: Priest Information Service of India; Diwali, E. Lumba; temple, S. Frazee; Buddha, S. Scheinberg; stupa, S. Scheinberg; bodhisattva, S. Scheinberg

Chapter Eleven: Bowl, Nelson-Atkins Museum, Kansas City, Mo.; cart, E. Lumba; Confucius, E. Lumba; Great Wall, horses and observatory, Embassy of the Peoples Republic of China; Buddha, L. Breese; landscape, K. Frazee

Chapter Twelve: Odysseus, Courtesy of the Trustees of the British Museum; vase painting, Metropolitan Museum of Art; trireme, J. Thompson; altar, K. Frazee; Erectheum, S. Frazee; theater, K. Frazee; Poseidon, National Archaeological Museum, Athens; gate, K. Frazee; frieze, K. Frazee; runners, Metropolitan Museum of Art, Rogers Fund, 1914; Olympia, S. Frazee

Chapter Thirteen: Lion, Greek Archaeological Service; mosaic, Museo Nazionale, Naples; Ephesus, C. Frazee; Artemis, K. Frazee

Chapter Fourteen: Temples, Etruscans, Forum, Regional Assessor of Tourism for Latium; priestess, Victoria and Albert Museum, London; battle, Art Resource; builders, J. Thompson; menorah, J. Thompson; road, E. Lumba

Chapter Fifteen: Augustus, Vatican Museum; synagogue, C. Frazee; Colosseum, Regional Assessor of Tourism for Latium; Pantheon, R. Miller; aqueduct, N. Woodard; baths, K. Frazee; Marcus Aurelius, Regional Assessor of Tourism for Latium; Constantine, R. Miller; church, R. Miller; Huns, E. Lumba; tomb, K. Frazee

Chapter Sixteen: Karnak, California Museum of Photography; pyramids, J. Thompson; Masai, California Museum of Photography

Chapter Seventeen: Head, W. Puzo; god, E. Lumba; Pyramid of the Sun, G. Shumway; temple, N. Woodard; glyphs, K. Frazee; cup, E. Lumba

Chapter Eighteen: Ka'bah, Aramco; mosque, Pakistan Tourist Development Association; Umayyad mosque, R. Hickman; Dome of the Rock, C. Frazee; minaret, J. Thompson; mosque at Kairouan, J. Thompson; pilgrims, Aramco

Chapter Nineteen: Dancers, S. Scheinberg; temples, Sir Bentley Travel; women and temples, Indian National Tourist Bureau

Chapter Twenty: Taizong, J. Thompson; gate, L. Breese; court lady, Victoria and Albert Museum; Kaifeng, Metropolitan Museum of Art; Silk Road, E. Lumba; silk processors, Courtesy of the Museum of Fine Arts, Boston, Chinese and Japanese Special Fund; Mt. Fuji, J. Thompson; shrine, K. Frazee; temple and palace, Japanese National Tourist Organization; pagoda, K. Frazee

Chapter Twenty-One: Salt workers, J. Thompson; bishop, Christine Molider, RSM, Catholic Near East Welfare Association

Chapter Twenty-Two: Mosaic, Soprindenenza per I beni e architecttonici Di Ravenna; church, K. Frazee; church, N. Woodard; battle, J. Thompson, medallion, Byzantine Visual Resources, © 1990, Dumbarton Oaks, Washington, D.C.; Cypriote church, C. Frazee; gate, C. Frazee; cross, J. Thompson; chalice, National Museum of Ireland, Dublin; Canterbury, L. Andersen; baptism, Granger Collection; Benedict, detail, Mellon Collection, National Gallery of Art, Washington, D.C.

Chapter Twenty-Three: Charlemagne, Granger Collection; coronation, E. Lumba; ship, Granger Collection; tower, K. Frazee; graphic, K. Frazee; farmers, E. Lumba; fields, K. Frazee; merchants, J. Thompson; Córdoba cathedral, Spanish National Tourist Office; Novgorod, C. Frazee

Chapter Twenty-Four: Crown, Kuntshistorische Museum, Vienna; Otto III, Bayerische Staatsbibliotek, Munich; Cluny, N. Woodard; tapestry, Tapisserie de Bayeux et avec autorisation speciale de la ville de Bayeux; cathedral, N. Woodard; Kaisariani, K. Frazee; Compostella, Spanish National Tourist Office; Russian church, C. Frazee; noodle makers, Corbis Bettman Archive; town, J. Thompson; towers, K. Frazee; Italian church, Regional Assessor of Tourism for Latium.

Chapter Twenty-Five: Warrior, J. Thompson; Chichen Itza, Mexican National Tourist Bureau; drawing, J. Thompson; village, Courtesy of New Mexico Latin American Institute, Univ. of N. Mex., Brazilians collection

Chapter Twenty-Six: Holy Sepulchre, C. Frazee; castle, C. Frazee; Cypriote castle, C. Frazee; Mongols, Courtesy of Love Tours; tomb, K. Frazee

Chapter Twenty-Seven: Sunrise, S. Frazee; Shiva, Art Institute of Chicago; priests, C. Frazee; herders, Courtesy of Love Tours; Anghor Wat, Cambodian Embassy; Malaysian mosque, K. Frazee

Chapter Twenty-Eight: Ghengis Khan, J. Thompson; Temple of Heaven, K. Frazee; animals, K. Frazee; samurai, K. Frazee; battle, Seattle Art Museum, Eugene Fuller Memorial Collection; Buddha, J. Thompson; Korean Buddha, K. Frazee

Chapter Twenty-Nine: Village, J. Thompson; Musa, E. Lumba; Female figure, Trustees of the University of Pennsylvania Museum, Philadelphia; Lalibala, E. Lumba; Zimbabwe, W. Puzo

Chapter Thirty: Florentine church, N. Woodard; students, E. Lumba; Aquinas, Art Resource; Notre Dame, French National Tourist Office; Cologne, N. Woodard; Assisi, N. Woodard; Abbey, K. Frazee; Saint Mark, N. Woodard; Warsaw, C. Frazee; Mongols, Corbis Bettman Archive; Amorgos, K. Frazee; walls, C. Frazee

Chapter Thirty-One: St. Sebastian interceding for plague stricken, Walters Art Gallery, Baltimore; army, Granger Collection; Parliament, Windsor Castle Library; Seville cathedral, K. Frazee; Avignon, J. Thompson; Rumeli Hisar, K. Frazee; Novgorod, C. Frazee; Moscow, K. Frazee; Lorenzo Di Medici, il Magnifico, Andrea del Verocchio, National Gallery of Art, Washington, D.C.; Florence, J. Thompson; Mona Lisa, Art Resource; people, J. Thompson; Isabella d'Este, Kunsthistorische Museum, Vienna; astrolabe, K. Frazee; Henry the Navigator, detail, Instituto Portugues do Patrimonio Cultural, Lisbon; Columbus, Metropolitan Museum of Art

Chapter Thirty-Two: chinampas, E. Lumba; sacrifice, Biblioteca Nazionale, Florence; Inca stone work, O. Arana

UNIT 1

BEGINNINGS: 2,000,000–3500 B.C.

CHAPTER 1

The First Humans

Anthropologists now have evidence that the first humans appeared on the earth approximately 2,000,000 years ago. Probably the men and women who made the gigantic leap from animal to human existence lived in Africa, evolving from hominids that walked erect and learned to share food with one another. In A.D. 1995, scholars in Africa announced their latest find of a bipedal hominid, *Australopithecus anamensis*, which pushed back the evolutionary record even farther than had previously been determined.

However, Asian origins for humanity are also possible, for researchers in China and Indonesia recently discovered skull fragments almost as old as those in Africa. No agreement among scientists yet exists on whether the first people appeared only once in a single place or whether humans appeared in different parts of Africa and Asia about the same time.

The Search for the First People

In the nineteenth century many people thought that there must be a "missing link" between humans and apes. One who sought to find that missing link was a Dutchman, Eugene Dubois, a doctor in the East Indies. In A.D. 1891, while exploring a river bank in Java, he found a skull, which he identified as having come from a manlike ape. After more fossils were discovered, he felt confident enough to announce to the scientific world that he had found the missing link. He returned to Europe with the bones he had unearthed, but few anthropologists believed him, and his discovery never obtained proper recognition. What he had discovered were the bones of *Homo erectus*, a true human.

Homo erectus

The name given individuals of these first people is *Homo erectus*, for one of their characteristics was erect posture. Unlike their apelike ancestors, they walked upright, which freed their arms for the many other functions that, as humans, they required.

The cortex, the outer layer of the brain, was much larger than in any other primate. To fit inside the skull, the cortex was folded and overlapped. Since it is in this part of the brain that memory is learned and behavior fashioned, its development was essential for human activity. The brain gives people those characteristics that identify them as humans.

They could remember the past and plan for the future, they could move from cause to effect, and they could use their reason to solve the problems of day-to-day existence. Above all, they could think in abstract terms and had a sense of self at a level that no animal has ever reached. Scientists can say that this occurred; they cannot tell why. Religion and philosophy attempt to provide the answer.

The human body proved to have exceptional qualities. It had a complex spinal cord that passed messages from the brain to the rest of the body instantly. The body's muscles were so arranged that men and women were able to run, walk, swim, or climb. Without the fur or hair that kept other animals warm, humans had to live in tropical regions of the world until they discovered how to use animal skins for warmth. On the other hand, the millions of sweat glands in the human skin provided an excellent cooling system for people when doing hard work in hot climates.

Human eyes were also special. Unlike many animals, humans see objects in color and in three dimensions. Since so much information to the brain comes from eyes, about 90% of the total, the placement of the eyes and their ability to see in the way they do gave humans a great advantage in the struggle for survival.

Anthropologists still do not agree about when exactly humans began to speak, perhaps it was 1,500,000 years ago. The organs for speech were present in the first humans: the larynx, the pharynx, and the tongue, which was attached to the throat in a special way. Combined, these three elements made it possible for humans to produce a wide range of sounds, pitched from very high to very low. The pharynx of *Homo erectus* was not so large as that found in humans today; therefore, the first men and women's capacity to speak was somewhat more restricted.

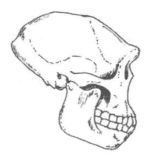

A reconstructed skull of Homo erectus *shows a sloping forehead and deep eye sockets.*

The skull shape of *Homo erectus* had several characteristics that made it a bit different from modern people. *Homo erectus* had a sloping forehead and deep ridges that projected over the eye sockets, a very small chin, and much larger teeth than modern people.

One of the distinguishing features of humans was the long period between the birth of a child and its ability to care for itself. The process requires many years, necessitating a great amount of socialization. The human brain takes 10 years for it to reach 95% of its development. Only at 20 years does the brain achieve full maturity. Parents, especially the mother, create a strong bond with the child, but the father, siblings, relatives, and friends all contribute to early education. The emergence of society was the only way to cope with the weakness of the individual. Mutual support, sharing, and devising ways to settle quarrels without violence contributed to the socialization process.

From the study of *Homo erectus* sites, it appears that many infants died at childbirth or in their early years. At Zhoukoudian in China, there is a cave where *Homo erectus* lived 400,000 years ago. Over half the human bones found there are of children under 14 years of age. Even for adults, life expectancy was probably under 25 years of age. Although many modern diseases were not present, and every indication suggests that the first people had nutritious diets, injuries were frequent. A broken arm or leg was not easily fixed, given the lack of knowledge about setting bones or infection in a wound. Hunting especially for large game, is a dangerous occupation, and many times hunters must have returned without all their party.

In the human species, unlike animals, sexual activity is a matter of the intellect. Custom and culture, the behavior of a society and the values it holds, dictate what is acceptable and what is not. Because choosing a mate can cause confrontation and friction in primates, the closest relatives of humans, students of prehistory surmise that one of the earliest concerns of *Homo erectus* was to put regulations on sexual activity. At an early date incest probably became unacceptable, thereby providing family stability. Choosing a partner from outside the immediate family had an advantage—it bound families together for mutual support.

The world in which *Homo erectus* men and women lived is known as the **Paleolithic Age** or Old Stone Age. It receives its name from the numerous stone tools that were and still are found at places where *Homo erectus* lived. After a stone tool is fashioned, it is almost indestructible. The most frequently found objects are spear points, which men fashioned to put on wooden sticks to hunt, and hand axes, which they used to hammer, hunt, and dig for roots. Hand axes are found in Africa, India, and Europe, but not in east Asia. They were exceptionally effective, which explains why their shapes stayed exactly the same for hundreds of thousands of years.

While men were hunters or fishers, women and children were gatherers. They looked for fruits, nuts, and roots of plants and for insects that could supplement their meat and fish diets. Anthropologists estimate that women furnished about 70% of the family food; nevertheless, because these activities leave no trace, women's contributions have not received the prominence they deserve.

After thousands of years of practice, hunters learned when animals migrated and were easier to kill, and women gatherers knew when wild rice could be harvested at a particular location. Families often lived near streams or lakes where fresh water, along with fish and crustaceans, were easy to secure.

It does not seem that *Homo erectus* men and women knew how to start a fire, that most useful instrument of nature, even though they must have been anxious to use it when they found it. Fire was obtained from a natural source, for example, when lightning struck a tree and started a blaze. At their homes *Homo erectus* families kept a hearth to provide light, warmth, and of course, heat for cooking. They also used fire to smoke food, harden wooden weapons, and dry animal hides. The first evidence of a hearth dates from a half million years ago.

It was probably the task of a woman to keep the fire going, since the only way to rekindle it was to seek out another friendly hunting group that would part with some of its flame. With a now-lighted torch, a courier sent out for fire returned to the hunting band. Sometimes weeks went by with a cold hearth since Old Stone Age bands were always on the move and many miles might separate them.

Cooperation was a key element for the hunters and gatherers of the Old Stone Age. Survival depended upon it. Sharing was more important than storing food or other material goods, which, in any case, were minimal. Therefore, when expeditions went out to look for animals, often much larger and more powerful than humans, a hunting band that was successful had to be sure that everyone knew what to do. Patience, as well as skill, were always required. Fortunately, the ability to speak made hunting easier, for the individuals in the band could alert someone nearby of any change in plans.

The bones of thousands of animals that were killed in a massive hunt can be found at some archaeological sites. Consequently, what occurred can be reconstructed. After hunters spied a herd of horses or elephants, they must have encircled them, passed out burning torches, and then, amid much shouting, rushed upon the animals creating a stampede that led their prey into a valley where there was no escape or over a cliff. So many animals died that there was enough food for weeks. In fact, because it could not all be taken home, the hunters probably smoked much of the meat to preserve it.

An artist reconstructs a scene of Homo erectus *hunters.*

Hunting and gathering societies usually had ample time for their own interests, for as long as there was a store of supplies, men and women could enjoy themselves telling stories, caring for their children, or making tools from stone, wood, or the horns and bones of the animals they killed.

Homo erectus lived on the earth for a very long time, from approximately 2,000,000 years ago until about 300,000 B.C. Over tens of thousand of years, these first people made their homes throughout Africa, Europe, and Asia in bands of 20 to 60 individuals. During this period, only slight modifications in the way people made their tools tell of change.

Gatherers and hunters are usually conservative, not wanting to take a chance with a new weapon or an untried plan. *Homo erectus* men and women must have been content with their way of life, for it offered a great deal of satisfaction.

Probably the most significant challenge came from climatic change, for four times in the last million years the earth became extremely cold during what we call the **Ice Age.** In the Northern Hemisphere great glaciers covered much of the land surface. When this occurred, those *Homo erectus,* living in cold climates, had to migrate toward the tropics. Once the world became warmer, some of the plants that once supplied seed and animals had become extinct, requiring adaptation to new circumstances.

Neandertals

About 230,000 years ago a distinctive type of people who bear the name Neandertal developed. They received their name in A.D. 1856 when the first fossils appeared in the Neander Valley of modern Germany. Their remains are now identified throughout Africa, Asia, and Europe. Most anthropologists believe that they were a type of archaic *Homo sapiens* but were a bit shorter—men were about 5.5 feet tall and women were about 6 inches shorter than the men. The size of their brains were the same as modern people, sometimes even larger, but they were stouter and had a heavier bone structure. The major difference was in their faces, which retained the sloping forehead and heavy eye ridges of *Homo erectus.*

Neandertals had to learn how to live in many different types of climate. When they first appeared, the earth was very warm. Then it turned colder and the kind of animals that they hunted changed from small game to large animals. During severe cold spells they made their homes in caves.

Tool making was a major concern of the Neandertals. They developed a wide variety of stone objects including hammers, awls, and knives. Hand axes similar to those of *Homo erectus* were also very common. Their most creative technique is called Levallois flaking. Finding just the right kind of rock that easily chipped, the tool maker, or **knapper,** shaped the Levallois flake with a stone hammer. The sharp edge produced a tool that could be used as a spear head, a knife, or a scraper. Wherever Levallois flakes are found, it gives evidence of a Neandertal campsite.

A Neandertal knapper's work is seen in the production of a Levallois tool.

The religious life of Neandertals probably paralleled that of modern hunting societies. If that surmise is correct, then they believed that the world was full of both good and evil spirits that they could not see but that actively played a role in their lives. They wanted to keep the good spirits on their side as well as to keep the bad ones at bay. Therefore, they developed rituals to manipulate this unseen world.

In Europe the cave bear, now extinct but much larger than the grizzly, was one of the Neandertal's prey. At several sites anthropologists discovered places where the skulls of the cave bears were neatly arranged in stone pits. This ritual was probably thought to appease the bears' spirits so that hunting these animals in the future would remain successful.

Neandertals place the skulls of bears in a pit.

Burial practices also testify to a belief in life after death. Corpses were buried in graves, sometimes in a horizontal position, sometimes in a fetal one, with grave gifts such as weapons and broken animal bones. One such burial site of 100,000 years ago in Shanidar, Iraq, had a body buried after it had been sprinkled with flowers. Death came early for many members of Neandertal bands, for the men hunted with spears requiring them to jab and thrust them into their prey. They never hit upon the idea of throwing the spear. Most male corpses found in Neandertal graves show numerous wounds and injuries.

About 30,000 years ago the Neandertals disappeared. Their last stand appears in caves located on Gibraltar. No one knows for sure what happened to them. Perhaps they were assimilated into *Homo sapiens sapiens,* all the people who now live on earth. According to some anthropologists, recent studies of DNA in fossils of Neandertals closely match those in modern European populations.

Homo sapiens

At the same time that Neandertals lived, archaic *Homo sapiens* shared the earth with them. Some anthropologists claim that they have found fossils (preserved remains found in the earth or in sedentary rock) that are at least 300,000 years old. If these fossils are correctly identified, then modern men and women have very ancient ancestors. Since fossils this remote from the present are so few and difficult to distinguish from *Homo erectus,* an exact date for the appearance of *Homo sapiens* remains speculative.

Recently some anthropologists, through DNA research, claim that they have found a male and female African ancestor of all people now living. They date their find from about 140,000 years ago. The same gene structure of modern men and women match these samples. Other anthropologists dismiss this idea, claiming that many ancestral groups of modern people exist.

Cro-Magnons

The oldest fossils of *Homo sapiens sapiens* come from East Africa, a place that very likely was the place of origin for modern people. The weather here was warm even at a time when most of the Northern Hemisphere experienced intense glaciation.

The first *Homo sapiens sapiens* are known as Cro-Magnons from the location in France where, in A.D. 1868, anthropologists first recognized their bones to be so old. Their fossils show that Cro-Magnons looked no different from modern men and women.

Cro-Magnon life centered on hunting and gathering, just as all previous human societies had done. Men and women used many of the same stone tools that their predecessors developed, but Cro-Magnon knappers could make just the right tool for whatever was required. Over 100 different kinds of tools exist. This was the world's first technological revolution.

The preferred stone for tool making was either obsidian or flint. These rocks have a high silicon content so that they leave a sharp edge when they crack.

A chisel called a **burin** fashioned bone and antler. These materials were in ample supply because deer and antelope were the favorite prey of Cro-Magnon hunters. Using a burin, skilled tool makers could fashion excellent tools or jewelry. In areas where the mammoth and elephant were present, tool makers made objects from ivory.

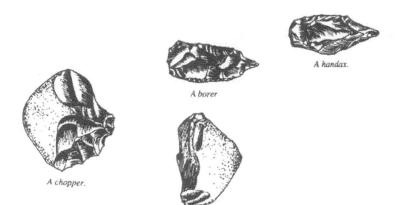

A handax.

A borer.

A chopper.

A burin.

Cro-Magnon hunters produced a variety of specialized stone tools.

A few artisans were so skilled that they would make a blade so thin that it had no practical purpose, but only demonstrated the art of the knapper. It was meant to be admired. Anthropologists call these blades **laurel leaves,** since they resemble leaves of this shrub.

Cro-Magnons made several new discoveries. Tool makers took a straight piece of wood or bone, about a foot long, and hooked it at one end so that the shaft of a spear could fit inside. The spear-thrower could eject the weapon more swiftly and accurately, up to 100 feet. By adding barbs to their spears, hunters made it much harder for animals to shake them loose.

About 18,000 years ago some inventive Cro-Magnon hunter discovered the principle of the bow and arrow. Using the tensile strength of a bent piece of wood combined with a sinew string, an arrow could be sent flying. When hunters used a bow and arrow, they could hide as they approached their prey; when they used a spear they had to stand upright.

The bow and arrow proved to be so effective that it soon spread from its first inventors all over the world. Until the discovery of firearms, it was the favorite weapon of hunters and afterwards of soldiers.

Cro-Magnons like their *Homo erectus* ancestors used stampedes to kill large numbers of animals. In one place in central Europe, bones of over 100 mammoths are found, whereas in France over 10,000 wild horses were killed in a single hunt.

Men and women of this period adapted their living conditions to many environments. In warm climates they built houses made of animal skins; in colder climates they used wood or even the tusks of animals to support the roofs over their heads. Ancient Siberians, who hunted the wooly mammoth, put up with the cold temperatures since this huge animal supplied all their needs for food and shelter.

Cro-Magnons in Siberia relax after a day of hunting.

Some people decided that, like many modern people, the beach was the best place to live. Fish and crustaceans were plentiful and required little effort compared to a mammoth hunt. Although we speak of Cro-Magnons as cave dwellers, caves were usually their homes only during severe weather because caves were usually damp and uncomfortable.

Language and Race

Cro-Magnon people were spread out over much of the world and were quite isolated from one another, living in bands of closely related men, women, and children. They were all biologically the same species, but at the same time variations appeared. Changes due to gene mutation, climatic shifts, and selection of marriage partners that appeared similar to one's self occurred. This has given people today concepts of race, although some scientists argue that the whole idea of separate races is false and should be abandoned.

Skin color among different groups of Cro-Magnons varied from black to white, hair might be curly or straight, body shapes large or short. In East Asia an eye-fold became a characteristic, while blond-haired people congregated only in northwestern European populations. Light skin also helped to synthesize Vitamin D, which aids in growth. Dark-skinned people, living closer to the equator, did not have the same need for this vitamin. Today, with marriage partners mixing from all over the world, racial characteristics in future centuries are bound to blur.

It was also during Cro-Magnon times that all of the modern spoken languages began their development. Today about 6,000 spoken languages can be found throughout the world. When a band of Cro-Magnons lived for months without meeting another human group, vocabulary and grammar evolved in thousands of different ways. In Cro-Magnon times the number of languages was much greater than today, for those spoken by larger populations gain an advantage and absorb others.

Cro-Magnons probably never numbered more than a million people, yet they eventually inhabited all the continents of the earth except Antarctica. They were the first people to come to the Americas, for neither *Homo erectus* nor Neandertals ever made it this far. The American Indians are all descendants of people who crossed the Bering Strait at a time when the ocean was so low that they could have walked or come in small boats from Siberia to the Aleutian Islands and from there to the Alaskan mainland. The same conditions probably made it possible for the Aborigines to reach Australia from Asia.

Inventions of the Cro-Magnons

One of Cro-Magnons truly important discoveries was how to make a fire. Some inventive person noticed how striking flint against a stone containing iron produced a spark that ignited dry leaves or wood shavings. No longer did people have to worry about letting their fire go out. The oldest extant firestone, nearly 10,000 years old, comes from a site in modern Belgium.

At some time during the Cro-Magnon period, one estimate is about 23,000 years ago, those people living in colder climates discovered a way to make fitted clothes. Women took hides, cut them to size, and sewed them together using needles of ivory or bone. Furs of the rabbit, fox, or another mammal kept all members of the family warm and enabled hunters to leave their houses in severe weather. Jewelry of claws, teeth, and shells completed the wardrobe of well-dressed Cro-Magnons.

Life for most Stone Age people required them to move about much of the time. Women gatherers had to conform to seasonal maturing of plants. The animal population upon which men relied could easily be exhausted from overhunting. In fact, this seems to have happened in several locations.

Certain places where fruits, seeds, or nuts were abundant must have seemed especially attractive to people weary of hiking over long distances. However, such food generally had to be eaten soon after it was collected so that it would not spoil.

Little is known of the religious views of Cro-Magnon people, yet it may be supposed that it differed little from that of their Stone Age predecessors. Efforts must have been made to maintain the favor of the spirit world. Rituals connected with birth, marriage, and death surely existed. In modern hunting and gathering societies, for example among the Amazon Indians, as boys and girls approach puberty, they go through an elaborate initiation rite to prepare them for adult life. It is highly probable that Cro-Magnons did exactly the same thing. A number of figurines of pregnant women point to a belief that human fertility was a concern. Some archaeologists see in these carvings images for worshippers to honor a Great Mother Goddess. Since life was so short, the very survival of a band depended on the life-giving power of women.

Cro-Magnon Artists

Carvings on a sandstone rock that were recently found in Australia push back the origins of art to 70,000 years ago. If these dates are confirmed, then the ancestors of the Australian Aborigines were the world's first artists.

Over a period of 20,000 years, Cro-Magnon artists in Europe worked to produce galleries of art that still astonish modern people. The European paintings are found deep inside caves in what is modern Spain and France. When they were first discovered, it was hard to convince people that they were the work of Stone Age artists. The paintings were made far from the entrance of the caves, so that the artists required torches or oil lamps to illuminate the cave walls. It is their location and subject matter that leads interpreters to suggest that they were connected to religious practice.

The most frequently painted subjects were animals, pictured in browns, reds, yellows, and blacks from pigments available to the Stone Age artists. The animals were the game for which Cro-Magnon hunters looked: reindeer, bison, cattle, deer, and horses. Very few pictures of human figures are present.

Spears are sometimes pictured piercing the animals, suggesting that the artists ritually killed the animals by representing them in this pose. The painting was a kind of prayer. After an animal died ritually the night before a hunt, it would be that much easier to kill it when the hunters stalked it the next day.

Another explanation suggests that artists painted the animals as if they were seeds. By sketching them on the cave walls, the animals were reborn even after they were dead, thus securing a constant supply of food for the hunters.

The most impressive of the galleries of Cro-Magnon painters is at Lascaux, a site in France. The paintings here were finished about 16,000 years ago. The wall is covered by a mural over 40 feet long that portrays many species of animals and includes paintings completed over several hundred years. This wall demonstrates that the tradition of using Lascaux was deep inside the minds of generations of Cro-Magnon people that lived in this part of Europe.

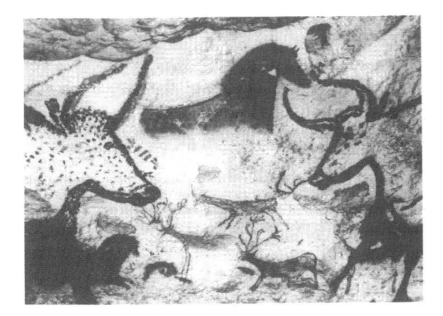

Painters in Stone Age Europe depicted the animals they hunted.

Conclusion

About 10,000 years ago the Cro-Magnon period of humans ended at the conclusion of the Stone Age in southwestern Asia. The Stone Age continued in other parts of the world for thousands of years.

Today only a very few hunting and gathering societies still exist, and even among them modernization has made an impact. These societies include the Inuit or Eskimos of the Arctic, the Khoisan of southern Africa, the Aborigines of Australia, and the Amazon Indians of South America. People in these societies live much as men, women, and children did over 10,000 years ago. Anthropologists learn from them what life in the Old Stone Age might have been like, for they provide a human museum of the past.

CHAPTER 1 REVIEW
THE FIRST HUMANS

Summary
- The search for the oldest hominids and first people is an ongoing process.
- *Homo erectus* was the first human species and lived in a hunting and gathering society where women were the main providers.
- Neandertal people, one of the first *Homo sapiens*, adapted well to their environment.
- *Homo sapiens sapiens* men and women are known as Cro-Magnons and are the immediate ancestors of modern people.
- Race and language developed during the Cro-Magnon period as isolated groups of people spread over the earth.
- The cave art of Cro-Magnons is the world's first major painting.

Identify
People: Homo erectus; Homo sapiens sapiens; Neandertals; Eugene Dubois
Places: Lascaux; Cro-Magnon
Events: development of race; use of fire; use of language

Define

culture	knapper	Paleolithic Age
language	cortex	burin
fossils	Ice Age	laurel leaves
obsidian	Cro-Magnons	

Multiple Choice
1. Humans appeared on the earth about
   (a) 2,000,000 years ago.
   (b) 20,000,000 years ago.
   (c) 200,000 years ago.
   (d) 20,000 years ago.

2. *Homo erectus* was able to speak because of a larger brain and the
   (a) location of the spinal cord.
   (b) size of the mouth.
   (c) structure of the jaw.
   (d) location and size of the larynx and pharynx.

3. A special characteristic of human children is that
   (a) they grow up very quickly.
   (b) they learn to walk on their own.
   (c) they must depend on their parents for many years.
   (d) they can see almost at birth.

4. The way of life for *Homo erectus* people was based on
   (a) fishing.
   (b) stone carving.
   (c) hunting and gathering.
   (d) agriculture.

5. *Homo erectus* hunters killed animals with
    (a) spears.
    (b) bows and arrows.
    (c) guns.
    (d) clubs.

6. Only human hunters
    (a) look for young and sick animals to kill.
    (b) hunt in large groups.
    (c) use fire in hunting.
    (d) stalk their prey.

7. Neandertal people
    (a) are a form of *Homo sapiens.*
    (b) were completely different from modern man.
    (c) are a form of *Homo erectus.*
    (d) are a species of *Australopithecus.*

8. Neandertals hunted large animals
    (a) since people did not eat vegetables.
    (b) during periods when the world was much warmer.
    (c) because they did not have boats.
    (d) when the climate turned cold.

9. Flaking is a technique
    (a) to hunt for fish.
    (b) to make a hand ax.
    (c) to start a fire.
    (d) to make a stone knife or blade.

10. Cro-Magnons are people who belong to the class of
    (a) *Australopithecus.*
    (b) *Homo erectus.*
    (c) Neandertal.
    (d) *Homo sapiens sapiens.*

11. A Cro-Magnon tool maker is called
    (a) a borer.
    (b) a carpenter.
    (c) a knapper.
    (d) a flapper.

12. The purpose of a spear-thrower is to increase
    (a) the size of the spear.
    (b) the distance the spear can be thrown.
    (c) the width of the spear point.
    (d) the length of the spear point.

13. When Cro-Magnons came to the Americas and to Australia, they probably knew how to make
    (a) fire.
    (b) wagons.
    (c) boats.
    (d) sleds.

14. Cro-Magnon women were usually responsible for
    (a) gathering and storing seeds.
    (b) hunting.
    (c) making stone tools.
    (d) serving as lookouts for animals.

15. Lascaux in France is a site for Cro-Magnon
    (a) houses.
    (b) tool-making industry.
    (c) temples.
    (d) cave paintings.

16. Race developed as Cro-Magnon people
    (a) held close together in large groups.
    (b) thought up different words for each other.
    (c) sought ways to show they were different.
    (d) moved about in isolated groups and intermarried with one another's close relatives.

Essay Questions

1. What explains the long time humans lived in the Old Stone Age without change?
2. Why was the role of women not emphasized when archaeologists first discovered Stone Age tools?
3. Why are Neandertals now considered little different from modern humans? What are the possible reasons for the disappearance of Neandertals?
4. How does the size of the brain affect human evolution?
5. What factors must be present for human language to develop?

Answers

1. a	5. a	9. d	13. c
2. d	6. c	10. d	14. a
3. c	7. a	11. c	15. d
4. c	8. d	12. b	16. d

CHAPTER 2

The New Stone Age

About 10,000 years ago when the last ice sheet began its retreat over the Northern Hemisphere, enterprising people in Southwest Asia, the lands between the eastern Mediterranean Sea and modern Iran, made a transition from the Old Stone Age to the New Stone Age. They were able to do this because they lived in a region of rich farmland, provided it had sufficient water, which is now known as the Fertile Crescent.

What gave the people living in the Fertile Crescent an advantage was the potential for irrigation in the valleys and an adequate supply of rainfall on the hills bordering them. They also found that the wild animals and plants that lived on these hills were extremely valuable.

The New Stone Age, or **Neolithic,** receives its name from the more sophisticated type of stone tools that artisans made. However, it was much more important for other reasons. This was the beginning of town life and the domestication of animals and plants.

The Neolithic first started in southwestern Asia, and its inventions and possibly its inventors spread from this center into surrounding areas setting the stage for civilization. The New Stone Age was the bridge between the world of hunters and gatherers and that of settled communities.

Town Life

As early as 11,000 B.C. men and women discovered while wandering about that there were certain places where there always seemed to be an abundance of plants—wild wheat or barley—or animals. Soon after 8000 B.C., men and women who once were nomadic found places where it was possible for them to settle permanently in southwestern Asia and in other selected regions of Asia and Africa. People were eager to take advantage of a regular food supply. Soon others who were not related by kinship joined them. The local population began to grow from 50 or 60 to several hundred.

Men and women found good reason to settle in one spot. They discovered that life within a larger group gave them greater satisfaction. A community of several hundred people could take on larger projects that needed many workers. They had a stronger sense of security. They could also share their stories and enjoy recreational activities within a much larger circle of acquaintances. Now that the choices for a mate increased, young men and women were encouraged to look among several other bands for a partner. Their children had a better chance of survival in a larger group, where childrearing could be shared with aunts and uncles.

In the western part of the Fertile Crescent—modern Syria, Jordan, and Israel—a people known as Natufians lived in settled communities after

9500 B.C. on a diet of wild barley and wheat. Archaeologists have also discovered grains of emmer wheat in Jarmo, a Neolithic village of modern Iraq. Emmer was a wild grain, not yet completely domesticated, but as early as 7000 B.C., the villagers of Jarmo crushed it to make flour. They used a **pestle**, a stone rolling pin, and a **mortar**, a flat surface on which the pestle was rolled to crush the wheat.

Specialization was one more outcome of the changes in New Stone Age life. A man who made very good arrowheads could use his skills to make these tools and forego actual hunting. A hunter would be willing to share his game in exchange for better arrowheads. A woman skilled in sandal-making could count on others willing to trade for the sake of her products. Mutual assistance proved to be a very good reason to take up a settled life within a larger community. Certain objects were now privately owned, and people lived in houses where their property could be securely kept.

Jericho and Çatal Hüyük

Easy access to water had a high priority for Fertile Crescent settlers. There was an especially favorable location in the valley of the Jordan River, located a three-day's journey inland from the Mediterranean. Now known as Jericho, it is where the first settlers arrived about 10,000 years ago.

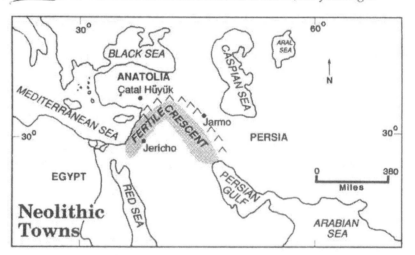

It is possible to speak of Jericho as the world's oldest known town, for as many as 2,500 people came to live in it. A spring that poured out gallons of fresh water made founding the town possible. Because of Jericho's location between the desert and the Mediterranean, it became a center for trade. Desert goods such as dates and salt could be stored and then exchanged for fish and timber from the Mediterranean. Jericho's merchants became prosperous overseeing the merchandise that passed back and forth.

Over generations the people living in Jericho continually had to build and rebuild their city, with its surrounding walls. A large stone tower gave its residents a sense of security against robbers or hostile invaders. Using mud brick as the construction material for houses was cheap, but heavy rain, infrequent as it was, played havoc with this material. The mud brick structures melted in heavy downpours and had to be rebuilt. Today Jericho rises on a mound 70 feet above its plain, an eloquent testimony to the willingness of the men and women who lived there to start over repeatedly. Its many layers of occupation draw archaeologists to study it as a remarkable guide to life during the New Stone Age.

The largest known town of the period is located in southeastern Anatolia, now modern Turkey, at Çatal Hüyük. The site is large enough, 32 acres, to have held as many as 6,000 people.

The houses at Çatal Hüyük were, like Jericho, made of mud brick. In fact, mud brick was and still is universally used in southwestern Asian villages. Its one defect is that once used to make bricks, it cannot be used again. This explains why the levels of the cities constantly rise in this part of the world. The citizens of Çatal Hüyük built on terraces, one house above the other much like a pueblo in the American Southwest. Ladders enabled people to get from one entrance to another.

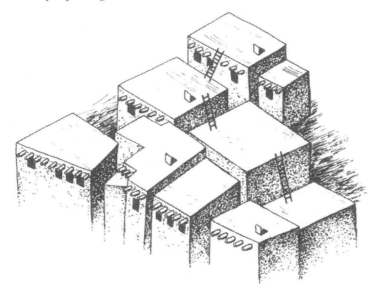

An artist shows a possible reconstruction of the houses of Çatal Hüyük.

The economic base for the people of Çatal Hüyük is thought to be trade in **obsidian**. Obsidian, a black stone like flint, was fairly rare and in great demand because its flakes provided excellent knives and arrowheads. Hunters who wanted the best blades possible traveled to Çatal Hüyük.

Archaeologists have discovered religious shrines in over a third of the houses that they excavated. On the walls of the shrines, people and animals are pictured worshiping a number of gods and goddesses, especially a Mother Goddess.

Çatal Hüyük's best days extended from about 7000 to 5600 B.C. Then the people abandoned their town for unknown reasons. Perhaps new sources of obsidian were found. One such site appeared on the Cycladic island of Milos at Phylakopi, one of Europe's first cities.

Another possible reason for the town's decline may have been a technological breakthrough that occurred when people learned how to hammer copper into weapons and utensils. This made stone tools increasingly obsolete. Copper smelting was known in the town, but apparently it was not fabricated in sufficient quantity to keep the population settled there.

Invention of Farming

The people who lived in eastern Mediterranean towns during the New Stone Age usually depended on hunters to bring them game or on gatherers to supply wild grains in order to have enough to eat. When there were years of small harvests or a lack of success in hunting, the citizens of the towns went hungry. The **Agricultural Revolution** now came to the rescue.

For the first time in human history, about 9000 B.C. farming made its appearance in the hill country of the Fertile Crescent. This happened when creative men and women discovered that certain plants could be domesticated. **Domestication** means that plants with wild ancestry can be brought under human control to provide a dependable source of food. Their seeds or roots can be gathered to provide a breeding population, which cannot survive without human intervention.

The Fertile Crescent provided the two essential ingredients for this Agricultural Revolution. Twenty inches of rain fell on the hill country of the Fertile Crescent offering sufficient water for the plants to grow. More importantly, plants that could be adapted to domestication were available.

As gatherers, women probably noticed those plants that produced the largest and most tasty seeds among the grains they harvested. They may have saved some of these seeds and put them into the ground where they sprouted. As a result, they had small gardens near their homes. Farming made life much easier, for now people had a source of plant food that did not require hours of searching. Gardens must have grown in size and variety.

After several years of farming, it probably became obvious that, despite the fact that they used their best seeds, the plants were no longer as vigorous. The first farmers recognized that the soil was wearing out. They looked for a new place to plant their seeds, usually in areas covered by trees.

The men then killed the trees, using stone axes to cut off the bark in a circle around the trunk. The leaves fell and sunshine could reach the seeds planted by women among the tree stumps. This type of farming, still in use today in tropical countries, is known as **slash and burn** agriculture. It got this name because, once the trees were killed, it was possible to burn them. The ash added further nutrients to the soil and prolonged its fertility. The increased sunlight, however, meant that weeds could also germinate and overwhelm the gardens. This was one more reason to clear a new section of the forest for planting.

Modern wheat's wild ancestor is a type of grain known as **einkorn**. When einkorn ripens, most of the plants scatter their seeds. People in the Fertile Crescent noted that the grains remained on a few stalks. Farmers kept these special grains for seeds, and in time they became one type of modern wheat.

The great advantage Fertile Crescent farmers had was that cereal grains grew in many places in southwestern Asia. Wheat and barley's ancestors flourished in the hills and provided men and women with a dependable source of food all year long. Cereal grains were very nutritious and could be easily stored.

After crop domestication was achieved, the idea of farming spread to nearby areas—Egypt, the Indus Valley, and Europe. The spread of a new product or way of doing something in a different way to new regions is known as **diffusion.**

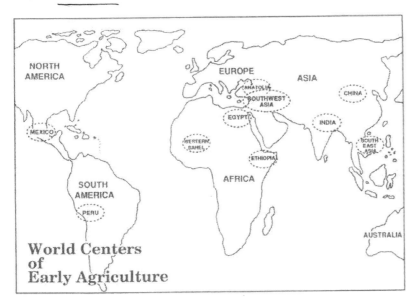

World Centers of Early Agriculture

There were also more distant centers of agriculture in the world. About 4000 B.C. people living along the Yellow River (in Chinese *Huanghe*) in northern China began growing domesticated millet. Like grains of wheat, its seeds were crushed to make flour. Although it is rarely eaten in the United States, much of the world prefers millet to wheat for making bread. Soybeans, one of the modern world's most important commodities, also first appeared in China.

In southeastern Asia, root crops including yams and taro were first grown. Farmers also cultivated peas and a variety of beans. Bananas, sugar cane, and orange and lemon trees also originated here. The most important domesticated plant was rice, which was first added to the human diet about 5000 B.C. Since rice in its early stages must grow in water, the damp tropical climate of southeast Asia helped it to gain popularity. Rice cultivation reached China about 2400 B.C. and soon became the staple of the population of the southern part of the country. Millet held its own in the north, since the climate there is too cold and dry for rice cultivation.

In the western **sahel** region of Africa, the dry area between the desert and grasslands south of the Sahara Desert, the first farmers discovered pearl millet, making it the major grain crop of this part of Africa. At that time the sahel still received ample rainfall, and Lake Chad was ten times its present size. The diffusion of agriculture from the sahel is still poorly understood. In time African farmers also discovered sorghum, a variety of gourds, cassava, watermelon, and the palm and kola nut. The coffee bean first became an important crop in the highlands of Ethiopia.

European farmers planted crops in Greece about 6000 B.C. Agriculture slowly moved westward, reaching Italy only 1500 years later.

In the Americas agriculture appears to have developed independently of the eastern hemisphere. The oldest center was located along the Pacific in modern Peru, where plants were first domesticated before 7000 B.C. The South American Indians who lived in the Andes Mountains, like the population of the Fertile Crescent, had many wild plants, over 200 species, which proved capable of domestication. These people cultivated lima beans, sweet potatoes, peanuts, tomatoes, tobacco, cotton, and, most importantly, the potato.

Mexico was a second region where domestication of plants proved feasible. Due to its diverse climate, from about 7000 B.C. the American Indians here grew a variety of pumpkins, squash, avocados, chili peppers, and cocoa beans for the making of chocolate. Cotton was also grown in Mexico.

By far the most important discovery for the Mexican farmers was corn, which was first planted after 5000 B.C. Its wild ancestor, a variety of grasses, became a natural hybrid thanks to crossbreeding. After much trial and error, human selection and genetic alteration gave birth to the modern ear of corn. Agriculture came to what is now the American Southwest after 1050 B.C., by means of the diffusion of plants first domesticated in Mexico.

Animal Herding

At about the same time that New Stone Age people were domesticating plants, they also learned that certain animals could be kept for human use as food or for transportation. No one is sure when people first learned that animals could be tamed, but it is thought to have happened in different parts of the world earlier or simultaneously with the discovery of agriculture.

Archaeologists theorize that the dog, descended from wolf cubs, was the very first animal that attached itself to humans, joining hunters so as to be rewarded with part of the game. Humans and dogs enjoyed the companionship that comes from shared experiences.

When hunters came across a young lamb or kid, they may have decided to take it back to their homes where they kept it as a pet, or perhaps put a rope around its neck until it was large enough to eat. Domesticated sheep and goats were very valuable to the people of southwestern Asia for they provided food, wool, and milk. These animals lived on grasses and leaves that are impossible for humans to digest, thereby offering a variety of meats to be added to the human diet.

The most valuable, but also the most difficult, animals to domesticate were cattle. The immediate ancestor of cattle is now the extinct **aurock**, an animal that was much larger than any human and that had massive horns on its head. Yet in time, through selective breeding (choosing the more docile animals to mate, while eating the more aggressive ones), the ferocious aurock was tamed, and modern cattle developed.

New Stone Age people were impressed with the powerful bodies and aggressive nature of bulls. They appeared to be nature in its most dynamic form. All over southwestern Asia they became objects of worship.

The hills of the Fertile Crescent also provided Neolithic people with the wild pig. However, pigs received a bad reputation because they foraged in human garbage. Many people avoided pigs for they were thought to pass on their foraging habits to anyone who ate them.

Horses have had a long history with humans. First they were hunted for food. They appear in Cro-Magnon cave art along with other prey. About 5,000 years ago people living in Inner Asia, the region between the Caspian Sea and the mountains of China, attempted to tame horses so that they could haul burdens. This effort was successful, but it was not until thousands of years later, about 2000 B.C., that men learned how to ride on horseback. Along with horses, jackasses, which were much more docile, became beasts of burden in Asia and Europe.

The domestication of the two-humped camel and the one-humped dromedary also took place in Inner Asia. The camel preferred cool mountain regions, whereas the dromedary made living in the desert possible because its body could store food and water.

In India people raised chickens for meat, eggs, and feathers. The elephant was another contribution of the Indian people to the number of domesticated animals. The elephant in Africa proved much more difficult to tame and still resists being used as a beast of burden. Southeastern Asians during the New Stone Age found that the water buffalo adapted well to carrying burdens.

Asia provided a large number of animals that were domesticated and able to breed in captivity, but not all continents were as fortunate. In Africa south of the Sahara, only the guinea fowl, similar to the chicken, became part of the human diet. In Northern Africa at the beginning of the Neolithic, the Sahara was a great grassland supporting huge herds of wild animals. The Saharan people hunted them for centuries but later turned to herding sheep, goats, and cattle, which were introduced from Egypt. A famous mural at Tassili in modern Algeria vividly portrays these herders with their animals. When the climate became too dry for grass to grow, the herders apparently left the Sahara with their animals, emigrating to eastern Africa where they introduced their way of life.

South American Indians had a limited number of animals suitable for domestication. Two animals were used as burden carriers, the llama and the alpaca, and one, the guinea pig, was eaten. Indians of North America had some success in raising turkeys, but what is now the United States and Canada did not have any animals fit for domestication.

The American Indians of South America domesticated the llama to carry burdens.

Neolithic Australians had no wild animals that could be tamed, so the Aborigines who lived there kept up a hunting and gathering way of life until European contact about 300 years ago.

It is possible that cattle were domesticated first in the Balkan peninsula, but for the most part Europeans had to borrow their domesticated animals from people living in southwest Asia.

Technology in the New Stone Age

For the people who took up farming and herding animals during the New Stone Age, life was very different. Herders had to adopt a nomadic way of life that depended on the grazing habits of their animals. They had to be tent dwellers, carrying with them only the material goods that could be loaded on the backs of their animals. Still they preferred this way of life to that of the farmer, for whom they had contempt. The Bible tells of the animosity between Cain, the herder, and Abel, the farmer.

Farming of necessity demands that people live sedentary lives. From sowing seeds to harvest time, plants need care—watering, fertilizing, and weeding. The earliest farming villages contained a dozen or more round houses, which were little more than huts, where poles held up the roofs and hides covered the sides. Every house had a hearth for the fire, which provided a place for cooking and, in cold times, for warmth.

After people discovered how to use mud bricks to build, houses became larger and more comfortable. They now roofed their houses with straw or tree branches and then added a layer of mud. Ovens built outside the house became more common because of the heat.

Baskets, which probably were used in the Old Stone Age, became very common in the New Stone Age. Easily made from grasses, the baskets were woven so tightly that they could even hold water.

An even greater advance in the making of containers occurred when people learned to make pottery. The first known use of pottery was in Japan, but a certain amount of experimentation with hardened clay probably took place all over the world.

From using unbaked clay for a container, artisans learned how to coil and heat clay in kilns to make it even more serviceable. The many uses of pottery for storage and cooking soon became evident. The various kinds of pottery from sites all over the world in the New Stone Age show how inventive this period was in human history. Artisans constructed pots, large and small, forming them in hundreds of shapes. Some were decorated; others were left plain. Different clays provided interesting contrasts. Pottery from Neolithic sites provides archaeologists with their best guide to time sequence during the New Stone Age.

Neolithic pottery appeared in many shapes and forms. Archaeologists use it as a way of identifying the movement of peoples and the length of their settlement.

The next great step in technology came with the development of metal-working. Although exact dates are impossible to ascertain, the oldest piece of worked copper, a piece of jewelry, comes from a cave in Iraq. The artisans in Çatal Hüyük could also hammer cold copper as could those American Indians in what is now Minnesota. Perceptive collectors can find copper ore on the ground for it appears in a natural state.

By 6500 B.C. hammering cold metals seems to have become more common in southwestern Asia. The next step in metal use appeared about 4000 B.C. and is known as **smelting.** Rock that contained metal ore was heated until the ore became a liquid. It was not easy to get a fire hot enough to reach the point where the ore liquified, so various experiments had to be tried. After many frustrations, one of the early smiths learned that blowing air into a furnace of coals raised the temperature to 2,000°F, the point when copper ore becomes a liquid.

About 3200 B.C. the smiths of the Fertile Crescent made one more advance. They mixed arsenic, and later tin, with the copper. The result was a much more useful metal, bronze. Unfortunately the ore that contains tin is scarce in southwestern Asia, so it had to be imported. Once bronze came on the scene, southwest Asia entered the age of metals that archaeologists call the Bronze Age.

Megalith Builders

The largest of the monuments left from the New Stone Age are the megaliths of Europe. About 6000 B.C. Neolithic farmers from Anatolia (modern Turkey) crossed into Europe. Some archaeologists identify them as Indo-European speakers, the first to arrive on the continent. They brought with them the plants and animals that they knew from experience would grow well in a cooler climate.

At this time Europe remained covered with a huge forest, lightly populated by hunting and gathering societies. The first farmers cleared patches in the forests, using the familiar slash and burn techniques.

For unknown reasons the farmers began the construction of huge stone monuments. This began about 4500 B.C. and continued for centuries, testifying to a growing population and an agricultural surplus that permitted people to engage in an activity that had no apparent economic value. Megaliths are the world's oldest stone constructions.

Archaeologists have identified some of the megaliths as tombs for chieftains, others appear to be temples entered through a long procession way. Some are considered to be observatories of the sun, planets, or stars. Knowing the time of year to plant or harvest was probably of great concern to the early European farmers.

Often the stones used in the monuments came from quarries located at a considerable distance. The masons at the quarries cracked the stone either by using wedges or by relying on the same principle as that which causes cement to break apart in weather from freezing and thawing. After the stones were cut, they were put on logs and rolled to the construction site. This laborious process required dozens of workers pulling their burdens over difficult terrain. After they arrived at the site, the workers used temporary earth mounds to haul the stones into place.

Stonehenge in England is the world's best known megalith construction.

Stonehenge in England is surely the best known of the megalith constructions. Although it has been studied for centuries, its purpose remains unknown. The largest group of megaliths was built in Brittany, which is in modern France. One stone, the Grand Menhir, weighs 385 tons. The fascination of modern people with the megalith builders comes from the mystery that surrounds their purpose and the skills needed to plan, organize, and build such massive constructions.

Since 1992 the discovery of an actual person who lived during the age of Europe's megalith builders has excited the archaeological world. He is known as the Ice Man. About 3300 B.C., while out on a high mountainside in the Alps, he died of still unknown reasons. Snow and ice covered his body and preserved it to the present. Examining his remains should tell a great deal more about the people who lived in Europe during the New Stone Age.

Conclusion

The domestication of plants and animals was a huge step for human society. For tens of thousands of years men and women had lived in small bands made up of relatives, who were completely dependent on what nature provided. Now they began to control their environment by growing food and keeping animals. The process of domestication involved generations of experimentation, but the effort proved worthwhile.

Climate determined how successful the first farmers and herders could be. Neither the tropics nor the Arctic, where temperatures were in the extremes, allowed farmers a place. Hunting remained the major occupation of people living here, for wild animals were abundant.

Farming has always entailed the willingness to accept risk and to put in long hours of labor. Early frosts, lack of or too much rain, plant diseases, insects, and rodents can be devastating. To compensate for the risks involved, farming and herding people now lived more comfortable, settled lives. Technology aided them in making containers and the use of metals marked a major improvement over stone for tools. Large numbers of their contemporaries still preferred the old ways and rejected the settled life. The future rested with the farmers, who, through cooperation and companionship, learned the skills that laid the foundation for the first world civilizations.

CHAPTER 2 REVIEW
THE NEW STONE AGE

Summary
- The first towns appeared in the New Stone Age.
- Agriculture first developed in southwest Asia.
- Life in farming villages led to many new inventions, such as pottery.
- Keeping animals, or herding, became a way of life for some people.
- New plants and animals were domesticated in East Asia, Africa, and the Americas.

Identify
People: nomads; farmers; megalith builders
Places: Fertile Crescent; sahel; Jericho; Çatal Hüyük; Jarmo
Events: Agricultural Revolution; selective breeding; smelting of metals

Define

megaliths	smelting	diffusion
Neolithic	obsidian	einkorn
mortar and pestle	specialization	auroch
domestication of plants and animals	kilns	
	slash and burn	

Multiple Choice
1. The Fertile Crescent is found in
    (a) Africa.
    (b) southeastern Asia.
    (c) southwestern Asia.
    (d) India.

2. Neolithic describes
    (a) the New Stone Age.
    (b) the Old Stone Age.
    (c) the Bronze Age.
    (d) a kind of pottery.

3. Nomads are people who
    (a) build cities.
    (b) develop pottery.
    (c) use mud brick for building houses.
    (d) wander about looking for food.

4. One of the features of early town life was the opportunity for
    (a) hunting.
    (b) domesticating animals.
    (c) specialization in one kind of work.
    (d) keeping animals close to one's house.

5. The oldest known town in the world is
    (a) Çatal Hüyük.
    (b) Beijing.
    (c) Jerusalem.
    (d) Jericho.

6. For a town to succeed it always needed to be near
    (a) water.
    (b) a forest.
    (c) mountains.
    (d) the sea.

7. The people of Jericho must have recognized the importance of private property because
    (a) they gave up stone tools for metal ones.
    (b) they invented pottery.
    (c) they built a wall and a fort.
    (d) they had a large spring from which to obtain water.

8. The people of Çatal Hüyük controlled the trade in
    (a) animals.
    (b) pottery.
    (c) gold and silver.
    (d) obsidian.

9. Domestication means that certain plants and animals
    (a) can be controlled by humans.
    (b) grow in dry climates.
    (c) grow in wet climates.
    (d) are found in houses.

10. A pestle and mortar give evidence of
    (a) the use of pottery.
    (b) the domestication of animals.
    (c) people crushing seeds to make flour.
    (d) the domestication of plants.

11. People who learned to make pottery probably used these containers first:
    (a) stone jars.
    (b) metal boxes.
    (c) baskets.
    (d) stone jugs.

12. The first metal used for practical purposes was
    (a) iron.
    (b) copper.
    (c) bronze.
    (d) silver.

13. In 3200 B.C. the world passed into
    (a) the New Stone Age.
    (b) the Iron Age.
    (c) the Copper Age.
    (d) the Bronze Age.

14. The auroch is thought to be the ancestor of modern
    (a) cattle.
    (b) horses.
    (c) pigs.
    (d) sheep.

15. Some of the wild nature of animals can be removed through
    (a) changing their environment
    (b) plowing
    (c) keeping them in cages
    (d) selective breeding

16. The ancestor of modern dogs is
    (a) the cat.
    (b) the wolf.
    (c) the bear.
    (d) the coyote.

17. One of the most impressive monuments of the first European farmers is
    (a) a step pyramid.
    (b) Jericho.
    (c) Jarmo.
    (d) Stonehenge.

18. The favorite grain of the first Chinese farmers was
    (a) corn.
    (b) wheat.
    (c) rice.
    (d) millet.

19. A common feature of Africa and the Americas was that they had
    (a) a lack of large animals that could be domesticated.
    (b) cool damp climates.
    (c) many species of wolves.
    (d) many breeds of horses.

20. The grain found useful to Mexican farmers was
    (a) rice.
    (b) wheat.
    (c) corn.
    (d) millet.

Essay Questions
1. What possible reasons existed for people to want to live in towns?
2. Why does specialization become a factor in town life?
3. What are the necessary ingredients for having plants and animals domesticated?
4. What is the relationship between monument building and political life?

Answers

1. c	6. a	11. c	16. b
2. a	7. c	12. b	17. d
3. d	8. d	13. d	18. d
4. c	9. a	14. a	19. a
5. d	10. c	15. d	20. c

UNIT **2**

THE FIRST CIVILIZATIONS: 3500–1200 B.C.

CHAPTER 3

The Fertile Crescent

The Fertile Crescent, that part of southwestern Asia extending from the Mediterranean Sea to western Iran, was the setting for the first world civilization. This is hardly a surprise because it was in this part of the world that the first towns were built and the domestication of plants and animals followed. It was here that village life moved from societies, or cultures, into civilization. The Sumerians were the first to make this transition.

Not everyone agrees on what makes up a civilization. Certain criteria appear to be present for historians to determine the difference, but the specifics differ throughout world history.

The people in the Fertile Crescent had an organized political system, an economy based on private ownership, social classes, and a religion that required a priestly class to intercede with the gods and goddesses. They built public buildings as well as private homes. They also had writing, a skill that demonstrates the level of sophistication that Fertile Crescent people had reached. Fertile Crescent men and women established a pattern of life that historians and sociologists now use to define a civilization. Once a society replicated the advances noted here, it qualified as a civilization.

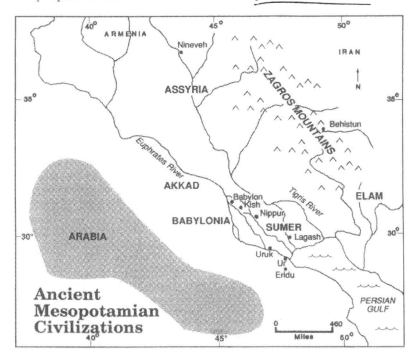

Ancient Mesopotamian Civilizations

Tigris and Euphrates Valley

The civilization of the Sumerians centered in the valley between the two great rivers, the Tigris and the Euphrates. These rivers rise in the mountain region of ancient Armenia and then flow through the flat terrain of Mesopotamia until reaching the Persian Gulf. Often they overflowed their banks and even changed their riverbeds. They now share a common mouth before entering the Persian Gulf, but 5,000 years ago they emptied into the sea separately. Today this area is a large swampy delta, called the Shatt al-Arab.

The ancient Greeks called the Tigris-Euphrates Valley Mesopotamia, the land between the rivers. It is a region that did not have much promise, for it was flat, wind-swept with little rainfall, treeless, and subject in the summer to intense heat. The monotonous landscape had, however, one great advantage. At the time of the annual spring flood, the rivers laid down a rich layer of fertile silt over the land, guaranteeing excellent farming. This rich soil attracted people into the Tigris-Euphrates Valley.

As early as 6000 B.C. there is evidence that the people who lived along the banks of the river dug channels alongside it to irrigate their fields. People brought plants, domesticated in the hill country surrounding the Fertile Crescent, into the valley. Irrigation replaced rainfall, and the plants adapted very well, producing far greater yields than before.

About 4000 B.C. a migration of people from the Arabian peninsula took up residence in the valley. They brought new skills with them for they had words for *weaver*, *potter*, and *carpenter*, which demonstrates their familiarity with these crafts.

Possibly about 3500 B.C. the people who are known as the Sumerians relocated in the Tigris-Euphrates Valley. Many archaeologists think that they came from the north, possibly from the Caspian Sea region. Others believe that the Sumerians may well have been in the Fertile Crescent long before 3500 B.C. Archaeologists are certain that there was a major growth in population, either the result of migration or an unforeseen jump in the number of indigenous people at that time.

The Sumerians were short of stature with black hair. Men wore woolen kilts, whereas women dressed in gowns tied over one shoulder. Hair fashion dictated beards for men and braids for women.

The Sumerian language was altogether different from any language spoken today. Yet, archaeologists are able to read the sources of Sumerian history for they wrote in a script known as **cuneiform**. It receives this name from the Latin word for *wedge*, because Sumerians wrote on soft clay tablets, in signs that appear like wedges. The tablets were then baked to make them permanent.

Towns of Ancient Sumer

In all there were about twelve large city-states in Mesopotamia, each with a strong wall about it. There was no concept of creating a single political unit. Instead, each city went its own way. Because the amount of arable land was limited, as was the water to irrigate it, conflict over property and water was endemic.

The cities held from 10,000 to 40,000 people. The oldest city was Uruk, giving it a claim to be the world's first city, which was surrounded by a wall that was 5 miles in circumference. Neighboring towns included Kish, Ur, Lagash, and Eridu.

From the few records of the earliest period of Mesopotamian history, it appears that an assembly of the more important people governed Sumerian cities. In time, however, this type of government proved unwieldy, especially in moments of crisis, and these times increased as the years passed. There was further need for strong personal leadership to keep the irrigation system working, dig canals, and build dams and reservoirs. Maintenance was a constant concern, as important as construction, and was very hard work.

In this scene the lugal and his court are entertained by a harpist as servants bring him gifts of animals and grain.

Agrarian conflicts or a breakdown in the irrigation network created the emergencies that led to the choice of a single ruler, called lugal, to command the army and manage the distribution of water. Later the lugal expanded his position to become a political and religious figure. Of course, as the years passed, the lugals of the city-states sought ways to pass on their rule to their sons, thereby creating an hereditary kingship.

Upon the lugal's death, burial was sometimes made in tombs befitting his importance. Servants and slaves were buried alive with one lugal's wife at Ur so as to accompany her into the afterlife where, it was supposed, she would need their services. These burials demonstrate the extent of the royal familiy's power, setting a pattern for southwestern Asian political expectations far into the future. Ordinary people presumably harbored no expectation of life after death.

Sumerian Religion

Religion and language were the two bonds that united the Sumerian people. The temple was an integral part of Sumerian religion, the focal point of religious as well as civic life. Here a staff of religious functionaries, priests, priestesses, and their employees carried on the prayers and sacrifices deemed essential to win the favor of the divinities worshipped there.

The Sumerians were fatalistic about life. The gods and goddesses created men and women to work on their behalf.

The Sumerians were **animists**, believing that the universe teemed with gods and goddesses, each with a task to perform, not too unlike human society. Every protecting deity required attention through prayers or festivals, lest benevolence turn to anger. Besides the main temple built for the town's patron, there were other places of worship, dedicated to additional divinities.

An or Anu was the god of heaven; Ki was the protector of the earth. Enlil brought storms and powerful wind, while Inanna and Dumuzi controlled fertility. Along with their companions, the gods and goddesses oversaw human affairs, intervening when it suited them.

The most important festivals occurred in the spring when nature began to stir. Sumerians became especially attentive to the needs of the gods and goddesses at this time in order to ensure a bountiful harvest and an increase in the herds. The waters rose in the Tigris and Euphrates, and the divinities had to be made aware of sending neither too much nor too little water into the farmers' fields.

As the population increased, so did the size and decoration of the Sumerian towns. Each city then sought to construct a **ziggurat** close by the main temple, a great mound to emphasize its importance. In a land where neither stone nor wood was available, the builders had no choice but to use mud brick. In a very creative way, they laid their bricks on ascending levels, creating an artificial mound that got smaller as it reached the top. The summit of the mound was reached by a flight of stairs.

An artist reconstructs one of the ziggurats of ancient Mesopotamia.

The Tower of Babel in the Hebrew scriptures is the most famous of the ziggurats. One of the largest was at the city of Ur, where the platform covered an area 200 feet long by 120 feet wide, rising to a height of 120 feet. Sumerian builders stuck cones of colored clay into the ziggurat exterior in a geometric pattern. Next to the mound, builders constructed the city temple.

Much of religious activity was directed toward preserving fertility. With that in mind, ritual prostitution was common, with the chief of the city having sexual relations with one of the temple priestesses.

A large number of goods and animals were stored in temple warehouses, for the religious establishment was a large landowner. The temple area also was a place to keep the harvests and tools of ordinary farmers who were not connected to the temple.

Development of Writing

One of the many gifts that the Sumerians gave to the world was writing. At first, clay tokens stamped with symbols of animals, tools, or cloth were used to keep an inventory of the temple's possessions. To perform a business transaction the tokens were wrapped in clay balls that were broken open when the goods arrived at their destination to be sure the shipment was correct. Eventually, some creative individual abandoned the clay balls and simply drew a picture of a cow or a sack of wheat and put a number with it on a small oval of clay.

These drawings are called **pictograms** and are the first steps in all writing systems. The scribe simply drew a picture of the object to be recorded. The first pictograms appeared about 3500 B.C. on baked tablets.

In time, scribes began to use a kind of shorthand rather than take the time to draw the object. They also combined symbols to make verbs and thereby conveyed an idea. These writing symbols are known as **ideograms,** for they present an idea. The last step toward a full writing system happened when the symbols for objects were used to convey the sound of the word. This sound could then be used wherever it appeared anywhere in the Sumerian vocabulary.

The cuneiform signs became very complex and even more abstract as time passed. A school boy studying to be a scribe had to memorize 6,000 signs, little lines with pointed heads and tails, written with a reed stylus while the clay was still soft. Women did not often receive the same kind of training to be scribes, so writing was usually a male occupation.

An ancient Babylonian tablet has an inscription beneath it in cuneiform script.

About 2800 B.C. the Sumerians began to employ cuneiform to write stories, myths, and hymns and to tell of their religious beliefs. These written records allow scholars to unearth the Sumerian traditions that had been preserved orally over the generations. It was also the start of world literature. For the first time, legal codes also appeared in written form.

Throughout the Fertile Crescent neighbors of the Sumerians adopted cuneiform writing. It became a common script throughout the world of Southwest Asian and continued in use for 3,000 years, when at last alphabetic writing replaced it.

Economic Activity

The size of the staff attached to the temples and the needs they generated added to the number of people who came to the temples as participants in the rites. This activity created a market for farmers and merchants to buy and sell their products.

As in all ancient societies, the most important sector of the economy was farming. The average Sumerian family lived on the land, at intervals coming into the city to sell handicrafts or to buy what was needed back home.

The greatest challenge to the farmer was to make sure that growing plants had enough water during the scorching summer season. Because the Mesopotamian valley was so flat, a major concern was to make sure that the water kept moving. Otherwise, if it stood in the fields, a buildup of salt occurred. Failure to provide a slope so that gravity would carry the water downstream was to risk the land becoming a desert. That, in fact, happened later. Today, where once prosperous cities covered the Mesopotamian plain, there is only desert.

The Sumerians took advantage of the large number of plants and animals that their predecessors cultivated. They grew both barley and wheat and a number of vegetables. Much of the grain they fermented into ale, the common drink of the Sumerians. The date palm gave them fruit and shade, as well as tall reeds for roofing their homes. Among the animals they kept were cattle, goats, sheep, and onagers, a kind of donkey.

It was Sumerian farmers who first learned that the use of a plow made planting crops much easier. Before the plow was invented, seeds were scattered by broadcasting them by hand. Once the plow appeared, the young plants could grow in rows and develop deeper root systems. Farmers could cultivate the plants during the growing season and harvest them much more easily after they matured.

The first plow was little more than a tree branch that, as one person pulled and another pushed, made a furrow in the ground. Later farmers put an arrow-shaped metal piece on the plow, making it go deeper and straighter. Oxen and donkeys now pulled the plow because the work was so hard.

The need for greater physical strength using plow agriculture was probably responsible for changing roles in the Sumerian family. Even though both women and men shared in agricultural work in the past, now the need for men to manage the animals pulling plows gave women a lesser role in the family's food production. Their lesser position increasingly relegated them to the home, with the result that patriarchal attitudes grew more prominent. Men made the decisions on economic matters, and they soon monopolized political decisions as well because they also filled the ranks of the armies. Patriarchal society became the norm in southwestern Asia.

In order to be certain of the boundaries of their fields, the Sumerians developed mathematics and surveying techniques. Instead of using 10 as a basis for calculation, the Sumerians preferred 60. Their calculations based on 60 explains why we use 60 minutes in an hour and 360 degrees in a circle.

The wheel was another invention of the Sumerians. As early as 3400 B.C. the potters of Mesopotamia discovered how much easier it was to shape their vases and jugs by spinning them on a wheel. This insight allowed them to find other uses for wheels. These first wheels were made of solid wood. They put wheels on sleds, using an axle to hold the wheels together, so that they could transport goods. The early carts were so light that when their drivers reached water they could be dismantled. Pulling a cart, rather than putting baggage on the back of a pack animal, increased the weight carried threefold. For travel on their rivers, the Sumerians first employed the sailboat.

Note the solid wood wheels on this Sumerian cart.

City people also had their share of discoveries. Jewelry of gold, silver, and precious stones was favored by the wealthy as a way to demonstrate their importance. Goldsmiths proved especially adept at hammering this metal, valued for its color and permanence. Cloth makers used cotton and wool to make garments that were dyed many colors. Often it seems that the weavers were slave women forced to work at this tedious job long hours each day. Workers tanned hides and used the leather for shoes and bags.

Sumerian businessmen used stone cylinder seals with a unique carving on them that could be rolled in soft clay to make an impression. This device served as the autograph of a Sumerian merchant. Sumerian cities also had pharmacists who dispensed drugs that the doctors, after examination, had prescribed for a variety of illnesses.

A lively exchange between the artisans who lived in the towns and the farmers who produced the food kept Sumerian cities filled with shoppers and traders. Since wood, stone, and metal ores were all absent from their valley homes, Sumerian businessmen took their wares to other nearby regions where they sought these products. Metal, especially copper and tin, had to be found, for these were used to make bronze cooking utensils for the kitchen and arms and armor for the army.

Houses in Sumerian cities were built of mud brick with reed roofs. They were built next to one another, sometimes sharing a common wall, because space was at a premium. Their houses lined the narrow streets that led away from the public square where the temple and its ziggurat were located. Homes of the wealthy were quite comfortable with wooden furniture and carpets. The bedrooms opened onto a courtyard, which offered a shaded place for conversation and a room to entertain guests.

Society in ancient Sumer was, as in all ancient cultures, divided between the wealthy and the poor. Land ownership was the major source of wealth, but merchants who prospered were also numbered among the rich. These families, along with the priests of the temples, comprised the social elite. The acquisition and exchange of costly items in the upper class was a major source of class differentiation.

Artisans formed associations with those who practiced the same craft. Often they appear to have pooled their resources for common projects. What we know of these associations, or **guilds,** comes from tablets that tell of business transactions that involved them in places as far away as India, Iran, and Egypt.

Women could keep their property separate from that of their husbands and were allowed to divorce spouses who did not support them adequately. A man could take a second wife if the family was childless.

Parents chose marriage partners for their children. Girls brought dowries to the marriage so that the new family could have a good start. The dowry remained the woman's property, and if her husband died she retained it. Children inherited the remainder of family property.

At the very bottom of Sumerian society were slaves. Usually captives in war, they were held in servitude unless their families could ransom them. Law codes gave slaves certain rights and sought to protect them from mistreatment.

Culture in Ancient Sumer

The Sumerians were interested in beautiful objects. Their artisans decorated not only jewelry but also household objects such as pottery and tableware with skill. Sculptors carved small statues that some people believe to be gods, whereas others think that they represent humans at prayer. Sumerians may have believed that these statues, as representatives of their devotees, could be left before a household shrine to make sure that the deity was continually honored.

A group of Sumerian statuettes with hands folded and eyes looking straight ahead.

Music was a highly developed skill. Stringed instruments included the harp and the lyre. One of the most famous lyres, which was found in an ancient tomb, has a bull's head on it. The Sumerians had pipes and flutes as well as tambourines to accompany their festivals.

Once writing reached a certain level, Sumerian authors began to record the stories they remembered. These compositions with their vivid imagery and descriptive qualities are one more great gift to the rest of the world. Later writers took these tales and made them their own, sometimes adding or subtracting parts, but the core remained the same.

The most prominent piece of Sumerian literature is the epic poem of Gilgamesh. It is known that one of Uruk's kings had that name, but one section of the story is universal: Why do people grow old and die? Gilgamesh had a friend who died in his youth. So traumatic was this loss that Gilgamesh set out on a quest to discover immortality. He found a wise man, Utnapishtim, who told him that there was a certain plant at the bottom of the sea that, if he had it, would enable him to live forever.

Gilgamesh, after many adventures, retrieved the plant from under the sea and with it started to return to Uruk. On the way home Gilgamesh stopped to take a bath in a pool of water, leaving the plant on the bank. While he was bathing a serpent found the plant and took it away. Gilgamesh returned to find the key to his immortality gone. It was the serpent, not he, who would enjoy eternal life. "I myself have gained nothing; not I, but the beast of the earth has joy of it now." The quest for immortality ended in tragedy.

Invaders in Mesopotamia

Sumerian civilization was threatened when neighboring peoples, living in the hill country surrounding the Mesopotamian plain, adopted its inventions. The plow was the most important because the land on which the hill people lived had sufficient rain for growing crops without irrigation. It enabled them to increase the amount of food they grew. This abundance translated into a larger population, bigger armies, and ambitious rulers who envied the life of the Sumerians.

The Elamites of the Zagros Mountains were first to take advantage of the Sumerians. Their city of Susa was comparable in size to many of the Sumerian towns, and their army was more aggressive. The Elamites came down from their hills and put an end to Sumerian city-state independence.

About the same time another group of people, the Akkadians, appeared on the scene. The Akkadians were Semitic-speaking people, belonging to a linguistic family whose origins are found in the Arabian peninsula. The Akkadians, who had adopted much of Sumerian culture with the exception of the language, now replaced the Elamites as the rulers of the Mesopotamian valley for the next 300 years.

About 2350 B.C., Sargon, one of the Akkadian kings, ruled from his capital, Akkad, but he certainly was not content to stay there. He built up a military force larger than any before seen. It was of such a size that historians believe it to be the first true professional army in world history. With his army he expanded his lands all the way to the Mediterranean Sea. His victories spread the use of writing, and hymns composed by his daughter Enheduanna are some of the world's oldest literature.

Sargon's empire did not long survive him. A volcanic explosion and prolonged drought caused people to move to the south, overtaxing its resources. Civil unrest followed, allowing one more people, the Amorites, to move with their herds of animals into Mesopotamia.

There was a brief Sumerian renaissance, led by Ur-Nammu, the king of Ur. About 2100 B.C. he built the great ziggurat, whose remains still rise over the Mesopotamian plain. All went well for a century and a half, then the Elamites returned, took Ur, and destroyed it.

The Amorites, the most recent arrivals in Mesopotamia, were, like the Akkadians, a Semitic-speaking people. Originally nomadic herders, some took up urban life when they moved into Mesopotamia, whereas others continued to keep their herds. By the time of their arrival, the wars in Mesopotamia had taken their toll on the infrastructure that had marked the Sumerian economy. Weeds now clogged the channels built by the Sumerians. The canals so carefully constructed in the past were left unattended. For the nomadic Amorites, finding pasture was their only concern.

About 1800 B.C., Hammurabi, one of the kings of the Amorites, appeared in the city of Babylon. Historians know him principally for his judicial concerns. His law code, written in cuneiform on a black stone column eight feet high, stands today in the Paris museum of the Louvre. It shows Hammurabi standing before the Babylonian god, Marduk, seeking his approval for the 282 laws written on it. The text says that Marduk and the king together intend to enforce the laws.

This portrait statue is thought to be the law-giver, Hammurabi.

In Hammurabi's code, penalties for breaking the law depended on the social status of the victim and the accused. What impresses legal scholars is the code's willingness to take up the cause of women and children to prevent their exploitation. Nevertheless, punishments remained strict, and the paying of a fine no longer sufficed to avoid retribution. Aiding an escaped slave could be punished by death. Overall, the code shows an awareness that the government has a moral obligation to order society and punish those who violate justice.

Anatolian Civilization

There is a good chance that, when thoroughly examined, archaeologists may be able to prove that a civilization parallel to the Tigris-Euphrates culture existed in Anatolia. The modern state of Turkey today encompasses this region.

The geography of Anatolia is quite different from Mesopotamia. Basically the region is a high plateau that in its higher regions is treeless. Its climate is harsh; in winter strong winds bring heavy snowfall, and in the summer the weather becomes very hot. Rain on the plateau is rare at that time of the year.

Ancient Anatolians preferred to live in the river valleys where they had a dependable source of water. Fertile silt enriched these lowlands, laid down by spring floods over many centuries.

The mountains of Armenia, rich in metal ores, dominated the eastern part of Anatolia, where winters were always harsh. Their tallest peak, Mount Ararat, is always covered with snow.

Hittites

About 2000 B.C. a people called Hatti occupied most of Anatolia. Then a new people came on the scene; they may have been invaders or people who had always been present but now emerged from the Stone Age to create Anatolia's first major civilization. These people were the Hittites. They spoke an Indo-European tongue, showing that they were not related to any other western Asian population.

The Hittite language was written down using a hieroglyphic script to represent ideas and less frequently the syllables found in its pronunciation. These hieroglyphs show pictures of objects in the Hittite vocabulary or stand for ideas. Some 25,000 Hittite tablets exist, dating from the seventeenth century B.C. They are the oldest writing in any Indo-European speech.

The first use of the name Hittite comes from records kept by merchants who speak of their presence in western Anatolia. They lived in the region of the Halys River (now the Red River), which makes a great arc on the Anatolian plateau and then empties into the Black Sea.

The Hittite capital was at Hattushash, near modern Boghazköy in Turkey. It was centrally located and easily defended. Within their empire, the Hittites themselves were but a ruling elite, for the population of the area remained extremely diverse.

Although the king was the sole ruler, the nobility of the nation kept a wary eye on his activities. Should he veer too far away from the interests of the aristocrats, they had the power to elect a rival monarch.

The ruler's title was Great King. The mythology of the state held that Labarnas, the first ruler, was reincarnated in each of his successors. During the period of the Hittite Empire, the king's title changed to My Sun, and the sun became the symbol of royal authority. One monarch explained, "The goddess, my lady, always held me by the hand. Since I was a divinely-favored man and walked in the way of the gods, I never committed the evil deeds of mankind." After the king died, he became a god.

When the Hittite ruler appeared in public, according to the monumental sculpture, he wore a long garment with a shawl over one arm. The sculpture depicts him with a close-fitting cap on his head and a staff, a sign of his power, in his hand.

The queen mother had an active role in public affairs as long as her son ruled. She had her own court and saw to it that the king was well advised. Her children and those of other relations belonged to the Great Family of Hittite royalty. Often the king's sons held governorships in the provinces.

The Hittite king was also the kingdom's high priest. Because he could not be everywhere, local priesthoods existed throughout the land. The most important deity was the god of weather, Teshub, in whose name the king ruled, while the chief goddess represented the sun.

At Yazilikaya a sculptor has carved in stone one of the great processions required of worshippers. The deities required those devoted to them to participate in a variety of rituals that kept the deities favorably disposed.

Building the Hittite Empire

About 1660 B.C. Hittite armies began a series of conquests to the south and east. The king Hattusilis I captured north Syria and brought it within his empire. His successor, Mursilis I, pushed down the Euphrates, making war on the Amorite kings who succeeded Hammurabi in Babylon. The great city of Babylon fell to them, but by now the Hittite armies were overextended.

The Hurrians, marching from a nearby kingdom to the east, challenged the Hittites for control of Mesopotamia. For a time the Hittite armies drew back, for palace coups had weakened the monarchy in Hattushash. About 1525 B.C. the kingdom revived when King Telipinus reigned, setting up a strict rule of succession so as to alleviate the confusion caused every time a king died.

The period of Hittite history from 1460 to 1190 B.C. is known as the period of the empire, a time when the Hittites were the most aggressive people of western Asia. Their great advantage now came from their knowledge of the process needed to smelt iron. Using iron weapons against bronze-armed enemies was hardly a contest. In 1500 B.C., the Hittites were the only people in the world to know how to kindle a fire hit enough to liquify iron ore. Their second advantage came from their mastery of the horse-drawn chariot. This kind of warfare was not known before the Hittites introduced it. A combination of iron weapons, iron-tipped spears, and arrows that archers and bowmen shot from the chariots made them invincible for several centuries.

The Hurrians and Mittani, other peoples of eastern Anatolia that had carved out kingdoms for themselves, felt the strength of Hittite arms as they swept across northern Syria. The Egyptian pharaoh, Ramses II, decided to challenge the Hittites over which of the two great powers of the eastern Mediterranean should prevail, for the world did not seem large enough for both.

In 1299 B.C. a great battle that was meant to settle the issue took place at Kadesh. Hittite and Egyptian forces fought each other with charge after charge, but the battle proved indecisive. Several years later Ramses offered to make peace, and the dispatch of a Hittite royal princess to Egypt sealed the agreement.

Agriculture was the major occupation of the population within the Hittite empire. Farmers grew wheat and barley, and tended olive and almond orchards. Beekeeping was also important. Mining was another major economic activity. Hittite miners learned how to dig out the copper and iron ore from the seams of the mountains.

The Hittites were anxious to keep the secret of iron-making to themselves for it gave them a great advantage over all other peoples of western Asia. However, this proved impossible, and soon the secret got out. This discovery of how to make iron is the most important contribution of the Hittites to the rest of the world. Unfortunately, its more lethal weaponry also had the effect of making empire-building more attractive.

Toward the close of the thirteenth century B.C., Hittite weakness became evident. The Assyrians, located in northern Mesopotamia, were anxious to take the place of the Hittites as the region's dominant state. On the coast, a variety of invaders, lumped together as the Sea Peoples, wreaked havoc on the empire's cities.

Syrian Peoples

The region south of Anatolia and west of Mesopotamia is known as Syria. It developed its own culture during this period, receiving influences from both Anatolia and Mesopotamia.

The first cities in this part of southwestern Asia were at Byblos and Ugarit, populated by people known as Canaanites. About 2700 B.C. Byblos and Ugarit began to extend their authority over neighboring towns. Herding animals was a major occupation of the Canaanite people, a way of life well suited to the semiarid plains of Syria.

In 2300 B.C. Sargon of Akkad had conquered the Canaanites, and about 300 years later the Hittites brought them into their empire. Between those two periods of occupation, a recently discovered city of Ebla flourished. Excavations show that Ebla covered an area of 140 acres. A large palace was the home of its king whose archives, containing 1,400 tablets, are now in the hands of archaeologists for decoding.

Even though the archives of Ebla are in cuneiform, those at Ugarit show the first steps taken toward alphabetic script. Scribes at Ugarit used 30 signs for consonants and 3 for vowels. All the alphabets of the world are derivatives of the Ugaritic script, for the alphabet's invention happened only once in the history of the world.

Conclusion

So much of our own culture is indebted to the Sumerians. Without their inventions and discoveries, it is hard to imagine the way we would grow our food, make our tools, build our homes, and think about literature.

The presence of cycles in history is very evident when studying later Mesopotamia. A strong leader appears and creates an empire, but after several generations the structure crumbles because of outside invasions or internal weaknesses. Then the cycle begins again.

The price people paid for living in settled cities was the development of a territorial concept that required violence and war to keep one's neighbors away. Since then finding new and deadlier weapons has occupied the attention of the warrior class in every society of the world.

CHAPTER 3 REVIEW
THE FERTILE CRESCENT

Summary
- The geography of Mesopotamia, the Tigris and Euphrates valley, shaped Sumerian civilization.
- The Sumerians were the first world civilization.
- The Sumerians built a dozen different city-states ruled by a king called the lugal.
- Sumerian society gave many rights to women.
- The Sumerian temples were built beside large mounds called ziggurats.
- The Sumerians invented a kind of writing called cuneiform.
- Semitic peoples invaded Mesopotamia and adapted its civilization to their own needs.
- Hammurabi, the Amorite king of Babylonia, published a law code.
- The Hittites of Anatolia first discovered how to smelt iron.

Identify
People: Hammurabi; Elamites; Sargon of Akkad; Hittites; Amorites
Places: Tigris and Euphrates valley; Uruk; Syria; Akkad; Anatolia; Babylon
Events: building Sumerian cities; development of writing; publication of law codes

Define

cuneiform	animists	pictograms
Semites	guilds	ziggurat
ideograms	lugal	epic of Gilgamesh

Multiple Choice
1. The discovery of ancient Sumer was made through reading about it in
    (a) Greek tablets.
    (b) Assyrian tablets.
    (c) Amorite tablets.
    (d) Eblaite tablets.

2. Mesopotamia is a great river valley formed by
    (a) the Nile.
    (b) the Orontes.
    (c) the Tigris and Euphrates.
    (d) the Red Sea.

3. The word *Mesopotamia* is Greek and means
    (a) between the rivers.
    (b) between the seas.
    (c) between the mountains.
    (d) this is where the Sumerians live.

4. Cities of ancient Sumer were always formed about
    (a) palaces.
    (b) springs.
    (c) temples.
    (d) mountains.

5. The oldest Sumerian town is
   (a) Uruk.
   (b) Nippur.
   (c) Sumer.
   (d) Lagash.

6. The Sumerians replaced the digging stick with the invention of
   (a) the spade.
   (b) the fork.
   (c) the shovel.
   (d) the plow.

7. Patriarchal society is one which
   (a) gives equal rights to everyone.
   (b) keeps slaves.
   (c) gives no rights to slaves.
   (d) gives men preference over women.

8. Sumerian arithmetic was based on the number
   (a) 6.
   (b) 60.
   (c) 10.
   (d) 12.

9. The need to irrigate farmland gave rise to
   (a) surveying techniques.
   (b) mathematics.
   (c) windmills.
   (d) the wheel.

10. A Sumerian king was called
    (a) ensi.
    (b) lugal.
    (c) archon.
    (d) priest.

11. Sumerian artisans joined together in
    (a) guilds.
    (b) companies.
    (c) unions.
    (d) partnerships.

12. A dowry is
    (a) a kind of boat.
    (b) a form of plowing.
    (c) a gift brought by a new bride.
    (d) a gift brought by a new husband.

13. Every city-state of ancient Sumer worshipped one or more gods because it was thought that
    (a) the gods brought fertility.
    (b) the city needed protection.
    (c) people were created to work for the gods.
    (d) all of the above.

14. Sumerian temples were built beside
    (a) artificial mounds.
    (b) mountains.
    (c) islands in the Euphrates.
    (d) palaces.

15. Writing grew out of the need
    (a) to tell stories.
    (b) to keep cows.
    (c) to keep records.
    (d) to make public signs.

16. An ideogram is a sign that reproduces
    (a) a map.
    (b) a letter of the alphabet.
    (c) an idea.
    (d) a picture.

17. The world's first story tells about the adventures of
    (a) Noah.
    (b) Gilgamesh.
    (c) Ur-Nammu.
    (d) Hammurabi.

18. Rolling a cylinder seal in wet clay provided the Sumerians with
    (a) a map.
    (b) a deed of trust.
    (c) a signature.
    (d) a cuneiform tablet.

19. Sumerian music had instruments of
    (a) strings, pipes, and tambourines.
    (b) drums.
    (c) only wind instruments.
    (d) clay whistles.

20. The Semitic people who lived north of Sumer were
    (a) the Eblaites.
    (b) the Greeks.
    (c) the Amorites.
    (d) the Akkadians.

21. The king of Babylon, famous for his law code, is
    (a) Sargon the Great.
    (b) Hammurabi.
    (c) Gilgamesh.
    (d) Ur-Nammu.

Essay Questions
1. What were the distinguishing characteristics of a Sumerian city?
2. What explains the origin of writing?
3. Explain the process of metal working and its importance for ancient societies.
4. What gave importance to trade in Mesopotamia?
5. Discuss the role of religion in ancient Mesopotamia.

The Fertile Crescent

Ancient Egypt

Egypt owes its life to a river, the Nile. Without this constant flow of water, human population of any size could not exist. Even in ancient times, it was recognized that "Egypt is the gift of the Nile."

Nile Valley

Once the mighty Nile, a river 4,100 miles long, carried a much greater volume of water than it does today. On its way to the Mediterranean, it hollowed out a trench 600 miles long and 30 miles wide through the limestone plateau that makes up northern Africa. Progressively the climate grew drier until, in historic times, the Nile retreated to its present state in Egypt.

The land adjacent to the southern Nile was called Upper Egypt. Where it enters the Mediterranean, the river created a huge **delta,** a marsh full of weeds and rushes, but the delta was extremely fertile once it was cultivated. This was Lower Egypt. Egyptians were always aware of the differences between the two regions of Upper and Lower Egypt. They called their country "the two lands."

On its descent from the African interior, the Nile passes through six cataracts, rapids where the water rushes over rocks preventing navigation. The first is at Aswan, now the site of a great dam and Lake Nasser, which was built to control the flow of water year round. In ancient times, during the annual summer flood, the Nile rose 25 to 26 feet, covering the land with a half inch overcoat of fertile mud. Much of the water remained in natural pools along the Nile.

The climate of the Nile Valley, so dry and practically without rain, is excellent for preserving artifacts and written materials. For this reason archaeologists know a great deal about ancient times in Upper Egypt. They have discovered an immense treasure in Egyptian tombs. In addition, since the ancient Egyptians had their own type of writing on monuments, called **hieroglyphs,** a continuous story of the life of ancient Egypt can be recorded.

Even though the knowledge of how to read hieroglyphs was lost during the Middle Ages, in A.D. 1799 the discovery of the **Rosetta Stone** made it possible to read them once again. The Rosetta Stone contained an inscription written in hieroglyphs, demotic Egyptian, and Greek. By comparing the three scripts, Jean-François Champollion broke the code that held the mystery of hieroglyphic writing.

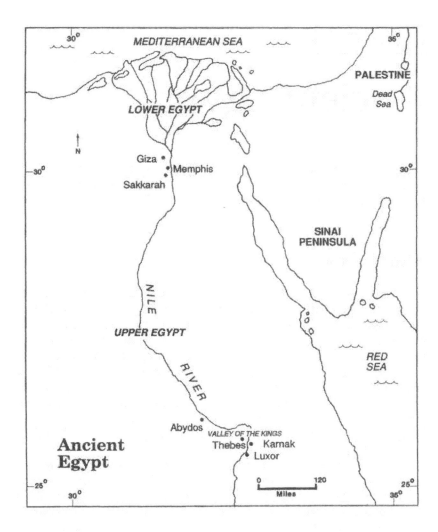

Ancient Egypt

Earliest Egypt

Ancient villages of Neolithic peoples are found throughout Egypt. Their tombs provide a rich assortment of grave gifts. About 3600 B.C. the skulls in the graves change, from narrow-faced people to those with broad foreheads. The broad-headed men and women brought plants from Asia, including flax and cotton, giving a hint of their origin. They began the reclamation of land along the Nile, clearing the marshes and building canals for drainage. They also built boats. From them they fished and caught birds in the marshes created by the Nile to supplement their diets.

Farming in Egypt was easier than in Mesopotamia for the flood came before planting rather than at the time of harvest as in the Tigris-Euphrates Valley. Egyptian peasants did not need the elaborate irrigation system of their neighbors to the north for it required little labor to tap into the pools of water left after the flood.

The Rosetta Stone provided the clue to the deciphering of ancient Egyptian hieroglyphs.

The Egyptians were anxious to take whatever was of value from their neighbors in Mesopotamia. They learned to make cylinder seals, to use brick for paneling and decoration, and most importantly, to use writing. The Egyptians kept their own gods and goddesses, however, and did not attempt to build any ziggurats.

As the population increased and the cultivated land extended farther from the Nile, the haphazard method of farming appeared more and more inefficient. Although there are no details, some village chiefs must have attempted greater control over water distribution. Little by little, larger and more important regions swallowed their smaller neighbors. At last there were but two **dynasties,** one in Upper Egypt and the other in Lower Egypt. (A dynasty is composed of rulers who succeed each other because of heredity.)

Tradition tells that the unification of the two regions of the country took place about 3100 B.C. under King Narmer of Abydos of Upper Egypt. He is given credit for uniting the two lands of Upper and Lower

Egypt, thus assuming the title of **pharaoh**, which means Great House. There is also an iconographic proof of the unification—a palette that shows the pharaoh defeating his enemies while wearing a double crown, symbolic of the unification. Pharaoh's rule of the two lands was visibly portrayed by his wearing the red crown of Lower Egypt and the white crown of Upper Egypt.

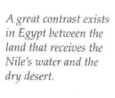

A great contrast exists in Egypt between the land that receives the Nile's water and the dry desert.

Old Kingdom

Narmer's capital was at Memphis, located very near modern Cairo. It was at the juncture of the delta and Upper Egypt, allowing him and his successors to keep a watchful eye on both parts of his kingdom, for separatism was still a factor. His realm was basically a land of villages rather than large cities. Those towns that did exist were administrative centers or religious sites.

Once established, Egyptian life lent itself to centralization. To supervise the irrigation of the land and to oversee the storage of the grain crop was essential to avoid famine, the greatest threat to the growing Egyptian population of about 4,000,000 people. Rebellions and revolutions severely disturbed the serenity that dominated the consciousness of the average Egyptian.

The Old Kingdom is that period of history that dates from about 2770 to 2200 B.C. During that time it has been customary to trace the several dynasties that held power. Later periods are known as the Middle and finally the New Kingdom, or Empire.

Egypt's unique rule of a single individual over hundreds of square miles received further confirmation when the pharaoh, or his advisors, came up with the idea that he must be a god. Whether the pharaoh believed this himself is unknown, but in their search for security the men and women of Egypt apparently accepted this view of him. It was a very consoling thought that one of the gods, not an ordinary human, guided the destiny of the nation and kept the world from falling back into chaos.

Egypt, in contrast to Mesopotamia, had very few law codes, since it was always possible to appeal to the living god. In Egypt the pharaoh's will was divine law.

Pharaoh could be any god that he wanted. One tomb text has it, "What is the King of Upper and Lower Egypt? He is a god by whose dealings one lives, the father and mother of all men alone, by himself, without equal." During the Old Kingdom he alone was immortal and therefore deserved a lavish funeral.

The notion that pharaoh was god obviously put him in a unique position in the nation's class structure. Most pharaohs kept large harems, where the queen mother ruled supreme. In their palaces they collected artifacts from all over the eastern Mediterranean, prestige goods that confirmed their importance.

The next step below the royal family consisted of the officials who served the pharaoh in multiple ways. The most important was an official who bore the titles Overseer of the Palace and Sealbearer of Lower Egypt. All officials served at the pleasure of the pharaoh. They lived in spacious homes and to the extent possible filled them with expensive furniture. A garden and pool helped break the monotonous brown of the hot season.

Both men and women dressed in tightly woven cotton garments and decorated themselves in jewelry. Children wore no clothes at all until reaching 12 years of age. Egyptians used a wide range of cosmetics. People wore dark eye makeup under their eyes to deflect the sun's glare. At banquets women put perfumed cones on their heads that melted as the evening progressed, giving off a pleasant odor.

Wives generally were given an equal status with their husbands. They conducted their own businesses and owned land in their own names, but they were denied entry into the class of administrators. In case of divorce, one third of the property went to the wife.

Titled office holders proliferated during the fifth and sixth dynasties. On the walls of their tombs, they were careful to make sure that their importance was noted. Governors of outlying provinces did their part to be noticed in hopes of a promotion to court.

Although pharaoh himself was a god, he had to share his divinity with a large group of other gods and goddesses in the Egyptian pantheon. Therefore, the priests and priestesses who served in the temples of these divinities held a special role paralleling that of the pharaoh's civil officials.

The Egyptian middle class, composed of lesser officials, private landowners, artisans, scribes, and army personnel, occupied their own niche. The vast majority of Egyptians, the peasant class, did not enjoy an easy life. Their day was spent from dawn to dusk working in the fields of their masters or watching over their animals. Pay was a scant portion of the harvest, hardly enough to feed their families.

The peasant's work—building canals, digging wells, sewing and reaping the crops—made Egypt wealthy. At times of high flood when the Nile crested 2 yards above normal, all the peasant's work was undone and had to be started over.

There were few slaves in Egypt, for in the Old Kingdom, military expeditions outside the country were infrequent. Without prisoners of war, a reservoir of slaves could not form. Men, women, and children of the peasant class worked together planting, tilling, and harvesting the crops.

Egypt depended on farming for its great wealth in the Old Kingdom. Trade outside Egypt was minimal, for the pharaoh's government kept a monopoly on what little export business existed. Scenes of farming, more than any other subject, are pictured on tomb walls.

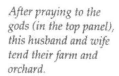

After praying to the gods (in the top panel), this husband and wife tend their farm and orchard.

Planting took place in October when the Nile was low, the ground was still moist, and plowing was easy. Oxen with a yoke tied to their horns pulled the plow. The fields resembled a checkerboard, each peasant responsible for a certain plot.

As the growing season progressed, government officials decided when and how much water should be released from the reservoirs built to hold water during the summer months. In early spring, before the flood, the harvest was brought in to threshing floors where workers drove oxen and donkeys over the grain to break it out of its husk.

Both wheat and barley were favorite cereal crops. With them the Egyptians made 15 different kinds of bread. Barley also furnished the ingredients for ale, the universal drink of ancient Egypt's peasants; the upper class preferred wine.

Mining and quarrying occupied a small number of Egyptians. The Sinai peninsula provided copper and precious stones.

Religion in Egyptian Life

The ancient Egyptians believed the world was alive with supernatural beings that they could not see, along with the pharaoh whom they could see. About 80 major deities existed, each with a share of devotees. Hundreds of priests served in the temples that dotted the Egyptian countryside.

Among the major divinities were Horus, the falcon god; Thoth, represented by the ibis and baboon; and Anubis, who was a reclining jackal and later a human with a jackal's head. The goddess Hathor was pictured as a cow. The fact that the gods appeared so frequently as animals was special to Egypt. The Egyptians believed that there was a divine quality in animals. In a world where little changed from day to day, the Egyptians found confirmation in each new animal generation reproducing its parents.

In addition to the animal gods, there were cosmic ones. The sun, earth, sky, air, and water were all divine. Myths recounted their origins and history. Re, the sun god, was the Creator, "Only after I came into being did all that was created come into being."

Each day Re sailed across the sky in a boat. Then at night when he disappeared, he had to fight a battle with darkness to rise again. The priests in the temple at Heliopolis had to offer prayers on a daily basis to make sure that the sun would rise.

Other deities, Ptah and Khnum, were also creators. During the Middle Kingdom, the story of Osiris and Isis gained great popularity. The myth held that a wicked brother killed Osiris and cut up his body into many parts. Then Isis collected them and wrapped them up restoring him to immortal life. He then became judge of the underworld. After death, Osiris weighed the heart of a person on a scale with a feather. If it was too heavy from bad actions it was eaten, and the person was denied admittance into the land of the blessed.

In Thebes, the major city of Upper Egypt, the favorite god was Amon, pictured with a ram's head. He was the Hidden One, who gave the breath of life and caused the wind to blow. Later Re was merged with Amon to become Amon-Re and as a hybrid became the nation's supreme deity. Long hymns of praise to Amon-Re give testimony to his popularity, especially at Thebes, which was the god's favored city.

One of the basic assumptions of the Egyptians, that the world was always the same, was challenged by death. This often came so quickly, sometimes violently, and made the Egyptians reconsider if they had their world view correct.

They believed that the cosmos was held together by a force known as **ma'at**. Although open to many translations, ma'at might be considered as the balance that provided right order. It governed the universe from the heavens to the earth, from plants to animals to humans. Even the Nile itself responded to ma'at.

Opposed to ma'at were ignorance, passion, pride, and anything else that upset the comfortable stability that enveloped the Egyptians. Death, of course, was the supreme contradiction. Therefore, it demanded great care and preparation, and consumed a large amount of the time of the living.

The first Old Kingdom tombs are called **mastabas**. They are found in two of Egypt's oldest sites, Abydos and Saqqara. The Egyptians probably borrowed the idea for their construction from Mesopotamian royal burials.

The first mastabas were brick and rectangular in shape, with sloping walls. A flat roof of cedar beams covered the ceiling. The Egyptians had plenty of stone, so rather than mud brick, later mastabas were made of stone shaped like brick.

During the fourth dynasty, from about 2560 to 2440 B.C., when the power of the pharaohs was at its peak, the mastaba became the pyramid. More than any verbal confirmation, the pyramid testified to the overwhelming power and majesty of the pharaohs. The first, called the step-pyramid, had Imhotep for its architect. He built it over 200 feet high, the first major stone building in world history, for his pharaoh Zoser.

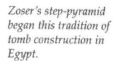

Zoser's step-pyramid began this tradition of tomb construction in Egypt.

Later pharaohs ordered the construction of the largest stone monuments ever to be constructed, the pyramids of the Giza plateau. They were built to last forever. Although some archaeologists believe they were more political statements about the pharaohs' power than tombs, most believe them to be the final resting place for the **ka,** the spirit of the pharaoh after death. The three largest are those of the pharaohs Menkaure, Khufu, and Chefren.

The largest of the three pyramids, built about 2530 B.C., was ordered when Pharaoh Khufu ruled the country. In addition to his own monument, a temple, pyramids for his wife and children, and even a building for his boat made up the complex.

Khufu's pyramid covers 13 acres and soars 481 feet into the sky. Over 6,000,000 tons of stone went into the construction, cut into blocks 2.5 tons each. The builders were so exact that a joint of 0.02 inch separates them. This construction was done without vehicles for delivering the stone, for the wheel had not yet reached Egypt. Humans and animals pulled the stones into place using sledges on temporary ramps of brick and earth that workers tore down after they finished the pyramids.

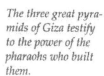

The three great pyramids of Giza testify to the power of the pharaohs who built them.

Herodotus, the Greek historian, says that the pyramid's construction required 100,000 men working for 20 years. Recent excavations prove that the builders were highly paid artisans living in permanent villages near the construction sites. Their skills were passed on from one generation to the next. The pyramids could be seen for a hundred miles away, reminding all Egyptians of their god-king.

Arts of Egypt

Egypt of the Old Kingdom was wealthy enough to support a large class of artisans and artists, in addition to those who worked on the tombs. Early on, these artists determined certain styles that were to last for the next 3,000 years. The conservative spirit of the Egyptians is best demonstrated in its art. For example, the painted human figure always has the face in profile, and the legs and shoulders bent forward. Statues of the pharaoh and his wife always have their eyes fixed, godlike, on the horizon. One foot is in front of the other. Facial expressions are always grim, as befit those with such heavy responsibilities that a whole kingdom depended on their will.

The extant architecture of ancient Egypt is confined to tombs and temples because they were built in stone. The obvious skill in planning and erecting them proves that the Egyptians far surpassed all other ancient civilizations in these areas.

Glass was an Egyptian invention, and its production extended from small perfume bottles to large vases. The Egyptians loved to carve in stone, as evidenced by numerous artifacts that survive. Hieroglyphic writing covers Egyptian monuments, each figure chiseled with great care. Carpenters approached the level of sculptors in their skillful decoration of furniture.

Egypt's neighbors always were impressed with the kingdom's many doctors. Sick people who sought healing in the ancient Mediterranean region journeyed to Egypt for cures.

The skill of the Egyptian doctors is closely related to their knowledge of human anatomy gained from the universal desire of Egyptians to be mummified at the time of their death. This required an elaborate ritual as well as dissection in order to remove those organs of the body that could be expected to hasten decay. As a result, Egyptian doctors knew more about the body than any other ancient people—how to use surgery, set bones, and even operate on the brain.

It was the Egyptians who developed the solar calendar, assigning 30 days to 12 months. At the close of the year, adding an extra 5 days kept the calendar up to date. Three seasons were reckoned according to the Nile's position: before, during, and after the flood.

Middle Kingdom

In the sixth dynasty of the Old Kingdom, the power of the pharaohs began to decline. About 2200 B.C. the Old Kingdom disappeared to be followed by an intermediate period. Drought caused famine to haunt the land. A text of the time complained, "The poor wear fine linen and the laundryman will not carry his burden." Obviously a social revolution had occurred. Perhaps too much of the nation's wealth had been lavished on the pharaoh and his court and not enough on a more equitable distribution of goods.

Then about 2050 B.C. the Middle Kingdom of Egypt appeared. The Middle Kingdom lasted for approximately 400 years, beginning with the eleventh dynasty. For 51 years Menthu-Hotep ruled the country after he made Thebes his capital and the center of Egyptian administration. Prosperity reappeared when once strong central power returned to the hands of the pharaohs, who ordered the canals and reservoirs of the Old Kingdom restored. To illustrate Thebes's importance, extensive building took place at Karnak, where the temple to Amon, protector of the city, was located.

Then about 1640 B.C. Egypt experienced an invasion from Asia. This was apparently unexpected, and no provisions were made to hold Lower Egypt against the invaders.

Hyksos Period

The Egyptians called the invaders Hyksos, or Rulers of the Uplands. They were a mixed people, speaking a Semitic language. Some archaeologists identify them with Syrians fleeing the Hittite invasion of their country.

The Hyksos introduced horse-drawn chariots and the composite bow to Egypt. It was their ability to use these new weapons of war that gave them their superiority over the Egyptians. Because they were but a ruling elite, the Egyptians assimilated the Hyksos into their lifestyle. Nevertheless, the native Egyptians identified them as foreigners and unwelcome. Beginning in 1552 B.C., Ahmose, a local ruler in Thebes, took up arms to expel them. Ahmose is the founder of the eighteenth dynasty that begins the New Kingdom in Egypt, a period that extends to 1087 B.C.

New Kingdom

Ahmose learned from the Hyksos how to use the weapons that they had introduced into Egypt. What he intended, once the Hyksos power was broken, was to make Egypt a military force that should be reckoned with in the future. Egyptian nobles were expected to fill his officer corps, and a standing army of recruits gave Egypt an opportunity to initiate a period of empire-building.

The result was a series of campaigns against Nubia in the south, now Sudan, and Palestine and Syria to the northeast. For the first time in history, an Egyptian army camped on the banks of the Euphrates.

About 1490 B.C. an Egyptian woman ruled in her own name, but as a king, not a queen. Her statues show her wearing the ceremonial beard of the pharaohs. This was Hatshepsut, who was both the daughter of one pharaoh and the wife of another. The Egyptian royal family, contrary to the fear of incest in other cultures, favored marriage with close kin. Apparently this kept the royal blood from dilution.

Hatshepsut ruled efficiently, and several times personally led the army in combat. Her tomb at Deir el-Bahri is one of the New Kingdom's finest pieces of architecture. By the time of her death, pyramids were no longer in fashion.

The tomb of Hatshepsut sits below the cliffs of the desert plateau. Its size testifies to her power.

Her son, Thotmes III, pharaoh from 1490 to 1468 B.C. was constantly at war, for the Syrian border defied all efforts to make it stable. At Megiddo, the key fortress in Palestine, Thotmes won a great victory. Most Syrian towns then held Egyptian garrisons.

Religious Reform of Akhenaten

The hereditary tradition of Egyptian kingship could often bring the unexpected. A warrior pharaoh, intent upon expanding the nation's borders, might well be followed by a ruler for whom military affairs were greeted with indifference.

In 1364 B.C. a new pharaoh ascended the throne as Amenhotep IV. As was the custom, he chose his sister Nefertiti to be his wife. The royal couple, despite following a long list of warrior pharaohs, turned their attention to a religious revolution. They announced to a startled court and populace that there was but one god in the universe who shared his divinity with the pharaoh. This was Aton, symbolized by the sun disk. The pharaoh and his family, in very lifelike poses, were sculpted receiving the sun's rays, invigorating them to rule the nation.

Amenhotep, to show his determination, changed his own name to Akhenaten, the spirit of Aton, and Thebes was to be known as the City of the Brightness of Aton. The pharaoh ordered the construction of three new cities, all of them, of course, dedicated to Aton, and he moved to one of them. This is the modern El-Amarna. Fortunately, when archaeologists dug the site, they discovered Akhenaten's archive, a treasure of information on the pharaoh's rule. While he busied himself with these religious activities, the Hittites pounced upon the Egyptian towns of Syria and Palestine. By the time of his death, not only was the empire considerably reduced in size, but all the multiple priests whom he had discharged along with their believers could hardly wait for his demise. Egyptians hastened to try and forget all about his Aton worship. They had an easy time, since Akhenaten's successor was only a boy of 11.

The boy was Tutankhamen. His 10-year rule was, in fact, rather uneventful. Only in the twentieth century did he reach fame, for his tomb was found nearly intact. The grave goods discovered in his tomb were one of the great archaeological finds of modern times.

The coffin of Tutankhamen shows the pharaoh holding the symbols of his authority, the shepherd's crook and a scourge.

Egypt's Decline

The last days of Egyptian military glory came in the nineteenth dynasty with pharaohs Ramses I, Seti I, and especially Ramses II. The latter was a warrior and builder on the scale of the pyramid pharaohs. He and his first wife, Nefertari, placed their capital, Per-Ramses, in the eastern delta. Ruling from about 1304 to 1237 B.C., Ramses II challenged the Hittites for control of Syria with a 20,000 man army at the Battle of Kadesh about 1299 B.C. The Hittite chariots struck hard at the Egyptians, but their lines held, resulting in a draw between the two armies. Ramses subsequently made peace with the Hittites.

Ramses's architectural triumphs included more temple additions larger than ever at Karnak and Luxor and four great statues of himself serenely overlooking the Nile at Abu Simbel. Late in A.D. 1995 archaeologists announced the discovery of a tomb holding the remains of the 50 sons he fathered during his lifetime.

The statues of Abu Simbel now stand on the Egyptian plateau. To save them from the waters of Lake Nasser, archaeologists cut up the stone and then reassembled them.

Ramses's rule brought to an end the impressive civilization of Egypt. After his death the enemies of Egypt gathered their forces on its borders.

Conclusion

Until now, ancient Egyptian civilization enjoys a longevity surpassed by none. It lasted for almost 3,000 years. The Egyptian view of the world was remarkably conservative, clinging to the past, eschewing change. Its cultural unity enabled it to withstand natural disasters, even the Hyksos invasion, without collapsing.

Ironically, Egyptian civilization's way of life did not travel well. The geography of the country made it unique. Because societies nowhere else in the world depended on a single river, no other people ever replicated Egyptian civilization.

CHAPTER 4 REVIEW
ANCIENT EGYPT

Summary
- The people of Egypt depended totally on the Nile.
- The Egyptian people were protected from invasion by the sea and the desert.
- A king named Narmer, according to legend, unified Egypt. He formed the first dynasty.
- The Old Kingdom, when the pyramids were built, was Egypt's first great historical period.
- Pharaohs of the Middle Kingdom moved the borders of Egypt southward into Nubia.
- During the New Kingdom Egyptian armies invaded Syria. Hatshepsut was a famous woman pharaoh of the New Kingdom.
- Akhenaten inaugurated a religious revolution.
- Egyptians worshipped pharaoh as a god.
- Egyptian inventions include the solar calendar, the discovery of many medicines, how to make a mummy, and how to write hieroglyphs.

Identify
People: Narmer; Hyksos; Nefertiti; Ramses II; Akhenaten; Hatshepsut; Tutankhamen; Zoser
Places: Nile River; Nubia; Thebes; Sahara; Sinai Peninsula; Karnak; Memphis; Abu Simbel
Events: Hyksos invasion; using irrigation for farming; development of writing; building the pyramids; religious reform of Akhenaten

Define

dynasty	pharaoh	mastabas
hieroglyphs	ma'at	Rosetta stone
delta	ka	

Multiple Choice
1. Lower Egypt is that part of the country formed by
   (a) the Mediterranean Sea.
   (b) the desert.
   (c) the southern river valley.
   (d) the Nile delta.

2. When the Nile flooded in ancient times, it left behind
   (a) pebbles.
   (b) silt.
   (c) grain.
   (d) islands.

3. The Nile flood depended on the rainy season in
   (a) Mesopotamia.
   (b) Lower Egypt.
   (c) the African interior.
   (d) the Red Sea.

4. Before farming could begin in Egypt,
    (a) the swamps along the Nile had to be drained.
    (b) the discovery of new plants and animals had to be made.
    (c) the country had to be civilized.
    (d) the trees had to be cut down.

5. The legendary king who united Egypt is known as
    (a) Narmer.
    (b) Tutankhamen.
    (c) Amenhotep.
    (d) Ahmose.

6. Egyptians believed that the world was kept in balance by
    (a) the Nile flooding.
    (b) the moon.
    (c) the sun.
    (d) ma'at.

7. The first pyramid was built for the pharaoh
    (a) Narmer.
    (b) Zoser.
    (c) Tutankhamen.
    (d) Imhotep.

8. A reason for building the pyramids was
    (a) to provide work for the slave population.
    (b) to build a temple to the gods.
    (c) to accent the power of pharaoh.
    (d) to provide a fortress near the capital.

9. The national drink of ordinary people in Egypt was
    (a) ale.
    (b) wine.
    (c) milk.
    (d) kummis.

10. About 1750 B.C. these people invaded Egypt:
    (a) the Assyrians.
    (b) the Nubians.
    (c) the Philistines.
    (d) the Hyksos.

11. This Egyptian woman served as a pharaoh in the New Kingdom:
    (a) Thoth.
    (b) Horus.
    (c) Nefertiti.
    (d) Hatshepsut.

12. The worship of Aton as sole god was promoted by Pharaoh
    (a) Zoser.
    (b) Tutankhamen.
    (c) Akhenaten.
    (d) Hatshepsut.

13. Ramses II had his statue carved facing the Nile at
    (a) Memphis.
    (b) Abu Simbel.
    (c) Thebes.
    (d) Karnak.

14. The name of the falcon god was
    (a) Osiris.
    (b) Thoth.
    (c) Aton.
    (d) Horus.

15. The Egyptian calendar, based on the sun, had
    (a) 8 months.
    (b) 3 months.
    (c) 12 months of 30 days.
    (d) 12 months of 33 days.

Essay Questions
1. Describe the art and architecture of ancient Egypt.
2. Why was irrigation so important to the political power of the pharaoh?
3. Contrast the world view of the Egyptians with that of the Sumerians.
4. How do you explain the longevity of Egyptian civilization?

Answers

1. d	6. d	11. d
2. b	7. b	12. c
3. c	8. c	13. b
4. a	9. a	14. d
5. a	10. d	15. c

CHAPTER 5

The First Indian Civilization

When geographers speak of South Asia, they include the modern nations of India, Pakistan, Bangladesh, and Sri Lanka. Several small kingdoms that lay beneath the Himalaya Mountains should also be counted. These are Nepal and Bhutan. Today political and religious differences as well as geography explain why the Indian subcontinent is divided.

Geography of India

India's shape resembles a triangle standing on a single tip. At the top of the triangle two great mountain chains seal India off from the rest of Asia. On the west are the Hindu Kush, on the east are the Himalayas, the tallest mountains of the world. Together the two ranges extend 2,000 miles east to west and are almost 150 miles north to south. Both ranges have passes that historically funnel invaders into India. The most famous is the Khyber Pass in the Hindu Kush. It permits travelers to ascend for 17 miles and then to descend the same number of miles into the hills of northern India. Great rivers tumble down the mountain chains, rising quickly in the spring when the snow melts and then decreasing as the year moves on. Two of these majestic rivers are the Indus and the Ganges.

Over the centuries both rivers created great fertile plains in India's north. It was in these valleys that India's first civilizations arose, and historically the people who lived here dominated the rest of the country.

The Indian people have a great respect for their rivers. Their annual floods give the plains their fertility, and their muddy waters offer spiritual cleansing as well. Modern Indians use the rivers today to be rid of their impurities, just as their ancestors did for many centuries.

South of the great Ganges and Indus Valleys is a region known as the Deccan plateau. Much of the land here is harsh and dry, covered with scrub forest and grasslands. The Deccan lacks the fertile soil of the north and traditionally has been the home of herders who pasture their cattle, goats, or sheep.

Along the southern coasts of India, tropical forests flourish thanks to the monsoon rains that wash the shores. Sri Lanka (formerly Ceylon), a teardrop-shaped island separated from the mainland by a scant 30 miles, is located off the southern coast of India.

The monsoon winds determine the climate of India. From October to mid-June they blow from the Asian interior, bringing cool dry air to the

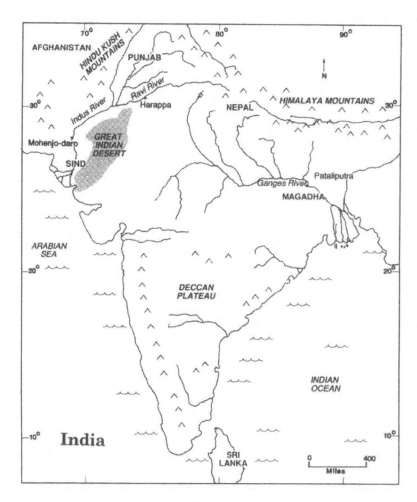

region. Then they reverse. The wind changes direction, blowing across the Indian Ocean from the southwest. These winds are heavy with moisture that falls upon the earth in torrential sheets of rain. The countryside turns green amid the intense heat and humidity of the summer season.

Peoples of the Indus Valley

The first known peoples who came into the Indus Valley were nomads who brought sheep and goats into the region for pasture. After the summer ended they retreated to the west. There was an abundance of wild animals in the dense forests and fish in the rivers. The presence of these nomads is known from the stone tools that they made. After domestication of plants occurred, some people took up farming, planted small gardens, and embraced a settled life. Wheat and barley bread supplemented what nature provided from the forests and grasslands.

These first Indians lived in mud brick houses clustered in villages. Over time they made pottery on the potter's wheel, a major advance over shaping containers by hand.

The first indian civilization was created either by these farmers or by invaders who came later and made the Indus Valley their home about 2500 B.C. Today their homeland is in modern Pakistan.

No one knows the name they called themselves, for the small amount of writing the Indus Valley people left remains undeciphered. As a result, the archaeologist, not the historian, tells us about their lives. Remarkably, it extended farther than any other ancient civilization, spread over thousands of miles with almost 150 sites now identified. For centuries no one knew what to make of the mounds that lay hidden under the sands. Discovered in the nineteenth century, it was only in the past hundred years that the Indus Valley civilization came to be appreciated.

Two Great Cities of the Indus Valley

Of all the sites of the Indus Valley people now known, two large cities stand out. These are Mohenjo-Daro and Harappa, located about 350 miles from one another. Despite the distance, they are carbon copies of each other. The building material was still mud bricks, some unfired, others hardened in a kiln, but all exactly of the same dimension. Both cities had wide streets off of which alleys wandered to people's homes. The major streets ran straight through the towns on a grid pattern, a regularity unknown to any other ancient civilization. Archaeologists estimate that 35,000 people could have made their homes inside each of the cities.

The builders of Mohenjo-Daro constructed their city of mud brick.

Mohenjo-Daro's main avenue had a 200-yard corridor that bisected the city. This was possibly a canal or a tributary of the Indus, diverted to run through the city. A large wall, about 3 miles in circumference, circled the town and protected the inhabitants from outsiders.

To construct such large towns required surveyors, engineers, and master builders. Whoever were the political leaders obviously enjoyed ample resources to put their projects into reality. Both reached the height of their prosperity about 2300 B.C.

The homes in the Indus Valley were not much to look at on the outside with no windows or decorations. Entrances led from alleyways into the homes. Surrounding a courtyard were rooms for the family to meet with friends, cook and eat, sleep, and store their belongings. The courtyard, open to the air, offered light and fresh air. Homes came equipped with indoor plumbing, the first in the world. Bath areas had drains leading to a municipal sewer. People bathed standing up, pouring water over their bodies. Some houses had their own wells that gave them ready access to water.

Both Mohenjo-Daro and Harappa have public buildings that archaeologists identify as citadels. When these cities were excavated, it appears that the Mohenjo-Daro citadel was five stories tall with a large complex of rooms. Here it is surmised that the city elite had their offices for administering the town. Attached was a granary that served the town in times of famine. City administrators collected taxes in the form of grain.

Close by the citadel buildings were large baths, resembling a swimming pool. Builders used asphalt between the bricks to make the pool watertight. Archaeologists believe that the baths served a religious purpose, possibly for the city priests to cleanse themselves before performing certain religious rites. Bathing is still a major devotional exercise for modern Indians, continuing this long tradition.

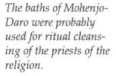

The baths of Mohenjo-Daro were probably used for ritual cleansing of the priests of the religion.

In order to make sure that the spring flood did not damage the citadels, they were built on artificial mounds made of earth and rubble, 40 feet above the plain. In fact, the cities themselves were elevated on similar platforms for the Indus and its tributaries are fickle, changing their course over the years. Layers of sediment show several rebuildings of the Indus Valley cities, the result of repeated flood destruction.

Because no temples seem to have existed, interpreters of the cities' remains surmise that worship to the Harappan deities took place outdoors. The names of the gods remain unknown, but statues show a multiheaded male deity and several bejeweled nude female figures who may either be goddesses or dancing girls. These statues are the only preserved artistic work of the Indus Valley people.

Indus Valley Economy

Most of the Indus Valley people were farmers, growing wheat, barley, and peas on land they had cleared from forest. Possibly they also cultivated rice. The Harappans were well aware of the need for levees and dikes to control the Indus and developed complex irrigation systems to sustain their crops during prolonged droughts.

Cotton was the most important commercial crop. Weavers turned it into cloth that became the major export of the Indus Valley people. Weavers also invented dyes to make clothing more attractive. Cotton cloth making is the major discovery of the Indus Valley people that still affects our own world.

Indus Valley peoples kept a wide variety of animals. Cattle were the most important. Some ancient historians credit them with domesticating the elephant and the chicken.

Merchants traded their goods not only in the Indus Valley but also in a large area extending beyond it. The products they offered consisted of copper tools, pottery, textiles, and wooden objects. The merchants of the Indus Valley, like the Sumerians, marked their goods with inscribed seals that served as their autographs. On the seals they inscribed a pictogram and a verse that is the only example of Harappan writing still extant. About 250 symbols appear on the seals. Standard weights and measures were used throughout the Indus Valley, but 16 rather than 10 was used as the base for calculation. Transportation was on barges on the river or on donkey caravans on the land.

About 1900 B.C. the quality of Indus Valley products went into decline. In the cities builders grew indifferent to fine construction. Obviously the Indus Valley civilization was in a slump.

Various reasons are put forward to explain what was happening. Some believe that the first Aryan invaders appeared in the Indus Valley and destroyed the levees. Other archaeologists attribute the decline to drought and overgrazing of animals, while others attribute it to flooding. The latter explanation appears more credible, given the location of the civilization.

A recent hypothesis notes that about 2000 B.C. the land at the mouth of the Indus River began to rise. Mud volcanoes were responsible. This is a type of volcanic action that causes lava to come to the surface like a thick soup, but without creating a cone.

By raising the land, this volcanic activity eventually completely blocked the Indus river from reaching the sea. Indus waters backed up, creating a great lake over the farmland with waves now lapping against the cities themselves. Merchants no longer sent out their ships, and farmers could no longer plant their crops.

The Harappan towns became islands, with people desperately trying to build higher and higher. About 1700 B.C. the fight appeared hopeless. The Indus Valley people abandoned their valley and its cities. They possibly moved eastward, joining the indigenous hunters and gatherers of other regions of India. Their descendants forgot about urban life and its culture.

Aryans Arrive

About 1500 B.C. a new migrating people arrived in India that soon changed the country's history. They called themselves Aryans, the noble ones. They were a part of the great Indo-European explosion of men and women seeking new homes in Asia and Europe. Originally settling in the lands between the Caspian and Black Seas, they poured into Iran, giving their name to that country. Most continued into India. Their language was **Sanskrit**, distantly related to English, Latin, and Celtic. For example, the word *father* in English is *pater* in Latin, *athir* in Celtic, and *pitar* in Sanskrit.

They were a very warlike people, among whom the display of courage was considered the highest ideal. They fought with bow and arrow from chariots. Charging the enemy in their chariots, they let loose a volley of arrows and then sped back to rearm. They smothered the opposition they met from what remained of the Indus Valley people who had no experience with chariot warfare.

A continuous arrival of more Aryans resulted in the occupation of the whole of northern India. The Deccan and southern India were not touched. Here remnants of the Indus Valley refugees mixed with the indigenous people, known as **Dravidians**. In this early period, the Dravidian cultures of southern India remained outside the thrust of the Aryans.

Aryan culture was quite different from that of the Indus Valley people. The Aryans were frontier people who loved horses and cattle and were indifferent to city life. Their chiefs were chosen because of their ability to fight. Their wealth and importance came from the number of cattle they owned and the victories they had won. Hunting, gambling, and rustling cattle from neighboring people kept boredom away. There were hundreds of small Aryan groups with no centralized authority as opposed to the Indus Valley cities of Mohenjo-Daro and Harappa. The Aryan people were always on the move, building their villages in simple wood and thatch, then driving on with their cattle to another valley.

Cattle gave the Aryans all the necessities of life, for these animals provided milk, hides, meat, and horn for tools. The deep reverence for cows in modern India has a long history. It recalls the close relation that Aryans had for the animals that made their way of life possible.

In addition to chieftains, the Aryan people had religious figures whose prayers and sacrifices served to worship the deities. With singing, dancing, and long complex hymns and chants, Aryan priests officiated at festivals. In this early period of Indian history, the priests memorized the ceremonies. They alone knew the correct formulas. The most celebrated of religious festivals was the horse-sacrifice that required the offering of dozens of animals to the divinities.

Conclusion

The people of the Indus Valley were forgotten for centuries, only to be discovered in the nineteenth century. Archeology alone can tell of their existence.

This is in contrast to the Aryans, whose sacred literature tells of their past. It is true that by 1200 B.C. the Aryans had been in India for at least 300 years and still had built no cities, had no writing, and except for music and the instruments needed to play it, had very little artistic concerns. They were now the masters of North India, the Indus and Ganges Valleys, and were poised to lead India into its classical period.

CHAPTER 5 REVIEW
THE FIRST INDIAN CIVILIZATION

Summary
- India has two great rivers, the Indus and the Ganges.
- The first civilization of India grew up in the Indus Valley.
- Two large cities represent the Indus Valley civilization—Harappa and Mohenjo-Daro.
- The Aryans came into India about 1500 B.C. and from that time onward dominated the civilization there.

Identify
People: Aryans; Dravidians
Places: Indus Valley; Punjab; Harappa; Mohenjo-Daro
Events: building of the Indus Valley cities; arrival of the Aryans

Define
Sanskrit

Multiple Choice
1. India receives water in the form of
    (a) thundershowers.
    (b) monsoons.
    (c) ocean squalls.
    (d) snow in the Deccan Plateau.

2. The Indus Valley people built their cities of
    (a) wood.
    (b) stone.
    (c) mud brick.
    (d) plaster.

3. The Indus Valley cities differ from other ancient towns because
    (a) they were fortified with stone walls.
    (b) they held thousands of people.
    (c) they were placed near rivers.
    (d) they were planned cities.

4. It is hard to follow Indus Valley history since
    (a) the people were isolated from Mesopotamia.
    (b) the people left few written records in a script not yet understood.
    (c) the cities were abandoned very early in history.
    (d) their cities were built in wood, which is not easily preserved.

Essay Questions
1. What factors of Indus Valley civilization make it unique?
2. Describe the life of the Aryans in India.

Answers
1. b
2. c
3. d
4. b

Prehistoric China

Of the four great ancient civilizations, the Chinese is the youngest, but it has also been the most enduring. Although the ancient Egyptian culture has disappeared, the Chinese civilization continues. Since it was the most isolated from the others, its characteristics were the most original, for what the Chinese borrowed, they soon adapted to their own way of life.

Geography of China

China's history, like the other three civilizations of Asia and Africa, began on a river. The Yellow River provided the rich soil for agriculture and the transition to civilization.

The Yellow River is hardly predictable. One year will find it too low, leaving areas once flooded high and dry. The next year it will flood, creating a huge shallow lake only 1 or 2 feet deep over the flat region that surrounds it. Whether the water in the river is too spare or too much, ancient Chinese farmers needed its refreshing waters and accustomed themselves to its moods.

From the earliest period of their history, the Chinese built dikes of earth to channel the river, but time after time it overflowed. When the water retreated, the Yellow River frequently created an entirely new channel, miles from where it once ran to the Yellow Sea, its outlet on the Pacific. Unlike the Nile, the unpredictability of the Yellow River has never allowed it to be tamed.

China has another great river in the south, and although its role has been less in history, the Yangtze has also provided a cultural stimulus to the people living close by. Unlike the Yellow River, the Yangtze is navigable, providing an artery of commerce from the eastern Sichuan region to the sea.

China's mountain ranges run north and south in some parts of the country and east and west in others. Their location has tended to create isolated valleys where communication and transportation proved difficult. People in one region of the country knew little about what was happening in others.

The size of China and the diversity of its landscape results in a varied climate. Northern China is dry with strong winds blowing from Siberia in the winter, making it very cold. Often the skies are a dull yellow at that time, for these winds carry dust from the topsoil of Inner Asia. Known as **loess,** it falls to the ground in northern China, giving the plain rich, fertile soil. Rain comes in the summer to the north, much as in the Midwest region of the United States.

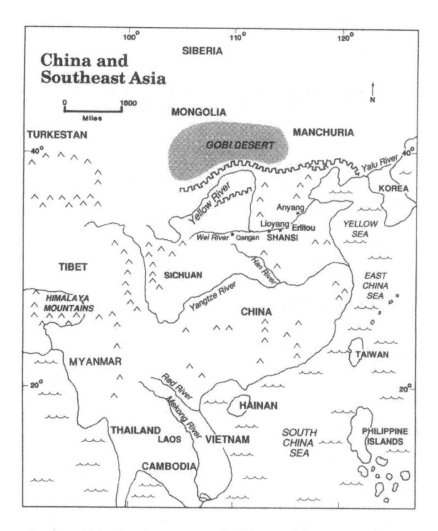

Southern China is quite a contrast. In this part of the country, the ocean determines the climate. Monsoon rains bring torrential downpours, and summer temperatures soar, while winter passes without the cold chill of the north. Climate determined the life of the farmers of both ancient and modern China. Cereal grains, wheat and millet, are the crops of northern China, whereas rice, which must grow in paddies of standing water, predominates in the southern regions of the country.

Chinese Origins

An ancient legend, confirmed from archaeological findings, says that the Chinese people settled along the Yellow River many centuries ago, about 5000 B.C. Archaeologists call this first culture **Yangshao.** Stone tools and pottery decorated with fish and bone motifs are found in grave sites, especially of women. In southern China, Homudu culture demonstrates a different style of pottery and grave gifts.

In the north the Chinese people were farmers, living in small villages on the banks of the Yellow River. Unlike in India, there were no great forests to clear before they began to cultivate the crops that furnished the bulk of their daily diet of bread. China was not rich in native plants that could be domesticated, but millet, a cereal grain grew well. Archaeologists presume that the seeds of wheat and barley entered China as a result of merchants who came all the way from India or even Mesopotamia.

Animals from other regions of Asia also found their way into China. These animals included cattle, dogs, chickens, and pigs. The remains of silkworm cocoons are evidence of **sericulture,** the production of silk, even at this early data. In southern China the water buffalo's introduction provided a beast of burden for the farmers living there.

To the northwest of China, in what is known as Inner Asia, a number of nomadic peoples herded sheep, camels, and horses, which were especially valuable from the point of view of the Chinese. These animals flourished in the cool dry climate of the region.

Chinese farmers both envied and feared the nomadic people—Mongols and Turks—who lived on their frontier. On the one hand there could be active trade, to the advantage of both, for many decades. Then suddenly, a warlord would appear from among the nomads. After recruiting an army, he would charge into China, pillage the farmers' villages, burn them to the ground, and then return to his homeland, his army loaded with booty. The great fertility of the Yellow River plain, despite attacks from the nomads, allowed the population to recover in a short time.

Workers plant seedlings in the rice paddies of southern China.

Legend has it that the first important ruler, Yu the Great, appeared about 2200 B.C. He gave the Chinese their first dynasty, the **Xia.** Yu, who may well be only a mythological figure, is famous for his efforts to control the floods of the Yellow River. A saying arose among the Chinese, "Only Yu saved us from becoming fish."

Yu and the Xia emperors made Erlitou, a town in the southern Shansi region, their capital. A square of buildings with thatched roofs stood upon a foundation of pressed earth. Among them was the royal palace.

Chinese Religion

It is possible that the Chinese people developed their religious beliefs during the Xia period. Among these beliefs, like the people of other ancient civilizations, was the idea that the universe and much of human life's events were the result of unseen forces at work in the world. This animistic belief gave a personality to all objects and required human concern if all was to go well.

The spirit of the heavens, **Tien,** was an all-pervading presence in the universe. Since the Yellow River also had a spirit, a young girl was put on a raft to float down the river as an offering to its god.

Spirits were also a part of the human world, strong or weak, depending on the social importance of a family. Ancestor worship became a major part of Chinese religion, for it was believed that a person's ancestors held on to existence as long as the living prayed and offered sacrifices in his or her name. This is an interesting parallel to the mummification of the Egyptians.

When the emperor died his spirit passed into the next world with servants and soldiers sealed in his tomb to assist him. How it was decided who was given this questionable privilege is unknown.

Certain ceremonies were to be performed in order to contact the spirit world. A religious figure, known by the Siberian title **shaman,** performed the rites that brought a living person into contact with the unseen world of spirits and dead ancestors. Often the shaman went into an ecstatic state. When that happened, the spirit spoke through the shaman, using him or her as a spokesperson.

The shamans were never organized into a class or had any kind of organization. They were charismatic individuals who were thought to have a special gift that allowed them to enter the unseen world.

Shamans often used **oracle bones** to predict the future. Some of the oldest remains of ancient China are the shoulder blades of animals that were heated over a fire until cracks appeared on them. Writing was put on the bones requesting guidance. When the shamans looked at the direction of the cracks, they presumed that they could see into the future. Many of the questions on the oracle bones make enquiries concerning the weather. Others asked questions on marriage or business. Men and women were very interested in knowing the future, a characteristic that has been a part of Chinese culture to the present.

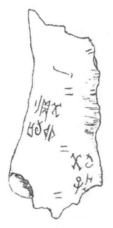

*Cracks on oracle bones
helped shamans of
ancient China to
predict the future.*

Chinese Writing

The signs on the oracle bones were first pictograms, but in time they became abstract symbols or expressions of an idea. In order to write Chinese, the scribe had to memorize every character, and the reader had to know the meaning. The number of characters approached 6,000 and took many years to learn.

Most Chinese words have only one syllable. Each syllable can have a different meaning depending on a high, middle, low, or very low pitch. Of course, this cannot be expressed in writing. That is why all Chinese characters must be memorized. Despite the fact that Chinese has many dialects, all literate people read the same characters and understand the same meaning.

Shang Dynasty

The first historical records from ancient times date from the Shang dynasty, which extended from about 1780 to 1050 B.C. Shang was the title they chose for their imperial name. The **Shang** rulers taught their subjects that they were the **Middle Kingdom,** Zhongguo. The Chinese were at the center of the world, with all other people outside China, the barbarians, surrounding them.

Anyang was one of the Shang capitals, a city located in northern China on the Yellow River. The buildings of the town were wooden and, hence, have not survived except for foundations. In addition to the palace in Anyang, large warehouses stored the grain that the rulers collected for taxes. Powerful aristocrats lived throughout China, anxious to enhance their prestige and wealth by making war or alliances.

Shang metalworkers shaped a ritual vessel in the likeness of two elephants.

Shang emperors took the title Sons of Heaven. They claimed that they were not mere mortals but that heaven had given them their authority to rule the Chinese people. When the emperors died, they were buried in huge tombs similar to, but not quite so grand as, the pyramids of Egypt.

Conclusion

Early China's history is not as well known as that of other civilizations, for its records are sketchy and buildings of perishable material no longer exist. Yet certain patterns of Chinese life, their notion that the emperor represents Heaven, their veneration of ancestors, and their great respect for the spirit world were molded in the experience of ancient China.

CHAPTER 6 REVIEW
PREHISTORIC CHINA

Summary
- China's first civilization was found in the great river valleys of the Yellow and Yangtze Rivers.
- Chinese religion consisted of spirits filling the world and a concern for ancestors.
- The Shang dynasty is the first of China's historical periods.

Identify
People: Yu the Great
Places: Erlitou; Anyang
Events: taming the Yellow River; development of writing

Define

loess	Yangshao	sericulture
Xia	oracle bones	shaman
Tien	Shang	Middle Kingdom

Multiple Choice
1. The first civilization in China was in
   (a) the Yangtze Valley.
   (b) the Yellow River Valley.
   (c) along the shores of the Pacific.
   (d) in the Han River Valley.

2. The Yellow River was dangerous because it often
   (a) ran dry.
   (b) ran between mountains.
   (c) flooded.
   (d) has cataracts.

3. Loess makes up
   (a) volcanic ash.
   (b) limestone.
   (c) the soil of northern China.
   (d) the great river of southern China.

4. The grain crop of southern China is
   (a) wheat.
   (b) barley.
   (c) millet.
   (d) rice.

5. The Chinese language has to be spoken
   (a) using three tones.
   (b) in four different tones.
   (c) with many grammatical inflections.
   (d) only in a low voice.

6. The horse nomads to the northwest of early China were the
   (a) Vietnamese.
   (b) Mongols and Turks.
   (c) Indians.
   (d) Tibetans.

7. Cracks on oracle bones helped ancient Chinese shamans
   (a) choose emperors.
   (b) tell how the animals died.
   (c) make soup.
   (d) predict the future.

8. Chinese religion was very much concerned with
   (a) writing sacred texts.
   (b) organizing priesthoods.
   (c) great processions.
   (d) honoring ancestral spirits.

9. The Middle Kingdom, or Zhongguo, was the Chinese way of talking about their
   (a) history.
   (b) religion.
   (c) concept of the world.
   (d) form of government.

10. Shang society was dominated by
    (a) powerful aristocrats.
    (b) astrologers.
    (c) the army.
    (d) the weather.

Essay Questions
1. Discuss how the first Chinese farmers coped with the Yellow River.
2. How does ancient Chinese religion differ from that of Mesopotamia and Egypt?

Answers

1. b	6. b
2. c	7. d
3. c	8. d
4. d	9. c
5. b	10. a

CHAPTER 7

Mediterranean Regions in the Ancient World

The Mediterranean Sea lies at the southern border of Europe and separates the continent from northern Africa and the **Levant,** the coastal region of southwestern Asia. For many reasons it is unique. Its size is impressive, covering over 1,000,000 square miles and extending east to west 2,300 miles. It is warmer, deeper, and saltier than other bodies of water because of its high evaporation rate during the summer. This gives it a deeper shade of blue. Two thirds of the Mediterranean's water flows into it from the Atlantic at the Straits of Gibraltar, a very narrow channel, 8 miles wide, between modern Spain and Morocco.

Because the Mediterranean is so large, some parts have their own names. The Aegean Sea, dotted with islands, is at the far eastern section of the Mediterranean. Some of the islands are but a few miles off the Anatolian coast, where the Hittites and other advanced cultures had been located.

Cycladic Origins

European civilization began on the islands of the Aegean known as the Cyclades, because the Greeks believed they formed a circle about the tiny island of Delos. *Kyklos* is the Greek word for circle. Here during the Bronze Age people turned from hunting and gathering to agriculture. This advance was the result of the introduction of three major crops that came from southwestern Asia: wheat, grapes, and olives. Together they are known as the **Mediterranean triad,** for throughout the course of history these three foods have always been the staples of Mediterranean peoples from the ancient world to the present.

There is no way to know exactly when farming began on the islands, but recent studies suggest about 3000 B.C. While wheat and olive oil, if not the olives themselves, could be stored for a long time, this was not possible with grapes. Grapes spoil easily. Then someone discovered that grapes could be squeezed and their juice extracted and, if conditions were right, fermented. Soon vineyards sprouted all over the islands as farmers planted more and more grapes on the hillsides to provide the wine that became the favored drink of the islanders.

The need for containers to store the wine was immediately evident, resulting in a major impetus for Bronze Age potters. Artisans also set to work on wagons and carts to transport the grapes to the wine presses and then to the island harbors where the containers were collected for export.

Out of this economic surge based on the wine trade, early political life on the Cyclades developed. Someone had to oversee the market, police the merchant stalls, establish weights and measures, and see that workers cleaned up after the day was over. This supervisor emerged into a political leader, responsible for keeping order throughout the island. The Cycladic islands produced a dozen petty chieftains, all intent on preserving their markets.

The artists of the Cyclades developed sculptures of people and faces that resemble modern abstract productions.

Along with wine, olive oil and metals made up the trade of the Aegean. Shipbuilding was also a major industry, putting a heavy demand on the fragile forests of the islands. The result is still evident, for the Cyclades today are bare and rocky with hardly a tree to be seen.

The island populations of the Cyclades had no room for expansion, limited as they were by the sea that surrounded them. They had done their part in igniting the spark of European civilization that now passed to the larger island of Crete.

Crete extends for 160 miles east and west and averages about 30 miles north and south, making it much larger than any of the Cyclades. Its size and location in the heart of the Aegean fitted it to take up a civilizing role.

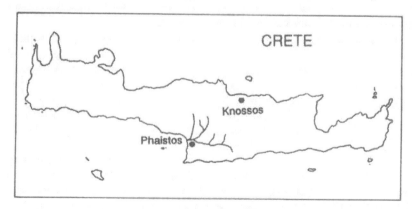

Discovery of Minoan Civilization

When European travelers visited Crete in the eighteenth and nineteenth centuries, they heard stories about a great civilization that once flourished on the island. There was little sign of that wonderful period at that time, except for some seals that looked a bit like those of southwestern Asia.

A British archaeologist, Arthur Evans, came to Crete to study the seals and then, in A.D. 1897, received permission from Ottoman officials to excavate a mound a few miles outside the city of Iraklion. Evans's workers soon discovered that they were on to a major discovery. From A.D. 1899 until 1914, Evans directed the excavations that resulted in the discovery of Europe's first civilization. He worked again from A.D. 1920 to 1932, allowing him to publish his finds in the five-volume work, *The Palace of Minos.* Since Evans finished his work, many other archaeologists have worked in Crete where proven sites number in the hundreds. Archaeologists now use aerial photography to discover additional ones. Once considered palaces, modern archaeologists identify Minoan remains as elaborate centers of civic life.

Minoans

Evans gave the name Minoans to the people who created the civilization of Crete. He borrowed the name from a Greek myth that the Athenians told about Theseus, the legendary founder of their city. In this story the Athenians recalled that Minos, a great and powerful king, once lived on Crete in a large palace. The king's life, however, was not altogether a happy one because his wife had proven unfaithful and had an affair with a bull. Their offspring was therefore half-bull and half-human and was something of an embarrassment for the royal family. The Minotaur was given his own pen, the **labyrinth,** constructed by a clever Greek, Daedalus.

Each year the Greeks sent six young men and six young women to Crete to satisfy the Minotaur's appetite for human flesh. Then Theseus volunteered to go to Crete to slay the Minotaur. Luckily, Ariadne, daughter of Minos, fell in love with Theseus, so that she provided him with a cord to spin out as he ventured through the labyrinth. Otherwise, even if he survived the encounter with the monster, Theseus might never have found his way out. The story then goes on to tell of Theseus's success and how he followed the cord, finding his way back to Ariadne and the royal palace.

Theseus and Ariadne got on board his ship to return to Athens, but he left her on the island of Naxos. Abandoned, her tears brought her a lover in the god, Dionysos, who gave her a crown in the sky as a wedding present. This is the constellation of the Pleiades, or the little crown. So despite her initial setback, she and her crown are still remembered, while Theseus is forgotten. The words *Minotaur* and *labyrinth* have entered the English language.

This story shows that the Athenians remembered that at one time they had to pay tribute to Crete. For Evans, the name Minos was entirely appropriate for the Cretans because the name they called themselves remains unknown.

The first people who lived on Crete came during the Stone Age. They left their tools and pottery in sites that are sometimes filled with debris several yards deep. There were also clay figures of goddesses that are similar to those found in Anatolia.

The Bronze Age on Crete is known as the Early Minoan and extends from about 3000 to 1950 B.C. During that time there was a great deal of trade between the island and Egypt. The Egyptians shipped much of the metalware that found its way into Crete.

Already the population was growing. People lived in villages of mud brick houses that grew larger as wheat and grape cultivation spread. Olive trees covered the sides of mountains. Silver and gold jewelry were part of the exchange with Egypt and Anatolia, as were the daggers that the well-dressed men of the towns favored.

The skill of the potters in Minoan society is evidenced with further development of fine pottery. One kind was so thin that it is known as **egg-shell ware.** It was so delicate that vases and cups of this variety could have been used only for decoration.

About 1950 B.C. there was an urban revolution. An increase in agricultural productivity allowed many people to settle in towns where they specialized in a variety of crafts. Unlike Mesopotamia or Egypt, architects built complexes of administrative, religious, and manufacturing centers rather than temples or ruler's palaces. Knossos held the largest center, but Mallia and Phaistos also had impressive constructions.

Arthur Evans reconstructed much of the palace at Knossos. This is how it appears today.

The Minoan cities had no walls, an exception to the general rule that ancient cities needed them for protection. On Crete, the rulers depended upon their navy to defend the island from attack.

A network of roads connected all the major cities, which has lead archaeologists to assume that there was only one king at Knossos. Probably it was members of his family or his appointees who lived in the other great centers of the island.

The Minoans city centers had certain common features. Large stone blocks were at the entrance, which led to a large rectangular courtyard with separate rooms built around it. Later the rooms were connected to form a single rambling structure. Some of the rooms appear to be living quarters; others are presumed to be halls used for public affairs. Ingeniously constructed shafts provided light and ventilation to interior rooms. Building materials were of brick, stone, and timber.

The walls of the rooms were painted with bright frescoes showing plants, animals, and the people of the center. The scenes with men and women in them demonstrate that the Minoans were interested in a wide variety of sports. These included boxing, wrestling, and fishing. The most interesting activity was bull-jumping. Acrobats, men and women, did somersaults on the back of a bull to the delight of festival crowds.

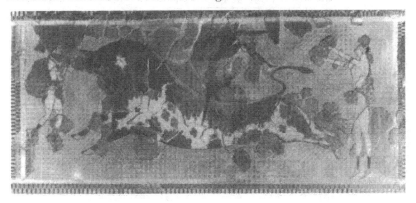

A fresco depicts skilled acrobats bull-jumping. The two lighter figures are women, the darker figure on top of the bull is a man.

The celebrations of the Minoans must have endeared the king to his people; however, the collection of taxes in the form of oil and grain to be kept in storerooms probably did not. The storage jars were so large that they had to be put in place by using ropes, for they were much too heavy for a single man to lift.

In order to keep records for their economic activities, the Minoans developed a script that archaeologists call **Linear A.** This script uses signs to record how many cattle or sheep the writer wanted to inventory.

It appears that the Minoan religion required no large temples to house gods and goddesses. They were content to receive offerings outdoors or in mountain shrines. Statues of a mother goddess show her with snakes crawling up her arms and in her hands. Sometimes she appears as a bird or a butterfly goddess. Another kind of worship was focused on the strength exhibited in the bull. Minoans built shrines that resembled a bull's horns, perhaps to give power to the rulers of the Knossos dynasty.

The Minoans had one serious problem. Earthquakes were very common on their mountainous island. On several occasions they shook the center buildings, causing them to collapse. Then the wealth of the nation had to be used to rebuild them.

About 1620 B.C. a major explosion blew up the small Cycladic island of Santorini, located about 80 miles north of Crete. All over the Aegean ash rained down on the cities of the region. A great tidal wave struck the harbors of northern Crete, destroying the ships and port facilities. Farmers found their vineyards and fields covered with ash and the sun blotted out because of the dust in the air. Multiple seasons passed when crops did not grow in this environment, and Minoans were never able to recover their earlier prosperity.

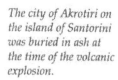
The city of Akrotiri on the island of Santorini was buried in ash at the time of the volcanic explosion.

In their weakened state the Minoans lay open to invasion. About 100 years later a band of Mycenaean Greek adventurers landed on Crete. They took over the Minoan centers and established their own dynasty. The Greeks adapted Linear A for their own purposes in a script that archaeologists call **Linear B.**

Once again prosperity came to the island, but there was an underlying discontent with Greek rule. Most Minoans resented the foreign presence, and the Greeks found it increasingly difficult to govern. About 1350 B.C. all the centers on Crete were burned down, yet few human bones and no gold or silver were discovered. In one room of the Knossos center, pots were left unfinished, leading archaeologists to believe that a Minoan artisan was unaware that the Greek masters had stripped the building of its wealth and were returning to the mainland. This marked the end of Minoan civilization.

In Homer's time he writes in the *Odyssey* that Crete has countless people in 90 cities, but nearly all are Greek newcomers who have settled there. The greatness of Minoan civilization, except for the legend of Theseus and the Minotaur, became a forgotten episode of history.

Indo-European Migrations

Although no one is certain of the origins of the Minoans, most people think they migrated to Crete from Anatolia and the Cycladic islands of the Aegean. At the same time that they crossed the sea to build their civilization on Crete, other peoples were on the move in the Balkans and spreading northward and westward into the Caspian and Black Sea regions. Ever restless, once they learned how to use horses, they continued their nomadic way of life until some reached as far as Ireland to the west and as far as India to the east.

These people belonged to the Indo-European language group. As they traveled, they left their name for noblemen, *aryan*, from Ireland to Iran to India.

Little by little the Indo-Europeans spread over the European continent, subduing the Neolithic hunters who were there before them. Some archaeologists believe that the modern-day Basques of Spain and France are the only remnants of the pre-Indo-European population of Europe that have survived until modern times.

By about 2000 B.C. Indo-European speakers had divided into the Slavic speakers of East Europe, the Italic speakers of the Italian peninsula, and the Celts in central Europe from the Black Sea to Ireland. The German people penetrated to the Baltic Sea and Scandinavia, and the Iberians traveled into the lands of modern Spain and Portugal. The farthest Indo-European penetration reached the Canary Islands of the Atlantic, a population that disappeared only about A.D. 1300.

Although the Indo-Europeans may not have initiated the megalith building that was so much a part of the Neolithic Age in Europe, they soon caught the fever. Some of the later megaliths are recent enough to evidence Indo-European construction.

A dolman in County Carlow, Ireland, was probably the tomb of an important chieftain.

The Balkan peninsula had three groups of Indo-Europeans prior to 2000 B.C. Those on the west were the Illyrians; those on the east were the Thracians; and advancing down the southern part of the Balkans, the Greeks.

Our knowledge of the Greeks far surpasses anything known about the other Indo-Europeans of the Balkans. They were first to record their history, having picked up the alphabet before all others. Their contact with the Minoans, who traded with them in the Peloponnesus, gave them a head start in learning how to construct a civilization. Sometime between 1900 and 1700 B.C. the Greeks reached the bottom of the Balkan peninsula, a region known as the **Peloponnesus.**

Mycenaeans

The first Greeks are known as Mycenaeans. When they arrived, they came as warriors, caring nothing for settled village life. Once they finished looting what wealth the Neolithic towns held, they started their own towns, making sure that they surrounded them with strong walls.

The largest of the settlements of these Greeks was at Mycenae in the northern Peloponnesus. Since it was the capital, its name now describes the culture of all the people who lived under its leadership.

The palace at Mycenae itself had an excellent position for defense, set on a hill about 900 feet high. Around it, builders constructed a strong wall of huge stones. A large lintel doorway permitted entrance to the castle. Over it artists placed a sculpture depicting two lions facing a pillar. After 3,500 years it still stands in place, with multiple explanations of its meaning.

The Lion Gate of Mycenae is at the entrance of the castle.

The kings of Mycenae wanted their graves placed inside the city walls where their successors could make sure that they would rest undisturbed. They are called shaft graves because their entrances passed along narrow passageways. Inside the graves the kings were laid to rest with a variety of grave gifts. The most striking are gold masks placed over the face of the dead ruler and beautiful inlaid daggers laid by their side. The precious metals used to bury the rulers came from the tribute that Mycenae levied on the towns under its control and from pirate raids launched against other people of the eastern Mediterranean.

A shaft grave at Mycenae held the remains of the royal family.

The Mycenaeans learned a great deal from the Minoans on Crete, especially shipbuilding. When they felt that they knew enough, about 1480 B.C., they invaded Crete and occupied Knossos. Archaeologists have found many Linear B tablets at both Knossos and on the Peloponnesian mainland. This was during the period of Mycenae's greatness, from 1500 to 1200 B.C.

At the close of the period of Mycenaean prosperity, a new wave of destruction struck the eastern Mediterranean. The Hittite Empire collapsed, and from Greece to Egypt and along the Syrian coast, cities went up in flames. A flash flood and an earthquake weakened Mycenaean defenses. Except for Athens, the cities of Mycenaean Greece were destroyed. Although invaders may have had a role, new interpretations argue that the Mycenaean collapse was more the result of its own weaknesses combined with natural catastrophes.

Mycenaean civilization came to an end, but the stories of past heroes and conquests were still remembered centuries later, when they reappeared in Homer's classic tales of the *Iliad* and *Odyssey*.

Rest of Europe

North of the Greeks, Europe remained a world without cities, writing, or significant technological progress. People still lived in small villages, in log homes, and grew crops or herded animals, but without writing little can be known about them. Because their dwellings were made from wood, they have perished.

Tools and weapons made of bronze replaced those of copper, yet it was only about 1500 B.C. that any kind of metal became known in Scandinavia. Mining developed into an important industry, and the man who controlled its production could lay claim to great wealth. Kings and nobles prized two-edged swords as their weapon of choice. The myths of the time tell of strong queens who were also warriors.

Graves are the clue to much that is known of life at this time. Subjects buried their chieftains in timber tombs, often in a chariot, that they covered over with earth. Gold and silver ornaments and weapons decorated the corpse. Another alternative was cremation, which apparently was thought to free the soul from the body and prevent the dead from returning to interfere in human affairs.

The islands of the Mediterranean were especially rich in stone tombs and forts. People in Sicily, Corsica, Malta, and the Balearic Islands gave their chieftains final resting places worthy of their position while on earth. About 1500 B.C. Stonehenge, in England, the most impressive of ancient monuments, received its final touches.

Conclusion

The advance of civilization across Europe did not move quickly. Generally the Indo-Europeans were content to live very simple nomadic lives, rejecting the notion that settling down in an urban setting offered a preferred existence.

Their contacts with the Minoans of Crete finally convinced the Mycenaean Greeks that city life and literacy, the fabric of civilization, were to be admired and imitated. Mycenae and other towns appeared at the tip of the Balkan peninsula. For better or worse, urbanization began its hesitant march northward into Europe.

CHAPTER 7 REVIEW
MEDITERRANEAN REGIONS IN THE ANCIENT WORLD

Summary
- The Mediterranean coast was the home of many cultures in the ancient world.
- The first Mediterranean civilization appeared in the Cycladic islands and then moved to Crete.
- Cultivation of wheat, grapes, and olives supported Mediterranean agriculture.
- The Minoans built large complex civic centers originally known as palaces.
- The Minoan cities were centers of trade and shipbuilding.
- The art of the Minoans demonstrates a keen aesthetic sense.
- The Mycenaean Greeks settled in the Peloponnesus, creating a culture based on the building of cities.
- Indo-Europeans occupied the whole of Europe but resisted urbanization.

Identify
People: Arthur Evans; Theseus; Greeks; Minoans; Indo-Europeans; Sea Peoples
Places: Levant; Knossos; Peloponnesus; Stonehenge; Cyclades; Aegean Sea; Mycenae
Events: beginning of agriculture on the Cyclades; Santorini explosion; building of Minoan centers; establishment of the Mycenaeans in Greece; Indo-European settlement

Define

Mediterranean triad	Linear A	labyrinth
Linear B	Levant	egg-shell pottery

Multiple Choice
1. The Mediterranean Sea extends east to west
    (a) 2,300 miles.
    (b) 1,500 miles.
    (c) 300 miles.
    (d) 23,000 miles.

2. Because of the fragile nature of grapes
    (a) Mediterranean people harvested them in the spring.
    (b) people allowed them to ferment into wine.
    (c) beer became the most popular drink of the Mediterranean.
    (d) they were not grown in the Cyclades.

3. The discoverer of ancient Minoan civilization was
    (a) Robert Leakey.
    (b) Donald Joanson.
    (c) Arthur Evans.
    (d) Heinrich Schliemann.

4. According to the myth of Theseus,
    (a) the Minoans built a capital in Greece.
    (b) the Minotaur represented King Minos.
    (c) the Greeks founded Minoan civilization.
    (d) Athens once paid tribute to Crete.

5. The defense of Minoan civilization was left up to
    (a) walls.
    (b) a professional army.
    (c) a navy.
    (d) castles.

6. Minoan taxes were collected in
    (a) coins.
    (b) oil and grain.
    (c) art works.
    (d) weapons.

7. Minoan writing is called
    (a) Linear B.
    (b) Linear A.
    (c) hieroglyphs.
    (d) pictographic.

8. Possibly the decline of Minoan civilization was due to
    (a) drought.
    (b) flood.
    (c) volcanic explosion.
    (d) disease.

9. The first Greeks established a town at
    (a) Athens.
    (b) Sparta.
    (c) Corinth.
    (d) Mycenae.

10. The Mycenaeans were noted for their
    (a) building a labyrinth.
    (b) use of iron.
    (c) writing Linear A.
    (d) burying their dead chieftains with gold masks over their faces.

Essay Questions
1. How do you explain the beginning of civilization on the Cycladic islands?
2. Discuss the religion of the Minoans.
3. Do you see a connection between the end of Minoan civilization and the myth of Atlantis, the city that sank beneath the sea?

Answers
1. a	6. b
2. b	7. b
3. c	8. c
4. d	9. d
5. c	10. d

CHAPTER 8

The First Americans

The discovery of America took place long before Columbus stepped onto San Salvador in the Bahamas. Although there is still no agreement on the exact date, as early as 36,000 B.C. or as late as 28,000 B.C., Cro-Magnons arrived on the North American continent. They came across the Bering Strait, possibly walking at a time when glaciers held so much of the ocean's water, that a land bridge existed between Asia and Alaska. Another theory holds that they made boats to carry them across the 60 miles of open water that now separates the two continents.

These first discoverers have no name, but they are the ancestors of the thousands of American Indians who came to populate the Western Hemisphere. There may have been only one small band of hunters who made the journey, for nearly all American Indians today have type O blood, and none have type A. Because all other people in the world have a mixture of blood types (the absence or presence of certain antigens on the membranes of red blood cells), it may be that there was only a single migration thousands of years ago.

Other anthropologists believe that physical differences among the American Indians are so distinct that a single migration cannot explain them. Evidence of human occupation does not appear until rather late. Certainly the last people to cross into the Americas are the Inuit, or Eskimos, who have close relatives remaining in Siberia, hunters like themselves of bears, caribou, and sea mammals.

Hunters of the Americas

Archaeologists have found the homes of a few of these first hunters. They were dug into the ground in order to hold warmth and are called **pit houses**. A frame made of limbs or large animal bones provided a structure when covered with hides.

The American Indian men were expert spear throwers, able to pursue bears, mammoths, and other animals much larger than themselves. Women and children gathered plant food, berries, nuts, and seeds of plants that would keep during the long winters. The numerous lakes and streams filled with trout and salmon supplemented the meat secured by hunters.

Little by little, Indian families began to move out of Alaska and Canada into regions where the weather was milder. When a small group of men and women, with their children, broke away from the group, over time their descendants changed the original language so much that a new one developed. The number of distinct Indian languages in the Americas is counted at several thousand, a testimony to the isolation of the early American Indian bands wandering over vast, empty lands.

Developments in Mexico

About 21,000 B.C. the first tool making appeared in Mexico. The American Indians who lived here needed spear points in order to hunt the mammoths, camels, and an early species of horse then found in Central America. They were possibly extremely skillful hunters, for today these animals are extinct in the Americas. The Spaniards brought with them all the horses now found in the Western Hemisphere.

About 8000 B.C. the hunters of Mexico took up a new way of life. The climate had changed so dramatically that only small animals like foxes and rabbits made up their prey. A food crisis loomed on the horizon.

Women probably experimented with the plants they gathered and soon discovered those plants that could be domesticated. The crisis passed. The plants included a variety of beans, squash, pumpkins, and chili peppers. Someone also discovered a species of cotton that could be woven into cloth.

Modern corn developed into its present form from wild grasses.

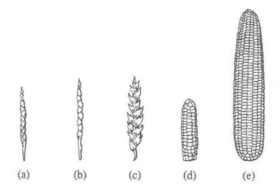

(a)   (b)   (c)   (d)   (e)

Of all the plants that the American Indians living in Mexico discovered, the most important was **maize,** or corn. When the first wild maize plants cross-pollinated with another wild grass, they had only small heads of grain. Over time, wild maize became cross-pollinated with another kind of grass. Therefore, when the American Indians first began to cultivate corn, perhaps as early as 5000 or as late as 3500 B.C., it was already a hybrid. The farmers then began helping nature. They pollinated by hand the corn stalks with the largest number of grains so that the cobs kept getting more kernels. Women took the corn and ground it into flour, using a pestle and mortar.

Women used a pestle and mortar to grind corn for thousands of years. It is still in use in some parts of the Americas.

The domestication of corn was a major advance in human nutrition. It enabled the population of Mexico to increase to a point that town life now appeared.

South America

The northern region of South America received its first human inhabitants about 20,000 years ago. The geography and climate of South America, with its tall mountains and impenetrable jungles, meant that the tip of South America, the land of Tierra del Fuego, saw no people until about 8000 B.C.

The rain forests of the Amazon presented a formidable barrier to early human settlement.

The peoples of South America continued to live in hunting and gathering societies until the Indians of Peru commenced experimentation in cultivating plants. This occurred between 7000 and 2500 B.C. The exact date remains illusive. Regions within the Andes Mountains were especially productive, for dozens of food plants could be successfully grown here and in the coastal region of Peru. After a stable supply of these foods was forthcoming, as in Mexico, the population began to increase.

Conclusion

The reconstruction of the distant past of the American Indian is ongoing. Archaeologists are still in the process of searching out sites of the early men and women of the continent who first made their homes in the Western Hemisphere. After further investigation, the exact time frame will become less subject to debate. Until then, historians can only speculate on the lives and travels of the first Americans and the developments that shaped their lives.

CHAPTER 8 REVIEW
THE FIRST AMERICANS

Summary
- The first Americans came many thousands of years ago to the Americas.
- They arrived in the Aleutian Islands and Alaska.
- The American Indians hunted large animals such as the mammoth and camel.
- When the climate changed, hunters had to look for smaller game.
- The first tool making appeared in Mexico.
- American Indians invented agriculture in Mexico and Peru.

Identify
People: First Americans; Inuit
Places: Alaska; Aleutian Islands; Bering Strait; Andes Mountains
Events: discovery of maize

Define
blood types   pit houses   maize

Multiple Choice
1. The first Americans were people who crossed into
    (a) California.
    (b) Alaska.
    (c) British Columbia.
    (d) South America.

2. The last people to cross from Asia to the Americas are
    (a) the Sioux.
    (b) the Tlingit.
    (c) the Inuit.
    (d) the Athabascans.

3. The first Indian hunters looked for
    (a) large animals like the mammoth.
    (b) rabbits and foxes.
    (c) birds and reptiles.
    (d) rodents.

4. Corn was first domesticated by the Indians of
    (a) Peru.
    (b) Mexico.
    (c) California.
    (d) the Mississippi Valley.

Essay Questions
1. How did climate affect the American Indian way of life?
2. Explain the variety and similarities among the early American Indian population.

Answers
1. b   3. a
2. c   4. b

UNIT 3

CLASSICAL WORLDS:
1200 B.C.–A.D. 500

Southwest Asia in a Time of Empires

Southwest Asia in the period from 1200 to 334 B.C. saw the rise and fall of many empires as one people held supremacy for several centuries only to be followed by another. It was a restless time, when rulers sat uneasily on their thrones.

Intense religious activity marked this period. Both Judaism and Mazdaism originated in the shadow of Southwest Asia's time of empires.

Assyrians

The rise of Assyria was the most striking event in Mesopotamia. The Assyrians were a Semitic-speaking people, who had long lived in the upper region of the Tigris and Euphrates Valley, but they were spectators rather than participants in the civilizations that developed to the south. On all sides they had hostile enemies; hence, they acquired a major concern for defense.

The Assyrians began to assert themselves only about 1350 B.C. In this early period they became noted for their military strength and the cruelty they used to make certain that subject people were aware of the price they paid for any hint of revolt.

The first victims of Assyrian imperialism were the Kassites of lower Babylonia. Then the Assyrian kings turned their armies against their northern neighbors in the kingdom of Urartu. The strongest of the conquerors was Tiglath-Pilesar I, ruling from 1116 to 1078 B.C. His ruthless shifting of population and merciless disposal of his enemies brought fear and trembling to all subject peoples from the Mediterranean to the Persian Gulf.

After Tiglath-Pilesar no king approached his level of competence so that Assyrian power languished for a century and a half, only to be renewed in the time of Shalmaneser III about 859 B.C. Each year this ruler led his armies into territories not yet incorporated into the Assyrian state. When the Assyrians overran new regions, the inhabitants were forced to move far away from their homeland, and new settlers from other parts of Southwest Asia replaced them. Assyrian chronicles speak of over a hundred such deportations. The idea was to break the will of the conquered.

Nineveh, the capital of Assyria, was the largest and most impressive city of Southwest Asia, if not the world, in the seventh century. From his palace, the Assyrian king set up a strong financial system for the state, ensuring that taxes would be assessed and collected on a regular basis. The

Assyrians created the first fully developed bureaucratic state to appear in world history.

Despite their skills in war, the Assyrians were anxious to excel in other ways. These areas included their interest in history, for palace scribes kept careful notes on all the campaigns of the kings. Needless to say, they were always "victors," even when they were not.

Sculptors had a special place in Assyrian society, for the rulers wanted posterity to gaze admiringly on their portraits. They are depicted receiving tribute from conquered kings and hunting in their chariots. The sculptors told the stories of their conquests carved in stone on successive panels. Sculptors also pictured hunting scenes. In fact so many lions died at the hands of Assyrian rulers that the animals practically became extinct in Mesopotamia.

An Assyrian sculpture depicts the king killing a lion.

The last major ruler of Assyria was Assurbanapal. The library that he collected at Nineveh, 25,000 tablets, is a storehouse of information on Southwest Asia. Here were housed collections of all previous Mesopotamian literature. His patronage of sculptors and painters made the Nineveh palace the wonder of his contemporaries. At his death in 627 B.C., it appeared that Assyria stood at the pinnacle of success.

Like all empires in their glory, appearances were deceptive. Assyrian energies were on the wane after years of campaigns that embittered so many people. Revolts, despite the ferocity of their repression, continued to flare, as enemies gathered outside the nation. In 612 B.C. the final blow fell on Nineveh when the Medes and Babylonians allied to destroy Assyria. The Babylonians now inherited the position of leadership in Mesopotamia.

Babylonians

For a century the greatness of Babylon was evident under kings who were known as the **Chaldean** or New-Babylonian dynasty. Having destroyed the Assyrians and checked the Egyptians, the renewed Babylonian state became quite formidable. The reign of Nebuchadnezzar II the Great, from 605 to 561 B.C. was the most brilliant.

It was then that Babylon surpassed all other southwestern Asian cities, with a population of nearly 100,000 men and women. The city wall of brick, with towers every 60 feet, extended for 10 miles. Built on both sides of the Euphrates, a great bridge connected the two parts of the city. A wide avenue led to the temple of Marduk, the chief god, and his ziggurat. The temple interior was covered with gold as well as the statue of the deity. Builders decorated the outside with glazed tiles.

Babylon's famous "hanging gardens" were a wonder of the ancient world. To please his queen a Babylonian king ordered a terrace of trees and bushes to be planted on an artificial mound that, at a distance, seemed to hang in the air.

From Marduk's ziggurat Babylonian wise men studied the heavens at night. The astronomers noted the rise of certain constellations during the year, enabling them to construct the zodiac and a monthly calendar. The Babylonians were competent in mathematics, enabling them to find the square root of numbers and to compute percentages.

The Babylonian supremacy, however, was to last no longer than its great monarch. It was now a new Southwest Asian power's turn to rise to prominence. This was Persia. Babylon, because of its wealth and presumed decadence, became a symbol of urban corruption in the literature of its neighbors long after the city disappeared.

Peoples of Syria

In 1200 B.C. the Canaanites were the dominant people of Syria, where they had settled, about the same time that Egypt was in its Old Kingdom. The Canaanite population increased considerably during the Bronze Age, with cities along the Mediterranean as well as inland increasing in size and wealth. Although often conquered by empire-builders of either Mesopotamia or Egypt, the bulk of the Canaanite people remained in place as tributaries of Akkadians, Hittites, Assyrians, Babylonians, or Egyptians.

In 1200 B.C. the Canaanite region consisted of three parts. The coastal area was Phoenicia, famous for its merchants that sailed the Mediterranean and the purple dye they sold. This dye gave its name to Phoenicia, for Greeks knew the region as the land of the purple merchants. Cities of importance in Phoenicia were Byblos, Sidon, and Tyre, which are now found in the modern state of Lebanon.

Inland from Phoenicia was the country of the Arameans, located between the desert and the Lebanon mountains. Damascus was its best-known city. The merchants among the Arameans traveled so extensively that their language spread all over Syria as the common idiom of discourse.

The third region was Palestine. Once a Canaanite preserve, it became a land contested between Philistines and Hebrews after 1200 B.C. The Philistines, part of the Sea Peoples that scourged the eastern Mediterranean, settled along the Palestinian coast, giving their name to the area. Inland, the Hebrews invaded Palestine in the thirteenth century B.C. after an escape from Egypt.

Hebrews

Despite their small numbers, the Hebrews have had a major impact on the history of Southwest Asia and later on Europe and the world. In fact, while Assyrians, Phoenicians, and Arameans are almost forgotten, the Jewish people, descendants of the Hebrews, are in the news daily. Their continued prominence demonstrates a remarkable tenacity to survive from ancient times to the present. The modern state of Israel is the result of a return of the Jews to their ancient homeland.

The Sea of Galilee empties into the Jordan River.

The region of Palestine that became Jewish territory was not an earthly paradise. It was a land of arid plateaus with but a few fertile valleys. Obtaining sufficient water was, and is, a major concern. The Sea of Galilee and the Jordan River were the only sources of fresh water in Palestine. The Jordan's terminus is the landlocked Dead Sea, so full of salt from centuries of evaporation that it is practically devoid of life.

If their numbers were so few that stronger nations constantly threatened their existence and the land they occupied so poor, then what explains their continued existence? The answer lies in their religious beliefs. No other people of Southwest Asia developed a faith that was able to bond its nation together so successfully.

The Hebrew Bible

The history of the Hebrews is told in one of the most remarkable books ever written, the Bible. This collection of literature includes many genres: history, myth, novels, poetry, songs, and works of practical advice. Through reading it carefully, it is possible to trace the story of the Hebrews from their origins to Hellenistic times.

The authors of most of the books of the Hebrew Bible are anonymous. The authors lived from approximately the tenth through the second century B.C. helping to explain the Bible's diversity. When they wrote, the authors drew extensively on an oral tradition that was centuries old. The first narrator, probably a court historian of either King David or Solomon, told the history of his people from Abraham to David.

The Bible is divided into three major sections: the Law, **Torah;** the Prophets, **Nebi'im;** and the Writings, **Kethubim.** The Hebrew Bible, as it now exists, was shaped by Jewish teachers or rabbis who decided what books should be included in the **canon,** or list of sacred books. This happened after the Roman destruction of Jerusalem in A.D. 70, at a time when the literature of the Bible was in danger of being lost.

Hebrew Beginnings

The origin of the Hebrews is told at the beginning of the Bible, known as the book of Genesis. According to Genesis, the creator of the universe was **Yahweh,** the Lord, or Elohim, God. What made Yahweh different from all other deities of the ancient Southwest Asian world was the conviction that he was the one and only divine being, neither male nor female, without any partners. He created the universe effortlessly, simply by saying it should be. He could also be a destroyer, as was remembered in the story of the flood. Most importantly, Yahweh was concerned with morality among humans and intended to reward the good and punish the evil. He was constant, but not immutable, and often interacted with the Hebrews.

These ideas about Yahweh were not there at the beginning. At first Yahweh was but one god among many, the deity that was the particular protector of the progeny of Abraham, founder of the Hebrew people. The biblical authors' conception of their god was always developing.

Out of his good will toward humans, the Bible taught that Yahweh intervened in human history. He chose a Semite from among the Habiru, a herding nomadic group, named Abram, later Abraham, to leave his homeland in Mesopotamia and journey into the hill country of Palestine. There his family, children, and grandchildren, settled sometime about 1700 B.C. The descendants of Abraham became known as Israelites, the name of Abraham's grandson, who took the name Israel.

The account in Genesis then tells how the Israelites went off to Egypt to avoid a famine in their own country. Here they received a welcome. This may have occurred while the Hyksos were ruling Egypt, for the Hyksos, like the Israelites, were foreigners in the country. Then the good fortune of the Israelites ended, for a new dynasty of pharaohs came to power and made them slaves.

Exodus from Egypt

According to the Bible, Mt. Sinai is where Yahweh gave the Ten Commandments to Moses.

According to the biblical author, Yahweh again acted to rescue the Hebrews. He chose Moses as his agent to deliver them from oppression in Egypt. This was not done easily. In fact, the writer describes that a series of plagues struck the Egyptians before Moses finally succeeded in leading the Hebrews across the Sea of Reeds into the Sinai peninsula, an event known as the **Exodus.** While in the desert, the second book of the Bible, Exodus, which received its name from this event, tells of Yahweh giving the Ten Commandments as rules for human behavior. In their desert experience the relationship between Yahweh and the Israelites was framed in terms of a **covenant** (a contract between two parties), "I will be your God, you will be my people."

A Canaanite priest is pictured in ceremonial dress.

After a long period of wandering in the Sinai, one of the world's most inhospitable places, the Israelites invaded Canaan. The conquest was a slow one for the local people put up a strong resistance. Later many in the local population joined them at Shechem, accepting the religion of Moses and the patriarchate of Abraham.

About this same time, around 1200 B.C. the Philistines appeared on the Palestinian coast, thwarting any plans that the Israelites had of conquering all the Canaanite territory. For a time it appeared that the strong military forces of the Philistines, armed with iron weapons and a full treasury, were going to win the land and defeat the Israelites. The Philistine city of Ekron, for example, held 103 olive presses that produced 1,000 tons of olive oil each year, making it the biggest industrial city of Southwest Asia. With this wealth the Philistine army grew to be an imposing force.

Hebrew Monarchy

About 1010 B.C., thanks again to a remarkable personality, David, the tribes of Israelites united. Prior to the unification, the Israelites formed a confederacy only loosely organized. David's armies took Jerusalem and made it the king's capital. David not only destroyed the Philistine threat, but his victories moved the border of Israel northward. For the Israelites, the rule of David has always been a golden age.

An artist's reconstruction of the Temple area is located in modern Jerusalem.

The height of Israelite expansion occurred under David's son, Solomon, who ruled from about 960 to 920 B.C. Solomon built a large temple to hold the **Ark of the Covenant,** a cabinet that held the Ten Commandments and was the symbol of Yahweh's presence. Nevertheless, the author of the book of Kings, which tells of Solomon's deeds, complained that the king lost the favor of Yahweh. Because he abandoned many of the traditions of Israel, Yahweh was not pleased, nor were many of his subjects. In response to Solomon's centralization and conspicuous wealth, there was a rebellion during the rule of his son.

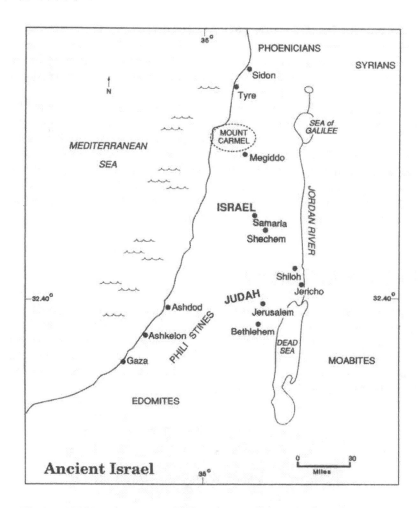

Ancient Israel

The ten northern tribes seceded from Jerusalem, called themselves Israel, and put their capital in Samaria. The kings who ruled in Jerusalem had to content themselves with the small territory occupied by the tribes of Judah and Benjamin. Over the next few centuries wars were frequent between Judah and Israel. They were small skirmishes, however, compared to the dangers posed when Egypt and Assyria began to test their armies after a period of relative quiet.

Foreign Conquest

The Assyrians were the first to strike. In 722 B.C. King Sargon II took Samaria and carried off the majority of Israelites, settling them, as was Assyrian practice, in provinces far away from their homes. Here they could be assimilated into the local population. Into their territory, Sargon moved Syrians and Babylonians, who eventually developed their own nationality, the Samaritan. The Samaritans worshipped Yahweh, but not in the Jerusalem temple, so the people of Judah considered them heretics.

Meanwhile, in Judah, the kings enjoyed a few more decades of peace. It was not to last. Once Nebuchadnezzar's Babylonia was ready to expand its borders to the Mediterranean, the several small states of Palestine stood in the way. In 586 B.C. the Babylonians marched on Jerusalem and captured it. They burned down Solomon's temple and took away the Ark of the Covenant. It disappeared at this time and has not been seen since.

Ten years later an uprising in Judah, once suppressed, caused the Babylonians to deport a still larger number of people into exile. Fortunately the exile did not last too long, for in 539 B.C. the Persian king, Cyrus, occupied Babylonia. Cyrus allowed the exiles to return to Judah as a satellite people of the Persian Empire. Judah remained such for the next two centuries, until the coming of Alexander the Great.

The exile caused a flurry of activity among writers whose works now make up parts of the Bible. An author, known as the Deuteronomist, composed the history of the Israelites from their arrival in Canaan to the fall of Jerusalem. Besides the book of Deuteronomy, most of the material in the books of Joshua, Judges, Samuel, and Kings I and II comes from his pen.

With their political independence gone, the people of Judah turned to their religious leaders to hold the nation together. These were the High Priests who served in the rebuilt Second Temple and the scholars, the rabbis, who culled the oral and written traditions to put the books of Torah into their final form. It is now possible to speak of this religion as **Judaism** and its adherents as Jews.

In addition to the five books of Torah, the sayings of the prophets and the advice of the sages of Israel and Judah were inserted into the Bible's corpus. The **prophets** were those men who spoke in Yahweh's name from the beginning of Israelite history until the second century, when the book of Daniel was finished.

Some of the ancient world's greatest literature appeared in the books attributed to the four great and twelve lesser prophets. The most fascinating piece of wisdom literature is the book of Job, which attempts to answer the age old question: Why do good people suffer?

The history of the Israelite people is better known than any of the ancient peoples of Southwest Asia. Its religious leaders wanted to make sure that, as each generation appeared, the traditions told of Abraham, Moses, and David, should not die. These stories were incorporated into the Bible in written form on scrolls considered so sacred that a scribe, making an error, had to bury a sheet of parchment in the ground, rather than burn it or throw it away. Temples—first, second, and in Roman times Herod's third construction—might disappear, but never, in Jewish opinion, the Word of God or his covenant with Israel.

Phoenicians and Arameans

An account of Southwest Asia during the first millennium B.C. would not be complete without a mention of the Phoenicians and Arameans; both peoples were members of the Canaanite nation. The name the Phoenicians gave themselves was Kena'ani, Canaanites.

The great gift of the Phoenicians to world history was their dissemination of the **alphabet**. The first of their alphabetic inscriptions used 22 letters, all of them consonants, dating from the eleventh century. The inscription is found on the sarcophagus of a king of Byblos. Later this Phoenician alphabet became known to the Greeks, allowing it to become the forerunner of all European scripts.

Their contemporaries knew the Phoenicians best for their extensive trading in the Mediterranean. As soon as spring came and the threat of storms passed, the Mediterranean became a lake criss-crossed with Phoenician ships headed for Egypt, Cyprus, North Africa, Greece, and even Spain. About 600 B.C. one Phoenician expedition is reputed to have gone around Africa, a feat not accomplished again until A.D. 1498.

Phoenician trade was in glass, metals, jewelry, lumber from the famous cedars of Mount Lebanon, wine, and cloth. Especially treasured was the purple dye (actually closer to scarlet than purple in modern terms) that the Phoenicians obtained from the murex mollusk. To make a pound of the dye, 60,000 snails gave their lives. Wealthy people all over the Mediterranean wanted to wear cloth of this color to set them apart as men and women of importance.

The most well known of the Phoenicians was Queen Jezebel, who was married to King Ahab of Israel. The Bible recounts how she pursued an aggressive policy to convert her husband's subjects to her religion. This brought down on her the wrath of Yahweh's prophet, Elijah; she was trampled by horses in a bloody death.

The Phoenicians were very active in colonizing other parts of the Mediterranean, establishing settlements all along the Syrian coast and on Cyprus and Malta. The two Phoenician colonies that grew into major cities were Carthage, now in modern Tunisia, and Cadiz, a port of Spain. The Phoenician cities became very wealthy from their dominance of Mediterranean trade allowing the kings of Tyre, Sidon, and Byblos to beautify their cities with temples to the Phoenician deity, El, his wife Asherah, and Baal, a fertility god.

Because each Phoenician city was independent of the other, little resistance could be offered Assyrians or Persians when they threatened. Sending the monarchs of these nations tribute allowed the Phoenicians the latitude they needed to pursue their economic interests. Like the rest of Southwest Asia, Phoenicia's history extends to the coming of Alexander the Great, when it was merged into the Hellenistic world.

The Arameans, the Canaanites of the interior, were also great traders of the first millennium B.C. Rather than ships, their merchants used caravans of jackasses and camels to carry goods from all over the region, from Phoenicia to the Euphrates. Damascus was at the hub of the Aramean trading network, but other cities such as Aleppo shared in the prosperity that its merchants generated.

So many Aramean merchants traveled throughout Southwest Asia that their language often displaced native tongues. In the seventh century Aramean replaced Akkadian and a century later Hebrew. The Aramean alphabetic script was the forerunner of the modern Hebrew and Arabic alphabets.

The rulers in the citadel of Aleppo from ancient times controlled the commerce of the city.

Persians

The Persians were to inherit the rule of all the peoples that once inhabited Southwest Asia. They were an Indo-European people, a part of the great migrations that took place early in the first millennium B.C. The Persians chose the plateau that extends from the Zagros Mountains to the Indus Valley for their homeland. Much of the plateau, except for the valleys of the Zagros and the immediate region south of the Caspian Sea, is very arid. For farmers, irrigation was needed, but for the herders of horses, the grass that grew on the plateau was sufficient for their needs.

The Persians had close relatives in the Medes, Sogdians, and Bactrians, all of whom found a place to settle on, or close by, the great Iranian plateau about 800 B.C. The Medes were the first to gain notoriety when their ruler, Kashtaritu (in Greek, Phraortes), was one of the allies that in 612 B.C. attacked Nineveh and brought down the Assyrian Empire.

For a moment the Medes created a small empire that reached into Anatolia. Their king became so impressed with his victories that he assumed the name king of kings, just in time for the Medes to be toppled, as the Persians came on the scene. The future belonged to the Persians.

The greatest of Persian kings was Cyrus, who ruled at the very beginning of his nation's prominence, from 549 to 530 B.C. The dynasty he founded receives the name Achaemenid, from Achaemenes, a legendary king believed to be the first of the Persian kings.

Not surprisingly, Cyrus led his armies, as was expected of a ruler in Southwest Asia, into Anatolia against the Lydian empire and Ionian Greek cities that were located along the coast. In 539 B.C. he turned his forces southward, where the Chaldeans of Babylon opened the gates of the city to him.

His tolerance made Cyrus popular with conquered people, for he allowed them to retain their own culture as long as they paid tribute. Cyrus forbade his troops to pillage and ordered them to respect the temples of those he defeated. Peoples who had once been exiled, like the Jews, were allowed to return to their homelands. Cyrus's victories created a multiethnic empire over all Southwest Asia, and Mesopotamia lost its preeminence to leadership when it became a province of Persia.

The son of Cyrus, Cambyses, invaded Egypt, opening a brief period of Persian rule over that country. Because he died unexpectedly, the kingship passed to Darius I, one of his close relatives and a member of the elite army corps, the **Immortals.**

Persian kings were not bashful about their accomplishments. Darius ordered an inscription to be carved on a cliff at Behistun of all nineteen of his campaigns. This **Behistun Rock**, written in three languages, proved to be the key to deciphering cuneiform writing in modern times.

One campaign that Darius was not so happy to record followed a successful invasion of western India. Because of a revolt in the Ionian Greek cities of Anatolia while he was away, Darius not only suppressed the rebels but also decided to punish the Athenians for sending help to the Ionians. Thus began the classic conflict between Persians and Greeks.

A Persian army marched across Thrace while the navy followed it along the coast. In 490 B.C. at Marathon, the Athenians met and defeated the Persians. Ten years later Darius's successor, Xerxes, tried once more to overcome the Greeks, but he, too, failed. Despite its strength, the Persian empire had reached its limits.

Darius and Xerxes, two Persian royalty in the center of the sculpture, receive a foreign delegation at Persepolis, the capital.

It was now the turn of the Greeks to intervene in Persian affairs. Because of a struggle over the kingship between two brothers, a Greek mercenary army fought on Persian soil, in vain as it turned out. On their departure from the country, one of the Greek generals, Xenophon, wrote a history of the expedition. This work, the *Anabasis*, is one of the most important sources for the history of both Greece and Persia.

The final page of Achaemenid Persia came in the fourth century B.C. when Alexander the Great concluded the conflict between the Greeks and Persians, with a win for the Greeks. The last Persian king, Darius III, was killed as his troops fled from the Greeks. According to legend, Alexander gave the king a drink of water just before his death.

Persian Culture in Achaemenid Times

The culture of Achaemenid Persia drew from many sources. Its character was especially dependent on the Assyrian and Babylonian influences that preceded it. The king held absolute authority, and all the land of the empire was his. When someone approached his throne, he or she had to prostrate before him. When speaking, subjects covered their mouth lest the monarch breathe "contaminated" air. The two capitals, Persepolis and Susa, were crowded with artisans and artists to decorate the palaces of the rulers with sculpture and painting to glorify their master.

The kings, who bore the title **shahinshah,** the Medean King of Kings, ruled their empires in the tradition of Cyrus. This meant that local language and culture continued as long as taxes were paid. Over all the empire there was a single standard of weights and measures, and a small gold coin, the **daric,** was used for currency. The Persian king's law, however, was supreme, supplanting all other local legal systems. For practical purposes, the law was written in Aramaic, so that the many Semitic peoples of the empire could read it.

A large bureaucracy served the Persian king, whose duties were to enforce the ruler's justice, to keep domestic order, and to collect the taxes that supported the army from the 20 **satrapies** or provinces. The taxes were collected in coin rather than goods, for the empire's daric was accepted everywhere within Persian borders.

Much of the monies that came to the kings supported the huge armies, which they kept for their campaigns. This imperial force held contingents from all the empire's peoples, from India to Egypt. To move their soldiers efficiently, the kings built a Royal Road that traversed the empire for 1,600 miles, from Susa to Sardis in Anatolia. Couriers on horseback made the journey in seven days.

The religion of the Achaemenids, **Mazdaism,** was based on the worship of a supreme deity named Ahura **Mazda.** Other Persian deities included Mithra, the sun god, and Anahita, a fertility divinity.

Worship was in temples where a fire was kept burning to symbolize the presence of Ahura Mazda. Keepers of the fire were the **magi,** a hereditary class of priests. One of Mazdaist teachings forbade either burial or cremation, since this polluted the earth or fire. Therefore the dead were exposed, to be consumed by scavenger birds.

Some authorities believe that a prophet, Zarathushtra (Zoroaster), in the early sixth century B.C. first introduced Mazdaism into Persia. Little is known for certain of Zarathushtra, but he is credited with writing about 570 B.C. the first hymns that now are found in the Avesta, the scriptures of the Mazdaists. The religion is sometimes known as Zoroastrianism in honor of its prophet.

Mazdaism also contained a dualistic concept of the divinity. It held that the cosmos was constantly a scene of combat between good and evil, between Ahura Mazda and the wicked divinity, Ahriman, who sought to win over the world of humanity to destruction. After death men and women faced judgment, the good going to a place of bliss and the evil to a fiery pit.

Anatolia

The Anatolian plateau and coastline held a great variety of peoples from 1200 B.C. onward. Among them were the Phrygians, who lived in much the same area as the old Hittite Empire. The Phrygians seem to have emerged just as the Hittites disappeared in Southwest Asia.

The landscape of Antolia contrasts valleys with mountains.

The Phrygian capital was located at Gordium, a site 50 miles from modern Ankara, Turkey. One of its early kings, Gordius, is reputed to have tied his cart to a pole with a knot so difficult to loosen that a story went out thatwhoever untied it would rule Asia. Phrygian importance peaked under its king, Mida (in Greek, Midas), who was reputed to be the richest man in the world. Everything he touched turned to gold, even his food, a problem that came close to killing him. He ruled from about 725 to 675 B.C.

Mida was buried in a structure that still stands. It may well be the oldest wooden tomb extant in the world and is built inside a mound 150 feet high and 900 feet in diameter. About 700 B.C. Cimmerian tribesmen fell upon Phrygia dealing it a devastating blow.

The Phrygian legacy is sparse because no archives have yet been found and the burial mounds of its kings have yet to be thoroughly excavated. A peculiar type of headdress, the Phrygian cap, a close fitted cone with a peak curling toward the front, was worn by freed slaves in Roman times. It was later revived during the French revolution.

The Lydians were another people of Anatolia, succeeding the Phrygians when they went into decline after 700 B.C. The Lydian capital was at Sardis, where their best remembered king, Croesus, was also their last. It was his wealth, like that of Mida, that gave Croesus his reputation.

The Lydian claim on history derives from the nation's invention of money. As far as is known, the first coins minted with the image of a king come from Lydia. The metal used was **electrum,** a combination of gold and silver. Aesop, famous for his animal stories, was probably a Lydian.

Lydia fell first to the Persian king Cyrus and later to Alexander the Great. In Hellenistic times, the rulers of Pergamum were its governors.

One other people was found in Anatolia, the Greeks who lived along the Aegean Sea coast and on the Black Sea shores. Those on the Aegean were known as Ionian Greeks, since most of them spoke this dialect of ancient Greek.

In fact, one of the first recollections of the Greeks dealt with the city of Troy and the conflict that took place between their warriors and the Trojans. Homer's epic, the *Iliad*, tells the story of that war. If he drew on historic facts, then an attack on Troy fits well into the declining years of Mycenaean Greece, sometime before 1200 B.C.

The Ionian Greek cities filled with immigrants from the Balkans and the Aegean islands. It was in these cities that Greek science was born. In many ways the cities of Ephesus, Smyrna, and Prirene rivaled those of the homeland.

At Troy, carpenters have reconstructed the Trojan horse. Later songs about Troy, but not Homer, tell how the Greeks entered the city in a wooden horse.

Conclusion

The coming and going of empires in Southwest Asia demonstrate how difficult it was for this part of the world to find stability, until the creation of the Persian Empire. Too many people with different cultures and religions lived in a very small part of the world. When one group attained ascendancy for a while, another was in the wings awaiting its moment.

At the same time advances were present. City life and its privileges extended to a larger number of people, and alphabetic writing became common as did coinage. The monotheism of the Jews laid a basis for religious belief that became a legacy for the world.

Chapter 9 Review
Southwest Asia in a Time of Empires

Summary
- The Assyrians built in Mesopotamia a strong empire noted for its bureaucracy and ruthless army.
- The Chaldean kings of Babylonia succeeded the Assyrian Empire.
- The Semitic Phoenicians became great traders, especially in purple dye.
- The Phoenicians spread the alphabet throughout the world.
- The Bible recounts the history, poetry, stories, and practical advice of the Hebrews.
- Cyrus, king of Persia, created an empire that was remarkably tolerant.
- Lydians first invented coinage.
- Ionian Greeks settled on the Anatolian coast.

Identify
People: Assyrians; Medes; Nebuchadnezzar II; Abraham; Tiglath-Pilesar I; Persians; Canaanites; David; Shalamaneser III; Moses; Jezebel; Cyrus

Places: Nineveh; Phoenicia; Jerusalem; Lydia; Ionia; Babylon; Canaan; Phrygia; Sardis

Events: rise of the Assyrian Empire; Israel's foundation; creation of the Persian state; accomplishments of Babylonia; writing the Bible

Define

Judaism	Ahura Mazda	Yahweh	satrapies
alphabet	magi	Nebi'im	Chaldeans
canon	Torah	Mazdaism	Behistun Rock
daric	covenant	exodus	
shahinshah	Ark of the Covenant	Book of Daniel	
electrum	Immortals	Kethubim	

Multiple Choice
1. The homeland of the Assyrians was
    (a) in the lower Tigris-Euphrates Valley.
    (b) in the upper Tigris-Euphrates Valley.
    (c) on the Iranian plateau.
    (d) in Anatolia.

2. The first great Assyrian empire-builder was
    (a) Ramses II.
    (b) Nebuchadnezzar II.
    (c) Tiglath-Pilesar I.
    (d) Shalamaneser III.

3. The Assyrian capital was at
    (a) Babylonia.
    (b) Jerusalem.
    (c) Nineveh.
    (d) Ur.

4. The destruction of Nineveh in 612 B.C. was a joint effort by
   (a) Hebrews and Phoenicians.
   (b) Arameans and Canaanites.
   (c) Medes and Phoenicians.
   (d) Medes and Babylonians.

5. The chief god of the Babylonians was
   (a) Ashur.
   (b) Isis.
   (c) Dumuzi.
   (d) Marduk.

6. The contribution of the Hebrew people to world civilization has been
   (a) the invention of sculpture.
   (b) the concept of one God.
   (c) writing.
   (d) metal working.

7. The part of the Hebrew Bible considered most important is
   (a) Torah.
   (b) Prophets.
   (c) Wisdom literature.
   (d) the Psalms.

8. The canon of the Hebrew Bible determines
   (a) when the books of the Bible were written.
   (b) the number of prophets.
   (c) who the biblical authors are.
   (d) what books will be in the biblical collection.

9. Tradition says that the Hebrews' common ancestor was
   (a) Moses.
   (b) Abraham.
   (c) David.
   (d) Joshua.

10. About the same time that the Hebrews entered Canaan, another people
    settled the Palestinian coast:
    (a) Arameans.
    (b) Philistines.
    (c) Babylonians.
    (d) Chaldeans.

11. Yahweh's presence with Israel after 1000 B.C. was signified by
    (a) the Ark of the Covenant.
    (b) the anointing of Israel's kings.
    (c) the Bible.
    (d) the exodus from Egypt.

12. A prophet is
    (a) a fortune teller.
    (b) a priest.
    (c) a spokesperson for God.
    (d) a scribe.

13. In 722 B.C. the Assyrians destroyed the northern kingdom of
    (a) Judah.
    (b) Israel.
    (c) Aram.
    (d) Egypt.

14. The people of Judah were sent into exile in
    (a) Babylonia.
    (b) Assyria.
    (c) Aram.
    (d) Egypt.

15. During the Persian period of Israel's history, authority was found in
    (a) the kings in Jerusalem.
    (b) the prophets.
    (c) the High Priests.
    (d) Moses.

16. One of the questions asked in the book of Job is
    (a) what are the rules for keeping the Sabbath?
    (b) what kind of worship is required in the Temple?
    (c) why do bad things happen to good people?
    (d) what should we believe about God?

17. The Persian kings who sought to conquer Greece were
    (a) David and Solomon.
    (b) Nebuchadnezzar II and Darius.
    (c) Cyrus and Darius.
    (d) Darius and Xerxes.

18. Sardis was capital of
    (a) Assyria.
    (b) Phoenicia.
    (c) Lydia.
    (d) Phrygia.

19. The oldest alphabetical inscription comes from
    (a) Tyre.
    (b) Sidon.
    (c) Byblos.
    (d) Nineveh.

20. The *Anabasis* is a work by
    (a) Cyrus.
    (b) Xenophon.
    (c) Darius.
    (d) Homer.

Essay Questions
1. Why was the Hebrew Bible written?
2. What were the contributions of the peoples of Southwest Asia after 1200 B.C.?
3. Discuss the life of ancient Persia. What were its unique features?

Answers

1. b	6. b	11. a	16. c
2. c	7. a	12. c	17. d
3. c	8. d	13. b	18. c
4. d	9. b	14. a	19. c
5. d	10. b	15. c	20. b

CHAPTER 10

India's Classical Age

India dominates South Asian history in the period after 1200 B.C. During this period two great empires appeared on the subcontinent. More lasting than the empires were the experiences of the Indian religious leaders, whose followers number in the millions in today's world.

The Aryan invaders continued to emigrate into India during this age, stamping Indian culture according to their traditions. Unfortunately, the Aryans showed no interest in recording their early history nor did they leave many remains of physical culture. It is from later myth and legends, written down hundreds of years after the events, that historians draw the threads to weave the story of India.

Political Life of the Aryans

After 1200 B.C. the larger Aryan chieftains began to expand their territories at the expense of their smaller, weaker neighbors. Villages where the chieftains made their residence became towns and eventually cities. The promotion of cotton farming and cloth making provided the rulers of these states with the economic basis to expand their territories.

War was a constant, both against the indigenous people and against their Aryan neighbors. Little by little several large kingdoms developed, so that by 600 B.C. there were 16 nations in the Punjab and on the Ganges and Indus plains. Below the Deccan plateau, Dravidians remained untouched by Aryan conquest, so that a major cultural division existed between the north and south.

The rulers of the Aryan kingdoms bore the name *raja*. Some went so far as to claim divine descent. Extensive wooden palaces were their residences, where attendants and royal officials kept their offices. Councils of noblemen consulted with the king on matters of war and peace. They joined the raja in his wars and his hunting expeditions and became his gambling companions.

At these palaces scribes appeared, not to record the king's activities but to write down the sacred literature of the Aryans. The rajas enjoyed lavish spectacles to entertain themselves and their courts. The peasants provided funds for the festivities, as tax collectors roamed the countryside.

Brahman Religion

The political history of India during this period cannot be understood without reference to the Aryan religion. While it is best to speak of it in this classical period as **brahmanism**, today, after centuries of development, its name is Hinduism. This term, which comes from the Indus River, was unknown until the Muslim invasion of the eighth century A.D.

Aryan society was very much structured according to classes. The Aryans would have argued that all men and women are born unequal and that at the very highest level of society were the religious priests, the **brahmans.** The brahmans were the only ones who knew how to offer sacrifices to the Indian deities correctly. They alone memorized the long and elaborate chants and prayers that, in their opinion, pleased the gods and kept them favorably disposed toward humans. It is not surprising that during the early years of the classical period, Indra, god of war, was the most popular divinity.

A brahman priest prays beside a river.

After 600 B.C., some of the songs were put into writing, possibly for the training of young brahmans. Four collections eventually appeared. They are known as *vedas;* the oldest of them is the Rig Veda. There is no agreement on the exact date of composition, but the present text dates only from about the first century A.D.

The Rig Veda is a book of songs, containing over a thousand compositions written in the sacred Sanskrit language. The brahmans used these songs to address the many deities who oversaw the universe. Along with Indra, the primary gods were Agni who gave fire, Varuna who directed the cosmic order, and Vishnu who became incarnate so as to help humans. Over all the other deities stood Brahma. He was the highest god, omnipotent throughout the universe. He made the statement, "All things abide in me, but I do not abide in them." For some brahmans, Brahma was the one reality. All other deities reflected him. He was the one reality. Religious ceremonies were held out-of-doors in India's warm climate, at altars used for animal sacrifices or for offering libations.

In addition to the vedas, two great epic poems appeared to supplement them. These were the *Mahabarata* and the *Ramayana.* They soon became the major literary works of ancient India. Probably, when first written, the Mahabarata was of moderate length, but over the centuries authors kept adding to it, now making it the longest poem in world literature. The *Ramayana* tells the story of Rama, once a prince who was unjustly removed from his throne. His efforts to regain it and to recover his wife make up the content of the poem.

The Feast of Diwali, a festival of lights, celebrates the restoration of Rama as told in the Ramayana epic.

Within the *Mahabarata* there is a section known as the Bhagavad Gita (the Lord's Song). The Bhagavad Gita teaches the major tenets of the Brahman religion.

The story takes place before a battle. Arjuna, a warrior, prepares for battle, but as he does, he has second thoughts. He knows that his relatives are soldiers in the enemy army. Then his charioteer speaks to him. The charioteer is **Lord Krishna,** who is one of the incarnations of the god Vishnu. He tells Arjuna that his duty is to fight no matter how reluctant he may be.

Krishna explains that the material body of every person is but one part of a human. When the body dies, the spiritual self lives on. This spiritual self will be reborn again. If Arjuna should, in fact, kill one of his relatives, he should remember that he has only destroyed a body that was fated to die eventually. The relative will be reborn, possibly to a better life.

Upanishads

From about 700 to 500 B.C. Indian philosophers expanded on the idea of the brahmans. Their commentaries on the vedas are known as **Upanishads.** This is the word for "sit near" in Sanskrit, for the disciples had to be close to hear the teaching of their master, the **guru.**

The philosophers taught the unity of all reality. The whole physical universe is really one but is expressed in individual bodies. All beings partake of the **atman,** the spirit that infuses reality. The atman is indestructible, but the bodies that it inhabits are corruptible; therefore, death and decay are an everyday phenomena.

A major concern of the teachers whose wisdom appears in the Upanishads was the stress on **dharma,** which means duty. Everyone who is human has certain responsibilities and obligations. Doing one's duty, fulfilling what is expected of one's role in this life, merits **karma** for a person.

Good actions add to karma throughout one's life. At death, when a person is done with earthly existence, a person's atman will be reborn, either into a higher or lower state, depending on the amount of karma accumulated.

Once a person has enough karma, it is possible to break the cycle of constant rebirth. He or she obtains **moshka** (enlightenment), which allows a person to be joined with Brahma. A person then loses his or her identity and becomes part of the spirit that inheres in the universe.

Classes and Castes

A distinctive feature of the brahman religion was an emphasis on human differences. The Aryans were extremely conscious of the possibility that the native peoples of India might well assimilate them. The caste system prevented that from happening. Brahmans taught that the caste system was, in fact, divinely ordained.

This story appears within the Rig Veda. One of the gods was responsible for human creation. The first people appeared from his mouth. This was the priestly class, the brahmans. The second class came out of his arms. The rajas and the **kshatriyas** (the warriors) were members of this class. From his legs the **vaishyas** came. These were the landowners, artisans, and merchants. Finally, there were the **shudras,** drawn from his feet. The consequence required the shudras to become peasant farmers. All who were of Aryan ancestry fit somewhere within these classes.

The indigenous Indian people, those Dravidians present before the Aryan invasion, were **dasas** or **pariahs.** They fell outside the Aryan classes. Another name for them was **untouchables,** for no one in a caste would get near them for fear of pollution. They formed the lowest group of all Indian society, doing the hardest work. Even within the class of untouchables, there was a distinction between sweepers and tanners and those whose jobs required dealing with human waste.

Each of the Aryan classes subdivided into what the Indians called **jatis** or **varnas,** but what Europeans knew as castes. The castes became thousands in number, each occupation having its own, and each thought of as better or worse than all others. A person's birth determined to which caste he or she belonged. The caste not only determined one's occupation but also the rank in society, diet, and choice of marriage partners. The brahmans saw to it that the walls between the castes were kept rigid. Anyone violating the rules of caste was punished with a beating and ostracism from the community, which could well mean death.

Should people in the higher castes associate with anyone of a lower one, they risked becoming ritually unclean. Brahman men or women had to be careful not to get too close to someone not on their level. They had to drink from their own wells, lest they incur defilement.

Recalling the idea of the indestructibility of the atman and the importance of gaining karma, the brahmans taught that whatever caste a man or woman happened to be born into was the result of an earlier life. If a person had good karma at the end of his or her life, then it was possible to ascend into a higher caste or class. Contrariwise, a person without good karma, even a brahman, could fall back a step. Therefore, the Upanishads gave Indian society a set of values that rewarded good actions and threatened punishment for bad ones. It held out hope, even to dasas, that they might do better in their next life. Eventually, when a man or woman had gained enough karma, **moshka** occurred and the person went out of personal existence.

What explains the caste system? There are several explanations, but the most probable was the fear of the light-skinned Aryans that they would be completely submerged by the larger, darker Dravidian population. The loss of their ethnic superiority appeared to them the ultimate disaster. To prevent this from happening, rigid class and caste lines prohibited intermarriage and social contacts with the indigenous people, allowing the Aryans to keep their superior status and ethnic purity.

When other peoples later arrived in India, the brahmans made room for them, placing them into a caste, ranking them with those who had come earlier. In this way they ensured the stability of society.

Among the Aryans, and it was their values that counted, families more than individuals mattered. Every member had his or her duties and responsibilities. When confronted with the need to chose between individual happiness or the family welfare, it was always the family's concerns that won out. Sometimes four generations lived under the same roof, especially among the wealthy. Most peasants had nuclear families, with only father, mother, and children living in the house.

Indian women had to cope with very patriarchal attitudes. They did not make their own decisions. Parents arranged their marriages, and once wedded, they came to live in the home of their husband. Here the mother-in-law assigned the tasks expected of the new wife. The major duty of a wife was to give birth to sons. Some outstanding women became teachers and poets in early Aryan society, but later these opportunities closed.

Jains Challenge the Brahmans

During the sixth century B.C. there were rumbles of discontent. Several individuals challenged the world system that the brahmans had constructed. Their ideas became permanent fixtures on the Indian scene.

The first of the challenges came from Mahavira. About 595 B.C. Mahavira, his name means Great Hero, was born into a noble family. For 30 years he lived a comfortable life but was constantly troubled over what was meaningful about existence. For 12 years he lived as a beggar, wandering about with only the necessities of life. In seeking to be rid of all material possessions, he hoped to find the way of understanding. One day the flash of insight came. Mahavira understood that it was desire that was at the root of the problem. Desire caused people to want things that made them clutter their lives.

Another insight made Mahavira understand the sacred character of all life. It became an absolute. Both human and animal life, even that of insects, must be preserved at all costs. Mahavira now looked upon all the prayers and sacrifices of the brahmans as useless.

A group of disciples soon gathered about Mahavira, calling themselves **Jains**, the word for conquerors. They learned from him how to avoid all impurity, to rid themselves of desire, and to respect all life. He taught them that they must only eat vegetables, for to eat the meat of animals was to violate the duty to preserve life.

The Jains lived in communities after Mahavira's death. They sought to imitate his way of life, ridding themselves of all possessions. Some became missionaries, adapting his teaching to an urban audience by making small accommodations to attract ordinary people. Others, the "sky clad" refused to modify any of his doctrine. The Jains, although not numerous, are still a part of the religious mosaic of modern India.

A Jain temple sits upon a mountainside in Rajastan.

Buddha

The second of the seventh century teachers in India was Siddartha Gautama, known as the Buddha, the Enlightened One. Siddartha's early life parallels that of Mahavira. Born about 567 B.C. in a kingdom just below the Himalayas, he grew up in a princely household. According to legend, his father heard a prophecy from a holy man that Siddartha would never become a prince, so the father sought to shield Siddartha from seeing or hearing anything that would cause pain or suffering.

There came a day, however, when Siddartha left the palace grounds and encountered an old man and a sick person and saw a dead body and the misery of a beggar. The shock overwhelmed him. He determined to find the meaning of life, whatever that should require. He abandoned his family and began a life dedicated to understanding the differences between good and evil, pain and suffering, truth and falsehood.

Siddartha's quest first led him to a serious study of the Upanishads, but their explanations did not satisfy him. Then he tried the ascetic life, eating but one grain of rice each day. Siddartha became so thin that he could feel his backbone when he touched his stomach. Still he remained puzzled at the mystery of existence.

At last Siddartha resolved to either discover the meaning of life or die. He sat down beneath a bo tree, waiting for 49 days. Then it happened. Enlightenment came. He became the Buddha.

Buddha's enlightenment showed him that to understand life was to assimilate four Noble Truths. The first truth was to acknowledge that suffering is a part of every human life. Then why do people suffer? The second truth answers this question. People suffer because of their ambition and desire. The third truth follows from the insight that the way to remove suffering is to be free of all ambition and desire. Finally, in the fourth truth, the Buddha outlined the way to liberate oneself in the Eightfold Path.

Each step along the path had to be completed before moving on to the next one. The eight steps include correct understanding, wishes, speech, conduct, employment, effort, kindness toward others, and meditation.

Once a person has completed the Eightfold Path, **nirvana** is attained. This is a state of serenity and tranquility, with no consciousness of personal existence, very similar to the brahman moshka. Siddartha's teaching modified the brahman's way of reaching enlightenment. He taught that it did not require complex sacrifices or prayers and that it had nothing to do with caste. He rejected the patriarchal attitudes of the brahmans, holding that men and women had equal opportunities to pursue the truth. He also rejected the idea that only male brahmans could read the vedas.

The Buddha is always pictured as a person of wisdom and serenity.

The Buddha's disciples, in imitation of their founder's efforts to teach about his vision of life and the way to reach nirvana, traveled throughout northern India seeking converts. They shaved their heads, wore a simple yellow garment, and carried a begging bowl to demonstrate their detachment from material concerns. To join a community of fellow Buddhists was encouraged, but this was not a necessity. The Buddha's moderate doctrine allowed people to go about their daily lives with confidence.

About 487 B.C., after 40 years of presenting his message, the Buddha died, leaving his disciples with the task of evangelization. It is doubtful that Buddha thought his teaching would be the basis for a new religion, yet his followers soon regarded him as a figure with divine qualities. His tomb, as well as the bo tree's site where he received enlightenment, became places of pilgrimage.

Disciples wrote down his sayings and collected legends about his life. Soon notions of an afterlife in heaven or hell supplemented the teaching on nirvana. Buddhism was now a religion that inspired thousands, later millions, of people to accept its values and live according to its doctrine.

Invasions from the West

At the very time that the Buddha was traveling about India preaching his doctrine, new invaders pushed into India across the Hindu Kush. These were the Persians, led by their powerful king, Darius I. In 521 B.C. the Persian army occupied much of the Indus Valley and annexed it. For the next 200 years northwestern India was a Persian province. The Persians raised the level of literacy and art as long as they remained.

The next invasion was by Alexander the Great's expeditions in his wars with Persians. Alexander's efforts to conquer the Persians meant that he should take all that kingdom's territories. Marching far away from their homeland, the combined Greek and Macedonian troops crossed into the Indus Valley in 326 B.C. The inhabitants of Takshasila welcomed him, but most of the Aryan rajas actively resisted.

For two years Alexander's armies battled the Indian forces, with their soldiers mounted on elephants. Although Alexander's troops could win battles, they were uneasy fighting so far from home. They demanded that he give up his ambition to conquer the world. Reluctantly, Alexander agreed and turned his army westward, back to Mesopotamia. Some Greek officers, however, remained in India for several decades.

Mauryan Empire

News of Alexander's army in India traveled across the countryside. The rajas were unsure of his goals, or whether the Greeks might return another time after they left. The result of the tension gave birth to the first native Indian empire.

Its origins were in the Ganges River state of Maghada. The architect was Chandragupta Maurya, a man who came to power in 322 B.C. Maghada was one of the wealthiest regions of India because of its cotton exports. Its capital, Pataliputra (now Patna) filled with merchants and farmers bringing their products to trade. Taxes on their gold and silver ornaments, silks, leather, and pottery enriched the royal treasury. In the city Chandragupta built himself a magnificent palace set among grounds planted with every kind of tree and shrub. Parrots were bred to decorate the palace grounds. One account says that among the palace guards were women warriors, whom Chandragupta trusted more than men. Concern for his security caused the emperor to build a great wall and moat to surround his capital.

There is no doubt that Chandragupta Maurya believed that war, not peace, would give him fame. According to chroniclers, he assembled an army of 700,000 soldiers, a cavalry of 30,000, and an elephant corps of 9,000. Although these numbers are an exaggeration, they nevertheless show the impression he made.

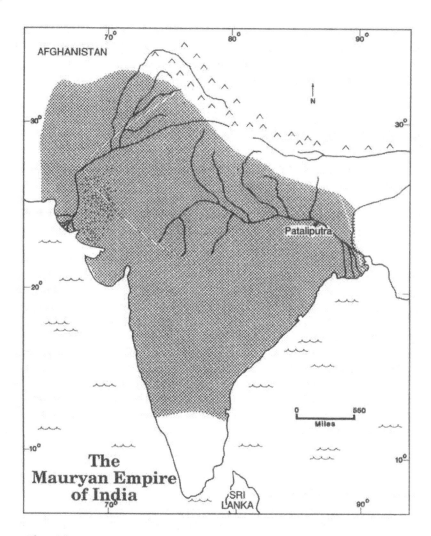

The Mauryan Empire of India

Chandragupta's armies rolled over neighboring states with little difficulty. He took the Punjab from the Greeks and went on to occupy the region that now makes up modern Afghanistan. All of India, except the far south, fell into his hands. His military victories brought the emperor little rest, for he lived in constant fear of assassination. Legends tell how he slept in a different place each night and how he paid spies to keep a check on possible rebels in Maghada.

The Greek ruler of Syria, Seleucus, was so impressed with Chandragupta that he sent his daughter to Pataliputra to seal an alliance with his Indian rival. In return Chandragupta sent him 500 elephants. As a matter of fact, using elephants in warfare had its risks. The large beasts in battle did not know which side they were on, and happily trampled friend and foe alike, who were usually drunk when they went into the fight.

Ashoka

The teaching of the Buddha would have made no impression on the warlike Chandragupta Maurya. It was a different story for his grandson, Ashoka.

Ashoka became the Mauryan emperor in 268 and ruled until 232 B.C. During that time he had a major conversion. In the early years of his rule, he entered upon conquests that would have made his grandfather proud. His armies marched against the few remaining kingdoms outside the Mauryan Empire. Reports say that his soldiers killed 100,000 people and made another 150,000 homeless refugees. At this point he was the most powerful raja ever seen on Indian soil.

Then Ashoka experienced his own enlightenment. Apparently Buddhist missionaries appeared at his court to explain Siddartha's doctrine. In time Ashoka became convinced that he should follow the Buddha's path.

To the astonishment of the court, Ashoka announced his regret for his many wars. The emperor ordered an inscription carved on stone pillars distributed throughout India. The inscription read in part, "The slaughter, death, and removal of captives is a matter of profound sorrow and regret to his Sacred Majesty."

From the royal treasury Ashoka now financed building programs and hospitals for the sick. He forbade the slaughter of animals by the brahmans in their sacrifices, nor were animals to be used for food.

Ashoka was so enthusiastic over his new view of the world that he sent Buddhist missionaries from Pataliputra into all the neighboring countries. Missionaries to Sri Lanka were especially successful.

Ashoka had a large **stupa** (a solid round monument of stone) built over the Buddha's relics. Upon a railing built about it, the teacher's sayings were inscribed for all to see.

Ashoka's stupa, a solid stone construction, contains the Buddha's relics.

With Ashoka's death, the security and good feeling that marked his times began to fade. The vast majority of his subjects, especially the brahman class, resented the personal views of the emperor now made a standard for all the country. Nevertheless, Ashoka's rule brought an era of peace and prosperity that his subjects and modern historians view as the high point of ancient Indian history.

Soon after Ashoka's death, the Mauryan Empire began to fall apart. Taxes no longer came in sufficient amounts to Pataliputra. With royal support gone, Buddhism shared in the general decline. In 180 B.C. the last Mauryan emperor gave up his throne. India fell back into small territorial states as the Mauryan central government fragmented.

Buddhists in western India were not discouraged. They continued to build temples with frescoed walls portraying the life of the Buddha, where those who were his disciples could draw inspiration.

India's weakness tempted neighboring peoples to take the well-traveled road through the Khyber Pass into the country. First came the Greeks of Bactria, a small Hellenistic kingdom of the north. Next came the Scythians, an aggressive nomadic nation whose home was originally on the steppes north of the Black Sea. Following them, the Parthians, known to the Indians as Pahlavas, poured into the plains of northern India.

The last in line were the Yueh-chih, who began the Kushan period of Indian history. The Kushans were Buddhist converts, so that the brahmans were once more on the defensive.

All these invaders were slowly absorbed by Indian society and soon lost their ethnic differences. The brahmans found room for them within the caste system, assigning them a place. The ability to absorb its conquerors has always been a quality of Indian life.

South India

The turmoil of the break-up of the Mauryan Empire in India's north did not affect the southern Indians. The Dravidian population went on its way, enjoying an economic boom that now extended to Europe.

Merchants came to South Indian ports from as far away as Rome in the west and Indonesia in the east. In 21 B.C. a group of merchants from India went to Rome bringing with them a miniature zoo of animals, among them tigers, which had never before been seen in Europe. The Romans thought India must be a marvelous place to live. In the first century A.D. trade between Rome and South India first brought pepper to Europe.

The Indian Ocean became the first sea to offer the setting for intense commercial activity. Sailors transported spices, textiles, and precious metals between African and Southeast Asian ports. This trade by sea paralleled the overland Silk Road from China.

Gupta Empire

The history of India's empires follows a certain pattern. A strong charismatic leader begins expanding against neighboring states. He sets up a central government, and for a time a period of prosperity comes to his capital as tribute pours in from conquered states. Then his successors appear, not so able, and soon the empire cracks apart with local leaders snubbing the king's officials and his tax collectors.

The founder of India's second great empire bears the name of the first. He is Chandragupta I, and the Gupta dynasty he founded is remarkably similar to the Mauryan Empire that preceded it. Even the capital, located in Pataliputra, was the same.

Chandragupta came to power about A.D. 320. He successfully incorporated most of northern India into his state, but he never reached the territorial limits of the Mauryans. Of great importance for Indian religious history, he and his successors were strong supporters of the brahman religion.

Fortunately for the brahmans and their supporters, Indian Buddhism had become a religion of monks whose interests were more and more defined by sterile arguments over interpreting Buddha's message. A great division took place within Buddhism between the Mahayana and Hinayana or Theravada Buddhists. **Mahayana** means "Great Vehicle," **Hinayana** the "Lesser Vehicle," and Theravada the "Teaching of the Elders."

Mahayana Buddhism was carried to China in the first century B.C. where it enjoyed much success. Its teaching there did not emphasize the monastic life but promised that ordinary men and women might, in a single lifetime, pass into nirvana. In addition many holy men and women appeared within Mahayana Buddhism who were known as **bodhisattvas.** A bodhisattva had earned enough merit to go to a heavenly nirvana but had remained on earth to help others. Buddhists venerated the bodhisattvas.

A bodhisattva is respected for remaining on earth as a teacher of Buddhism.

Theravada Buddhism remained predominantly monastic. It enjoyed favor in Sri Lanka, Burma (now Myanmar), and Southeast Asia. Both divisions of Buddhism created impressive temples with the Buddha portrayed sitting crossed-legged and dressed as an Indian prince.

In order to make Hinduism more attractive, the brahmans advanced the importance of several more popular deities. These were Lakshmi, who favored business people; Genesha, with the face of an elephant; and Shiva. Wisely, the brahmans decided that Vishnu had appeared on earth in the Buddha, thus making Buddhism a part of their own religion.

The worship of Shiva was important for gaining power and for increasing fertility, both human and animal. While Shiva was a creator, his wife Kali was pictured as a destructive force. Kali might destroy crops and bring famine to the countryside.

It was probably during the Gupta period that Christianity first arrived in India. No doubt Christian Syrian merchants, trading in South India's spice market, spread their faith to the people living there. Christians in India called themselves after St. Thomas, for tradition claims he came to their country late in life and died there. They point out the apostle's tomb in Kerala, the location of his missionary work.

The artistry of the Gupta period is to be seen in the many Hindu temples built at this time, both in northern and southern India. Frequent festivals and colorful pageants attracted people away from Buddhism or Jainism. Towns grew about the temples to serve the thousands of Hindu pilgrims who came to them in hopes of gaining favors. Statues of gods and goddesses, dancers and musicians covered the exteriors of the temples.

It was a time of great literary works, as classics were written in Sanskrit in the north and Tamil in South India. The most revered poet of the times, Kalidasa wrote in Sanskrit. Kalidasa's play *Shakuntala* became the most popular of his works. It remains to this day one of the favorite presentations for the Indian people.

The Guptas set up centers for the study of astronomy, physics, and mathematics. In these schools scholars first invented the zero and the use of the numerals that Europeans call Arabic. Astronomers discovered that the world moved on an axis. Great libraries, sponsored by imperial grants, aided the research. Doctors used inoculations to control smallpox and invented surgical instruments for operations.

A Buddhist monk from China, Faxien, described the wealth and prosperity of the country in a work he wrote after his trip to India early in the fifth century A.D. At this time in addition to textiles, Indian merchants also exported sugar to all parts of the Indian Ocean. Everywhere Faxien was impressed at the renewed vigor of Buddhism, especially at Nalanda, on the Ganges River, where monks studied the philosophy of the scriptures.

Hinduism became more rigid as the Guptas saw to it that its views on caste should be made universal. Untouchables were forbidden to enter brahman temples, enjoy the pageants, or even live in the same part of town with people of higher castes. Women also lost out. They were excluded from much of public as well as religious life. Wives could not inherit family property and, if widowed, were forbidden remarriage.

In the late fifth century the prosperous Gupta period began to fade. Once more invaders waited to pounce on a divided nation.

Sri Lanka

The history of Sri Lanka, lacking records, is unavoidably brief. The first people in the island were the Veddahs, who lived in a hunting–gathering society. About 500 B.C. a large migration of northern Indians, the Sinhalese, arrived and set up a dynasty that ruled the country over the following centuries.

Conclusion

India's contribution to the world in its classical period was its great religious leaders. Millions of people in the past and in the present regard their teaching as the way to happiness. The teaching of respect for all life was in sharp contrast to the practice of the rajas, but for India's masses it offered consolation, especially for those in the lower castes or outside the system. Indian thought and religion have had a remarkable staying power.

The arts and sciences of Gupta India contributed much to India and later the world. Its culture remained in the collective memory of the country long after the names of its emperors were forgotten.

CHAPTER 10 REVIEW
INDIA'S CLASSICAL AGE

Summary
- Aryan kingdoms fought one another for supremacy in the subcontinent.
- The sacred literature of the Aryans was written in the Vedas.
- Four classes were found among the Aryans with hundreds of castes.
- In response to the Persian and Greek invasions, the Mauryan Empire was founded.
- Ashoka, a Mauryan king, converted to Buddhism but failed to make it India's faith.
- The Gupta state, India's second empire, made many advances in science and the arts.

Identify
People: brahmans; Mahavira; Darius I; Kushans; dasas; Kshatriyas; Jains; Chandragupta Maurya; Siddartha Gautama; Ashoka; Chandragupta I
Places: Himalayas; Maghada; Hindu Kush; Pataliputra; Ganges River
Events: writing the vedas; constructing the Mauryan Empire; defining class and caste; Buddha and Mahavira found new religions

Define

Mahabarata	Ramayana	Krishna	atman
Upanishads	dharma	Theravada	stupa
bodhisattva	moshka	nirvana	karma
brahmanism	brahmans	kshatriyas	shudras
guru	vaishyas	dasas	
jatis	Mahayana	Hinayana	

Multiple Choice
1. Aryan warfare involved the use of
   (a) light chariots drawn by horses.
   (b) large ships.
   (c) the phalanx.
   (d) none of the above.

2. The Aryan way of life demanded keeping large herds of
   (a) sheep.
   (b) goats.
   (c) horses.
   (d) cattle.

3. The priestly class of Aryan India is known as
   (a) kashitryas.
   (b) brahmans.
   (c) vedas.
   (d) soma.

4. Aryan history is best seen through sacred literature written in
   (a) hieroglyphs.
   (b) Assyrian.
   (c) Iranian.
   (d) Sanskrit.

5. The Bhagavad Gita is a story told about
    (a) Lord Krishna.
    (b) Arjuna.
    (c) reincarnation.
    (d) all of these.

6. The good acts people perform in this life enable them to obtain
    (a) vedas.
    (b) karma.
    (c) dharma.
    (d) heaven.

7. A person's caste in India set up rules for
    (a) work.
    (b) marriage.
    (c) proper behavior.
    (d) all of these.

8. Women in Aryan society joined the household of
    (a) their husbands.
    (b) their uncles.
    (c) their aunts.
    (d) their father.

9. Jainism teaches that
    (a) all life must be protected.
    (b) only cattle should be eaten.
    (c) Hinduism is the correct religion.
    (d) only pork should be eaten.

10. Siddartha Gautama received the name Buddha because
    (a) he fasted for a long time.
    (b) he founded a community of disciples.
    (c) he was enlightened.
    (d) he taught a way of meditation.

11. The goal of the Buddhist is to reach
    (a) karma.
    (b) nirvana.
    (c) bodhisattva.
    (d) utman.

12. He led Greek armies against India:
    (a) Themistocles.
    (b) Sargon.
    (c) Darius I.
    (d) Alexander the Great.

13. The capital of Mauryan India was at
    (a) Delhi.
    (b) Calcutta.
    (c) Bombay.
    (d) Pataliputra.

14. Ashoka is remembered for his renunciation of war and
    (a) conversion to Buddhism.
    (b) conversion to Islam.
    (c) conversion to Hinduism.
    (d) conversion to Jainism.

15. The Gupta Empire had a flowering civilization in which
    (a) the people became Buddhists.
    (b) there was a great interest in astronomy and scientists discovered that the world turns on an axis.
    (c) a mathematical system was developed using 60 as a base.
    (d) sculpture, not painting, became an important art.

16. A bodhisattva is a person who
    (a) is a Hindu priest.
    (b) is a Jain priest.
    (c) is a Buddhist holy person.
    (d) is a Gupta priest.

Essay Questions
1. What are possible reasons for the Aryan's putting people into castes?
2. What are the positive and negative aspects of the caste system?
3. Describe the major tenets of Buddhism. How does one explain its success?

Answers

1. a	5. d	9. a	13. d
2. d	6. b	10. c	14. a
3. b	7. d	11. b	15. b
4. d	8. a	12. d	16. c

China and Its Neighbors

The first historical dynasty of China, the Shang, ruled from about 1520 to 1050 B.C., a time in which much of the culture of later Chinese life was set. At the last Shang capital, Anyang, architectural and art forms developed. This work so impressed the Chinese that it set a pattern for what was recognized as distinctively "Chinese" for centuries to come.

This period of Chinese life is also famous for the special role of the Qin dynasty because of the monumental buildings of the time. It is also the moment in history that produced the Chinese wise men, Confucius and Laozi, who are credited with laying the foundations for the spiritual life and value system of the Chinese people.

Later Shang Period

The family has always been at the core of the Chinese understanding of society, and its values were imposed on the nation at large. At the top was the emperor, who claimed to be a Son of Heaven. This meant that he was not simply an ordinary person but rather had his origins in a divine plan that made him a companion of the immortals. It was his responsibility, like a father, through elaborate ceremonies and sacrifices, to keep heaven well disposed to the people of the country. Should he fail, the world of the Chinese might well collapse and his commission from heaven be withdrawn.

The emperors commissioned huge tombs for their final resting place. The wife of one emperor was buried with a treasury of 200 bronze vessels and a collection of oracle bones reciting her accomplishments. Servants and slaves were also entombed alive in order to serve their masters in the next life.

In Shang times the rulers governed areas in different ways. Some were directly under the emperor, and others paid him tribute. He did not interfere with the local authorities.

Beneath the emperor and the royal family were the nobility scattered throughout the country. The nobles were important because of their inherited wealth in land that was augmented by the rents they charged the peasantry that worked on the lands they owned. Strong class distinctions separated them from the peasantry. The payments the nobles received allowed them to lead lives of leisure, filled with games, sports, and hunting.

When these entertainments proved tiresome, the Chinese nobles went to war with each other. They rode into battle in bronze armor-covered chariots, armed with spears and bows with bronze-tipped arrows. Because horses were needed to fight battles from chariots, they were of great importance to the Chinese aristocrats. However, breeding stock was never sufficient in China, so new horses had to be purchased from the nomads to the north.

In the Chinese family, from peasant to aristocrat, the oldest male enjoyed preeminence. It was his decision to dispose of property, find marriage partners for the children, and guarantee the family honor. The oldest woman was in charge of all the other females in the family, often a large group of daughters-in-law, to whom she assigned their tasks. The most respected of virtues was filial obedience.

Artisans perfected casting bronze, not only for weaponry, but also for tableware, bells, and ceremonial vessels, some of them weighing a ton. This was a major feat of casting. Animal motifs decorated these vessels that mark them as some of the earliest distinctive Chinese art forms. Other crafts were also a part of this period. Working in jade, ivory, and soapstone, master artisans produced articles both useful and decorative. Because music and dance were so much a part of Shang entertainment, a collection of percussion, wind, and string instruments came into prominence.

A Shang cauldron was used to offer sacrifices to ancestral spirits.

Scribes and Silk

As society progressed with increased trade, Chinese writing developed further. The officials who worked in the emperor's palace or for aristocratic employers needed to keep an inventory of taxes and rents. In Shang times there were thousands of characters, all of which had to be memorized. The characters were usually painted with a brush on bamboo; consequently, the writer had to be an artist as well as a calligrapher.

In economic life the Shang period witnessed a significant expansion within the silk industry. Making silk thread was not an easy process. When the silk moth lays its eggs, they grow into larvae that must be fed mulberry leaves several times each day. During this crucial period in their lives, the larvae must be kept at just the right temperature so that they will move into the pupa stage when the weaving of the cocoon begins. Once they have matured, the pupae are put into hot water. This kills them and allows the silk maker to begin the careful unwinding of the cocoon's strands in order to make the silk thread.

The time and skill needed to make the silk thread resulted in textiles that had astronomically high costs. It became the most evident sign of wealth for an aristocratic woman or man to be clothed in silk garments. The Chinese also created a demand for silk among their neighbors who could afford it.

Zhous Come to Power

The end of the Shang period came about 1050 B.C. when a chieftain in the region of the Wei Valley, to the west of the Yellow River's great bend, challenged the Shang for control of the state at a time when a rebellion of slaves was in progress. His dynasty is known as the Zhou.

The Zhou moved the capital to Qangan, now Xian, where it remained throughout the period of their ascendancy. Their palace, the Luminous Hall, was renowned throughout the Chinese world. However, because the Chinese built in wood rather than stone, little remains of early Chinese buildings.

During the Zhou period the wealth of the country continued to grow as agricultural production expanded. Rents paid in kind by the peasants kept the upper classes comfortable and the peasants miserable. When the emperors prepared to launch a campaign against their enemies, they expected the nobility to provide detachments of troops. The problem was to keep the loyalty of the great landowners, for often the interests of the nobles and the emperor were not the same. The aristocrats built their own palaces, walled them, and ignored their duties to the emperor.

Chinese nobles travelled in horse-drawn carts.

In 771 B.C. an invading army killed the Zhou emperor, and his son and heir was forced to flee to the east. Here he set up a new capital at Luoyang and a new Eastern Zhou dynastic period started. Once broken, the power of the emperors could not be regained, with the result that dozens of small principalities sprang up across the Chinese countryside. These principalities were at war with each other so often that Chinese historians call this period the Time of the Warring States.

Iron-working began in China about this time. This new technology made possible a change in the way that farming was done. Iron axes and plows became common and allowed large numbers of people to move into the forests of the Yangtze Valley. With their axes the peasants cleared the trees from the land that was now placed under cultivation. As the northern Chinese assimilated the peoples of the Yangtze, they advanced a common Chinese civilization over a much broader area.

Warfare became more deadly as a result of iron weapons. The chariot was abandoned as individual horsemen, covered with iron armor, made up a mounted cavalry. During the Eastern Zhou period warfare over land and prestige was common, for the emperors were too weak to prevent quarrels among their vassals. Many Chinese despaired of ever finding harmony or security as long as ambitious princes thought warfare was the way to reach their goals.

Confucius

At this moment of despair, wise men appeared on the scene urging peace to be a more important value than military skills. This was the message of the most famous of Chinese philosophers, Kung Fuzi, whom Westerners recognize as Confucius.

Confucius was born about 550 B.C. into a family of lesser nobility. He was convinced that something needed to be done to alleviate the constant fighting inside China. He tried to find a position in one of the noble courts but did not succeed. Then deciding to be a teacher, he gathered disciples about him who would seek careers at court and thereby change the Chinese values of the aristocracy.

Confucius became the most famous wise man of ancient China.

Confucius found a large number of students who adopted his teaching. Basically his instruction focused on moderation in all things. The family was to be the model of good relationships, where each member had his or her own role. The father was the source of authority, the mother devoted to him, the children dutifully following the guidance of the parents. In order to achieve harmony, each family member needed to be aware of his or her responsibilities, and this same attitude carried over to the state. According to the view of Confucius, "Let the ruler be a ruler and the subject a subject; let the father be a father and the son a son." All conflict in China would stop, once the nobility in the provinces recognized imperial authority and saw themselves as brothers in a unified family.

Ethical considerations were important for Confucius, but even an evil ruler should be obeyed. The ideal ruler would have a devotion to truth and justice, would govern generously and fairly, and would have the same concerns for his subjects that a father has for his family. Confucianism confirmed family values, already China's strongest tradition.

Women did not fare well in the Confucian teaching. They had no role to play in public life and, even in the family, their role was always to be humble and obedient to the father. Parents arranged the marriage of young girls. They had no opportunity to choose their partners for life. The welfare of the family was the highest concern of all its members.

Confucius said little about religion, leaving this aspect of Chinese life untouched. Nor did he leave any literature, trusting the memories of his students to preserve what they had learned. Later a body of classics, principally a book called the *Analects*, were attributed to Confucius, but these were written long after he was dead. They are the work of those who learned from him.

Laozi and Meng Ko

The wisdom of Confucius did not win a complete victory over all other values held in China. Competitive schools of thought sought to modify or even reject what he taught.

One view grew out of a combination of Chinese attitudes toward nature and long-held respect for spirits, good and bad, that shamans conjured to heal people or bring them good fortune. This was known in Chinese as **Daoism,** the way. Its basic tenet was to learn from nature, for it was always the best teacher.

Daoists felt that Confucianism did not have any room for emotion and was much too rigid; that life is best that imitates nature. Nature is often unruly and tempestuous and so too was the human personality. The artist especially could not function in a world where everything was reduced to following rules.

The Daoists found their teachings in the book Dao-de Qing, Classic of the Way of Power. They attributed it to the teacher Laozi, which means the old master; he was a contemporary of Confucius. There is no evidence to support this claim. Perhaps Laozi believed in one of Daoism's favorite sayings, "The one who knows does not speak; the one who speaks does not know."

Meng Ko, anglicized to Mencius, modified Confucian teaching on governance. He argued that citizens should resist an evil ruler. The right to rule is forfeited when he does not consider the welfare of his subjects. Mencius's proposition did not convince another philosopher, Xunzi. This teacher asserted that a dictatorial emperor was best because men and women were basically selfish and unwilling to work unless forced to do so. Xunzi's opinion on humans later received a welcome in a group known as the **Legalists.**

Another belief that appeared during the Zhou dynasty's last years was a notion explained in terms of **Yin and Yang.** Within this concept was the idea that all things are predominantly either Yin or Yang: light and darkness, hot and cold, male and female, earth and sky. However, within everything that is Yang, there is a bit of Yin, and in everything that is Yin, there is some Yang. Therefore, there is always contrast in every object or event, but in time a balance will be restored. Nothing lasts forever because change is endemic in this world. Yesterday will never return, and tomorrow is unpredictable.

China During Qin Dynasty

The Qin dynasty was one of China's shortest, extending only 15 years, from 221 to 206 B.C. Yet its influence lasted for centuries. Its founder created the first true dynasty in Chinese history bent upon imperial expansion.

This first of the Qin rulers was Shi Huangdi, whose name means First Emperor, born about 246 B.C. in one of the poorer and smaller provinces of Zhou China. However, in this region the rulers paid great attention to the army. Equipped with crossbows, Shi Huangdi's forces toppled the last of the Zhou emperors and then established his own centralized state over provinces that had long shown independence from Luoyang. For the first time northern and southern China had a single ruler.

Shi Huangdi brought the nobles to his capital, once more at Qangan, where he could watch them and nip in the bud any tendencies toward rebellion. In a law code he issued, he took away the privileges they once enjoyed.

The emperor envisioned an empire far beyond the borders he inherited from the Eastern Zhou. His armies campaigned in Southeast Asia, where the Vietnamese people first experienced the might of Chinese arms. Next to fall to Shi Huangdi was Korea, a nation that inhabits the peninsula that juts into the Sea of Japan from the Asian mainland. The spread of Chinese arms also meant the diffusion of Chinese culture, which the Vietnamese and Koreans now experienced in close fashion.

Moderation was not found in Shi Huangdi's character, hence his contempt for Confucian values. His advisors, the Legalists, assured him that might makes right and supported all the imperialist ambitions of the First Emperor. The emperor's rage at Confucianism translated into a purge of scholars at his court (several hundred were buried alive) and the destruction of any books that carried Confucian doctrine. The only exceptions were books dealing with farming and medicine, which the First Emperor deemed harmless. Many Confucianists hid their scrolls, convinced that their cause would prevail.

The most lasting monument to Shi Huangdi's activities is still to be seen. While other rulers built sections of walls to keep out the Mongol and Turkic nomads who raided China, Shi Huangdi sought to connect these partial barriers into a single Great Wall. To accomplish this huge construction effort, his government conscripted tens of thousands of workers from all over China. Built and rebuilt many times after Shi Huangdi's time, the Great Wall now traverses 1,400 miles across the north of the country.

The Great Wall of China was Shi Huangdi's construction to defend his empire's northern border.

To provide for his tomb, he chose a mountain near Qangan to be hollowed out so as to contain his body. According to one estimate, half a million people labored for 30 years to complete this project, which compares favorably to the pyramids of Egypt. To guard his final resting place, artisans cast 7,500 life-size soldiers made of baked clay, each with his own individual characteristics, to be buried with their master. Lost for centuries, the emperor's tomb was only discovered in A.D. 1974.

The list of Shi Huangdi's accomplishments is impressive. He standardized a system of weights and measures, reformed the Chinese script so that the writing of characters should be more uniform, and centralized both the bureaucracy and the tax system in Qangan. His minister Li Ping is still held in honor in modern China, for he found a way to control the worst of the annual spring flood of the Yellow River.

The Chinese remembered the burdens Shi Huangdi placed on them during his rule. His less than able successors could not enforce the rigid rule of First Emperor. Only four years after Shi Huangdi was buried in his magnificent tomb, rebels overthrew the third of the Qin emperors, his second son. A new dynasty came to the fore, and ancient China entered its most prosperous era.

Han China

In 202 B.C. an officer in the army, Liu Bang, assumed the imperial throne. As a Confucianist, he restored the honored place of the practical philosophy of the master to its former place. His dynasty, known as the Han, received its name from a tributary that flows into the Yangtze. Although Liu Bang could not foresee it, his dynasty was to last for 400 years, and the empire he ruled looks very much like the borders of the modern Chinese state.

The people of China supported a return to more moderate ways. The Hans relaxed the amount of labor demanded of the peasants and the rigid tax system of the Qins. Many of the Chinese provincial nobles were able to return to their ancestral estates. This encouraged them to support the Han emperors. The monarchs lavished much of their wealth on beautifying Qangan with lovely parks and a great palace. They enjoyed hunting in their leisure time, when not attending to imperial duties.

Every Han emperor kept a harem of wives, and among the children one would be chosen as the successor. The mother of this child became the empress and had many privileges that were denied to the other women of the harem. For example, Lady Wu, one of the empress mothers, saw to it that her relatives held the major state offices.

The Han emperors wisely selected as many officials as possible from men who were not from the nobility. These office holders were thought to be much more loyal than nobles who often tried to build up a separate power base. Throughout China Han bureaucrats collected grain, wax, or cloth and other commodities. After the palace took what it wanted, the army was provisioned. Officials were also responsible for recruiting laborers to work on the many public projects of the government. One of the constant problems of China was the many debts that the peasantry accumulated because of their absence when working on imperial projects.

To better prepare its civil servants, in 124 B.C. a Han emperor opened a school for their training. Candidates came from all over China to study in order to pass the rigorous examinations that allowed a person to enter government service. Students received training not only in Confucian etiquette but also in ritual, archery, and physical skills. From a small beginning the government school grew to hold 30,000 candidates. China was unique in its concern that all its officials should obtain positions because of intelligence and merit rather than the accident of birth.

The examination system that rewarded those who passed gave China a great deal of stability, for the governing class was made up of administrators who had a similar experience and recognized what was expected of them. On the other hand, the system dampened creativity in the ruling elite. Knowing the Confucian classics was supposed to answer all questions.

Animals decorate a Han general's tomb in Xangan.

Despite the wealth that China enjoyed from trade, merchants were looked upon with contempt since Confucius considered that profession unworthy of a gentleman. Prestige was limited in the upper classes to government officials, soldiers, or owners of property.

The most important economic investment was made during the first century B.C. in the export of silk to the Mediterranean. Merchants might not enjoy the praise of the ruler and his officials, but they knew how to make money. Mediterranean societies were so anxious to obtain Chinese products that they were happy to hand over their gold coins to obtain them. A vast caravan route extended from China, across Inner Asia, where oases developed to offer stopping places, all the way to Syria and Egypt. This route, the great **Silk Road,** was the first major international trade link between Asia and Europe.

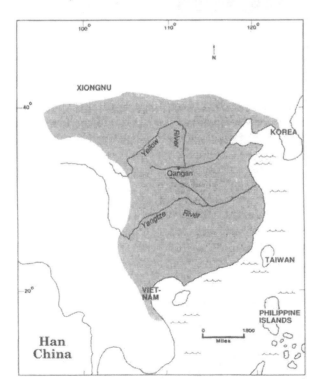

Han Court

Although Confucian thought influenced the ritual and ceremonies of the court in Qangan, most of the emperors who lived there turned to **shamans** to know what the future held. The shamans used a wide variety of methods to probe the future, most of all through a study of the heavens. The position of the planets and stars were all important for knowing how to adapt to the future.

Court astronomers studied the heavens from twenty-seven observatories of ancient China.

It is little wonder, therefore, that the Chinese became eager students of astronomy. Emperors patronized the building of observatories throughout the country so that court astronomers, a notch above the shamans, could chart the heavens and thereby learn its secrets. The astronomers thought in terms of Five Directions, north, south, east, west, and center. Each direction was imbued with certain divine powers. During Han times Confucius himself was regarded as a deity, something the teacher would never have expected.

Daoism had its proponents at the Qangan court, but it was Daoism that reflected much of the traditional lore of shamanism. Therefore, only certain foods should be eaten, a regimen of physical exercises prescribed, and the color red was elevated to a status above all other colors. Confucianists expressed disdain for what the Daoists taught, but this did not silence the advice of the Dai-de Qing.

Arrival of Buddhism

One of China's characteristics was its self-sufficiency. Since its earliest history, the spirit of the people who made decisions in China was to reject out of hand any influences coming from abroad, especially if they tended to trouble the Middle Kingdom. In their view of the universe, China alone was the land of civilization, and outside its borders there were only "barbarians."

There was one exception to this generalization. During the first century B.C. Mahayana Buddhist monks journeyed to China, teaching the wisdom of their master. Many Daoists recognized in Buddhism's attitude toward nature a reflection of their own beliefs. As a result, Daoists formally or informally became converts to Buddhism as a way to explain suffering, evil, and human restlessness.

Thousands of Chinese men and women flocked to monasteries where they studied the path of the Buddha. Cave temples carved from rock became places of refuge from the harsh realities of life. Worshipping the ever-peaceful Buddha's statue, sometimes 30 or 40 feet tall, confirmed pilgrims in their search for enlightenment. For the next 2,000 years, Buddhism was a part of the Chinese value system.

Buddha's image has been carved from rock at this Chinese pilgrimage site.

Later Han Period

In the first century A.D. the condition of the peasants was once more approaching disaster. After paying rents to their landlord and taxes to the emperor, there was little left to sustain their own families. The peasants found a champion in Wang Mang, a minister at the court. In A.D. 8 Wang overthrew the reigning Han emperor and began a series of reforms over the next 14 years.

He despoiled the landlords of much of their property and emptied their warehouses of grain. He then put the grain under state control so as to distribute it from government-run stores. He introduced an income tax to distribute the burden of payments more equitably and tried to limit the interest poor farmers had to pay their creditors. Wang Mang's experiments in socialism did not survive him. In A.D. 23 a cousin of the last Han emperor ousted him, and his reforms came to an end.

The second or later Han period now began. It lasted for the next 200 years, a time when China's population reached 60,000,000 people, by far the most populous nation on earth.

The emperors of the later Han period expanded their domain even further. The Silk Road was under their control all the way to the Caspian Sea. Chinese armies wore down the Xiong-nu, their most troublesome enemies north of the Great Wall. The Xiong-nu were so demoralized that they decided to move westward, where they reappeared in Europe as the Huns several centuries later. In Korea and Vietnam, Chinese culture became ever more intense.

Inventions and technological improvement characterized later Han times. Farmers began to use the mold board plow in the millet-growing parts of the nation, causing a considerable increase in the amount of grain they were able to harvest. A collar that put the weight of plowing against the shoulders of oxen rather than around their necks considerably increased their pulling power. New and improved ways to mine salt increased production of this commodity. For the first time water mills were used to grind grain.

One more important invention was developed about A.D. 100, the process for making paper from rags. This discovery made it much easier for scribes, since parchment made of animal hides was so expensive. Another technique appeared about this same time, the way workers glazed pottery so as to make porcelain. Later, when Europeans came to China, they were so impressed with the quality of the porcelain, they called it china, after the country of its origin.

The later Han period was rich in literature, especially historical writing. Simaqian's *Historical Records* and Bangu's *History of the Han Dynasty* reconstructed the past in exemplary fashion.

The Chinese people remembered the years of the Han dynasty as a period of prosperity. They still call themselves **Han;** only foreigners call them Chinese.

About A.D. 200 the Han dynasty began to decline, the result of provinces breaking away and asserting their independence from central rule. Twenty years later a group of Daoist extremists, the Yellow Turbans, claimed that the court in Qangan was full of corrupt officials and justified their resistance to the emperors.

Three Kingdoms

Weakened central authority caused China to break into three separate states and a number of smaller ones early in the third century. Frequently the monarchs in these states were too ineffective to keep avaricious landlords and bandits from preying upon villagers. The Silk Road was no longer safe. In Korea and Vietnam, Chinese governors could not suppress movements for independence. The Chinese people, for the most part, felt that a return to strong central government was necessary, but this would not happen until the close of the sixth century.

China's Neighbors

To the north of China, the Koreans lived in a mountainous country speaking a Uralic-Altaic language quite different from Chinese. The first major contact that they had with their powerful neighbor came in 194 B.C. when a Chinese rebel sought sanctuary in their country founding a state known as Choson, with his capital at Pyongyang. This encouraged an emigration of Chinese to enter the country, which grew even faster after northern Korea's capture during the rule of the Han emperor, Wu Di.

Korea's fertile valleys attracted the Chinese northward.

In the fourth century A.D. the Koreans threw out the Chinese and established three sizable states: Kogoryo in the north, Paekche in the southwest, and Silla in the southeast. Conflicts among the three kingdoms generally meant victory went to Kogoryo. The size and magnificence of its kings reflected those of China. Buddhism, another import from the south, entered Korea late in the forth century, forever imprinting itself on the history of the country.

The Japanese remained in a culture known as Jomon until the third century B.C. About that time bronze, iron, and a new style of pottery brought Japan into the Yayoi period of history. Tombs from the time are built under large mounds of earth, similar to those in Korea. The largest is 120 feet high.

About 250 A.D. the last immigration from Korea entered the islands, fierce warriors riding on horses. Their military strength swept all previous leadership away.

The Japanese have two chronicles to recount the mythical origins of the nation, *Kojiki* and *Nihon-shoki*. They tell of the goddess of the sun, Amateratsu, giving birth to the Japanese islands. Later her grandson became a human, Jimmu Tenno. The symbols of his authority were a sword, a mirror, and a jewel. According to the story, Jimmu Tenno ruled Japan in 660 B.C., but if he is an historical person, a date closer to A.D. 300 would be more accurate.

In the fourth century A.D. it appears that one of the chieftains living on the island of Kyushu moved to the island of Honshu, taking for himself the imperial title, and in Chinese fashion, calling himself Son of Heaven. The now-reigning Japanese dynasty traces its beginning back to this event, making it the oldest dynasty in the world.

Vietnam fell within the Chinese orbit, but never completely since Indian influences were also present in the country. In 111 B.C. the Chinese emperor annexed the northern part of Vietnam, and with this event Chinese culture commenced its growth. The Red River Valley, with its rich soil, was excellent for rice cultivation, making it very valuable to the Han emperors.

Conclusion

The Chinese divide history into dynasties rather than centuries, as is done in the West. Each dynasty has its own unique characteristics. Certain dynasties enhanced China, promoting the farming that gave the country its wealth. Inventors abounded in this environment, as did the sages of China who grappled with life's problems.

Unlike other world societies of that age, the Chinese sought harmony on secular rather than religious terms, so that China never produced an institutionalized religion with scriptures or a priesthood until the arrival of Buddhism. In political terms the Chinese were quite willing to accept authoritarian government as long as it offered stability.

CHAPTER 11 REVIEW
CHINA AND ITS NEIGHBORS

Summary
- The Shang emperors claimed to be Sons of Heaven.
- The noble class in China fought from chariots in constant wars.
- Silk production became a major industry in China.
- Confucius's teaching on how to seek harmony became the norm for human behavior.
- Shi Huangdi, the first emperor of the Qin dynasty, was the builder of the Great Wall and his huge tomb.
- The Han dynasty brought prosperity to China for 400 years.
- Han emperors began the examination system for positions in the government.
- Buddhism came to China, and millions of people accepted its teaching.
- The first Japanese civilization appears.
- Korea and Vietnam come under Chinese culture.

Identify
People: Shangs; Zhous; Confucius; Laozi; Shi Huangdi; Liu Bang; Jimmu Tenno
Places: Qangan; Luoyang; Wang Mang; Korea; Vietnam; Kogoryo
Events: production of silk; teaching of Confucius; building the Great Wall; beginning the examination system

Define
Daoism   Legalists
shaman   *Kojiki*
Yin and Yang   *Nihon-shoki*
Silk Road

Multiple Choice
1. The Zhou capital was at
   (a) Luoyang.
   (b) Anyang.
   (c) Qangan.
   (d) Annam.

2. The title of the Chinese emperor was
   (a) Great Khan.
   (b) Mighty Lord.
   (c) Son of Heaven.
   (d) Ruler of the Five Directions.

3. The Great Silk Road extended from China to
   (a) Vietnam.
   (b) Mediterranean cities.
   (c) Indonesia.
   (d) Mongolia.

4. A major Shang metal-working industry was
   (a) iron.
   (b) silver.
   (c) copper.
   (d) bronze.

5. The material used for Chinese building was
   (a) wood.
   (b) stone.
   (c) brick.
   (d) stucco.

6. Confucius's doctrine emphasized
   (a) religion.
   (b) economics.
   (c) politics.
   (d) human behavior.

7. Confucius taught that women should
   (a) find employment outside the home.
   (b) obey the male head of the household without question.
   (c) assert themselves as equals to their husbands.
   (d) never leave home.

8. Daoists argued that Confucianism was contrary to
   (a) law.
   (b) nature.
   (c) the emperor's will.
   (d) the role of the father in the family.

9. Shi Huangdi's armies invaded
   (a) Korea and Vietnam.
   (b) Manchuria and Japan.
   (c) Korea and Japan.
   (d) Japan and Vietnam.

10. Peasants often fell into debt because of
    (a) long absences away from home.
    (b) a fall in grain prices.
    (c) taxation.
    (d) military conscription.

11. Buddhism in China arrived in
    (a) the fifth century B.C.
    (b) the fifth century A.D.
    (c) the first century A.D.
    (d) the first century B.C.

12. Wang Mang directed his reforms against
    (a) government officials.
    (b) military chieftains.
    (c) landlords.
    (d) merchants.

13. The later Han emperors were unable to
    (a) collect taxes.
    (b) control outlying provinces.
    (c) pay their army.
    (d) all the above.

14. Silla was a kingdom in
    (a) Vietnam.
    (b) Korea.
    (c) Manchuria.
    (d) Tibet.

15. Amateratsu was the Japanese goddess who
    (a) brought fertility to the land.
    (b) gave birth to the Japanese islands.
    (c) punished evil.
    (d) brought Buddhism to the nation.

Essay Questions
1. How do you explain the style of Chinese government?
2. Assess the rule of Shi Huangdi as ruler.
3. What explains the spread of Chinese culture to its neighbors?
4. What teachings of Confucius do you find positive? What do you find negative?

Answers

1. c	6. d	11. d
2. c	7. b	12. c
3. b	8. b	13. d
4. d	9. a	14. b
5. a	10. a	15. b

CHAPTER 12

The Rise of Greek Civilization

The first great European civilizations emerged in the period from 1200 B.C. to A.D. 500. Two peoples stand out for their accomplishments, the Greeks and the Romans.

The Greeks turned to the sea, because their country had no rivers of importance and irrigation was out of the question. Three fourths of their country was mountainous, giving them little land for food production.

The Athenians of Greece attempted Europe's first democracy, while the Romans took republican government a step forward. Their legacy laid a permanent foundation for the development of Western civilization.

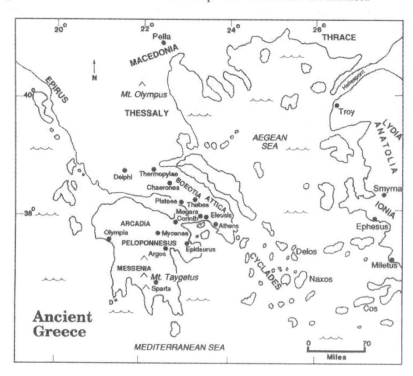

Dorian Invasion

Before Greece reached its golden age in the Western world, it first had to pass through the Dorian invasions. The Dorians were themselves Greeks and probably associated themselves with the Sea Peoples who wreaked such havoc on the inhabitants of the eastern Mediterranean.

There is no completely adequate explanation for the migration of the Dorians into Greece. It was probably due to the restlessness of the Indo-European people who were always anxious to seek out new homes for themselves and their flocks.

The Dorians forced out the Greeks who preceded them into the mountains or to the islands, except in the region of Attica. Here the Athenians and their neighbors held their territories against the newcomers.

The Dorians occupied most of the Peloponnesus, and in the fertile valley of Lacedaemonia they reduced the original residents to serfs. Little was left of the rich Mycenaean civilization. Writing was lost, public buildings were no longer constructed, and pottery decoration turned from human and animal representation to simple geometric designs. When potters pictured humans, they drew stick-people and made no effort to show perspective.

The major political organization was the tribe, people united by presumed kinship, under a chieftain who was usually the war leader, the judge of disputes, and a religious priest. Life was very simple in its externals. In time the larger tribes tended to assimilate smaller ones, especially through marriage alliances.

Greek Renaissance

In the half century after 750 B.C. the Greek world came out of its underdeveloped state. It experienced a renaissance that many historians credit to a dramatic rise in population due to the use of the plow for farming and increased economic links with Egypt and Phoenicia. Not only did merchants from these countries bring wares to sell, but they also brought new ideas, none of them more important than the Phoenician alphabet.

Inventive Greeks adapted the alphabet to their own needs, using the letters that did not have corresponding sounds in the Greek language to write vowels. Alphabetic writing put literacy in the grasp of a much larger population than in Mycenaean times.

Remarkably, probably less than 100 years after learning alphabetic writing, Greece produced its first outstanding writer, Homer. Although very little is known of his life, his two books, *Iliad* and *Odyssey*, have become classics of world literature. No other author had such an influence on Greek culture. Young boys learned to read from his books, and old men died listening to his verses.

The subject of the *Iliad* is the story of the Trojan War, an expedition led by Agamemnon, king of Mycenae, to rescue his wife, Helen, whom the Trojans had kidnapped. The story is told of the many years the Greeks camped outside Troy, besieging the city, and of the many heroes in the Greek army. Homer is interested in individuals, not the armies. No one knows if the Trojan War is historical or merely fiction written in a dramatic way to provide the Greeks of the seventh century B.C. with an introduction into their heroic past.

The *Odyssey* tells of one of these mighty warriors, Odysseus, on his way home from Troy, meeting one dangerous encounter after another. It is the first piece of adventure literature in the West. Later stories about the siege of Troy talked of the Trojan horse that led the Greeks to victory. This story is not in the *Iliad*.

On this vase painting, an artist portrays Odysseus bound to the mast of his ship lest he succumb to the siren's songs.

In A.D. 1871 Heinrich Schliemann began excavations in Turkey at a site that he felt certain was ancient Troy. He discovered artifacts that convinced him of the historicity of the *Iliad*, and additional digs continue to this day.

Colonization

From the Phoenicians the Greeks also learned improved techniques for shipbuilding and the advantages that come from founding colonies outside the homeland. The Dorians not only pushed other Greeks across the seas but engaged in colonization themselves, to Crete, Rhodes, and Cyprus. Colonization was especially attractive for the farmers who did not own their own land and the unemployed.

Before leaving Greece, the person in charge of recruiting for the colony went off to Delphi, the most popular religious shrine of all Greece. There Apollo had an oracle that gave the god's blessing to the expedition as well as advice on what should be done to make the venture a success. Once this was done, the colonists set out, taking with them fire kindled in the mother city's hearth.

Large numbers of colonies dotted the Ionian coast of Anatolia, the islands of the northern Aegean, Macedonia, and the Black Sea region. One colony was set up in Egypt, Naucratis, and another in Libya, Cyrene. Sicily and southern Italy received so many colonists that this region was named **Great Greece**. Other colonies went to the Iberian and Gallic coasts. Massalia, now Marseille, at the mouth of the Rhone River, was a Greek foundation.

The two major towns of Greece itself were the city-states of Athens and Sparta. The Greeks knew these towns as poleis, or city-states. A polis included the city and the agricultural region about it. Greeks in other poleis were foreigners, despite the fact that they might be less than 50 miles away. Ancient Greece was united by culture, language, religion, and common participation in athletic events, but not politically. There was never a single, unified Greek nation.

Athens

The people who lived on the Attic peninsula had settled there about 1900 B.C. Slowly among the dozen sizable towns, Athens took the lead in attracting new settlers and in imposing its will on the smaller poleis. In time, all the people living in Attica were pleased to call themselves Athenians. When the Dorian invasion struck the other poleis of Greece, Athens escaped for unknown reasons. The physical location of Athens was one factor, for it had a mighty rock fortress, the **acropolis,** that was so steep on three sides that it was impregnable to invaders.

On the Road to Democracy

Kings originally governed the Athenians, as was common in all other Greek city-states. As time passed, the Athenian nobility, well aware of its importance as the king's cavalry, began to chip away at monarchical powers. Eventually the king lost his authority, keeping only a religious role. An official known as an **archon** took over his executive powers, while the **polemarch** assumed his military duties. The legislative authority of the king fell to a council of nobles grouped in the **Areopagus.** In this way an aristocracy ruled Athens, a type of government that placed power in the heads of important landowning families.

The military needs of the state contributed to a demand for change. Aristocratic warfare was the province of the cavalry, which was a relatively small force, for ordinary citizens could not afford horses. However, military tactics evolved with the emphasis switching to the infantry, armed with iron spears and swords. Athenian farmers, city merchants, and artisans now enlisted in the army to fight as **hoplites.** The soldiers fought in a **phalanx,** eight men deep.

These citizen soldiers recognized that it was their participation in the Athenian army that gave the city its victories. With that realization came a demand for a role in the decision-making of the government.

Most aristocracies, in historical perspective, are noted for their short-sightedness and greed. The Athenian upper class tended to govern only with its own interests in mind, ignoring the common good. The mass of ordinary people found themselves increasingly impoverished and in desperation looked for anything that promised relief.

A young hoplite and a woman, possibly his sister, offering a libation before leaving for war.

First came a call for a written code of laws, to fend off the arbitrary nature of a judicial system in which the landowning class passed judgment on peasant farmers. Draco, a judge elected in 621 B.C., fulfilled this charge. He issued a written code of laws, carved in stone, that was erected in the **agora,** the heart of downtown Athens.

In 594 B.C. the archon, Solon, determined to further limit the power of the Athenian nobility. He freed all enslaved citizens who were in debt to the landowners and forbade any further enslavement of citizens. Then he classified the male population according to their wealth, not birth, for purposes of elections and the administration of the state. All were now allowed to vote in the **ekklesia,** the citizen assembly. He also broadened the number of jurors who sat on trials, so that ordinary people should form the majority and permitted any citizen to bring charges if he had a grievance.

In 546 B.C. the march toward democracy took a side turn. An Athenian general, Peisistratos, well known for his bravery, seized power in the city.

Peisistratos was known as a **tyrant,** and our word *tyranny* comes from that title, but in Athens Peisistratos' main object was to break the power of the aristocrats. As a tyrant, he actually improved the lives of ordinary citizens, fulfilling the promises that he made.

Ordinary Athenians, despite better times, did not long abide tyranny after the death of Peisistratos. Most citizens agreed that the rule of a dynasty threatened their freedom. Therefore, assassins struck down one of Peisistratos' sons, and the second fled into exile. The Athenians acclaimed the assassins heroes.

Cleisthenes, archon in 508 B.C., completed the process of transforming the Athenian state into a complete democracy. Every citizen, regardless of wealth or birth, was now eligible for office in the Athenian government. Each was registered in a **deme,** and every deme belonged to one of ten artificially constructed tribes. Fifty men of each tribe, chosen annually by lot, formed a **Council of Five Hundred,** which supervised the day-to-day running of the state.

The Council prepared an agenda of legislation that was submitted to the ekklesia for its approval or dissent. On the hill of Pnyx, facing the acropolis, anyone who was a citizen now had an opportunity to vote on the major issues facing the city. The vote was a yes or no, decided by acclamation.

Note, however, that the number of citizens only included adult men born Athenian, thereby excluding women, foreigners, and, of course, slaves. As a result, even though Athens has always been the model of ancient democracy, only a minority of the total population made policy. From Cleisthenes's time until the Macedonian conquest of the fourth century B.C., with few interruptions, the Athenian democracy persevered.

Women did not have a role in public life in ancient Athens nor in any other Greek city-state, except for minor duties in some religious cults. The norms of society dictated that the closest friendships should be had with people of the same sex, thus homosexuality was commonplace. Older men took young boys to educate them, but also as sex partners. Women, often slaves, entertained at the dinner parties of rich Athenians, which excluded wives, and enjoyed the most freedom of any females. Athenian wives spent the day at home cooking, caring for the children, and weaving the family's clothes. Their most important task was to give birth to male babies.

Sparta

Spartan citizens have always excited the imagination. Their way of life, which demanded a discipline seen nowhere else among the Greeks, was a wonder both to their contemporaries and to modern historians. Scholars have found this Spartan discipline simultaneously admirable and repugnant.

The Spartans were Dorian Greeks who settled in Laconia, the valley of the Eurotas River in the southern Peloponnesus. Uniquely, during the monarchical period in their history, the Spartans allowed the concurrent rule of two kings. Later they limited them to military commands, where they alternated in directing the army.

The Spartan senate of 30 members, the **gerousia**, assumed the right to enact legislation on the approval of the citizen assembly. The assembly could be manipulated rather easily because voting was done by shouting.

The assembly chose the gerousia's members for life from among men over 60. Five elected **ephors** acted as executives. Spartan society was very egalitarian. In fact, citizens called themselves the Equals.

As the population increased, the Spartans decided to forego foreign colonization with one exception, and instead concentrated on conquering the land of Messenia, the neighboring polis. This contest, begun about 725 B.C., proved to be long and brutal, and Sparta succeeded only after 19 years of fighting. With victory in hand, Messenian land was divided among the Spartan citizens, and the conquered Messenians were reduced to the state of serfs, known as **helots.**

For a while all went well. Then, about 600 B.C., the Messenians revolted, and the Spartans found themselves in a struggle that lasted a full generation. This rebellion proved so traumatic that the Spartan ephors and gerousia agreed to make its citizens into a standing army. Each Spartan had its Messenian helot family to supply his food.

The regimented society of Sparta required that every baby born should be examined for defects. If a handicap was found, the infant was left to die.

Boys over 7 years of age were enlisted in the army. "Captains of youth" supervised them in physical training, self-reliance, and unquestioned obedience to the state. A secret group of the young men were encouraged to prey on the helots, killing those who threatened to get out of line.

At the age of 20, the young men entered the army and took up life in a barracks. They were not permitted to marry until 10 years later. Girls in Sparta were given the same physical education as boys, and as married women, they managed the household.

The Spartan view contrasted with that of the poet Archilokos:

> *Some Thracian now carries a perfect shield*
> *I could not help it, so I left it in the woods.*
> *Oh well, I'm still alive, so what's the loss*
> *A new one will be just as good.*

Persian Attack

Athenian support for a revolt of the Ionian cities of Anatolia deeply touched the sensibilities of the Persian king Darius I. Darius was convinced that Athens must pay a price for its interference. Therefore, the Persian king began preparations for a Greek invasion.

In Athens, appraised of Persia's intent, the archon Themistocles, elected in 493 B.C., urged his countrymen and women to use state monies to construct a fleet to balance the Persian advantage on land. Themistocles's advice was well taken. The Athenians were in a much better position to resist the Persians 3 years later.

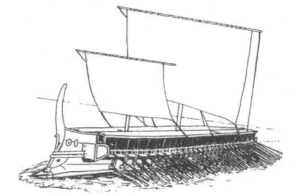

In a naval battle the Greek trireme sought to ram its opponent and sink it.

In 490 B.C. the Persian fleet disembarked its soldiers at Marathon, a bay on the east coast of Attica. The Athenians attacked, forcing the Persians back to their boats. A runner hurried off to Athens in a 26-mile run to inform the citizens, with a shout of "Nike!," or Victory! The army soon followed so that it was at its stations when the Persian fleet arrived. The Persians, finding the army on guard, did not attempt a landing but rather withdrew. In Athens there was jubilation.

Ten years later Xerxes, the son of Darius, took up the plans of his father to incorporate Greece into his already huge empire. Sparta and Athens allied to defend their homeland. The Spartan general Leonidas elected to defend at Thermopylae in northern Greece with 7,000 men, only to be outflanked. He ordered the soldiers of the other poleis to withdraw, but he and his 300 Spartans remained until all were killed. The Persians therefore were able to march on Athens without further resistance.

Themistocles, who directed the Athenian defense, ordered the Athenians to leave the city, so that when the Persian army arrived, Athens was empty. The Persian commander had the city burned.

The Athenian navy was still intact, so Xerxes then had to confront it in the narrow straits off Salamis, an island close by Athens. In this naval engagement, the Athenian sailors proved their fighting spirit was very much alive. The Persians were beaten and in the following year at Plataea, the Spartan forces dealt the Persian land troops a decisive defeat. The Persians never again came to Greece.

It is hard to overestimate the enthusiasm that spread through Greece over this victory. Tiny Greece had taken on and defeated the Persian giant. Athens became the undisputed leader of the Greeks, forging an alliance, the **Delian League,** that was meant to keep the Persians at bay.

Soon it became evident, however, that Athens intended to create an empire itself, forcing any rival to its power to submit to the city's policy. This did not sit well with many other poleis. Athens's allies especially resented the decision of the Athenian general Pericles to divert money from the upkeep of the Delian League's fleet to a building program on the acropolis and to pay salaries to the city's officials.

Priests sacrificed offerings to the gods on this altar from Delos.

War clouds began to gather as pro-Athenian and anti-Athenian alliances formed. Athens's enemies naturally looked to Sparta, and in 431 B.C. the storm broke. The two great cities of Greece were now in an exhausting struggle for the leadership of the Greek nation.

Peloponnesian War

Pericles was the acknowledged leader of Athens when the conflict began. As one of the Athenian generals, he stood for reelection over a period of 30 years. Apparently he felt his city was better prepared than ever before. The walls that extended the 4 miles from Athens to Piraeus, the port of Athens, were thought to be so strong that no matter what happened on land, Athens could be supplied from the sea and eventually wear down the Spartans.

In 431 B.C., as expected, the Spartans marched into Attica, leaving a scorched earth behind them. Refugees poured into the city. From the walls, they watched their homes go up in smoke. The following year a plague spread through the overcrowded city, a misfortune that Pericles had not foreseen. He himself fell victim and died, along with one third of the population. The Athenians sought terms to end the fighting, but the Spartans saw no reason to bargain while Athens was in such a state.

No politician in Athens was of the same caliber as Pericles. Demagogues rose up in the ekklesia advocating radical and unwise expeditions. The greatest disaster took place in 413 B.C. when the Athenians voted to send an armada against Syracuse in Sicily, an ally of Sparta. The Athenians outfitted 134 triremes and placed 27,000 men on board. The Syracusans defended themselves with vigor, sank most of the Athenian fleet, and took thousands of war prisoners.

At last, in 404 B.C. Athens sued for peace, agreeing to tear down its walls, limit its fleet to 12 ships, and give over its foreign policy to Sparta. The Spartans now set up a garrison on the acropolis and chose a group of 30 Athenians from among the peace party to govern the city in their name. The Athenians knew them as the **Thirty Tyrants,** for they killed over 1,000 of their enemies and exiled another 5,000. The Athenian public did not tolerate them for long. They rose in revolt, ousted the tyrants, and restored the democracy.

Architecture of Ancient Greece

The age of Pericles has always been thought to be the golden age of Greek culture, a claim justified because of the artistic and architectural accomplishments of that era. Pericles's building program enhanced the acropolis of Athens with four structures—three temples and a magnificent gateway—which are considered to be the finest examples of construction in ancient Europe. These are the Parthenon, the Erectheum, the Temple of Athena the Victor, and the acropolis entrance or Propylaea. Their continued existence brings over a million tourists to modern Athens each year.

The Erectheum was the favorite temple for the Athenians. Inside it the cult object, a wooden stump, signified the presence of the goddess.

These buildings exist because the Athenians built them in Pentelic marble, a white stone with just a touch of color, that was available from nearby quarries. Modern tourists, however, do not see the temples as the Greeks did, for the architects painted the marble capitals and the statues of the pediments in reds, blues, and yellows.

The temples were houses for the statues of the gods and goddesses. Unlike churches or synagogues, the general public did not go into the temples, for entrance was reserved to priests and priestesses. Sacrifices to the deities took place on outside altars where everyone could see.

Originally temples were wooden rectangular buildings with sloping roofs. A porch supported by columns was at the entrance. In the late eighth century B.C. architects first used stone, but the plan of the building remained the same. The style became more complex, with columns added to the back and sometimes encircling the structure. The shape of the capital on top of the column gave the style its name: Doric, Ionic, or Corinthian. The skill of the architect, working within the limits required of each style, appeared in the refinements of the building.

The Doric column was the simplest and heaviest. The top of the column was a simple square stone resting on a round base. The column rose directly from the floor with no decoration on it except for fluting, the semicircular ridges that were carved from the base to the capital. A frieze ran around the Doric temple that told one of the myths associated with the god or goddess. The triangular pediment that supported the roof held statuary that was so finely carved that the sculptor took into consideration the perspective of someone viewing it from the ground.

Ionic buildings were narrower and their capitals were curved. Corinthian-style temples were the latest to be built and had taller columns with capitals that resembled acanthus leaves. The Parthenon is a Doric temple, whereas the Erecthium is in the Ionic style. The largest temple of Athens, dedicated to Zeus Olympus, is below the acropolis and over many centuries was built in the Corinthian style.

Public buildings in Athens, Corinth, Olympia, Epidaurus, and other sites in Greece included gymnasiums, hippodromes for horse racing, theaters, and stadiums. In the center of every town, the agora was surrounded by shops called **stoa** where people came to shop. A fountain house was important for there was no indoor plumbing in Greek homes. The site of ancient Sparta, in contrast to Athens, holds few memories of its past because the Spartans built in wood rather than stone and did not wall their city.

In contrast to their public buildings, the ancient Greeks paid little attention to their homes. These were constructed in mud brick and clustered side by side. A few pieces of furniture—chairs, a table, and a chest—were sufficient. Behind the house, pigs had their pens. The smell encouraged the men of the household to walk down to the agora as early as possible to do the day's shopping.

Theater

The ancient Greeks were first to develop theater in the Western world. The earliest performances grew out of religious beliefs, for the Greeks thought of the gods as being very similar to humans, except that the gods were immortal. Because people liked to be entertained, the Greeks reasoned that their gods would also enjoy it. Even though every polis had a theater, only those plays composed in Athens are still extant. These are the tragedies of Aeschylus, Sophocles, and Euripides and the comedies of Aristophanes and Menander. For their efforts playwrights received an ivy wreath.

In the early plays, a chorus did most of the singing and dancing in unison. There is a tradition that in about 534 B.C. an author, Thespis, wrote a part for a single person to dialogue with the chorus. Later Aeschylus added a second actor. Soon there were three, always male, playing different roles. The audience had to watch the actors change face masks in order to know which character was speaking.

Greek plays did not contain much action. Violence might be spoken of, but it occurred offstage. The audiences knew the stories because they drew on myths everyone recognized. The skill of the playwright was in his handling of the story and his use of language. Tragedies drew on the accounts of heroes who overreached themselves and fell into disaster. Comedies poked fun at the politicians of Athens and even the gods and goddesses. Because plays have a timeless quality that continues to entertain, they are still presented in theaters throughout the world.

The actors were not paid very much, but they enjoyed the celebrity that working in the theater gave them. The chorus, on the other hand, required long hours of rehearsal, and private citizens paid the expenses. Unlike today, the plays had to be staged in the daylight, since oil lamps of the ancient world were not bright enough to illuminate a stage at night. Competition for a prize during the festival season required three plays to follow one another in a single morning.

Theaters were always located in places where a natural amphitheater allowed an audience to hear the actors' voices at a distance. The stage was first a full circle, with an altar to the god Dionysos in the center. Dionysos was the patron of the theater, and performances were dedicated to him. A tent nearby the stage allowed the actors to change costumes. Over time the stage was elevated and a backdrop of masonry added so as to provide a setting for the action of the play. The oldest theater is located at the bottom of the Athenian acropolis and is dedicated to Dionysos. The largest, still in use today, is located at Epidauros in the northern Peloponnesus.

The Theater of Dionysos is the oldest in the world. Its present shape dates from Roman times when gladiators fought there.

The Arts

Painting was highly regarded in the Greek world, but none of it has survived. Archaeologists now must study the work on vases to pass judgment on ancient painting. Actually, the vase painters probably do show in miniature some of the best work of Greek artists.

Few bronze statues are extant because these were melted down for ammunition in war times. Those statues that do exist often come from under the sea, as underwater archaeologists find them in centuries-old shipwrecks. Most marble statues in modern museums that are examples of Greek sculpture are usually Roman copies. There was a major trade in statuary in the ancient world and a great demand for copies of the master sculptors.

At first the Greek sculptors looked to Egypt for inspiration, especially to the statues of the pharaohs. As a result the early figures, **kouroi**, are very stiff with the eyes looking straight ahead. By the sixth century the sculptors carved the human body in much more realistic, but also idealized, poses. Sculptors found models in the nude athletes who were in the peak of physical fitness and attributed poise and serenity to them.

No ceremony or public event was without music. The ancient Greeks made both vocal and instrumental presentations. Often musicians competed for prizes. Several pieces of musical notation are extant, but no one today knows exactly how it sounded.

A bronze statue of Zeus or Poseidon demonstrates the qualities of strength and poise the Greeks expected of their gods.

The literature of ancient Greece was abundant, both in poetry and prose. Sappho of Lesbos was Greece's first major woman poet, famous for her lyrical poems that spoke of friendship and love between women. She gave the name "lesbian" to women lovers. Training in poetry and music was considered a basic part of an education for the young.

Historical writing in the Western tradition had its origins in Greece. Two names stand out because of the literary merit of their compositions, Herodotus and Thucydides. What we know of the Persian and Peloponnesian Wars we learn from their works. Although their concerns were with conflict, they used the wars to discuss and analyze much broader political and social issues.

Philosophers

Ancient Athenians loved to hold conversations on a wide range of topics, for they valued the person who could think as well as act. Among the wealthier Athenian young men, the pursuit of wisdom was as important as physical fitness and social prestige.

A group of teachers known as sophists promised to educate the young, to teach them wisdom (*sophia*, in Greek). This is how they made a living. Some of them, however, gave the rest of the teachers a bad reputation. They taught that to win an argument was all important. In order to persuade people to a given position, flattery and lies were as effective as telling the truth. An honest pursuit of evidence became lost in the pursuit of a better salary.

Among those teachers considered Sophists, one person demonstrated that integrity mattered. His name was Socrates, and his reputation for seeking truth is still honored. He refused to take any pay for his lectures, a reason for most other Sophists to dislike him. Socrates loved to begin a conversation in the agora by questioning young men who thought themselves bright and well educated. Through his questioning he demonstrated that what was accepted as true or good was not often the case.

Socrates wanted explanations for human behavior. What was the norm for deciding the difference between a good act and a bad one? Socrates concluded that people always act for the good and that they cheat, steal, or lie because they choose a subjective over an objective good. Moral evil, therefore, grows out of ignorance. If a person knows what is right, he or she will act accordingly.

Socrates lived during the age of the Peloponnesian War and fought in the Athenian army. He was not, however, convinced that the government was always acting in the best interests of the people. He feared a democratic system that was open to emotion rather than reasoned discourse. Some of his students became critics of democracy and were among those who came to power in the period of the Thirty Tyrants. Therefore, in 399 B.C. when there was a restoration of the democracy, his enemies put him on trial for disrespect for the gods and corruption of the youth.

Socrates, now 70 years old, eloquently answered all these charges, proving them false, but the jury found him guilty. When given a chance to choose his penalty, he suggested that the government provide him free meals, just like the polis's athletes. His boldness did not sit well with the jury. They voted that he should die. He was jailed in a place where it would have been easy to escape, but Socrates refused to leave. When offered the cup of poisoned hemlock, he drank it.

One of Socrates's friends and admirers, Plato, was shattered when he learned of his teacher's death. For years he sat at his master's feet recording the dialogues Socrates had with his students and critics. Because Socrates himself never wrote anything, all that philosophers know of his ideas comes from the pen of Plato.

After the death of Socrates, Plato left Athens and traveled about the Mediterranean. When he returned to Athens, he opened a school at a gymnasium, the **Academy,** located just outside the city's main gate. At the entrance to the Academy, Plato erected the sign, "Let no one enter here who does not know geometry." How effective this warning was, no one knows.

Plato's philosophical speculation built upon what he learned from Socrates. He was especially concerned with the question of how do we know what we know? What is reality? Plato's answer was that all that exists, exists in forms. These have an actual reality, but human senses cannot know these **forms.** The senses can grasp only expressions of the forms in individual things. The mind has these forms in it when people are born.

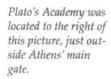

Plato's Academy was located to the right of this picture, just outside Athens' main gate.

The purpose of education is to get rid of the ignorance that misguides men and women when they think they know reality, but in fact, see only images. Plato uses the analogy of people sitting outside a cave, looking into it and seeing shadows on the wall of objects outside the cave. The people think they are seeing reality, but in fact, they are viewing shadows.

Plato argued that the purpose of life is "doing all things for the sake of truth." He believed that individuals should find in society the means to that truth. Because society, in the ideal state, needed government, then its leaders should be those men and women who would function as guardians because of their superior intelligence. The guardians would make the laws under a leader, the philosopher-king. It is noteworthy that Plato allowed women into the guardian class.

Just as Plato was Socrates's student, Aristotle was eager to learn from Plato. After Plato's death in 347 B.C., Aristotle became the leading intellectual of Greece. Although he was Plato's student, he did not always agree with his teacher. Aristotle believed reality did exist outside the mind, in individual objects. We know them through reliable information gathered through our senses.

Aristotle started his own school to the east of the acropolis, a competitor to the Academy, called the **Lyceum.** Here he and his students got the name **peripatetic** because Aristotle walked up and down with his students while he taught.

More than Plato, Aristotle took great interest in ordering and classifying objects, from embryos to Greek constitutions. His curiosity knew no bounds. Speculating on origins, Aristotle taught that a single god was the First and Final Cause of creation. He had begun the world, and one day everything would return to him. For humans, that life is happiest that seeks moderation in all things and enjoys enough leisure to pursue philosophical questions.

Aristotle did not just live in an ivory tower. His reputation for learning was so great that King Philip II of Macedonia prevailed upon him to become the tutor of his son Alexander. Without a doubt, Alexander's interest in the natural world owes much to the years he spent with his teacher.

Aristotle's work in biology and physics made him the final authority in these matters. No one challenged his opinions until 500 years ago. To quote Aristotle was to settle the question until the invention of the microscope and telescope made the world much more complex than Aristotle ever dreamed.

Science

The first scientists of the Greek world appeared during the sixth century B.C. in the cities of Ionia in Anatolia. Their special interest was in explaining the essence of matter and the reasons for change or motion. Technological inventions were not of much interest because slaves did the hard work in the Greek world. The idea of building machines to make labor easier did not really enter the Greek mind.

New methodology caused the scientific breakthrough. While contemporary societies and even for most Greeks the world was explained only through the intervention of good or evil spirits, or unknown magical causes, scientists explained natural phenomena through observation, experimentation, and analysis. They placed human reason at the heart of understanding. Their great contribution to the world was the **scientific thinking** that now dominates the search for facts in the present, very technically oriented, world.

Thales, one of the first known scientists of Ionia, sought to explain matter, arguing that everything is made up of water or a liquid very similar to it. Anaximenes had a different view. He stated that **prime matter,** limitless and eternal, composed the universe. These early Greek scientists were of the opinion that there was only one uniform substance found in all things. Diversity appeared because of the forms that the universal substance took.

Empedocles later moved the discussion further, disputing the idea of a single substance in matter, arguing instead that the world held four elements: earth, air, fire, and water. Combinations of these four substances determined individual objects.

The next contributor to scientific enquiry, Pythagoras, came from a Greek colony in Italy. Pythagoras was a multitalented individual who was interested in physics, cosmology, music, and especially mathematics. The Pythagoreans, members of the school he founded, placed numbers at the center of understanding. This was especially useful in explaining how music sounded when playing a stringed instrument and how harmony resulted from playing chords in combination.

The Pythagoreans were also great students of both plane and solid geometry. One of the most famous of geometric theorems still bears the name of Pythagoras: the sum of the two squares of the two shorter sides of a right triangle is equal to the square of the third.

In the next generation of Greek scientists the challenge was to explain motion. Heraclitus of Ephesus proposed that everything is always in motion and nothing ever remains the same. His famous statement sums up his opinion, "You can never put your foot in the same river twice." Critics of Heraclitus claimed that, yes, you can. Appearances may change but not the underlying reality, which always remains the same.

In the field of healing, the name of Hippocrates of Cos stands out as the father of modern medicine. Rather than assume an evil spirit or demon entered a person to bring on sickness, Hippocrates treated illness after examining symptoms and then prescribing a cure.

Religion

The Greeks were a very religious people, although they never developed a priestly class or a sacred scripture. In a world where scientific explanation had only begun to be acknowledged, men and women sought answers in religion. The calendar, the festivals, and the celebrations of the passages of human life all bore a religious connotation.

Many gods and goddesses inhabited the Greek pantheon. According to Homer, Mount Olympus in northern Greece was their home where they lived in leisure, sometimes quarreling with each other, sometimes in harmony. Zeus was the sky god who conquered the world and then gave his two brothers parts of it. Hades received the underworld, and Poseidon got the sea.

The Ionian Greeks adopted Apollo as their patron, although other Greeks also celebrated his festivals. Athena was the protector of Athens. She gave her name to the city, and her temples on the acropolis overshadowed the town. Inside the Parthenon her gold and ivory statue stood 39 feet tall.

The favorite holiday of every fourth Athenian year was dedicated to her, the **Panathenaea.** During this celebration her statue received a new garment, carried in a large procession from the nearby city of Eleusis.

The frieze of the Parthenon, now in the British Museum, pictures horsemen in the Panathenaea.

These gods and goddesses were city protectors, but they left much to be desired in the personal life of individual men and women. The **Orphic religions** filled that vacuum for they offered individual contact with a god, usually Dionysos, through song, prayer, and dance. Since Dionysos was patron of the grape vine, wine flowed freely at his celebrations, and excessive drinking added to the ecstatic state experienced in his worship. Women known as **sibyls** led the festivities on the mountains at nighttime.

The Orphic cults were a part of what became known as **mystery religions.** They received their name from the fact that they held secret rites that only those who were initiated knew about. The most frequented shrine of the mystery religions was at Eleusis. Here Demeter, goddess of fertility and prosperity, was honored along with her daughter, Persephone. At Eleusis priests presented a drama that told how Hades stole Persephone to take her to the underworld. For six months of the year, during the winter, she lived with him, but she returned to earth to give it new life when spring came.

Athletics

Exercise and training for physical fitness held the highest priority for ancient Greeks. Competition in physical games took place throughout the year, contributing to the value the Greeks placed upon athletic prowess.

The gymnasium was a place set aside for physical training. Here men could practice running, boxing, wrestling, or whatever other sport they enjoyed. Adjacent to the gymnasium were baths and massage rooms. Slaves oiled the bodies of the athletes and then scraped off the oil with curved blades.

Runners compete in a race on this vase painting.

Four major centers for games were located in ancient Greece: Nemea, Delphi, Isthmia, and Olympia, the most famous site of all. Dozens of other cities also had their games. All the cities of Greece, so often at war with one another, called a truce every 4 years so that they could attend the competition at Olympia. Each city sponsored its favorite athletes, many of them professionals. Winning one of the major events guaranteed a man celebrity status for the rest of his life. In addition the winner's city might give him prizes such as bronze cauldrons, oxen, cloth, or free meals for showering such glory on their polis.

Although the games lasted only a week, every man and unmarried woman of Greece who could do so poured into Olympia for the event. Days were filled with religious ceremonies, banquets, and speeches. Each contestant swore on the altar at the temple of Zeus that he was a Greek and that he would not cheat. Foreigners could attend the games, but they could not enter them. Women competed in running a race in honor of Hera, the wife of Zeus.

While the winners were heroes, the losers went home in disgrace. Some contestants preferred death, especially boxers and wrestlers, to defeat. These contests continued until one fighter signaled that he had enough.

The **Olympic games** were so important to the Greeks that they based their calendar on **Olympiads,** the four year periods that began in 776 B.C., when the first contest was held.

The entrance to the stadium at Olympia. Through it both athletes and spectators passed during the thousand years that the games were held.

Conclusion

The people of ancient Greece laid the cornerstone for Western civilization. For this reason, in the study of world history Greek culture has received more attention.

It is difficult to give a full explanation for the outpouring of accomplishments in ancient Greece. Its contributions to the arts, philosophy, science, athletics, theater, and government are remarkable. A combination of natural gifts in an environment congenial to innovation and competition provided the setting for one of the great ages of Europe and, later, the world.

CHAPTER 12 REVIEW
THE RISE OF GREEK CIVILIZATION

Summary

- The Dorian period of Greek history demonstrates a decline from the rich cultural life of Mycenae.
- Due to population pressure, Greeks colonized the coasts of the Black and Mediterranean Seas.
- The Greeks were the first to establish the *polis*, or city-state, in Europe.
- Greeks believed in many gods and goddesses who protected their cities.
- The interaction of the Phoenicians and Egyptians gave an impetus to the Greek renaissance.
- Political life in Athens moved from monarchy to oligarchy to direct democracy.
- Sparta developed a social system that made it a military state.
- Persian attempts to conquer Greece failed.
- The Greeks excelled in architecture, arts, philosophy, athletics, and science.

Identify

People: Homer; Draco; Solon; Peisistratos; Cleisthenes; Pericles; Socrates; Plato; Aristotle; Philip of Macedon

Places: Acropolis; Delphi; Athens; Sparta; Messenia; Delos; Olympia

Events: Olympic games; development of democracy in Athens; beginning of philosophy and scientific thought; rise of Macedon

Define

scientific thinking	Great Greece	Panathenaea	phalanx
peripatetic	oligarchy	polemarch	Academy
Orphic religion	Areopagus	hoplites	helots
Olympic games	tyrant	Delian League	deme
ekklesia	agora	Council of Five	gerousia
olympiads	forms	Hundred	Thirty Tyrants
archon	kouroi	acropolis	stoa

Multiple Choice

1. Geometric painting refers to the decoration of
   (a) weapons.
   (b) pottery.
   (c) walls.
   (d) public buildings.

2. One gift of the Phoenicians to the Greeks was
   (a) the calendar.
   (b) weapons.
   (c) the alphabet.
   (d) shipbuilding.

3. Establishing colonies helped the Greeks
   (a) trade with the Assyrians.
   (b) relieve population pressure.
   (c) improve shipbuilding.
   (d) prepare for war against Persia.

4. Apollo's most famous oracle was found at
   (a) Delos.
   (b) Delphi.
   (c) Athens.
   (d) Corinth.

5. The wife of the Greek god Zeus was
   (a) Aphrodite.
   (b) Artemis.
   (c) Hera.
   (d) Penelope.

6. The home of the Greek gods was
   (a) at Athens.
   (b) at Troy.
   (c) on Mt. Pentele.
   (d) on Mt. Olympus.

7. A tyrant was a person who
   (a) wanted to be an archon.
   (b) wanted to be the sole ruler in a polis.
   (c) wanted to attack Persia.
   (d) had a bad temper.

8. People said Draco's laws
   (a) were not strict enough.
   (b) were just fine.
   (c) needed constant changes.
   (d) were written in blood, not ink.

9. Solon gave more power to
   (a) the archons.
   (b) the tyrants.
   (c) the Areopagus.
   (d) the ekklesia.

10. Peisistratos was a
    (a) general.
    (b) archon.
    (c) demarch.
    (d) tyrant.

11. Cleisthenes put political authority into an executive body that was called
    (a) the agora.
    (b) the ekklesia.
    (c) the heleia.
    (d) the Council of Five Hundred.

12. Women in ancient Athens were found in
    (a) the ekklesia.
    (b) the Council of Five Hundred.
    (c) the demes.
    (d) none of the above.

13. Sparta's need for a military way of life arose from a fear of revolt in
    (a) Athens.
    (b) Messenia.
    (c) Arcadia.
    (d) Mycenae.

14. Leaders of the Spartan government had the title
    (a) archon.
    (b) ephor.
    (c) general.
    (d) king.

15. Spartan servants were known as
    (a) archons.
    (b) helots.
    (c) Athenians.
    (d) none of the above.

16. A trireme was
    (a) a sailing ship.
    (b) a two-oared warship.
    (c) a merchant vessel.
    (d) a three-oared warship.

17. The first Persian invasion of Greece failed at
    (a) Thermopylae.
    (b) Marathon.
    (c) Plataea.
    (d) Salamis.

18. The Athenian Empire was formed within
    (a) the Delian League.
    (b) the Peloponnesian League.
    (c) the Arcadian League.
    (d) the Areopagus.

19. This Athenian statesman commissioned the buildings of the Acropolis:
    (a) Solon.
    (b) Cleisthenes.
    (c) Pericles.
    (d) Aristagoras.

20. After the Peloponnesian defeat Athens was ruled by
    (a) kings.
    (b) the Persians.
    (c) the Thirty Tyrants.
    (d) Pericles.

21. The Parthenon is built in this style:
    (a) Attic.
    (b) Ionian.
    (c) Corinthian.
    (d) Doric.

22. The best woman poet of ancient Greece who wrote lyric poems was
    (a) Electra.
    (b) Sappho.
    (c) Hera.
    (d) Artemis.

23. The historian of the Peloponnesian War was
    (a) Thucydides.
    (b) Herodotus.
    (c) Aristotle.
    (d) Hippocrates.

Essay Questions
1. Contrast life in Athens with that of Sparta.
2. What were the steps that led to democracy in Athens?
3. Discuss the importance of Greek theater.
4. Which of the Greek philosophers is your favorite? Explain.

Answers

1. b	9. d	17. b
2. c	10. d	18. a
3. b	11. d	19. c
4. b	12. d	20. c
5. c	13. b	21. d
6. d	14. b	22. b
7. b	15. b	23. a
8. d	16. d	

Alexander the Great and Hellenism in Southwestern Asia

The recovery of Athens from the Peloponnesian War was remarkably swift. Fear of Spartan intentions encouraged the Athenians to forge an alliance with other Greek poleis against Sparta. By the mid-fourth century B.C., the citizens of Sparta were no more than a thousand, yet tradition forbade granting any new people the privilege of citizenship.

A shift in power now took place in the Greek peninsula. North of the city-states of the classical period, Macedonia lived in isolation until the mid-fourth century B.C., its people in villages scattered over the mountains. Monarchy remained the rule for no major political evolution had occurred. In 359 B.C. the potential for a strong king to come to power was realized when Philip II mounted the throne at 23 years of age.

Rise of Macedonia

Philip had great ambitions. His goal was to bring all Greece under his single rule, a project that no one before had ever attempted. By conquest, bribery, and deception Philip expanded his borders. His major contribution to strategy was to increase the size of the phalanx to double its depth to 16 men.

In Athens most people were concerned about Philip's intentions, but not enough to vote funds for a larger army. The orator Demosthenes in the ekklesia gave speech after speech, pointing to the need to prepare. Finally the Athenians acted, and gathering allies along the way, the army marched to Chaeronea in Boeotia to meet Philip's forces. In 338 B.C. the battle was joined. The Macedonians won the day, and classical Greece came to an end.

Philip treated both Athens and Sparta gently, allowing the two poleis to continue to run their internal affairs. The rest of Greece he placed in a league, based at the city of Corinth, where his Macedonian representatives dominated the proceedings. Having won Greece, Philip planned, with the help of the Corinthian League, to invade Persia. Unknown to him, a plot against his life was forming in the ranks of his trusted friends. In 336 B.C., at his daughter's wedding, assassins struck Philip down.

This Macedonian lion marks the battlefield of Chaeronea.

Philip's son, Alexander, had no great affection for his father and, with his mother Olympia, had gone into exile a year prior to Philip's death upon the occasion of Philip's remarriage. The report of his father's murder now allowed Alexander to return to claim his inheritance. Fortunately several of Philip's generals came to his aid. After suppressing a revolt in Thebes, the other Greek cities, taking note, fell into line.

Alexander then announced his idea for completing his father's plan to invade Persia and revenge that country's earlier attacks upon Greece. At the age of 22 he crossed the Dardanelles leading an army of 30,000 infantry and 5,000 horsemen. Of the cavalry units, 2,000 were his Companions, so named because he took his position with them when he went into battle. He never saw Europe again. The history of Greece now becomes the history of Alexander and his successors.

Alexander

In 334 B.C. Alexander took his army across the Bosporus Strait into Asia. His goal was not only to complete the project of his father but also to break the Persian hold on southwestern Asia and to annex its lands into an empire that he alone would rule. Alexander had a remarkable hold on the loyalty of his army.

Alexander commanded more than soldiers when he crossed into Anatolia. He brought with him geographers, scientists, philosophers, and even poets, for Alexander did not want to be known only as a military leader but rather as a ruler concerned with expanding knowledge of the world. He ardently believed in the superiority of Greek culture, and he wanted its advantages spread into a much larger area than the Balkan peninsula and the cities of the Anatolian coast.

The Persian king, Darius III, forewarned of Alexander's plans, believed that if only he could be killed the invasion would not proceed. He was probably right. So when the first battle between Alexander and Darius commenced at Granicus River, the Persians tried desperately, but unsuccessfully, to kill the Macedonian king.

In this mosaic, Alexander and Darius meet in desperate battle.

His victory at the Granicus allowed Alexander to march through Anatolia meeting no resistance. In the Greek Ionian cities he announced that he had come as a liberator and that henceforth the citizens living in them could choose their own government. The Macedonian army then moved to southern Anatolia where once more a Persian force had gathered at Issus. Darius sought to reach a bargain with Alexander, but the Macedonian king refused. He saw no reason to negotiate. Once again, his troops carried the day.

The army then marched through Syria and Palestine and finally crossed into Egypt. Alexander was in awe at the great monuments of Egypt. When he visited the shrine of Amon in the desert, the oracle that resided there told him that he was a god. It appears that Alexander considered himself to be one after this encounter. During his stay in Egypt, Alexander picked a site for a harbor to be built on the western edge of the Nile delta. He graced it with his name and ever since it has been known as Alexandria. Alexander left Egypt, never again to return, so he never saw the completion of his dream.

Because Darius was still in Persia recruiting a new army, Alexander turned back toward Asia, hoping to catch the king before he finished his plans. The two forces met in northern Mesopotamia, at Gaugamela, and again Alexander proved the victor. He marched on Persepolis, the Persian capital, and set fire to the royal palace. At this point, the Persian generals despaired, killed Darius, and announced their acceptance of Alexander as their ruler.

Now Alexander decided to push eastward to make sure that the satraps of eastern Persia should acknowledge him as their king. He believed that these provinces lay on the border of the ocean, and after he gained sovereignty over them, all of Asia would be his. He plunged into this campaign with his usual enthusiasm. Long and difficult campaigns in Inner Asia, in parts of modern Uzbekistan and Afghanistan, awaited him and left his army with more victories but few rewards.

Never content, Alexander then turned his forces southward into the Indus Valley, modern Pakistan, where his forces for the first time had to confront Indian warriors fighting from the backs of elephants. At last his soldiers, who had sojourned with him for so long, decided that they wanted to return home. Seven years of fighting was enough. Disappointed, for Alexander had not yet reached the ocean, he agreed to follow the Indus to its mouth and then to return to Mesopotamia.

Alexander set up headquarters in Babylon and began projecting a campaign against Arabia, when he fell ill. When he recognized that he would not recover, he requested to review his soldiers a last time. In silence, they filed by in the room where he lay. On June 13, 323 B.C., not yet 33 years of age, Alexander died.

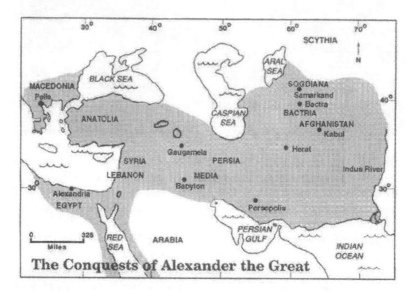

The Conquests of Alexander the Great

Alexander's achievements as a military leader were remarkable. No general ever accomplished more. He also wanted to be seen as someone who would fuse the Greek world with other "barbarian" societies. Initially he brought Persians into his service and took a Persian wife, but toward the end of his life, he wavered, reserving the highest offices for Greeks. He bears the name Great because many people feel he deserves to be remembered as one of history's noble personalities that changed the world. Others see him as an ambitious man whose life was dedicated to his own aggrandizement no matter what it cost in blood and suffering for others.

Hellenistic World

The world that Alexander left behind, the **Hellenistic age,** extends from his death in 323 B.C. until the coming of the Romans in the first century B.C. Its history was marked by the rule of Greeks over the indigenous people of Southwest Asia, the founding of Greek cities throughout the region, and the spread of European institutions including the Greek language. All memories of Athenian democracy seem to have evaporated in the absolute control demanded of keeping empires intact.

The generation after Alexander's death was very turbulent as the generals who accompanied him struggled among themselves for precedence. When the dust cleared, two of his generals founded great empires.

Seleucus set up one dynasty in the city of Antioch on the Orontes in Syria. The second was located in Alexandria in Egypt where Ptolemy and his successors ruled.

Seleucus fell heir to most of Alexander's Persian possessions. He constructed a second capital, Seleucia, near ancient Babylon in order to keep an eye on events in Mesopotamia. Often he did nothing to disturb local rulers as long as they paid tribute and acknowledged him as sovereign. He, and for a long time his successors, were careful to keep their armies entirely Greek, forbidding entrance to the natives.

The Seleucid bureaucracy and higher society were also a Greek preserve and unquestioned loyalty to the ruler was demanded for advancement. A cult of the emperor developed. The ideology of the state encouraged people to offer his statue divine honors.

In southwestern Asia the garrisons left by Alexander's conquest grew to become important cities as Greek teachers, merchants, and professional people poured into them. With their arrival, separatist tendencies arose. The Seleucids could not contain them.

Places like Bactria, modern-day Afghanistan, broke away from the Seleucid monarchy and for a time flourished under its own Hellenistic dynasty. Armenia, once a part of the Seleucid empire, declared independence, setting up a double kingship. Pergamum on the Aegean coast in Anatolia also broke free. The Seleucid leaders were simply unable to find resources sufficient to hold their empire together. A revolt by the Macabees in Palestine also meant the revival of a small Jewish state.

The theater of Ephesus, built for thousands of spectators, demonstrates the size of Hellenistic city populations.

This weakness on the borders did not stop the kings in Antioch from constructing magnificent buildings in their cities. All the Hellenistic towns of any size had their temples, theaters, baths, gymnasiums, parks, and illuminated streets. Scholars, writing in Greek, brought Western learning into southwestern Asia to fill Seleucid libraries. Artists of the times carved stonework to decorate public buildings.

Realism and size attracted Hellenistic artists. At Ephesus, the **Temple of Artemis** was built three times larger than the Athenian Parthenon. The statue of the Colossus of Rhodes, set beside its harbor, illustrates the point. It was the largest statue of Hellenistic times.

The worship of Artemis at Ephesus attracted people from all over the Hellenistic world. This cult statue portrays the goddess as she appeared in the now destroyed temple.

In religion, there was a turning away from the Greek gods and goddesses of classical times to a more personal and emotional faith. Syncretism, the blending of the Greek pantheon with local Asian deities, became common. Some Asian deities came to the fore, such as Cybele, the mother goddess of Anatolia, Isis of Egypt, or Mithra of Persia and were associated with Greek deities.

For some people, all religion seemed suspect. They turned to philosophy to give their life meaning. The two major schools of the time were **Stoicism** and **Epicureanism.** Both taught that the pursuit of the good life demanded a calm response to whatever life brought, either good or bad. A Stoic found satisfaction in doing one's duty, whereas an Epicurean discovered satisfaction in pleasure. According to Epicurus bodily pleasure was fine, but the greatest pleasure was in a good conversation. Stoicism also stressed the idea of the natural law, which was found in all men and women. It rejected the notion of a world divided between barbarians and Greeks.

Conclusion

Each year thousands of tourists visit the eastern Mediterranean countries to view with admiration the monuments of Hellenistic towns now deserted and forlorn. They must use their imaginations to reconstruct the vibrant life of the hundreds of cities that once were scattered over this part of the world.

Perhaps this is how the people of this age expected their society to end. The literature of the time shows an uneasiness about life that could not be shaken off. The Greeks provided the ruling and cultural elite in Southwest Asia, but their values never eliminated local people's beliefs and customs.

CHAPTER 13 REVIEW
ALEXANDER THE GREAT AND HELLENISM IN SOUTHWESTERN ASIA

Summary
- Alexander the Great conquered the Persian Empire, placing huge territories under his rule.
- The generals of Alexander divided his territories among themselves.
- The Seleucid dynasty ruled southwestern Asia for 200 years. The rulers retained their Greek culture, but many of their subjects resisted it.

Identify
People: Alexander the Great; Darius III; Antiochus III; Seleucus
Places: Granicus; Bactria; Ephesus; Antioch; Babylon; Ctesiphon
Events: Alexander's conquest of the Persian empire; the spread of Hellenistic culture throughout southwestern Asia

Define
Temple of Artemis at Ephesus   Hellenism
Stoicism   Epicureanism

Multiple Choice
1. He warned Athens of its danger from Macedonia:
    (a) Demosthenes.
    (b) Pericles.
    (c) Cleisthenes.
    (d) Themistocles.

2. Alexander's armies reached in the east as far as
    (a) Syria.
    (b) the Indus Valley.
    (c) Cyprus.
    (d) the Persian Gulf.

3. Alexander's last days were spent in
    (a) Macedonia.
    (b) Alexandria.
    (c) Babylon.
    (d) Ctesiphon.

4. Greeks usually considered people who did not know the Greek language as
    (a) barbarians.
    (b) dumb.
    (c) Hellenes.
    (d) Illyrians.

5. Antioch in Syria became
    (a) the capital of the Romans.
    (b) the capital of the Persians.
    (c) the capital of Ptolemy.
    (d) the capital of Seleucus.

6. A characteristic of the Hellenistic age was
   (a) the spread of the Greek language.
   (b) the extension of Greek democratic ideals.
   (c) building canals on the Tigris.
   (d) the spread of the Latin language.

7. Pergamum was a Hellenistic city in
   (a) India.
   (b) Persia.
   (c) Anatolia.
   (d) Greece.

8. Stoicism stressed
   (a) aggression.
   (b) emotion.
   (c) self-indulgence.
   (d) duty.

9. Modern Afghanistan was once the Hellenistic kingdom of
   (a) Bactria.
   (b) Syria.
   (c) Lydia.
   (d) Armenia.

Essay Questions

1. What are the reasons for calling Alexander great? Does he deserve this title?
2. How did southwestern Asia profit from Hellenism?
3. Describe why Epicurus might be correct in his view of life.

Answers

1. a	4. a	7. c
2. b	5. d	8. d
3. c	6. a	9. a

CHAPTER 14

The Roman Republic

The Romans were one of the ancient world's extraordinary peoples. Their legacy in law, politics, and building still has an impact on the present. Of all European peoples, they were the only ones to create a world state that extended the length of Europe's southern Mediterranean shore from Spain to Greece. The expansion of city life in these regions and the economic unification that followed was a major contribution to the subsequent history of the continent.

It is a tribute to their political skills that most of the people who lived under Roman rule were proud to be known as its citizens. Even people who were born far away from the city of Rome and never knew a word of Latin, the language of the Romans, considered themselves Romans for several centuries.

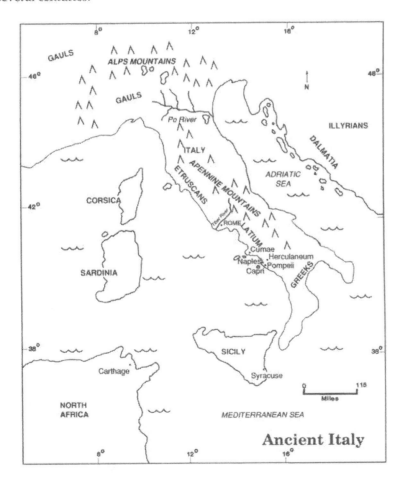

Ancient Italy

Italian Peninsula

Italy is a peninsula, shaped like a boot, that juts into the Mediterranean Sea. To the north the Alps, a great mountain chain, separate Italy from the rest of Europe. The Alps are rugged mountains and in ancient times were a barrier to easy movement into other parts of Europe. However, several passes in the Alps allowed access to the northern Italian plain. It was through one of them that the first Latin-speaking people came into Italy.

Down the length of the Italian peninsula are mountains called Apennines. They are not very tall, but low and rolling so that, unlike the Alps, crossing them was relatively easy. In southern Italy, two small peninsulas, the toe and heel of the peninsula, extend into the Mediterranean. Just a few miles south of mainland Italy is an island known as Sicily. Shaped like a triangle, it gets its name from the Sicels, the people who lived there before the coming of the Romans. There are also two large islands, Corsica and Sardinia, that lie to the west of Italy, but they have never played an important role in history.

The soil of Italy is more fertile than that of Greece, and the countryside gets more rain. Rivers such as the Po in northern Italy have deposited a layer of rich mud through the centuries so that Italian farmers can produce good harvests. The climate in the summer is hot and dry, and in the winter cool and rainy.

Peoples of Italy

About 1000 B.C. the ancestors of the Romans picked an area along the western side of the peninsula for their home, a region they called Latium. Farmers and shepherds made up the bulk of the population. A few artisans worked in bronze and iron, which were first introduced into Italy about 900 B.C. In many ways these early Italian villages were self-sufficient because they could easily supply all that they needed for their simple existence.

The people of Latium, however, were not destined to keep themselves apart from the rest of the world. Italian grain was much in demand, and merchants from other countries wanted to trade their metal tools, glassware, leather goods, and slaves for grain.

The Greeks were the most important of the merchants who traveled to Latium, coming from the many Greek city-states of southern Italy and Sicily. The Greeks taught the Latin farmers how to cultivate the olive tree and the grape vine. Soon wine-making became a major industry. What the Latins did not consume themselves, they could easily sell to Celtic peoples to the north where grapes could not survive the colder winters.

The Greeks also taught the Italians how to construct stone buildings, how to mix pigments in order to make paints, and how to carve a statue from stone. They also shared the technology for better weapons and armor. Most importantly, they shared their alphabet with the Italians. The Italians soon adapted it to the sounds of their own Latin language, changing the shape of some letters and adding several new ones.

Greek temples were a part of the southern Italian landscape as migrants to Italy continued to worship their deities.

The Greeks of Italy established over 50 city-states on models drawn from their homeland. They built temples to their gods, large marketplaces, and harbors for trade. Phoenicians and Carthaginians were also busy forming cities on the island of Sicily. Much of western Sicily was dominated by the Phoenicians, so the Greek colonies had to stay in the east.

The Etruscans lived in the area today known as Tuscany, to the north of Latium. In many ways they are a mysterious people, for no one knows for sure where they came from. Some authorities believe them to be a remnant of the Neolithic population of Italy. Others argue, following the lead of the Greek historian Herodotus, that they were immigrants from Anatolia. Their language, unrelated to Indo-European, survives in only a few inscriptions.

By 700 B.C. the Etruscans were settled comfortably in large impressive towns, wealthy because of agriculture and mining, for their land held copper, iron, and tin ores in abundance. In their towns two large streets, paved and drained, crossed in the middle. Temples, similar to those of the Greeks, were built, with statues of the gods sitting on the rooftops.

At the head of the Etruscan cities were kings who wore purple robes, colored with Phoenician dye, to emphasize their dignity. During religious processions, servants carried bundles of rods and an ax, symbols of the power of the kings. They did not have to share authority with an assembly or senate but were absolute rulers. The magistrates who served them came from the nobility in what was a very stratified class structure.

The Etruscans, like many other men and women of the ancient world, spent a great deal of time preparing their tombs for death. They laid out

A husband and wife are pictured atop an Etruscan sarcophagus.

large cemeteries with rooms cut into soft rock for the burial of whole families. On the walls of these tombs, painters drew scenes of their gods and goddesses as well as pictures of torture or sacrifices. These images suggest that the Etruscans had a gloomy picture of life after death.

This dark picture of Etruscan life, however, must be balanced by the carved statues of the dead that appear on their sarcophagi. Smiling husbands and wives who in life were happy together appear to be hoping for a pleasant reunion after death. The religion of the Etruscans was based on revelation, which made it very different from that of either the Greeks or the Romans. It required belief both in public gods, protectors of the cities, and in personal gods, who watched over individual fortunes.

The Etruscans performed many rituals that were meant to help them know the future. One of these demanded the slaughter of an animal and then an inspection of its liver. Priests studied its size and shape and interpreted what each bump and dip in it meant. Other means of determining the will of the gods included watching the paths of birds in flight and the direction of lightning bolts. Later the Romans took over these rituals in their religious practices so that they, too, could predict the future.

The Etruscans, like the Greeks, never formed a nation. Each city-state had its own interests to protect, although there were meetings to discuss policy and to share in religious ceremonies common to all. Neighbors frequently quarreled about land and water, and warfare was the result. Their divisions made the Etruscans vulnerable to Rome, once it began its expansion.

Early Rome

Early Rome lay in a generally flat open plain with some low hills surrounding it. In the eighth century B.C. several villages of Latium located overlooking a ford on the Tiber River agreed to form a single town on a site 15 miles inland from the coast. Tradition placed this foundation of Rome in 753 B.C. The location was a good one, for merchants from the Greek city-states could bring their wares here on their way to the Etruscans.

In later history the Romans invented two different legends to explain their city's foundation. In one, a Trojan warrior named Aeneas fled his city after it was taken by the Greeks and established Rome. According to the second legend, Rome was founded when a mother abandoned her two babies, named Romulus and Remus, on the banks of the Tiber. A flood carried them down the river where a female wolf discovered them and took over their nursing. She cared for them until they were old enough to move away and build a home for themselves.

Romulus and Remus settled down on the banks of the Tiber, but quarreled over which of the seven hills surrounding the area should become a town. Romulus killed his brother and therefore named the future city for himself.

Since it was a long time before Roman history came to be written, it is difficult to know exactly what happened in the early days of the city. It does appear that by 500 B.C. Rome held as many as 80,000 people and was ruled by an Etruscan dynasty of kings.

One of these Etruscan kings was Tarquin the Proud. In order to enhance the city, he drained a marshy area to form a paved square. This square, built to hold the merchants' shops and centers for exchange, was the **Forum.** Ever after, the Forum was the center of Roman life and the square around which Rome's public buildings clustered.

The Roman Forum as it appears today contains buildings from both the republic and the empire.

Formation of the Republic

About 509 B.C. Roman nobles, known as **patricians,** in concert with another Etruscan town, expelled Tarquin and set up a new form of government, a republic. The word comes from the Latin *res publica*, the peoples' state, to differentiate it from *res privata*, the private state that existed when the Etruscan king ruled Rome as his personal property. The patricians formed a **Senate** to direct the government's policies. To be sure that power would never be given to a single man, the patricians determined that elected officials should remain in office for only 1 year.

Another means of controlling the power of Roman officials was to divide their offices. There were two **consuls** at the head of the state and two **censors** in charge of numbering the men in the army. Later **praetors** and **quaestors** appeared, magistrates in charge of legal and financial affairs, respectively. One official could cancel out an order of the other. Only in times of crisis could the Romans vote to give supreme authority to a single person, the **dictator,** and then only for 6 months. This division of power meant that change came very slowly. Custom and tradition governed Rome more than decisions of the consuls or other magistrates.

In addition to the Senate, Rome's citizen army gathered in the Centuriate Assembly to vote on matters put before it by the consuls. This body received its name from the military unit of the **century,** which in theory should have held 100 men. In fact the number of men in a century was variable. The patricians dominated the Assembly's activities thanks to its method of voting.

Conflict of the Orders

In early times the Roman patricians, like the Greek nobility, were the only judges in the state. If a plebeian (a citizen who did not have sufficient credentials to be considered noble) went to court, he had to depend on the judge's memory for a fair trial. Pressure was put on the patricians to have a written code of laws just as had happened in Athens under Draco.

In 451 B.C. a committee of ten judges wrote out the Roman law. They put it on **Twelve Tables,** which were set up in the Forum for all to see. The Twelve Tables forbade people from taking the law into their own hands. Only the state could exile a person or execute a criminal, and the right to appeal a sentence to the highest court was guaranteed. The Twelve Tables was only the first of many law codes that continued to be produced throughout Roman history.

The patricians constituted only about one tenth of Roman society, the remainder fell into the plebeian class. Although citizens, the plebeians were forbidden to become Senate members or to be selected to hold office as a magistrate. In the Centuriate Assembly they were powerless to outvote the patricians.

Unhappy over this denial of equal civil rights, the plebeians at one time threatened to leave Rome but instead sought a compromise, organizing their own Plebeian Assembly, with two, and later ten, **tribunes** at its head. In 387 B.C. the patricians finally agreed to allow the plebeians to stand as candidates for all offices in the government. The Plebeian Assembly won a complete victory exactly 100 years later when a decree, called the Hortensian Law, gave all its **plebiscites** binding force on the Roman state. After this, patricians and plebeians cooperated in making policy for Rome.

Roman Society

The Roman patricians were the great landowners and, like the Indian brahmans, were the only ones who could perform certain religious ceremonies. They controlled the power and wealth of the nation through membership in the Senate and received enough income from their lands to spend their time in politics or in entertainment. To be in business was considered beneath their dignity, although buying and selling land was acceptable. The two major classes of the elite were the senatorial and the equestrian orders. Families that had a member who held the consulate were at the pinnacle of society, the **nobiles.**

The **toga,** a garment that was 18 feet long and 7 feet wide, which the men in the upper classes wore, severely restricted their physical activity. This long sheet of material was draped over the shoulder and fastened with a pin, but its size made manual labor almost impossible. Women in Rome wore **stolae,** long dresses that reached to the ground.

In order to further emphasize their position, the patricians drew clients from among the plebeians. Their clients accompanied them to the Forum and to all public events; in return for this service, the patricians gave them gifts of money and food and helped them when they had difficulties.

In every family, patrician or plebeian, the father held absolute authority according to the law. He was the **pater familias,** controlling the activities of his wife, children, household servants, slaves, and all the property. As long as he lived, family wealth was exclusively his. Upon his death, the power of the pater familias went to his eldest son. If he had no son, he might adopt a young man to carry on the family name.

Roman women upon marriage became integrated into the husband's family, even to the point of adopting his ancestors for her own. She managed the household, cared for the children, and provided for their education. In plebeian households women worked alongside their husbands in shops and on farms and were not as secluded as they were in Greece. Women in the upper orders attended public events and served as hostesses in their homes. Their testimony was taken in court. Boys and girls played and went to school together in their early years. Girls often married at 13 years of age; boys married at about 20 because their schooling in grammar and public speaking took more time.

Women had a role serving in a religious capacity. On this ivory a priestess of Bacchus offers a libation.

Rome's many wars meant that prisoners for the slave markets of the cities were never empty. Here men and women, tablets around their necks advertising their origin and skills, awaited sale. Their future was a bitter one, especially those purchased for work in the mines or on large estates. Slave rebellions were repressed with the utmost cruelty.

Roman Expansion

Rome and the other cities of Latium were located in a part of Italy that was open to invasion from the mountain people of the Apennines. Early in their history, they organized an army of citizens in the Latin League to defend themselves.

Every able Roman man over 17 years of age was expected to spend some time in military service. The patricians were rich enough to own horses so they made up the cavalry. The plebeians served in the infantry, carrying a spear and a short sword. They wore helmets and a suit of iron over their tunics and held a large wooden shield covered with leather on their arm. The infantry was organized in **centuries** led by a centurion. The largest army unit was the **legion,** which was composed of 60 centuries.

The Romans were typically the victors in conflict with their neighbors over land that they both claimed. After 450 B.C. the Roman legions rolled over their enemies, culminating in the capture in 396 B.C. of their most feared rival city, Etruscan Veii.

Once a city or region came under Rome's control, one third of its territories were directly added to the public domain. However, often the Romans did not take their share. They trusted that their generosity would inspire loyalty among the conquered people. Certain cities were given privileges of Roman citizenship; the citizens were permitted to trade with Rome and marry its citizens.

The conquered were permitted to keep their religion and to continue their old form of government. Rome demanded only that they pay taxes, supply a certain number of men to the military, and allow the Senate to make foreign policy decisions. On the whole, within a generation, bitterness between Romans and conquered peoples tended to fade.

These close relations served Rome well when the city itself came under attack by the Celtic Gauls. In 390 B.C. an army of Celts descended into the Italian peninsula. With their long swords and wild charges, the Celts swept away the Roman forces sent to meet them. The Celts occupied most of the city, leaving only the Capitoline hill in Roman control. For 7 months they endured a siege, until the Celts withdrew. This event made the Romans more concerned than ever about defense and the strength of the army. They hastily put up a new, stronger wall around the city.

A battle between Celts and Romans is depicted on this sarcophagus. While the Romans wore armor, the Celts fought naked.

The Romans soon recovered from the Celtic invasion, and its former prosperity returned to the city. The policy of expansion commenced once again, with Rome enlarging its Italian frontiers at the expense of its neighbors. The Etruscans proved no match for the Roman armies. In the same way, the Romans gathered in the Greek cities and their territories. Rome was now supreme in Italy, but a new challenge appeared on the horizon. This came from Carthage, the strongest power next to Rome in the western Mediterranean.

In 264 B.C. a conflict began between the Carthaginians and the Romans, supporting two opposing cities on the island of Sicily. Three wars between Carthage and Rome were fought during the next century. They were known as the Punic Wars because *Punic* is the Latin name for Phoenicians. Due to superior leadership, Rome won all three, but it had a major scare when a Carthaginian general marched into Italy.

The Carthaginian general Hannibal led an army of 50,000 men from Spain into Italy in 218 B.C. His army came equipped with a corps of 50 elephants. Hannibal crossed over the Alps with his elephants but suffered heavy losses because of avalanches and deep snows. Nevertheless, Hannibal defeated every Roman force sent against him. At Cannae he won his greatest victory, and the Romans suffered 50,000 casualties. For the next 15 years his army remained in Italy, but he was never strong enough to attack Rome.

Carthaginian officials then recalled Hannibal to return to fight his last major battle with the Romans. This time he lost to the general, P. Cornelius Scipio, who added *Africanus* to his name after his victory.

In 146 B.C. Carthage was so badly defeated a third time that a Roman army completely destroyed it. The Roman Republic had no more serious opposition in the west.

Now, more confident than ever, the Romans turned eastward. Although they had no long-range plan for conquest, they wanted no rival power in the east to threaten their position in the Mediterranean. First, they conquered Macedonia and took over the Greek cities that the Hellenistic kings of Greece ruled. Then their forces moved against the Seleucid king of Syria, Antiochus III. Other armies fought in Spain and southern Gaul, and these regions were successfully added to Rome's territories. Rome often sent out colonies of veterans or the unemployed to make their homes in these lands and to help spread the Latin language and culture throughout the Mediterranean region.

When not involved in combat, Roman soldiers built fortifications on the frontier.

Coming of the Romans to Southwestern Asia

When Alexander turned his armies eastward, he failed to notice Rome's growing power in the west. He could hardly be faulted for not recognizing the potential of Rome, for it had not yet launched its expansionist program. The luxury of ignoring Rome was not afforded his Hellenistic successor, Antiochus III the Great, ruler of the Seleucid empire from 223 to 187 B.C. When he ignored warnings to disengage from a campaign in Egypt, the Roman fleet defeated his navy and later his army.

For the first time a Roman army entered southwestern Asia. Its presence meant that Antiochus lost his Anatolian possessions, which the conquerors awarded to its allies, Pergamum and the island of Rhodes.

Henceforward, Rome kept an eye on events in southwestern Asia. It was only a matter of time until its armies were to intervene again. In 64 B.C. the Roman general, Pompey, overthrew the last Seleucid and made Syria a Roman province.

At first the Romans set up several client kingdoms in southwestern Asia, where monarchs ruled because of their ties to Rome. They preferred to govern other regions directly as Roman provinces. They established a client kingdom in Jerusalem where the High Priest of the temple was placed in charge as Rome's representative. Later the Romans recognized Herod, a foreign general, as king of Judaea.

Roman rule built upon the area's Hellenistic foundations. Greek remained the language of business and literature, and Hellenistic artistic models continued to receive esteem. City councils debated and ruled on local matters and collected the taxes. Tax-farming, the sale to private individuals of the right to collect taxes, put a crushing burden on the peasant population and caused great discontent. Equally distasteful was the presence of garrisons that enforced the laws of Rome in an arbitrary way. Locals often accused them, correctly or not, of brutality and contempt for their traditions and culture.

While the Seleucid and later the Roman emperors held unchallenged supremacy in the Mediterranean regions of southwestern Asia, a competing state, the Parthian kingdom, grew up on the Iranian plateau. In the mid-third century B.C. the Parthians took advantage of Seleucid weakness to free themselves from Greek dominance. They placed their capital in Ctesiphon on the Tigris River.

The Parthian kings who lived here proved to be excellent military strategists, and in 53 B.C. the Romans suffered a major defeat at Carrhae when fighting them. In the second century A.D., the Romans occupied Ctesiphon three times and had to retreat each time.

Jews and Romans

Of all the peoples in southwestern Asia, the Jews proved the most difficult to assimilate into the Roman world. Many Jews were never reconciled to Roman occupation of their land and hated the imposition of the foreign family of the Herods in Jerusalem. Once Rome commenced to rule Judaea directly, leading Jews were equally dismayed over the caliber of the procurators sent out from Rome to govern them. They proved to be corrupt and venal to an extreme.

In A.D. 66 the Jewish population in Caesarea, a major coastal city, commenced an uprising. It was the first battle in a long drawn out conflict between the Jews and Romans. The struggle was hardly an equal one, since Roman resources were so much greater.

After 4 years of resistance, the Roman legions broke through Jerusalem's walls and pillaged and destroyed the city. The last Jewish survivors of the rebellion died by suicide at Masada rather than fall into Roman hands. Titus, the victorious general, came back to Rome bringing with him thousands of prisoners and much of the wealth of the country. In Rome Titus's arch, built to commemorate his victory, still stands.

A drawing based on a panel of the Arch of Titus shows Roman soldiers carrying a menorah from conquered Jerusalem.

There was still one more revolt of the Jews, the Bar Kochba revolt, from A.D. 132 to 135. This ended tragically once again for the Jewish cause. After the rebellion's suppression, Emperor Hadrian forbade any Jews to make their residence in Jerusalem. The failure of these two revolts contributed to the **diaspora,** the establishment of Jewish colonies throughout the Roman world. It also resulted in an agreement on the canon of the Hebrew Bible at a meeting of the rabbis at Jabneh, so that in their dispersion all Jews might have the same text.

Roman Religion

The most important deity in early Rome was Janus, the god who guarded doors. A small temple was erected to him in the Roman Forum. Whenever Rome was at war, the temple door stayed open. It was shut in times of peace. Despite the fact that he lost his importance in later times, Romans always called on Janus first when they prayed.

Jupiter, originally a god of the oak forest, eventually took the leading place among the Romans. When the leaves blew in the wind, people believed that Jupiter was sending a message. Later he became a god of thunder, lightning, and rain. Jupiter always stood for law and order, the authority of the Roman state. He became Jupiter Optimus Maximus, which means Jupiter, the best and the greatest.

A Roman temple, built during republican times, combines Greek and Roman styles.

Diana was the goddess of hunters, forests, and fertility. Venus, like the Greek goddess Aphrodite, was the patroness of love. Another important goddess was Vesta. This goddess protected the hearth in every Roman household. Rome itself needed her protection so a temple in the Forum was built to her. A fire was kept burning there all the time. Young women, the Vestal Virgins, cared for this fire and made sure that it never went out.

In addition to the public Roman gods and goddesses, there were divine spirits who lived in or around Roman homes and were attached to particular families. **Penates** were in charge inside the house, where they were thought to live in cupboards.

The Romans believed that the gods should be honored with many holidays. Sacred dances, music, processions, and sacrifices were offered the gods on those days that were special to them.

The Romans never made fun of their gods the way the Greeks did. They kept their distance and covered their heads with their togas when they stood before a temple in a respectful attitude called **pietas.**

In the later years of the Republic, after Rome had conquered many foreign lands, other peoples brought their gods to the city, in the form of mystery religions. From Greece came Dionysos and Orpheus. From Anatolia came Cybelle, the Great Mother Goddess, and Egyptians in Rome gained converts for Isis and Osiris. All these religions promised a happy life after death, which made them very attractive to poor people whose existence in this world had not been a happy one.

Political and Economic Problems of the Late Republic

The extensive training that prepared the Roman citizens for war made them the best soldiers in all Italy, but this also had a negative result. Citizens were called into service so often that they neglected their farms and families. The women and children who were left behind could manage their households only by using slaves. When their husbands returned from service, they often had little taste for farming. Frequently they sold out and took their family to Rome hoping to find work. Too few citizens found work; therefore, the capital filled with the unemployed.

Wealthy Romans expanded their holdings by purchasing the farms of veterans and joining them into large estates, **latifundiae,** run with slave labor. The remaining free peasants could not compete, adding to the emigration to the towns.

The huge numbers of unemployed in Rome and the gap between rich and poor caused the consul, Tiberius Gracchus, to look for a solution that would both help the poor and ensure a sufficient supply of soldiers. To join the army, a person had to own property. Gracchus intended to extend the citizenship to outsiders and to open public land for purchase to people of modest means. Since this reform was to be done at the expense of the wealthy, his program came under fire. The landowners saw to his assassination, and when his brother tried the same later, he committed suicide rather than be arrested. The nobility would brook no interference with the system that made them rich.

The social decline of Rome became increasingly evident in the first century B.C. Roman generals fought each other as readily as they battled foreign enemies and Italian allies. The city became the scene of riots. The Republic, once the model of ordered government, was thrown into anarchy and confusion.

Out of this chaos strong men appeared. Their fame as generals gave them the support they needed to direct public affairs. One such man was Pompey. His soldiers moved across Asia, bringing Syria and Palestine under Roman control. Another was Julius Caesar who fought in Spain and Gaul. For a time in 60 B.C. Pompey, Caesar, and a third general named Crassus formed a **triumvirate,** a three-man government. Caesar, however, was not a person who liked to share power.

Roman senators were well aware of Caesar's ambition, for he sent reports of his battles back to Rome. He was very rich and had many friends in Rome who shared in his success. In 49 B.C. Caesar and his army approached the capital. The Senate told him he must disband his army, but Caesar refused and crossed the Rubicon, a small river in Italy, with his army. The Senate appointed Pompey to stop him, but he was unable to do so. Caesar marched into the city of Rome, while Pompey fled to Greece. Caesar pursued him and destroyed his army at Pharsalus.

The Appian Way, the first paved road between Rome and Capua, was built to facilitate the movement of Roman troops.

Pompey again fled, this time to Egypt. When Caesar caught up with him, he was already dead, killed on the orders of the king of the country, Ptolemy XIII. Caesar then found himself involved in a civil war between Ptolemy and the king's young sister and wife, Cleopatra VII. Caesar and Cleopatra joined forces, her husband drowned while in flight, and Caesar was able to establish her as queen of the country.

Caesar went on to add new conquests in Anatolia, sending word back to Rome, "Veni, vidi, vinci," which means "I came, I saw, I conquered."

In Rome, the Senate elected Caesar dictator, consul, tribune, sole commander of the army, and chief of the city's treasury. He gained additional prestige by spending state funds as well as his own to build new temples, libraries, and buildings around the Forum. In order to attempt a solution to Rome's unemployment problem, he ordered landowners to hire free workers as at least one third of their work force. Twenty colonies left Rome so as to decrease the population pressure. He altered the course of the Tiber River to stop it from flooding and ordered a review of the Roman calendar to make it more accurate. From this study came a new **Julian calendar.** The seventh month, July, was named in his honor.

Most Romans believed that Caesar's one-man rule was preferable to the chaos that had gone before, even though it violated the Republic's constitution. Other Romans, especially some of the senators, secretly hated Caesar and plotted to get rid of him. When Caesar brought Cleopatra to Rome and had a statue of her placed in a temple, his opponents were outraged.

A group of disgruntled senators hatched a plan to kill him. They approached Caesar on the Ides of March (March 15) in 44 B.C., pretending that they wanted to question him about a petition. After they gathered around him, the conspirators brought out daggers that were hidden in their togas. Caesar saw his friend Brutus with a dagger. His last words were, "Et tu Brute?" (And you, too, Brutus?).

Marc Antony, one of Caesar's generals, claimed his body and took it to the Forum to be placed upon a funeral pyre. Here he made a speech about Caesar that made his audience furious over Caesar's assassination.

Caesar's closest male relative and heir was Octavian, a grand-nephew and adopted son, who was but 18 years old. He quickly returned to Rome where he found Marc Antony in charge. Octavian, Marc Antony, and a third general, Lepidius, formed a second triumvirate, but like the first, it soon crumbled because of the personal ambition of its members.

Among those who perished during the conflict between Antony and Octavian was Cicero, the most famous of Roman orators. After many years of battle between Marc Antony and Octavian, the latter won at Actium in 31 B.C., becoming in fact, if not in name, the sole ruler of Rome with the title **princeps,** or first citizen. History knows him by the name Caesar Augustus.

Europe's Other Peoples

The Romans were of course not the only people of Europe. To their north were the Celts, a people who lived in an area from Ireland across Europe to the Black Sea. They were most numerous in Gaul, or modern France, where several thousand made their home in the second century B.C.

Their language was also Indo-European, and closely related to Latin. The Celts are the ancestors of the Irish, Scots, and Welsh of the modern world. The Celts of the contienent were the primary victims of Roman expansion in Europe for it destroyed their way of life.

Celtic villages were built on hills with log walls and stockades around them for defense. The Celts were experts in making iron weapons and tools.

As warriors, they battled as individuals without much discipline. As they rushed into battle, they wore only helmets, a necklace called a torque, and a belt. To make themselves look more fierce, Celtic warriors washed their hair in lime, which made their hair stand out from their heads in spikes. On more peaceful occasions they wore trousers and highly ornamented jewelry.

After a battle the Celts took the heads of their enemies and brought them home where they displayed them for all those who had not seen their bravery. The head of an enemy supposedly held magical powers that a victorious soldier wanted to become his own.

Every Celtic tribe had its own elected chieftain. He led the army and made its major decisions. His wife was an important person who received special privileges just as her husband did, sometimes joining him in battle. When the chief and his wife died, they were buried in a wagon and a mound of earth was put over them.

Celtic priests were called **Druids.** Because the Celts did not have writing, the Druids served as record keepers by memorizing the laws and traditions of the tribe. They remembered long poems and entertained people by reciting them; they were also the only ones who knew magical spells to cure illnesses.

One custom among the Celts sought to bind families together. When boys and girls were about 7 years old, their parents sent them to live with another family. That other family perhaps had a child of their own to send back, and these foster families raised the children. After their education, ages 14 for girls, and 17 for boys, they were sent home. This bonding helped reduce the clan violence that was so common among the Celts.

Other peoples in Europe of this time include the Germans and the Slavs. Their early history is known only from archaeological discoveries, for as yet they had no writing.

Conclusion

The Roman Republic moved from its origins as but one Italian city among many to the construction of a mighty empire. Even though the battles it fought were cruel, the government it offered afterward was benign, showing considerable tolerance to local sensibilities. Roman government proved flexible enough until the first century, when problems still not addressed finally overwhelmed the Republic.

CHAPTER 14 REVIEW
THE ROMAN REPUBLIC

Summary
- The Italian peninsula offered fertile farmland to the people living there.
- Greeks lived in the southern part of the peninsula, Etruscans in the north, and Latins in the central region.
- The Roman aristocrats overthrew an Etruscan king to begin the Republic.
- The government of Rome was placed in magistrates elected in the Centuriate Assembly, but the real power lay in the Senate.
- Roman expansion began as the result of insecurity and later continued because of the wealth it provided.
- Romans replaced the Seleucids in southwestern Asia.
- The Roman Republic collapsed in the first century.

Identify
People: Celts; Hannibal; Pompey; Julius Caesar; Etruscans; Carthage; Cleopatra; Marc Antony; Parthians
Places: Tiber River; Rubicon; Gaul; Actium; Britain; Masada; Ctesiphon
Events: formation of the Roman Republic; expansion of Rome; conflict between patricians and plebeians; Punic Wars; Roman rule in the eastern Mediterranean

Define

Forum	Senate	patricians
plebeians	tribunes	consuls
triumvirate	legion	Twelve Tables
censors	consuls	praetors
dictators	legion	diaspora
pietas	Druids	centuries
plebiscite	nobiles	toga
stolae	penates	Julian calendar

Multiple Choice
1. Rome was located in the region called
    (a) Tuscany.
    (b) Dalmatia.
    (c) Etruria.
    (d) Latium.

2. The Greeks taught the Romans
    (a) the alphabet.
    (b) how to grow olives.
    (c) how to grow grapes.
    (d) all the above.

3. The Romans learned from the Etruscans about
    (a) building towns.
    (b) making stone buildings.
    (c) republican government.
    (d) growing grapes.

4. Rome is located on this river:
    (a) the Po.
    (b) the Tiber.
    (c) the Tigris.
    (d) the Arno.

5. In a republic, officials are
    (a) appointed.
    (b) chosen by the governed.
    (c) in politics because of birth.
    (d) in politics because of their relation to a king.

6. Roman censors
    (a) provided the army's generals.
    (b) oversaw public buildings.
    (c) counted citizens.
    (d) all the above.

7. A dictator held power
    (a) for 1 year.
    (b) for 6 months.
    (c) for 2 years.
    (d) until tossed out of office.

8. Tribunes represented
    (a) the plebeians.
    (b) the patricians.
    (c) the army.
    (d) the senate.

9. In every family the male with the most authority was
    (a) the pater familias.
    (b) the mater familias.
    (c) the grandfather.
    (d) the paternal uncle.

10. Roman women
    (a) managed the household.
    (b) cared for the children.
    (c) provided education.
    (d) all the above.

11. In 390 B.C. Rome was invaded by
    (a) Etruscans.
    (b) Greeks.
    (c) Sabines.
    (d) Celts.

12. The Punic Wars were fought between
    (a) Sparta and Rome.
    (b) Carthage and Spain.
    (c) Rome and Sicily.
    (d) Rome and Carthage.

13. The Roman god of love was
    (a) Jupiter.
    (b) Minerva.
    (c) Venus.
    (d) Janus.

14. Protecting spirits of a Roman house were the
    (a) penates.
    (b) lares.
    (c) ancestors.
    (d) vestals.

15. An example of a mystery religion was the worship of
    (a) Mars.
    (b) Isis and Osiris.
    (c) Jupiter.
    (d) none of the above.

16. The Roman Republic broke down in the first century B.C. due to
    (a) the invasion of the Celts.
    (b) economic causes.
    (c) ambitious generals.
    (d) corruption in the Senate.

Essay Questions
1. What were the checks and balances in the Roman government?
2. Discuss the Gracchi brothers' reform.
3. How did religion play a role in Roman life?
4. Discuss why conquered people usually were loyal to Rome.
5. Why did the Roman Republic fail?

Answers

1. d	5. b	9. a	13. c
2. d	6. d	10. d	14. a
3. a	7. b	11. d	15. b
4. b	8. a	12. d	16. c

The Roman Empire

With the rise of Caesar Augustus to power, the Republic ended and the Roman Empire began. It had become evident that the many responsibilities of overseeing such a great expanse of territory could not be effectively performed by the Senate, the city's assemblies, and officials who held office for only a year. A strong government was needed under a single individual.

Augustan Age

The appearance of Caesar Augustus begins a new era in European history. Augustus kept all the forms of the Republic even though everyone knew he was now in charge. In 27 B.C. he told the Senate,

> I shall lead you no longer, and no one will be able to say that it was to win absolute power that I did whatever had to be done . . . . Receive your liberty and the republic. Take over the army and the subject provinces and govern yourselves as you will.

A grateful Senate responded, naming him **Augustus.**

Caesar Augustus's rule marked the beginning of the Roman Empire.

For the next 41 years Augustus gave the Romans good government. To better the administration, he appointed men whom he knew could be trusted to office from every class. In order to solve the problem of so many people without jobs, he put Rome's citizens to work on construction projects building forums, granaries, baths, temples, libraries, and roads. He boasted of his accomplishments, "I found Rome built of sun-dried brick; I leave it clothed in marble."

Augustus appointed able men to supervise the postal service and the grain trade. It was extremely important that enough wheat come into the city to provide bread for a population now approaching a million men and women. Hunger led to urban unrest. The emperor also gave Rome its first fire department. This answered a great need for the city because fires were so frequent in the tenements where most Romans lived.

Education was another major concern for Augustus. He paid the salaries of school teachers and librarians and urged that students be given a basic training in citizenship.

The emperor was well aware that the army had become bloated during the wars of the Late Republic. He intended to do more with less. Therefore he reduced the size of the army from 60 to 28 legions. Dismissed soldiers, 100,000 of them, were settled in different parts of the Empire furthering its Romanization. Nevertheless Augustus thought that one of his responsibilities as emperor was to expand Rome's borders even farther to the Elbe River in Germany.

The Teutonic tribes of Germany, however, proved too strong. In A.D. 6 they soundly defeated a Roman army. Fighting from behind trees, the Teutons would not come out to battle the Romans in the way the soldiers of Augustus were used to fighting. The Romans withdrew to the Rhine River, which became a permanent boundary between Germans and Romans for the next 300 years. In eastern Europe all the territory south of the Danube was brought under Roman rule. In Anatolia, a bargain struck with the Parthians divided Armenia between them, placing the Roman border on the Euphrates River.

The Roman Empire
at the Time of
Caesar Augustus

The reign of Augustus lasted until A.D. 14 when he died at 76 years of age. He had truly become a father to his countrymen. His vision for the Empire was to unite all people for service on behalf of Rome. He came close to success. It is not too surprising that some people thought him a god. After his death the Senate erected temples to him where his spirit was given divine honors. In Rome itself, men and women could visit the great Altar of Peace that Augustus erected to commemorate his restoration of the Roman world.

The age of Augustus was also a time for Roman literature to flourish. The most important author was the poet, Virgil. His epic, the *Aeneid*, was narrowly saved from destruction because he was dissatisfied with it. Augustus appreciated its value and saw to its preservation. Other authors of the time include Horace and Ovid, both poets of exceptional talent, and the historians Livy and Tacitus. All Roman writers and authors looked to Greek models that seemed the standard for good literature.

Successors of Augustus

Augustus failed to set up a system to choose a successor. He had no children to take his place as ruler, so there was considerable confusion over who should now govern. Finally, his stepson, Tiberius, became emperor. The Romans were reluctant to establish a formal system for choosing an emperor, causing a period of crisis whenever an emperor died.

The next several emperors were in some way related to Augustus, either naturally or by marriage. None of them had his ability. Tiberius started out well but ended his reign spending the last 10 years of his life on the Isle of Capri. There he was almost completely cut off from the situation in Rome.

Caligula followed Tiberius as emperor. Tiberius had said of Caligula, "I am raising a viper for the Roman people." Caligula proved him correct, ordering a statue of himself cast in gold so that people could worship him as a god. Sacrifices of flamingos and peacocks had to be made to this "god." He demanded that his horse be given a marble stall and a purple blanket and insisted that the horse be elected consul. At last a group of army officers could take this no more and murdered him.

In A.D. 41 Claudius was picked to be emperor by the **Praetorian Guard**, the army unit that served as the imperial bodyguard. Despite the fact that Claudius had never shown any ability before, he showed himself to be more able than anyone believed possible. He added five more provinces to the Empire, the most important of them, Britain. Years before, Julius Caesar had invaded the island, but he later withdrew his forces. In A.D. 43 the army sent by Claudius occupied Britain and claimed it for Rome. The Romans built Londinium to be their capital.

The rule of Claudius ended when he died at the hand of his wife. She served him a dish of poisonous mushrooms so that her son, Nero, could become emperor. At first, Nero was rather popular. Later he decided that he was a gifted singer and commenced tours around the Empire to give concerts. Instead of caring for Rome's business, he let his advisors run the Empire in his name. Guided by their advice, Nero had thousands of innocent people arrested, tortured, and killed to satisfy his paranoia.

In A.D. 64 a great fire struck Rome. Nero confiscated the land that had burned to build himself a new palace. He told people that the fire was started by a group of arsonists, who were followers of a certain Chrestus. Nero's persecution was the first state attack upon the Christian church. Four years later, when Nero was threatened by a rebellion, he committed suicide.

It is remarkable that, despite such emperors, the administration did not break down. Augustus laid the foundations so well that the government continued to work. Even when incompetent people were at the top, provincial administrators and local officials were able to keep the Empire intact.

With Nero out of the way and no heirs in sight, the Empire had four rulers in the following year. With the support of his army, a general, Vespasian, managed to gain power. Vespasian commissioned the largest of Rome's temples, dedicated to Jupiter, the chief Roman god. An even more famous building constructed at this time was the Colosseum.

The foundations of two synagogues built atop one another remain at Capernaum. Jesus would have worshipped in the lower building, built of darker stone.

Jesus of Nazareth

While Romans and Jews contested what should be the future of Judaea at the time of Caesar Augustus, a man was born who changed the history of the world. His name was Jesus of Nazareth, for he lived in this town of Galilee, in upper Palestine. His followers used the name Christian, followers of the Christ, to identify themselves. (The word *Christos* is a Greek translation of the Hebrew *Messiah*, meaning the anointed one.)

Christians believed that Jesus was the Messiah, in popular Judaism a figure who would usher in a new era of peace and prosperity. For those who became Christians, the death of Jesus was followed by his bodily resurrection, therefore fulfilling not only his claims to messiahship but a testament to his divinity as the Son of God. Only a small percentage of Jews, however, were convinced, with the result that Christianity after A.D. 70 became a religion of Gentiles, non-Jews.

All that is known of Jesus is contained in a book Christians call the New Testament. Four gospels, a collection of letters, a history of the early Christian community called Acts, and an apocalyptic work, Revelation, make up the corpus of the sacred scriptures for Christians. The New Testament was written in Greek, not Aramaic, Jesus' own language, testifying to the strong influence of Hellenism at the time the authors wrote.

In the New Testament, Jesus is portrayed as a wandering rabbi, teaching people that the kingdom of God had arrived among them. He was also seen as a wonder worker, able to perform miracles on behalf of those who trusted him. His message called for repentance and the directing of a person's life toward keeping the Ten Commandments. He associated with him a small band of men, called **the Twelve,** as well as a group of women who traveled with them on journeys about his native region of Galilee.

The Roman Colosseum was built during the rule of Vespasian to provide a place for public spectacles.

Over a period of about 3 years, according to the Gospels, the books that tell of Jesus' teaching and activities, some Jews, especially among the priests of the Temple, opposed him for they believed that he was causing trouble within the Jewish community. They resented his public teaching, for he had not studied to be a rabbi, and felt threatened by his messianic claims. Jesus was arrested and then taken before the Roman procurator of Judaea, Pontius Pilate, who condemned him to die on a cross. Three days later, in Christian tradition, Jesus appeared alive.

Christians

These disciples of Jesus organized themselves into their own community, called a church. While some of the early Christians wanted to keep Jesus' followers within Judaism, others did not. Among the latter was Paul of Tarsus, or Saint Paul, a later convert to Christianity who had not known Jesus when he was alive and was not among the Twelve. Paul argued that

Christians did not need to be circumcised like Jewish men or to keep the dietary rules of Judaism. He taught this to the Christian groups that he formed throughout the Mediterranean world. The letters he wrote to these early churches are preserved in the New Testament, as well as some later attributed to him.

Christians also elected their own leaders, the chief of whom was Peter, one of Jesus' Twelve. Like Paul he traveled about the Mediterranean, organizing communities of believers. Tradition holds that he died a martyr in Rome, during the persecution of Christians launched by the emperor Nero.

Christians also developed their own distinctive worship that became known as the **Eucharist**. It was celebrated weekly on Sundays, rather than on the Jewish Sabbath, on Saturdays. At the Eucharist the blessing that Jesus used at the Last Supper, the Passover Seder, over the bread and wine, was repeated by the congregation's president. Christians believed that at the repetition of the words, "This is my body; this is my blood," Jesus became present to them again in the bread and wine of the Eucharist.

To be initiated into the Christian church, individuals had to be **baptized**. This ceremony required candidates to be immersed in water, or to have water poured over their heads, while the minister of baptism invoked the name of the Trinity. The concept of the Trinity, that within the one God, Yahweh, there was Father, Son, and Holy Spirit, was one more doctrine distinguishing Christianity from Judaism.

Throughout the cities of Southwest Asia, Egypt, and Europe, the message of Jesus became known as Christian missionaries formed small communities of believers. After A.D. 100 leadership was vested in a leader known as a **bishop**, who had a group of clerics associated with him called **presbyters**. After the mid-second century, they became known as priests. There were also deacons and deaconesses, people who ministered to the physical needs of Christians. The most important bishops lived in Rome, Alexandria in Egypt, and Antioch in Syria. Others were in Ephesus, Miletus, and Smyrna in Anatolia and Corinth and Thessaloniki in Greece. In the fourth century, the heads of the churches of Alexandria and Rome reserved the title of pope to distinguish them from the other bishops of Egypt and Italy.

Second Century

The second century proved to be the best of times for the Romans. Five able emperors followed one another in succession providing good government and fair treatment to all the Empire's citizens.

Trajan, emperor from A.D. 98 to 117, extended Roman rule over the Dacians, who lived north of the Danube, and eastward over Mesopotamia. While Trajan ruled, the Empire reached its largest size. It extended from the Persian Gulf all the way to Britain.

Within its borders the **Pax Romana** prevailed over up to 80,000,000 people. What military action took place was on the borders and affected only the areas nearby. Everywhere people traveled for both business and pleasure. The silver **denarius** was accepted as the coin of the realm, making travel and commerce easy.

Taxation was mild for the imperial bureaucracy needed few employees. Local town councils made the decisions affecting people's lives in their own region, not someone in the capital. The **tributum,** which taxed individual wealth, provided most of the state's revenue. Anyone living in Italy was exempt, as were Romans abroad.

Administrators were drawn from the ranks of the senatorial and equestrian orders, but at this time many non-Roman provincials were a part of these classes. They eagerly embraced Roman values, studied their literary works, and spoke excellent Latin or Greek, depending on whether they lived in the west or east. Skill in public speaking, or rhetoric, was the key to a public career. Audiences expected their public officials to know the classics, to use clear argument, and to speak with elegance.

During the Pax Romana there was a flurry of public building, much of it financed by private individuals. Romans expected the wealthy to spend their fortunes on beautifying their cities building baths, libraries, fountains, or temples that everyone could enjoy.

Roman law developed further, presuming certain principles that have come into the American understanding of the legal system. Some of these principles are: everyone should have access to judgment from a court of law, an accused is innocent until proven guilty, and a law that is irrational has no validity.

Roman Buildings

The Romans in imperial times excelled in architecture and engineering. This did not happen at once. During the Republic, Rome and other Italian towns were quite inferior to Hellenistic cities in the eastern Mediterranean.

The Etruscans first introduced the Romans to the techniques of building drains and sewers, paving roads, and constructing bridges. The Romans perfected the principle of the arch, using it to construct vaults and domes. Another invention was concrete, a material that was stronger than anything used before to hold bricks together.

The first Roman buildings were temples, followed by **basilicas,** or courtrooms, and a Senate building. Statues, triumphal arches to commemorate victorious generals, and a platform for speakers were placed within the Forum. The area became so crowded that other forums were built, and wheeled traffic was banned in daylight hours. Cities throughout the Empire were built with pedestrians in mind.

Roman builders used both stone and brick to erect many large projects, including theaters, baths, and amphitheaters. The Colosseum held as many as 50,000 people. The **Circus Maximus,** the largest of Rome's race tracks, seated 250,000 spectators at one time.

The most impressive construction in Rome was the **Pantheon,** which still stands as a church in the modern city. Plans for this building were made in Augustus's day, but the building was not completed until about A.D. 120, while Hadrian was emperor. It was a domed structure with seven recesses that were meant to honor the gods of the planets. At the top there was an "eye," an open circle to let in sunlight.

The exterior of the Pantheon, Rome's most important temple in early imperial times, was dedicated to the planetary deities.

Among other major engineering accomplishments were the construction of aqueducts to bring water into Rome and other cities of the Empire. The aqueduct builders first tapped into a spring or lake. With only gravity to help, the water was carried in the aqueducts into the city. Sometimes the water traveled a distance of 30 miles. The aqueducts in the territories of Gaul and Spain had to cross ravines, requiring one course of arches to be placed atop another.

A Roman aqueduct of Gaul carried water to a nearby city.

The most enduring of Roman engineering feats was the network of roads that traversed the length of the Empire. These spun out from the city in all directions from the Forum's milestone. Built by the army during the imperial period, they covered over 180,000 miles. The roads were finished with great paving stones on top of layers of small rocks, gravel, and sand. No cement was needed because the paving stones were masterfully fitted together.

The contractors of the Empire found opportunities awaiting them from the patronage of Rome's wealthy families. They received commissions to construct their city houses and country villas that were equipped with every comfort, including running water, central heating, and a pool. The rooms of the houses, built around an atrium, had mosaic floors and walls covered with paintings. Often sculptors were brought in to carve the faces of the Romans who wanted to be remembered by their descendants in portraits remarkably faithful to their models.

The poorer people in imperial cities lived in large tenements called islands, **insulae.** These were usually four or five stories high with shops on the bottom floor. The apartments did not have running water or heat and were little better than slums. The Tiber served as Rome's garbage disposal.

Entertainment in Rome

It is unfortunate that a people so gifted in many ways should find it entertaining to watch animals and people fight and kill one another. This cruel streak in the Romans is hard to explain.

The Etruscans believed that when one of their important men or women died, his or her spirit required the shedding of blood. Therefore, they had slaves or prisoners of war fight one another as part of a funeral, and the Romans adopted this custom.

In 264 B.C. the Romans began gladiator fights. The gladiators were usually men who were prisoners of war or slaves whose lives were so difficult that they enlisted in gladiator schools. There they trained to hunt animals or each other in the amphitheaters. On certain holidays, Roman crowds streamed into the gates of the Colosseum to see them fight lions, leopards, and bears. On other days spectators came to watch fights between the gladiators themselves.

For those who refused to attend these bloody spectacles, there were other sources of entertainment. People could go to the chariot races in the Circus Maximus and bet on the drivers. More sophisticated Romans went to the theater or to a musical performance.

Many people preferred spending a day at the baths. There they received a free rubdown and had a choice of warm, hot, or cold pools. The baths had libraries, gardens, lecture rooms, a gymnasium in which to work out, steam rooms, and courts for ball games.

A Roman bath in the town of Bath, England, still holds water.

211

The bath was a very democratic institution. Both rich and poor, men and women, attended them. An emperor found no better way to please Roman citizens than to build a bath. Eventually Rome had over a hundred of them. Daily life escaped boredom since there were as many as 150 holidays a year. Religious celebrations were frequent as were market days.

In imperial times women were much freer to make their own decisions, and the old power of the pater familias was now a thing of the past. Ownership of property was possible for all, regardless of sex.

Armenians and Persians

Roman problems on their Asian frontier did not end when the Parthian kingdom faded. The Sasanian Persian empire soon appeared as a successor state of the Parthians. In A.D. 224 Ardashir, a prince of Fars, took the lands once Parthian under his control. Within a few years, building on the light cavalry tactics of the Parthian cavalry, the emperor Shapur I occupied Antioch. In A.D. 258 the Persians captured the Roman emperor Valerian I, who in captivity had to serve as a footstool when the king mounted his horse. The caravan cities on the Syrian frontier went into serious decline as a result of the never-ending wars between Persians and Romans.

The Sasanian dynasty was anxious to promote the native Mazdaist faith, especially after the Romans adopted Christianity. It gave the kings a chance to draw more firmly the line between the two peoples. In the fourth century Shapur II almost succeeded in destroying the Persian Christian community because of its ties to the west.

Both Parthian and Sasanian art has in large part disappeared. Some of what remains shows hunting scenes, always a familiar theme in southwestern Asian art.

Armenians first appeared in history with a mention of their nation on the Behistun Rock in the sixth century B.C. They were then a part of the Achaemenid, later of the Seleucid empire. Finally, after 189 B.C. and the Roman defeat of the kings of Antioch, two Armenian dynasties took shape. The high point of Armenian independence was at the time of Tigranes the Great when Armenian rule extended from the Black Sea to the Caspian Sea in northern Anatolia. His capital was at Tigranocerta close to the Tigris River. Later both the Persians and Romans successfully challenged Armenian independence, beginning a long sad history of occupation of their nation.

Pax Romana Evaluated

The Roman presence in the Mediterranean was long-lasting. It extended until the Muslim invasions of the seventh century. During this time of Roman rule, there were both positive and negative aspects.

On the positive side, Rome provided the Pax Romana, the Roman peace. This was a time when external enemies, with the exception of Parthians and Persians on the eastern frontier, were nonexistent. Citizens of the cities of the Mediterranean shores knew security and prosperity without war or disturbances over a period of hundreds of years.

During the Pax Romana economic activity expanded throughout the Mediterranean region. People and goods traveled widely during the summer months. Lavish displays of wealth were evident in the extensive construction of public buildings throughout the Roman world.

The negative side of Roman rule was also present. The miserable condition of slaves with no rights whatsoever was in glaring contrast to the pride the Romans expressed in their legal system. Tax-farming and the coarseness of the army, which also served as the police, made life difficult for local people. The ultimate cruelty, death by crucifixion, was inflicted on criminals, but not on Roman citizens.

Rome in Jeopardy

Marcus Aurelius was the last of the Five Good Emperors. He studied philosophy and was especially interested in Stoicism, which taught that the ruler must be a model for his people, more just than anyone else. Though he preferred sitting in a library and reading, he felt it his duty to lead the Roman armies personally against the German tribes crossing the Danube frontier.

An equestrian statue of Marcus Aurelius depicts the last of the Five Good Emperors.

The campaign against the Germans proved to be more deadly than anyone anticipated. When Marcus Aurelius and his troops returned to Rome, they brought with them the plague. This disease soon swept Rome, killing 2,000 people each day. A few years later another deadly disease, smallpox, struck Rome, carried by Roman soldiers who had fought in Asia. After the death of Marcus Aurelius in A.D. 161, conditions in Rome became even worse because his son proved himself utterly incompetent.

It is not often that an empire that is so prosperous in one century collapses so quickly in the next. Yet that is what happened to Rome. One historian described the third century by saying that a century of gold was followed by a century of iron.

The emperors were now all generals of the army. Often they were ignorant men who knew little and cared less about Roman civilization. They were anxious to gain wealth and power, no matter what the cost. Most spent their time in distant provinces fighting others who wanted to take their place. Between A.D. 235 and 284 fifteen legitimate emperors ruled while dozens of would-be candidates for the throne arose.

Such internal weakness came at the worst time. During the decade of the 230s, the Germans struck the Romans in Europe, and the Persians surged across the border in the east. A generation later Visigoths, originally from Scandinavia (Gotland in Sweden), occupied Anatolia, destroying the temple of Artemis in Ephesus. The cities of Greece were next to suffer pillaging.

The Roman people were now heavily taxed to provide defense, but no amount of money was enough. Roman coins, once made of precious metal, were minted out of lead. Businessmen closed their shops and locked the doors rather than take money they knew was worthless. Farmers hoarded their grain and refused to bring it into the cities.

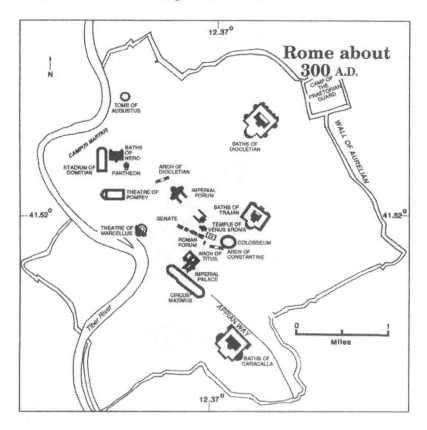

On the sea, pirates made long voyages impossible with the result that foreign trade among the provinces was no longer important. Investments in this atmosphere simply dried up as wealthy people left the towns to live behind the walls of their villas in the country.

With conditions so bad, many people believed the Empire was all but gone. However, two able emperors arrived on the scene and commenced a restoration.

These were Diocletian and Constantine. Both men recognized that the greatest need was to get the Roman armies under control. They saw to it that soldiers were paid on time and that any sign of rebellion was at once put down. The old Roman discipline returned. New strategies, especially the creation of mobile cavalry units, enabled the legions to win their battles with the Germans and Persians.

Diocletian and Constantine

Diocletian began his rule in the year A.D. 284. He made his capital in the east, in Anatolia rather than Rome, so as to be closer to the Persian frontier. He appointed a co-emperor to govern the western part of the Empire, for at last it was evident that a single individual could not handle the many responsibilities that went with the office. This division worked well. It allowed one emperor to concentrate on European affairs while the other could focus on Asian matters.

Later, after this arrangement had proven itself, two other men joined the emperors. They were given the title of **caesar** and appointed successors to the emperors. There was to be no confusion who the next emperors would be. Laws of the Empire were issued in the name of all four officials. However, Diocletian acted as the highest authority.

Diocletian wore a crown and rich clothes to emphasize his importance. He claimed he was Jovius, the earthly representative of Jupiter. Those who came near him had to first kneel on the ground. The emperor was seldom seen in public, adding to the awe about him.

To stabilize the economy, the emperor issued new coins minted in gold, silver, and bronze. Wage and price controls were initiated in an attempt to halt inflation. After men and women were counted in a census, Diocletian ruled that they were not permitted to change jobs. When the tax system failed to bring in enough revenue, he demanded that town councils deliver a certain amount of grain, oil, or timber. People grumbled about these harsh measures, but for a time stability was restored to an empire in serious political and economic trouble.

Religious affairs were also matters of concern to Diocletian. He held a strong conviction that everyone should worship the Roman gods. He was convinced that their neglect had caused the problems of the past decades and blamed the growth in the number of Christians for much of the Empire's difficulties. As a result, in the year A.D. 302 he ordered all Christian writings burned and churches destroyed. People known to be Christians were arrested. If they would not make sacrifices to the gods, they might lose their property, be tortured, or even be put to death. This persecution, lasting for ten years, was the worst that Christians had known.

Diocletian later resigned his rule and returned to his palace near Salona, now the city of Split in Croatia. There he tended his cabbage garden until his death.

For a time, the two caesars became emperors as Diocletian had arranged. It was not long, however, before a single individual once more sought to be the sole emperor.

Constantine was the son of one of the caesars with an ambition to govern Rome by himself. When, in A.D. 306, his father died, the army in Britain lifted him on a shield and shouted their loyalty to him as their leader. Constantine used his army to bring Spain and Gaul under his command, and then he was ready to march on Rome.

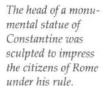

The head of a monumental statue of Constantine was sculpted to impress the citizens of Rome under his rule.

Outside the city Constantine believed he had a vision. In the sky he saw something shaped like a cross with the words, "Conquer with this." He marked his soldiers' shields with this symbol. When the battle was fought to gain Rome, his army followed behind the emblem of Christ's name. At Milvian Bridge Constantine won a great victory, and the rival emperor drowned in the Tiber. Constantine entered Rome believing that the Christian God, whose sign was the cross, had given him victory. The Senate reluctantly voted to raise an arch to commemorate his success.

In the winter of A.D. 313, Constantine met with the emperor of the eastern part of the Empire at Milan. Here the two men agreed, in the **Edict of Milan,** to make Christianity a lawful religion. Christians could rebuild their churches and had all their rights restored as Roman citizens.

Several years later, in A.D. 324, Constantine at last became sole ruler after defeating his co-emperor. He then decided that his capital should be located in the east and found the Greek town of Byzantium ideally situated.

Byzantium was an excellent site because it lay on the Bosporus Strait where the waters of the Black Sea pass into the Sea of Marmara and thence into the Aegean. It had an excellent harbor, the Golden Horn, for all the ships that passed back and forth. Its location meant that it could hold out indefinitely during a siege. From the palace Constantine had constructed in Byzantium, he could easily direct his armies in the Balkans or in Asia.

Although Constantine called his city New Rome, everyone knew it as Constantine's city. Thus, it came to be called Constantinople and today is known as Istanbul.

Rome Under Attack

From the time of Constantine's death through the rest of the fourth century, the Roman Empire was again divided at a time when new challenges arose thanks to the Germanic peoples' movements on the Rhine-Danube frontier. The Visigoths and Ostrogoths were now settled in Ukraine and north of the Danube in modern Romania.

In A.D. 372 the Visigoths discovered to their discomfort that another group of emigrants planned to share their homeland. These were the Huns, a Turkic people whom some historians identify as the Xiong-nu, the tribal confederation that for centuries plagued the Chinese. After the Han emperor defeated them, according to this scenario, a number of their chiefs moved eastward rather than accept Chinese rule. If correct, they were still a powerful military force, a fact that first the Ostrogoths and then the Visigoths learned very quickly.

Rather than continue to live with the Huns nearby, the Visigothic king requested permission from Emperor Valens to cross the Danube into Roman territory. Valens was in a difficult position. It was a completely unique request. His decision was to allow the Visigoths to enter if they agreed to be disarmed. However, many corrupt Roman officials charged the Visigoths steep prices for food and land on which to settle and accepted bribes to let them keep their weapons.

The upshot was a rebellion on the part of the Visigoths. Valens, then on the Persian border, returned with his army to face them at the battle of Adrianople (now Edirne in European Turkey). Both Valens's infantry and cavalry collapsed in the face of the Visigothic charges. The emperor, wounded, was carried into a house that subsequently caught fire, killing Valens. Only one out of three Roman soldiers who fought that day survived. It was the worst defeat since Hannibal won the battle of Cannae 600 years before.

The walls of Constantinople were adequate to stave off its capture, so the Visigoths made their way into Greece. Meanwhile the army sent to aid Valens from Italy arrived, and its commander, Theodosius, assumed the throne. Theodosius decided that a policy of accommodation was superior to confrontation, enlisting Gothic services as **foederati,** troops in alliance with Rome who kept their own leaders. When the Ostrogoths also sought security inside Roman borders, a similar arrangement was agreed upon.

Progress of Christianity

Although the Emperor Constantine delayed his baptism into the Christian church until a week before his death, after the victory of Milvian Bridge he threw the support of the Empire to the once persecuted religion. His mother, Helena, was a Catholic and may well have influenced his sentiments. He also kept a number of Christian bishops in his court as advisors, in particular Hosius, bishop of Córdoba in Spain.

Money that formerly went to support the temples and celebrations of Roman gods and goddesses now was given to Christians. The emperor provided funds for buildings in Constantinople, Bethlehem, and Jerusalem in the east, and in Rome he donated the Lateran Palace to be the pope's residence.

Some historians believe that Constantine's turn to religion was due to his hopes to unify the empire more closely around his throne, aware that the old religions no longer enjoyed much credibility. If this is true, what he did not foresee was that divisions could also shake the unity of the church. Early Christians were extremely concerned to speak of their faith accurately. It was not enough to quote biblical verses for these were often ambiguous. As a result Christian teachers used concepts taken from Greek philosophy, but these too were not always clear.

Constantine's conversion appeared at the very time a major dispute was troubling the eastern churches. The issue was a correct understanding of the Trinity. Was the Son, the second person of the three divine persons, of the same nature as the Father and his equal, or was he created by the Father? A priest in Alexandria, Arius, preached that the Son was a creature, although this deviated from earlier understandings about God. To settle the issue, Constantine summoned the first Christian ecumenical council to meet at Nicaea (modern Iznik in Turkey).

Bishops from all over the east and delegates from the Roman pope journeyed to Nicaea at government expense to debate the question. There they almost unanimously rejected Arianism. The council issued the **Nicene Creed,** a statement of belief, affirming the same divine essence to be in all three persons.

Constantine accepted the decision, ruling that bishops holding Arian doctrine must go into exile. While at the time the bishops were pleased to receive the state's assistance in branding Arianism a **heresy,** a deviation from church belief, a dangerous precedent arose. The church became dependent on the state to effect its decisions. The emperors claimed that it was their obligation to oversee the enforcement of conciliar acts because in the Roman view religion was a public matter.

Toward the close of the fourth century, after A.D. 381, the union of church and state was made official. Emperor Theodosius I declared Christianity the state religion of Rome. Only Jews and Samaritans were permitted to worship outside the Christian church, and disabilities were placed on them for their determination to remain in their traditional faiths.

Christians in the Empire were a majority of the urban population by A.D. 400, but more disharmony in the church arose over the doctrine that Jesus was God, having in his person united both a complete human and divine nature. In A.D. 451, at the Council of Chalcedon, most Syrian and Egyptian Christians broke away from the Greek and Roman churches in a schism that remains unhealed to this day. Later the bishops of Armenia and Ethiopia also rejected the Chalcedonian Council's decision.

These arguments over doctrine were also ethnic in origin, since a large number of Eastern Christians resented the Greek domination of their civil as well as their religious lives. Over the next three centuries the emperors in Constantinople sought to find a compromise acceptable to both sides but failed.

Despite these disputes the fourth and fifth centuries were the golden age of Christian literature. By this time the Catholic bishops had become the carriers of Greek and Roman culture even modeling their administration on that of the Empire. The talent of the age was to be found in the works of bishops and scholars who wrote commentaries on the Bible, ethical treatises, and theological tracts. St. Augustine, bishop of Hippo, dominated thought in the Latin west; St. John Chrysostom was the major intellectual of the Greek east.

*The church of
St. Sabina in Rome
was built in the fifth
century, modeled
on the structure of
a basilica.*

Western Problems

In A.D. 395 Theodosius died and left his two sons to follow him in a divided empire. One assumed the throne in Constantinople; the other made Ravenna in Italy his capital. Since Ravenna was a port city, it was much more defensible than Rome. Both emperors were dominated by their chief ministers who were Germans.

From Ravenna the Western court watched the steady growth of the Visigoths under their leader, Alaric. Twice Alaric threatened Rome, but he then turned back after terrified Romans bribed him to go away. Once more outside Rome's walls in A.D. 410, he broke into the city. The panicked Romans fled their homes while the Goths pillaged the riches found there. Only the churches were spared, for the Goths were converts to Arian Christianity.

Alaric then turned to the conquest of southern Italy but died before that was done. The Gothic army turned to the north, receiving from the feeble emperor in Ravenna title to southern Gaul and the emperor's sister, Galla Placidia, to wed the new Gothic king.

A shock wave sped around the Mediterranean world on the news of Rome's capture. Who was to blame became the topic of the day. In Hippo, St. Augustine answered the charge in his classic, *The City of God*, claiming that it was hardly the fault of Christians. Augustine pointed out that Christians were not identified with any specific political system, but that they recognized the value of the Roman state and acted to defend it.

The most serious challenge to the Roman Empire of the fifth century came from the never-ending war with the Persians. Once more Rome's perennial enemy in the east sought to reach the Mediterranean by marching through Syria. By concentrating the army on its eastern frontier, Constantinople had allowed the Germans of the Rhine and Danube to break across these river boundaries and occupy large areas of the western part of the Empire.

The Visigothic gain at the expense of Rome was followed by other migrations of Germanic peoples into the empire. In A.D. 406 Vandals, who were so destructive that their name has became a synonym for senseless behavior, laid waste Gaul, moved on to Spain, and then crossed into Africa. The Vandal ruler made Carthage his capital and stopped the important grain supplies that Rome depended upon for food.

In Roman Britain a surge of Angles, Saxons, and Jutes poured over the island on an invitation to defend the country from the Picts and Irish. The Roman army had abandoned their British camps on orders from Ravenna. The German migrations into Britain were so large that Roman culture disappeared nearly everywhere along with the Latin language. People recalled the Roman presence in Wales and a few other places in the west, but they spoke their native Celtic language. Here a Christian Briton named Patrick was destined to become the apostle of Ireland.

In Gaul the invading Germans belonged to a variety of tribes, the largest and most important were the Franks. It was their presence that changed the name of the country from Gaul to France.

For a long time the Franks lived across the Rhine River from the Romans. They had learned many Roman ways and had no intention of destroying a culture they admired. Romans in Gaul did not abandon their homes as they had in Britain, for they were familiar with the Franks in their midst. Farmers stayed on the land even when the Franks became their rulers. On the other hand, people in towns, who depended on trade or had jobs in the imperial service, were likely to leave. One major effect of the coming of the Germanic peoples into Gaul was a decline in the size of towns. Large cities became small towns; small cities became villages.

Just after the Germans swept across western Europe, the Huns, who initiated the Germanic migrations because of their pressure on the Goths, decided to move farther west. The Huns had a very strong ruler named Attila, whose name meant little father. The Romans had a different view of him, calling Attila the scourge of God. He was a fierce warrior and in A.D. 450 was more powerful than either the emperor in Ravenna or Constantinople. This was true even though he could not read or write and lived in a palace built of logs.

In A.D. 452 the Hunnic army marched into Gaul. Near Orléans a combined Roman and Visigothic army attempted to halt his advance. Thousands of soldiers died in battle, but there was no clear winner. As long as Attila had an army he was very dangerous, and although he turned away from Gaul, he directed his forces into Italy.

The frightened Romans watched while the Huns reduced to ashes many cities in the north. Heading southward, the Huns camped outside Rome. The pope of Rome, Leo I, and two senators arrived in Attila's camp to plead with him to spare the city. Surprisingly Attila agreed, and the Huns headed out of Italy. On that journey, Attila died and his Hunnic Empire collapsed. Only a very strong leader could keep the Hunnic army together, and Attila had no able successor.

The threat of the Huns may have ended, but only a year later, in A.D. 455, a Vandal fleet from Africa landed in Italy. This time Pope Leo was not so fortunate. The Vandals robbed Rome of all its wealth and took many prisoners, even the empress and two princesses, with them back to Africa.

Attila led his army into Europe. As commander of the Huns he was the most powerful man in Europe in A.D. 450.

All of Italy reeled from the destruction caused by these invasions. Rebellion among the soldiers, who often could not be paid, was a constant menace. A German, not a Roman, led what remained of the Roman army in the west. He appointed his Roman friends and relatives to official positions. After over a decade of these puppet rulers, another general, this time a Roman, promoted his son Romulus Augustulus to become emperor.

The Germans in Italy

In A.D. 476 a German army of several different tribes appeared in Italy. Their leader was Odovacer, a German who once had served in the Roman army. He killed Romulus Augustulus's father and forced his son to abdicate. Odovacer then asked the emperor in Constantinople to be made general of the Roman army in Italy. The emperor agreed and gave him the title **Patrician**. Odovacer did not call himself emperor, nor did any of his successors. In western Europe no one held that title for the next 300 years.

Many people believe that the Roman Empire fell in A.D. 476, but nothing so important occurred in that year. Only one more German ruler had imposed his will on Italy, something that had been happening for the past 60 years. In fact, the legitimate western emperor whom the court in Constantinople recognized was still alive in exile and held his title until his death in A.D. 480.

Why did the western part of the empire fall to the Germans? The major reason appears to be military. The Germanic forces were simply stronger than the Roman armies. The Germans were enthusiastic, loyal to their commanders, and anxious to gain the rewards of victory. The Roman armies were larger, but they lacked competent generals. Their armies held more German recruits than Romans in the fifth century so pay, rather than loyalty, held them together. When that pay did not arrive, there was no reason to fight for Rome.

Internally the Roman government in the west had many problems. It did not take in enough taxes to keep up its army because the Roman aristocrats did not pay their fair share of taxes. The emperors in the west, when they sought help from Constantinople, were usually ignored. The constant battle in Italy over who would rule the Empire dissipated what strength remained. The economy inevitably declined as markets in northern Europe were lost to Italian merchants when Germans or Huns occupied these areas.

There is no indication that the way the Romans of the fifth century lived had anything to do with the imperial decline. In the fifth century most were Christians and were held to high ideals of conduct.

In the eastern part of the empire, life was much better for people. Constantinople increased in size and wealth, becoming the largest city of Europe. City life and trade inside and outside the empire kept the standard of living high. In the fifth century the eastern part of the empire prospered at the very time the Roman government it was extinguished in the west.

In A.D. 493 the western part of the empire underwent a change in the German leaders who now dominated Italy. On the encouragement of the court in Constantinople, an Ostrogothic king, Theoderic, led his tribesmen into the peninsula. Theoderic killed Odovacer and assumed his title. He was quite willing to employ a Roman staff at his capital in Ravenna.

The exterior of the tomb of Theoderic still can be viewed in modern Ravenna.

Conclusion

The Roman world was a much different place in A.D. 500 than it was in 400 B.C. The one-man rule of an emperor had replaced the Republic. There were Senate houses in both Rome and Constantinople, but the senators were now no more than city councilmen. The only strong institution left in the west was the Catholic church. Rome, though no longer the home of emperors, was still the home of popes.

CHAPTER 15 REVIEW
THE ROMAN EMPIRE

Summary
- Caesar Augustus restored stability to Rome in his role as princeps.
- The life and teaching of Jesus of Nazareth inspired his followers to begin the Christian religion.
- After Augustus a series of incompetent rulers followed, but the Empire proved strong enough to survive.
- At the end of the first century A.D., the Pax Romana covered the Mediterranean world.
- Roman entertainment varied, but generally included gladiatorial contests.
- Ambitious generals and foreign invaders shook the Empire in the third century A.D.
- Diocletian and Constantine returned the Empire to strong central rule.
- Christianity became a tolerated faith under Constantine, who moved Rome's capital to Constantinople.
- In the late fourth century, the Empire was divided into an eastern and western part and experienced new invasions.
- Roman culture survived in western Europe in the Catholic church.

Identify
People: Caesar Augustus; Jesus of Nazareth; Paul of Tarsus; Nero; Virgil; Constantine; Theodosius; Augustine of Hippo; Valens; Trajan; Theoderic
Places: Dacia; Milan; Constantinople; Adrianople; Rhine River
Events: Augustus lays the foundation of the Empire; Constantine moves the capital and legitimated Christianity; Goths and Huns invade the western part of the Empire

Define

Praetorian Guard	bishop	presbyters	foederati
Pantheon	insulae	Circus Maximus	*Aeneid*
empire	heresy	Nicene Creed	Pax Romana
basilicas	tributum	denarius	caesars
the Twelve	Eucharist	baptism	Edict of Milan

Multiple Choice
1. Romans accepted the rule of a single emperor because
   (a) Augustus expanded the army.
   (b) Augustus paid off all his opponents.
   (c) they feared a return to the chaos of civil war.
   (d) Augustus's opposition was scattered in many factions.

2. Borders of the Roman Empire in northern Europe followed these two rivers:
   (a) the Rhine and the Elbe.
   (b) the Danube and the Morava.
   (c) the Rhine and the Tiber.
   (d) the Rhine and the Danube.

3. The border between Rome and the Parthians was
   (a) the Sahara desert.
   (b) the Black Sea.
   (c) the Euphrates River.
   (d) the Tigris River.

4. The Praetorian Guard was the imperial
   (a) fire department.
   (b) bodyguard.
   (c) customs officers.
   (d) police.

5. Emperor Claudius conquered this land for Rome:
   (a) Gaul.
   (b) Spain.
   (c) Britain.
   (d) Germany.

6. Prisoners of war taken by the Romans were
   (a) executed.
   (b) made slaves.
   (c) exiled.
   (d) returned to their homes.

7. The emperor Trajan
   (a) expanded the Empire to its largest extent.
   (b) set up an order of succession.
   (c) moved the capital to Dacia.
   (d) reorganized the Roman army.

8. When the Roman army was not fighting it often
   (a) constructed ships.
   (b) built roads.
   (c) played cards.
   (d) went home.

9. The center of Rome was the
   (a) temple of the Pantheon.
   (b) agora.
   (c) Forum.
   (d) Colosseum.

10. The race course of Rome was
    (a) the Pantheon.
    (b) the Forum.
    (c) the Colosseum.
    (d) none of the above.

11. Roman insulae were
    (a) apartments.
    (b) boats.
    (c) streets.
    (d) aqueducts.

12. This Roman general conquered Jerusalem in A.D. 70:
    (a) Hadrian.
    (b) Nero.
    (c) Vespasian.
    (d) Titus.

13. Christians believed that Jesus of Nazareth was
    (a) only the Son of God.
    (b) Messiah and Son of God.
    (c) only the messiah.
    (d) God the Father.

14. The New Testament was written in
    (a) Aramaic.
    (b) Hebrew.
    (c) Greek.
    (d) Latin.

15. Paul of Tarsus called for Christians to reject
    (a) circumcision.
    (b) Sabbath worship.
    (c) the Hebrew scriptures.
    (d) the Ten Commandments.

16. The third century A.D. was chaotic until the appearance of
    (a) Marcus Aurelius.
    (b) Tiberius.
    (c) Caligula.
    (d) Diocletian.

17. The Christian doctrine of the Trinity holds that
    (a) there are three Gods.
    (b) within the one God there are three persons.
    (c) Jesus is equally man and God.
    (d) God appears in three different roles to humans.

18. Divisions in the Christian church appeared in the fifth century causing
    a break between the emperor and
    (a) Syrian and Egyptian Christians.
    (b) Parthians.
    (c) Romans in Palestine.
    (d) the Roman pope.

19. Constantine moved the capital to this Greek city:
    (a) Sirmium.
    (b) Alexandria.
    (c) Antioch.
    (d) Byzantium.

20. The Edict of Milan gave Christianity
    (a) toleration.
    (b) official status as the Roman religion.
    (c) new leadership.
    (d) a new period of persecution.

21. The last emperor to rule the undivided empire was
    (a) Constantine.
    (b) Diocletian.
    (c) Vespasian.
    (d) Theodosius I.

22. Romulus Augustulus is the last person in the west to hold the title
    (a) emperor.
    (b) Bishop of Rome.
    (c) patrician.
    (d) general of the West.

23. The Sasanian Persian empire promoted
    (a) Judaism.
    (b) Egyptian religion.
    (c) Mazdaism.
    (d) Christianity.

Essay Questions
1. How did the personality of the emperors affect Roman government?
2. What accounts for the Roman weakness in repelling invaders in the third and fifth centuries A.D.?
3. What were the effects of moving the capital to Constantinople?
4. What were the advantages and disadvantages of living within the Roman Empire?
5. What made it possible for the Christian church to become the imperial religion?

Answers

1. c	5. c	9. c	13. b	17. b	21. d
2. d	6. b	10. d	14. c	18. a	22. a
3. c	7. a	11. a	15. a	19. d	23. c
4. b	8. b	12. d	16. d	20. a	

CHAPTER 16

African Societies

The classical period of African history begins with Egypt, its major civilization subject to numerous invasions of foreign peoples. It will close the era as part of the Roman Empire. Egyptian decline is not the only story. In other parts of the continent, history was just beginning, especially south of the Sahara, with the formation of two formidable states, Kush and Axum.

Invaders in Egypt

Foreign invaders constantly harried Egypt after 1200 B.C. First to appear were the Sea Peoples, the mysterious confederation that also brought down the Hittites and Mycenaean Greeks. Although Egypt recovered from this attack, the structure of the country began to weaken.

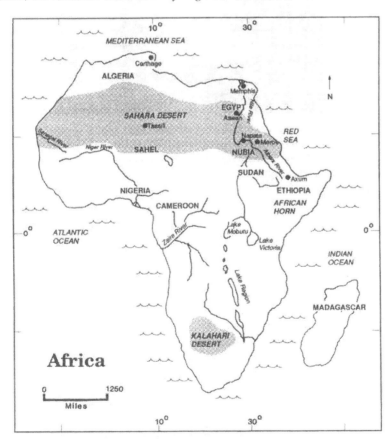

The pharaohs, living in the delta town of Tanus, were unable to collect the taxes to support an army sufficiently strong to repel the country's invaders. Much of the reason for their weakness was the growth of lands dedicated to the upkeep of the priesthood of Amon Re at Karnak. Revenues that formerly went to the state now supported the clerics who had their own uses for Egypt's wealth. Thebes in Upper Egypt became a theocracy, where priests rather than secular rulers were dominant.

Massive pillars support the roof of Karnak's temples.

The pharaohs of the 22nd dynasty, ruling from about 935 to 725 B.C., went on the offensive to reunify the nation, but the effort collapsed in the face of an unexpected invasion from the Kushites, a people found in Nubia, now the Sudan.

Kush

The Egyptians had long been aware of the importance of Nubia, the land to the south of Aswan. Since the days of the Old Kingdom, traders on the Nile below Aswan exchanged gold, frankincense, ivory, ostrich feathers, and slaves for Egyptian commodities. The pharaohs were always pleased to recruit Nubian soldiers into their armies. During the Middle Kingdom, in order to protect their economic interests in Nubia, pharaohs built over a dozen forts south of Aswan. After the Pharaoh's power declined, the Nubians were ready to assert their independence.

About 1100 B.C. a dynasty of Nubian kings established a capital at Napata. Their state was called Kush, the Egyptian name for Nubia. Kushite rulers took the name pharaoh for themselves and were very eager to support the familiar Egyptian culture in their capital. Religious ceremonies honored Egyptian gods and goddesses, and tomb builders constructed pyramids of a modest size to hold the remains of the Kushite pharaohs.

The next step was to create an empire. In the mid-eighth century B.C. a Kushite army marched northward, occupying Thebes. Then about 710 B.C. the strongest of the Kushite pharaohs, Piankhy, overran the rest of Upper Egypt. His brother completed the conquest, so that the Kushite pharaohs became Egypt's twenty-fifth dynasty.

The Kushite pharaohs were not able to hold onto Egypt for long, since the warlike Assyrians were now on the march. In 671 B.C. they wrested control of the country away from Taharqa, the Kushite king. The Assyrian iron weapons proved far superior to the bronze ones of the Kushites.

King Taharqa returned to Nubia, still faithful to his belief that in Kush authentic Egyptian traditions might still be maintained. He continued to wear the double crown of the pharaohs and ordered that Egyptian should be the court language. It was now the turn of an Egyptian army to invade Nubia. As a result, the capital at Napata was destroyed, but resilient Kushites moved farther south, establishing a new base at Meroe, which soon flourished as a new capital.

The kings of Kush built large pyramids in imitation of the Egyptian pharaohs.

Merchants from East Africa came to Meroe to exchange their goods for the cattle that made up much of the export trade of the Kushites. Then a new product, iron, came into production at Meroe. After 500 B.C. Meroe's smiths were the most important iron workers of East Africa. Ore was abundant, and nearby forests offered the raw material for charcoal needed to fuel the furnaces for smelting. Great heaps of slag that still exist testify to this industry that made Meroe so wealthy.

Despite a rather unfavorable location, for Meroe was far from the sea and isolated by desert, it grew into a major center for trade. Caravans from India brought the goods of the Orient to the Kushite capital. Elephants became an exciting addition to the parades that accompanied the ceremonies of the Kushite rulers. Up to the third century A.D. the pharaohs of Meroe held their kingdom together. At that time rival trading cities diverted the merchants that once came to it. Overgrazing of the land and the destruction of the forests contributed to the decline. In A.D. 330 the last Kushite king lost his throne to a rival, Ezana, the king of Axum. East Africa's first kingdom below the Sahara passed into history.

Hellenistic Egypt

The attacks from Kush and then Assyria left Egypt reeling. Thebes, the most important Egyptian city of Upper Egypt, was in ruins after the Assyrians passed through. The Egyptians had native rulers for just over 100 years during the time of the twenty-sixth dynasty, when the capital was at Sais. This revival was short-lived, for the Persians soon entered Egypt. They arrived in 525 B.C. and with but two interruptions held Egypt until Alexander's conquest. Alexander met no resistance when he moved into Egypt.

After Alexander's death, his Macedonian general, Ptolemy I, made his residence in Alexandria and wisely brought Alexander's gold coffin back with him, a symbol that he intended to succeed him. He placed Alexander's tomb in the very heart of Alexandria, at the crossroads of its two major streets.

The Ptolemies developed their capital to such an extent that Alexandria surpassed all other cities in the Mediterranean. Unlike other Egyptian towns, it was a planned city, with the streets on a grid pattern crossing at right angles.

About 290 B.C. Ptolemy I laid the foundation of the **Museon**, a building to collect the many wonders of Egypt. It has given its name, *museum,* to all subsequent collections. After recognizing the value of the Museon, Ptolemy then ordered construction of a great library, the largest ever to be built. It was filled with scrolls from all over the Mediterranean.

His son, Ptolemy II intended to collect every known book in the world and then to have a Greek translation made. The library bulged with 900,000 scrolls, among them a very important translation of the Jewish scriptures, known as the **Septuagint.**

The Museon and library attracted scholars from all over the Greek world. Astronomers, scientists, and doctors all converged on Alexandria where the Ptolemies were pleased to pay their salaries. Euclid was among them, publishing *Elements,* a book on geometry and its methods that remained the standard text until about 100 years ago.

Eratosthenes was one of the geographers. He sought to discover the size of the earth through an experiment that gave a remarkably accurate answer. On the longest day of the year he set himself up in a dry well 500 miles south of Alexandria, while an assistant did the same in the capital. At high noon Eratosthenes could see no shadow, but in Alexandria there was one. By measuring the angle between the observations, Eratosthenes found it to be one fiftieth of a circle. By multiplying 500 miles times 50, he concluded that the earth was 25,000 miles in circumference. Modern measurements place it at 24,902 miles. Unfortunately, this discovery of Eratosthenes was lost, and the true size of the earth had to be rediscovered in the sixteenth century.

The Ptolemies, the richest sovereigns of the Hellenistic world, embellished Alexandria with numerous palaces and public buildings. At the city harbor they put up the **Pharos,** the most famous lighthouse of the ancient world. It reached a height of 400 feet and projected a light that could be seen for 100 miles. Workers continuously tended a fire that mirrors reflected to ships at sea.

The building program of the Ptolemies was very costly, requiring heavy taxation on the Egyptian peasantry. Greek civil servants told the farmers what they must plant, when they must plant, and how much of the harvest the government demanded from them. Salt, papyrus, and textiles were government monopolies as were mining gold and quarrying stone. One positive feature of Hellenistic rule for the Egyptian farmer was the introduction of the dromedary for hauling and plowing. Until then this animal was unknown in the country.

The Greek ruling class monopolized the political and military life of Ptolemaic Egypt. They lived in towns with their own separate quarters, away from the Egyptians.

Carthage and North Africa

If Alexandria was the metropolis of the African shore in the eastern Mediterranean, Carthage played the same role in the western region. This city, unlike Alexandria, is now in ruins. Carthage was located just outside the city of modern Tunis in North Africa.

From 1000 B.C. the Phoenicians had a colony at Utica on the North African coast. The native peoples of the region were Berbers, who spoke a language that was common from the Atlantic to the Libyan border with Egypt. The ancestors of the Berbers were the descendants of the herders that once lived in the Sahara before it became so dry that their way of life was no longer possible.

The most important Phoenician settlement was put down about 814 B.C. at a site with an excellent harbor. The settlers called their town Carthage. Its position on the Mediterranean made it a great maritime power, the strongest in the western Mediterranean.

It was not acceptable to the Carthaginians when Greek sailors advanced beyond Sicily into what they considered their lake. Allied with the Etruscans of Italy in 535 B.C., the Carthaginian navy fought and won a battle off the coast of Corsica, allowing the Carthaginians to keep their dominance in the western Mediterranean. After this victory the navy patrolled the Straits of Gibraltar to see to it that no other ships came through but their own. In this they were successful. Carthage grew to be so large that it started colonizing other parts of the western Mediterranean. Carthaginians founded towns on the Balearic Islands, Sicily, and Corsica.

Egypt Under the Romans

For both Alexandria and Carthage the growing power of Rome presented a very real threat to their independence. Already in 200 B.C. Roman ambassadors arrived in Egypt to make known their interest in events there. Members of the Roman Senate now hovered over Egypt, knowing it to be the richest region of the Mediterranean. When the Seleucid emperor Antiochus the Great sought to add Alexandria to his kingdom, Rome forbade it and forced the Syrians to withdraw. When his brother overthrew Ptolemy VI, Rome required his restoration.

In 51 B.C. upon the death of the eleventh Ptolemy, he left his two children, Ptolemy XII and Cleopatra VII, joint heirs. Then the brother ousted his sister. Cleopatra planned to seek revenge and her restoration by allying herself with Rome. This opportunity arrived when Julius Caesar and his legions embarked in Egypt on the trail of his arch-enemy, Pompey. While the Romans fought her brother, she arrived in Caesar's camp. One day he received the gift of a carpet, and when it was unrolled, there was Cleopatra. In time Caesar's armies overwhelmed Ptolemy's troops, and the Roman general put Cleopatra back on the throne. She and Caesar were lovers, and Cleopatra became pregnant with his son. Later Caesar brought her to Rome, a decision that lost him some of his popularity. After Caesar's assassination she and her son, Caesarion, returned to Egypt as joint rulers of the nation.

Cleopatra found a new champion and lover in Marc Antony. She joined his efforts to take over the Empire, but they lost their chance at the battle of Actium. Octavian was now the undisputed ruler of Rome. Recognizing her impotence, Cleopatra committed suicide rather than be taken prisoner, and Octavian had Caesarion put to death. These events signaled the end of the Hellenistic period in Egypt and the beginning of the Roman.

The Roman emperors made Egypt an imperial province, sending governors from Rome to reside in Alexandria. Their main task was to collect revenues and send them back to Rome. Egyptian wealth, built on the backs of the peasants, poured into the city.

Alexandria's reputation as the intellectual center of the Mediterranean world continued in Roman times. Claudius Ptolemy called the city home while he pursued his research. In his work as an astronomer, he theorized that the sun, moon, planets, and stars revolved around the earth, a view that was accepted for the next 1,300 years. In his study of geography he made an estimate of the earth's size, which was not as accurate as Eratosthenes, and listed places on its surface according to latitude and longitude.

While the Romans ruled Egypt, Christianity came into the country, according to tradition, through Jesus' disciple Mark. The bishops of Alexandria became the leading personalities of the early church, responsible for all of East Africa. They held the title **pope**, just as the bishop of Rome, to emphasize their special position. Under their direction the first Christian school was organized. Here Origen, the most creative scholar that the new religion produced, taught for many years.

After the Roman capital moved to Constantinople, the Alexandrian bishops looked upon Constantinople's head as a rival, and frequent disputes broke out over precedence. When Christianity became the official religion of the Roman Empire, the Egyptian church grew even larger. Within its ranks the first Christian monks were to be found. In fact, the monastic life became so popular that in the neighborhood of Alexandria the desert became a city of monks and nuns.

In the fifth century, the Egyptian church broke with the Latin and Greek Christians over the correct understanding of Jesus' humanity. Calling itself the Coptic church it became autonomous, with its own leader, the pope of Alexandria.

Roman North Africa

Carthage and Rome for many decades were friendly powers since Carthage was far enough away that interests did not clash. Carthage was a huge city of 250,000 people, three times the size of Rome. Rome's concerns were in Italy, Carthage's were on holding a commercial supremacy in the Mediterranean. This all changed when a conflict between two Sicilian cities spilled over, drawing in Carthage on one side and Rome on the other.

The First Carthaginian War erupted in 264 B.C. It was fought in Sicily for over a generation. During this conflict the Romans sought for the first time to compete with the North African city for control of the sea. Rome built a navy, blockaded Carthage's Sicilian cities, and won the war. Henceforth, Rome was both a land and naval power.

Carthage sought to recoup its fortunes by occupying eastern Spain. The Roman Senate was not at all pleased, resulting in a Second Carthaginian War from 215 to 202 B.C. The Carthaginian general Hannibal recruited an army in Spain and, with an elephant corps in the lead, crossed the Alps, arriving in northern Italy. Despite a series of victories, Hannibal had to withdraw back to Africa, and in 202 B.C. the Carthaginian forces were beaten at Zama. In the treaty that followed, Carthage lost all its navy and overseas possessions.

The city tried one more time to reverse its defeat in the Third Carthaginian War, but it failed again. This time the Romans thoroughly destroyed the town. Carthage later was rebuilt as a Roman city, and its lands were handed over to veterans of the Roman armies.

The country that is now Morocco was annexed to Rome in the first century A.D. with its capital where Tangier now stands. In modern Libya major building of Roman cities took place. Leptis was the birthplace of the emperor Septimus Severus. North Africa provided most of the wheat shipped to Rome in imperial times, making it essential to the economy. Veterans settled on the lands in northern African in large numbers, Latinizing the coastal regions. The poorer interior was the land of Berber tribal peoples.

Roman Carthage developed as a major trading center, approaching 100,000 inhabitants. Christianity sank its roots here, producing the author Tertullian, the first major Christian scholar to write in Latin. By A.D. 200 seventy bishops resided in Roman Africa.

The most important Latin Christian writer of the fifth century was St. Augustine, bishop of Hippo. Two of his classics, *The Autobiography* and the *City of God*, are still on college reading lists. He was both a preacher and a writer; 113 of his works are extant demonstrating the reputation he held among his contemporaries. Augustine urged Christians to become involved in this world as well as to look forward to the next.

Toward the middle of the fifth century A.D., the Vandals, a Germanic tribal people, invaded North Africa. Augustine died in A.D. 431 while his city was under siege. It was fortunate that he did not live to see so much of Latin culture destroyed. A Vandal king now set up a throne in Carthage and in A.D. 455 was powerful enough to send a fleet against Italy. Vandal Africa contributed little, destroyed much, but in the end had only a short time to make North Africa in its own image.

Bantu

The history of the people in western, central, and southern Africa is not so easily known. Writing did not appear until much later, with the result that history must be reconstructed through archaeology, botany, and linguistics to trace the movements of men and women in this part of the world.

Just when western African people adopted agriculture is still not precisely known. Certainly by 1500 B.C. a number of people in western Africa were cultivating millet and sorghum, Africa's basic grain crops. In the African Horn, the region of eastern Africa adjacent to the Red Sea, Ethiopian farmers planted root crops and cow peas.

In the vast savannah regions of Africa, farming provided a chancy way of life. Rainfall was fickle, and insects were a constant problem. Mosquitoes carried malaria, and the **tsetse fly** was deadly for both people and animals since it spread sleeping sickness. Wherever it was found, no herding of cattle was possible.

About 1500 B.C. a major migration of Bantu-speaking people left their homeland in the Nigerian-Cameroon region on the Atlantic coast and commenced a migration into the African interior that gathered momentum after the first century A.D.

Some Bantu were farmers; others herded cattle or goats. For a time one generation settled, only to have their children pick up their belongings and move again. Today there are over 400 Bantu languages, demonstrating how isolated each group must have been when they found a new location. Often the Bantu moved into empty regions or into lightly populated areas, the home of Mbuti (Pygmy) or Khoi Khoi hunters.

About 500 B.C. iron-working became known among many of the African nations. Before iron came into use, it seems that all tools and weapons were made of wood, horn, or stone. Archaeologists have yet to find any copper or bronze artifacts, so it appears that the use of metal was still unknown until the introduction of iron. Two sources of the technology are probable. One came from Carthage; the other came by way of Kush. The spread of iron-working subsequently spread across the continent.

In some nations ironsmiths were considered very special people, given certain privileges because of their skills. In others, the smiths were apparently a group held in contempt despite their usefulness to society.

Cattle were the most important animals for those people who lived in regions free from the tsetse fly. Their hides provided clothes; their horns, milk, and sometimes even blood were used as food products. A family's wealth could be reckoned according to the number of cattle it owned.

In the rain forests of Africa, thin soil and too much rain were problems. Serious farming commenced only when southeastern Asian plants were brought to this part of Africa. These were root crops, such as Asian yams, gourds, and Abyssinian bananas. Game was so plentiful that forest people had little incentive to change their way of life.

From what is known of modern African political and social institutions, it is probable that similar ways of living were present in ancient times. People were organized under a chief who had a council of elders to advise him. Bonds of kinship, a common language, and religion gave men and women a sense of belonging.

The Masai are an African people who count their wealth in the number of cattle they own.

Axum

The strongest kingdom of eastern Africa south of the Sahara was Axum. Once King Ezana conquered Meroe, Axum then took the place of Kush as the political and economic power of East Africa.

Adule (now Mitsiwa), the Axumite port on the Red Sea, was the transfer point of goods coming from the African interior with merchants from the Mediterranean, India, and Persia trading there. Enabled by their wealth, the rulers decorated their capital with a stone palace and fortress. They also built churches, for on Ezana's orders, the Axumites adopted Christianity as their religion. Originating in Axum, a distinctive type of art and architecture later transferred to the kingdom of Ethiopia, the successor of the Axumite nation.

Conclusion

This period of African history shows several major developments. North Africa and Egypt, after enjoying an independent existence for several centuries, became part of a greater empire when the Romans extended their rule over the African coast of the Mediterranean. These regions later became centers of the new Christian faith.

South of the Sahara the discovery of iron-working and the Bantu migration are the focal points of history during these years. The vast African continent, due to the natural barrier of the Sahara desert, could easily accommodate the two very divergent cultures of the period from 1200 B.C. to A.D. 500.

CHAPTER 16 REVIEW
AFRICAN SOCIETIES

Summary

- A series of invaders struck Egypt after 1200 B.C.
- Kush, the kingdom of Nubia, pressed Egypt on the south, eventually conquering it for a short time.
- Kushite pharaohs sought to imitate Egyptian models.
- Under the Ptolemies, Alexandria was an intellectual center with its museum and great library.
- Carthage on the North African coast developed into the Mediterranean's most important commercial city.
- Rome went to war with Carthage over which city would dominate the western Mediterranean.
- Julius Caesar allied with Cleopatra and brought Egypt under Roman rule.
- South of the Sahara Bantu farmers and herders began a migration into eastern and southern Africa.
- About 500 B.C. iron-working became a major industry in Africa.
- Axum, a Christian African kingdom, followed Kush as the dominant state of eastern Africa.

Identify

People: Taharqa; Euclid; Ptolemies; Eratosthenes; Cleopatra VII; Bantu
Places: Sahara; Nubia; Kush; Meroe; Napata; Aswan; Carthage
Events: invasion of Egypt; growth of Alexandria as a center of learning; Punic Wars and defeat of Carthage; Romans make Egypt a province; Bantu migrations

Define

tsetse fly	Museon	Pope of Alexandria
Septuagint	Pharos	Eratosthenes

Multiple Choice

1. A major effect of Alexander's conquest of Egypt was
   (a) the end of the Old Kingdom.
   (b) an immigration of Greeks into the country.
   (c) the founding of Cairo.
   (d) building a canal to the Red Sea.

2. The famous library in Alexandria sought to house
   (a) a museum.
   (b) books from all over the ancient world.
   (c) only books written in Greek.
   (d) the private collection of the Ptolemies.

3. Greeks in the Hellenistic Age were
   (a) anxious to adopt foreign customs.
   (b) very democratic.
   (c) willing to share power.
   (d) none of the above.

4. Kush lost out to the Assyrians in Egypt because
    (a) the Assyrians had iron weapons.
    (b) of revolution by the Egyptian peasants.
    (c) of the intervention of Rome.
    (d) of the intervention of Antiochus III.

5. Iron-working in southern Africa resulted in better
    (a) bridges.
    (b) weapons and tools.
    (c) houses.
    (d) public buildings.

6. The original Bantu homeland was in
    (a) Nigeria and Cameroon.
    (b) Zaire.
    (c) Zimbabwe.
    (d) Tassili.

7. The African kingdom that grew up in Nubia was
    (a) Nigeria.
    (b) Kush.
    (c) Thebes.
    (d) Memphis.

8. Meroe was famous for
    (a) iron-making.
    (b) pottery.
    (c) stone pyramids.
    (d) irrigation works.

Essay Questions
  1. Describe a visit to Ptolemaic Alexandria.
  2. Why did Rome win its wars with Carthage?
  3. Discuss the importance of Kush to African history.
  4. Why was agriculture difficult in Africa?

Answers
1. b   5. b
2. b   6. a
3. d   7. b
4. a   8. a

CHAPTER 17

Indian Civilizations of the Americas

The civilization of the American Indians had to develop completely on its own. Their experience told the American Indians that they were the only people on the earth. Therefore inventions discovered in the Americas were made without diffusion because the centers of civilization in Asia, Africa, and Europe were so far away.

Great civilizations appeared despite two major handicaps. The first was the absence of large animals in the Americas for transportation. The second was the very limited use of writing. On the other hand, the large number of plants fit for domestication, ensuring a regular food supply, proved a great benefit. Where there was a surplus of these foods, the First American civilizations appeared.

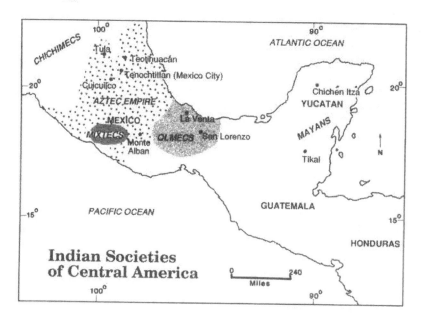

Indian Societies of Central America

Olmec Civilization

The very first civilization in the Americas carries the name Olmec. The people who created it were the American Indians who lived along the Atlantic coast of southern Mexico, in a climate of hot, humid weather. About 1150 B.C. they occupied a site known today as San Lorenzo. There are still Olmecs in modern Mexico, but they are not the same people as the ancient ones.

This part of Mexico has rich soil, and the weather produces the right amount of rain for growing corn, which was the staple of the Olmec diet. Farmers learned to channel water to their fields through a network of ditches. The ancient Olmecs were merchants as well as farmers, trading obsidian for tools and jade, which they used to carve jewelry. The exchange of goods with the nearby highlands was extensive.

The American Indians who lived at San Lorenzo worshipped gods who were a mixture of humans and jaguars. The speed of the jaguar, the fastest animal in the world, probably convinced the Olmecs that these animals had a divine spirit in them.

The sculptures of human heads is one of the most intriguing aspects of Olmec culture. The largest one is 9 feet tall. The heads, wearing helmets, have the features more of a baby than an adult person. No one knows for sure, but archaeologists theorize that these were heroes of a ball game that the Olmecs played.

The heads were carved out of basalt rock that was located 50 miles away. Apparently, the stone was quarried, dragged to a nearby river, put on barges, and floated to the San Lorenzo site. The largest head, weighing 44 tons, required a very large work force to move it. Because the sculptors had no metal tools, the features on the faces were carved by pecking and pounding with stone tools. Their productions make the Olmec sculptors the first great artists of the Americas.

Olmec Indians fashioned the giant heads of heroes, using only stone tools.

About 950 B.C. invaders struck San Lorenzo. They knocked over the stone sculptures and threw them down a ravine where they were ceremonially buried. Olmec civilization, however, continued at another site on a river island, today called La Venta.

La Venta was the paramount center of religious activities for the Olmec people. Priests ministered to thousands of pilgrims who came here to worship the gods and goddesses. In 800 B.C. La Venta was the largest town in North America, holding this position for the next 200 years.

At the center of La Venta, workers built a large mound, 100 feet high, of packed earth. Archaeologists believe the mound served as a tomb for a chief, or chieftains of a dynasty, that governed the town. Other mounds, or tombs, are also found within the city. A variety of grave gifts—little figures of **jaguar-men gods**, pottery, jewelry of jade, and mirrors that people wore around their necks—were laid to rest with the dead.

One of La Venta's favorite gods combined both human and jaguar traits.

Sculptors continued to work in stone at La Venta, carving the figures of their gods. These deities are identified as the gods of fire, rain, and corn. One is a feathered serpent, a familiar deity that continued to appear in many Mexican religions through the centuries.

Another Olmec site was located approximately 200 miles from La Venta at a place called Monte Alban. This was also a religious center. A series of carvings that depict a scene of slaughter can be found there. The notion of death as a religious act was a part of Central American belief that lasted through the centuries, until the arrival of the Europeans.

Some Olmec carvings resemble markings on a calendar, making them the first American Indians to record the passage of time. These three elements—the worship of jaguar-men gods, the connection of death with religious ceremonies, and the recording of time—became an integral part of Central American culture.

About 600 B.C. invaders captured and destroyed the Olmec site at La Venta. What happened to the Indians who lived here? One guess is that they decided to migrate to the Yucatan peninsula and that centuries later they emerged as the Mayan Indians.

Possibly other Olmecs traveled northward to the Valley of Mexico, where Mexico City now stands. Characteristics of Olmec civilization appear here, too. Either they were adopted by other Indians or were brought by the Olmecs themselves. About 300 B.C. a pyramid made of packed earth 75 feet high was put up at a site called Cuicuilco.

City of Teotihuacán

By the year 200 A.D. a city called Teotihuacán lay in the Valley of Mexico. It was located about 30 miles northeast of modern Mexico City. The word *Teotihuacán* means the place the gods call home. A large settlement emerged when corn-growing became so common that there was a significant food surplus. Because the people believed the gods were responsible for their prosperity, they built a religious shrine to keep the gods favorably disposed to them.

As the population of Teotihuacán increased, the city spread over the plain until it covered almost 7 square miles. From the years A.D. 400 to 700, it is estimated that 200,000 people lived here, making it one of the world's largest cities in this time-period. Nothing else compared to its size in all the Americas.

Teotihuacán was a planned city. Its founders were concerned that it should show the order that the universe demonstrated. Indian pilgrims from less-developed societies must have stood in awe at the huge pyramids that the citizens of Teotihuacán constructed to be the largest in all the Americas.

The pyramids line a street that the Spanish conquerors called the **Avenue of the Dead,** although there is no reason to give it that name. On one side of the street stood the Pyramid of the Sun, at its base covering 700 square feet. The pyramid rose to the height of a 20-story building. Packed earth and sun-dried bricks, all carried there by human laborers, made up the building material. Stone-facing covered the exterior. A smaller construction, the Pyramid of the Moon, stood at the north end of the avenue.

Teotihuacán's Pyramid of the Sun was built in the first century B.C.

Other buildings lined the avenue, one of them was a temple dedicated to the Feathered Serpent god, Quetzalcóatl. His many images were prominently placed on the front of his temple in Teotihuacán. Another god was Xipe Totec. This god required his priest to dress in the skin of a human victim to perform the ceremonies connected with his cult. Central American religion always required human sacrifice. Apparently it was believed that unless men and women were sacrificed to them, the gods would die. A spiritual transfusion of blood from living people to the deities meant that the world would continue.

Excavations in the area that was once Teotihuacán turned up the ruins of the houses of the priests, nobles, and ordinary people. Although the upper class had homes that were bigger and more comfortable, even farmers and artisans had dwellings of moderate size. Homes were without windows, but on their walls paintings recounted the myths connected to the deities.

It is hard to imagine the magnificence of the ceremonies that took place in this city as great processions marched along the avenue. Music, chanting, and dances must have had a profound effect upon those who came to Teotihuacán. Stories about the great city spread throughout the Central American world, causing people to send tribute and offerings to its gods and goddesses.

Mayan Achievements

Some archaeologists trace the rise of the Mayans to a migration of Olmecs, who left their homeland and moved into southern Mexico, specifically the Yucatan peninsula, and the neighboring regions of what is now Guatemala, Belize, and Honduras. More likely, their culture, rather than the Olmecs themselves, sparked the beginning of Central America's great Mayan civilization.

The Mayan world depended upon temple sites to locate their cities. Markets here provided a place to exchange corn, beans, leather goods, jewelry, and pottery. Apparently priest-rulers, the elite of Mayan society, supervised market activities.

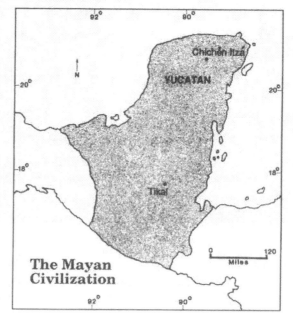

The Mayan Civilization

Population growth in the Yucatan became possible as farmers increased the yields from their fields of corn. To clear land from the rain forest, they used the same slash-and-burn method, common in Asia and Europe. Once they cleared the land of trees, they built raised fields so that the crops would not rot because of stagnant water standing in the fields. An elaborate network of channels drained the fields and required constant surveillance.

About the year A.D. 250, many of the agricultural villages of the Mayans were wealthy enough to begin the construction of stone temples and public buildings to honor their gods. People brought earth to the religious site and then covered it with stone or stucco. Finally, they placed a temple on its summit.

So successful were the priests who supervised the work that over 100 temples were built. The largest were at Tikal, now in Guatemala, where two monumental temples still stand side by side overlooking a great plaza. A special characteristic of these temples was an ornamental roof built of stone placed in cement.

The great temple at Tikal recalls the days of Mayan glory.

The Mayan idea of beauty demonstrated a very different view of how the body should be ornamented. The Mayans enjoyed putting tattoos all over themselves. If any space was left, it could be painted. Priests used blue paint, warriors black and red, and slaves black and white.

Some Mayans filed their teeth and tried to make their noses longer. Artificial noses with holes for jewels apparently were a help for those to whom nature did not provide enough length. Ear plugs were enormous. A really handsome Maya tried to become cross-eyed to add to his or her appearance. In fact, parents often hung objects in front of a baby's eyes in the cradle hoping to get a crossed focus.

Religion of the Mayans

The Mayan religion was very complex. The chief creator god was **Itzamna,** who was also patron of knowledge. Heavenly bodies such as the sun, moon, and planets were also divine. The gods of corn and rain had to be worshipped lest the food supply of the Mayans diminish.

Each god and goddess had to receive just the right kind of offerings or prayers to be kept well disposed. Sometimes the gods required fasting and offerings of incense, animals, and sometimes even humans.

The priest-rulers of the Mayan world spent many years studying texts in order to perform their duties correctly. Young men destined to be priests lived in barracks near the temples. When performing the sacred rites, they wore beautiful costumes of colored cloth and headdresses of flowers or feathers. The priests traveled widely. They visited each others' temples to compare their concerns and discuss their building programs.

At every major temple site there was a court shaped like a capital *I* where ball games took place. The object of the game was for two contesting teams to get a rubber ball, weighing several pounds, through a goal without kicking or throwing it. The Mayans took the games very seriously so that the players for the losing team might be put to death. The course of the ball game was supposed to tell the future, or it might open an especially holy season.

The Mayans believed that physical and spiritual beings were part of a universe composed of heaven, earth, and an empty void beneath the earth. They thought that the heavens were held up by four great trees and that unseen creatures filled the sky in the day and the night.

Writing

To record events of importance, the Mayans invented a type of writing more complex than any other ever to appear in the world. Their script has been difficult to interpret, but much of it is now deciphered. It consists of a mixture of people and animals in certain positions. Some 850 characters or **glyphs** are now identified. Some stand for ideas; others are phonetic, representing sounds.

Mayan glyphs combined animal and human characters.

Archaeologists have found three books from this civilization, written on bark and folded like a fan. They are the only specimens of writing in a book in all the Americas.

Numbers were written as combinations of dots and bars or as human faces. Twenty, rather than ten, was at the base of the Mayan system. The zero was also known. Because Mayan writing was so complex, probably only priests could read it.

The Mayans were fascinated with the passage of time so it is hardly surprising that they invented a calendar that was completely accurate. There were two cycles in the Mayan calendar. One for recording the time for ceremonies had 20 months of 13 days, while the second counted 18 months of 20 days with 5 extra days left over. The two calendars recorded the same dates only every 52 years, a time of great celebration among the Mayans. In addition the Mayans used a Long Count Calendar of 360 days for ordinary events.

South America's Pacific Coast

The landscape in this part of the world is very forbidding, an unlikely spot for the origin of the South American civilization of Peru. Along the coast there is a desert that practically never gets any rain. From May to October there is fog, but this does not bring showers. The fog appears because the cold Humbolt Current parallels the Pacific coast. When the current's cold water hits the warmer land, fog appears just as happens along the California coast in late spring.

Rugged mountains also present a challenge for people living in Peru. Fortunately, mountain rains in the summer create rivers that flow through the desert, depositing rich silt along their banks. This makes it possible to farm alongside the rivers.

Well-watered valleys exist in the mountain ranges. In historic times these valleys became the major areas of human settlement. Barren and cold plateaus surround the valleys, and finally the tall Andes appear with peaks up to 20,000 feet in height. On the eastern slopes of the Andes, the rain forest begins. Its rivers form the headwaters of the mighty Amazon River.

Peru is also an area subject to many natural disasters such as earthquakes and landslides. About seven major earthquakes occur there every century.

Chavín Culture

In one of the Andes' high mountain valleys, archaeologists believe they have found the ruins of South America's oldest city, built by people who belonged to the Chavín civilization. In this valley, where it is said, "There is summer every day and winter every night," Indian people constructed a town surrounding a great temple to their god.

Construction of the Chavín temple started about 1000 B.C. The temple was built and rebuilt several times as new galleries were added. Inside the temple the Chavín Indians placed an image of the god, a figure 12 feet tall, part man and part jaguar. Because he wears a smile, archaeologists suggested calling him the smiling god.

The Chavín people also put up adobe temples to other deities, but none match the grandeur of the smiling god's stone residence. Men and women

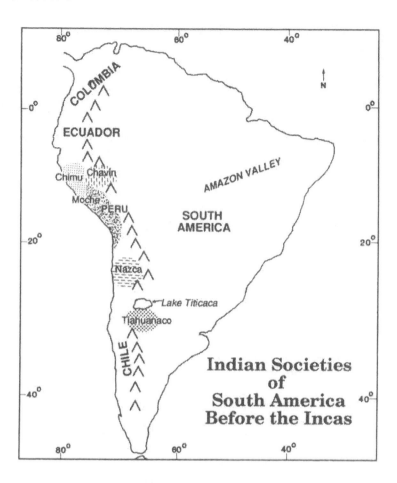

**Indian Societies
of
South America
Before the Incas**

from all over Peru must have organized pilgrimages to visit his temple and, on their return home, spread Chavín culture.

A number of smaller subcultures developed after the influence of the Chavín Indians declined. Some were more important than others, but all depended on better agriculture and fishing to give them a surplus of food.

Coastal people relied upon fish and shellfish for much of their diet. The Humboldt Current's cold waters made it a haven for huge schools of fish. The fish, in turn, attracted millions of birds to the coastal islands. The Indians learned to harvest **guano,** their droppings, to fertilize their fields.

Indians of northern Peru learned to make cups out of gold.

In northern Peru a new discovery was made about 900 B.C. that rivalled the stone construction found in Chavín culture. This was goldsmithing. The American Indians here learned how to hammer gold and to smelt and polish it. Gold mining became an important industry for making jewelry and instruments, but gold never was used for money.

About A.D. 300 a new people, the Moche, created a society where irrigation brought food production to a larger number of people. This society abounded with artists and potters who favored depicting scenes of daily life on their work. The Moche traded their extra corn and cotton, grown in a warm climate, for the wool and potatoes of the interior.

Conclusion

The major American Indian civilizations were remarkable for many reasons. Foremost was their aptitude for farming and fishing, which no other part of the world could rival at this time. Moreover powerful leaders proved able to direct massive building projects requiring the labor of thousands of people. Metallurgy, carving in stone without iron tools, the construction of sophisticated calendars, and the Mayan writing system demonstrate their skills.

CHAPTER 17 REVIEW
INDIAN CIVILIZATIONS OF THE AMERICAS

Summary
- The first civilization of the Americas was formed by the Olmec Indians of Mexico.
- The Olmecs are noted for their stone sculptures made at their religious centers.
- The largest city of North America was located at Teotihuacán in the Valley of Mexico, where immense pyramids were built to honor the gods.
- The Mayans created their civilization and built many temples in the difficult environment of a rain forest.
- Mayan calendars and accounts of historic events were recorded in their glyphs.
- The first South American cultures were located in Peru; the oldest was the Chavín.

Identify
People: Olmecs; Mayans; Chavín
Places: San Lorenzo; La Venta; Teotihuacán; Yucatán peninsula; Avenue of the Dead; Tikal
Events: carving heads at San Lorenzo; building the pyramids of Teotihuacán; Mayan ball games

Define

jaguar-men gods	glyphs	Itzamna	Mayan calendars
Avenue of the Dead	guano		

Multiple Choice
1. San Lorenzo was an early site of these people:
   (a) the Chavíns.
   (b) the Toltecs.
   (c) the Chichimecs.
   (d) the Olmecs.

2. A feature of Indian religion in Central America has been to
   (a) connect death with worship.
   (b) worship jaguar-men deities.
   (c) record time exactly for festivals.
   (d) all the above.

3. Teotihuacán could become such a large city because it had
   (a) discovered the arch.
   (b) conquered many areas far away.
   (c) large draught animals.
   (d) a food surplus.

4. Teotihuacán was famous throughout the Americas because of
   (a) its art.
   (b) its pyramids.
   (c) its language.
   (d) its horses.

5. The feathered-serpent god was
   (a) Quetzalcoátl.
   (b) Huitzilopochtli.
   (c) Xipe Toltec.
   (d) Pixe Toltec.

6. Mayan civilization was centered in
   (a) Panama.
   (b) Peru.
   (c) the Valley of Mexico.
   (d) Yucatán.

7. Mayan civilization was unique in that it
   (a) was built in a rain forest.
   (b) had no writing.
   (c) had no calendar.
   (d) none of the above.

8. Mayan ball games were exciting for the players because
   (a) they were played with a lead ball.
   (b) they were played on a large open field.
   (c) losers might be killed.
   (d) winners were given many gold coins.

9. Mayan fashion preferred people with
   (a) tattoos.
   (b) long noses.
   (c) ear plugs.
   (d) all the above.

10. Among all food crops in Peru, the most important was
    (a) peanuts.
    (b) apples.
    (c) beans.
    (d) potatoes.

11. South America's oldest civilization is known as
    (a) Moche.
    (b) Chavín.
    (c) Nazca.
    (d) Inca.

Essay Questions
1. Discuss what is known about Olmec civilization. What makes it special?
2. What do the pyramids at Teotihuacán tell of political and social organization?
3. How might you explain the Mayan concern for calendars and writing?

Answers

1. d	5. a	9. d
2. d	6. d	10. d
3. d	7. a	11. b
4. b	8. c	

UNIT 4

EXPANDING HORIZONS:
A.D. 500–1100

The Islamic World of Southwest Asia

Southwest Asia has always been at the center of religious origins. Here Judaism and Christianity, the Western world's most important religions, were born. In the seventh century a new faith, Islam, emerged in Southwest Asia.

Some historians claim that the life and teaching of Muhammad, the founder of the Islamic religion, was the single most important event in the Middle Ages. Muhammad certainly changed the world of Southwest Asia. Before Muhammad, most Arabs lived outside the major civilizations. Within 100 years of Muhammad's death, they became the principal actors in much of Southwest Asia and northern Africa.

Arabian Peninsula

The Arabian peninsula resembles a large rectangle, surrounded on three sides by the sea. On the fourth side lies the Syrian desert. Most of Arabia is desert with a forbidding landscape. There are no lakes, no forests, and no prairies. The few rivers dry up very quickly in the summertime. Although it can become very hot during the day, the lack of humidity on the peninsula makes it cool in the evening.

The regions of Yemen and Oman in the southern part of the peninsula have rather tall mountains where clouds collect giving off 4 to 8 inches of rain a year. The peninsula's southern interior, however, practically never gets rain. For this reason it is called the empty quarter.

On the coast near the Red Sea there is a narrow plain. To the east of the plain is a line of hills that rise several thousand feet. They reach up to a plateau that subsequently tilts eastward down to the Persian Gulf. In ancient times merchants along the southern coast of Arabia were famous for the incense that they exported to the rest of the world. Incense was made from the gum of a tree that grows in this region.

In the desert there are a few places, oases, where water rises to the surface. From ancient times farmers used the springs of the oases to irrigate date and fig trees. Nomadic dromedary herders, the **Bedouin**, came to the springs for watering the animals they kept. The Bedouin way of life was made possible because of the dromedary, the one-humped camel, an animal well suited for desert life. It could go for several weeks in winter without eating or drinking. The tough skin in its mouth allowed it to eat almost anything, including thorny cactus.

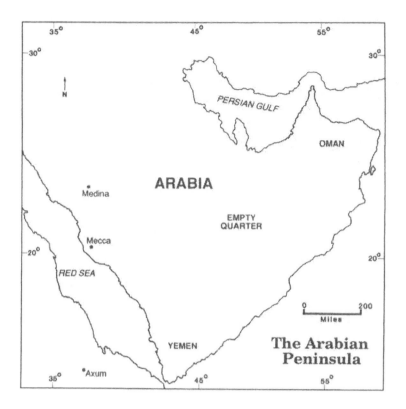

Bedouin life was difficult. Often the only food and drink to be had was camel's milk. Raiding and fighting among tribes went on constantly except during the time set aside for religious pilgrimage.

A tribe took responsibility for all its members. To be without its protection meant that a person had no security. The Bedouins' code of ethics made courage the highest virtue. In the second place, hospitality for strangers was required of all Arab chieftains. Unfortunately, for weaker members of their own society, such as orphans and widows, there were no safeguards from abuse.

Town life in the peninsula was possible only in regions where water was present. Yemen was such a place, for the rain that fell in its mountains could be trapped in reservoirs. Elaborate irrigation systems and terracing made it possible for farmers to grow crops here that supported the town populations.

In the northern and central parts of Arabia, towns grew up around oases. One of these towns was Mecca. Because it did not have enough water for agriculture, its citizens lived from commerce. In Mecca it was possible to exchange products brought by caravan from the Red Sea with those of the desert.

Mecca was also the site of the most important religious shrine of the peninsula. Here stood the **Ka'bah,** a cube-shaped building sacred to the gods and goddesses of the Arabs. Annually, during a time of truce when fighting among the Bedouin was forbidden, thousands of pilgrims traveled to Mecca to worship at the Ka'bah. Built into one corner of the Ka'bah was a large black stone considered especially sacred.

Prophet Muhammad

The exact year of Muhammad's birth is not known, but it was about A.D. 570. He was born a member of the Hashimite clan that included many of Mecca's important merchants. His father died before Muhammad was born, so that as a child his mother sent him out to the desert to be brought up in a Bedouin tribe. This was a common practice among families in Mecca. His sojourn here allowed the young Muhammad to learn the language of the desert, considered the ideal form of Arabic.

After several years with the Bedouin, Muhammad returned to Mecca. Little is known about his life during this time. A widow named Khadijah hired him to oversee her business, organizing caravans to carry exports to Syria. In time, Muhammad and Khadijah were married.

Muhammad was a thoughtful person and was therefore discouraged by the religious views of his contemporaries. The Arabs worshipped many different deities, and the stories told about them were hardly worthy of belief. Muhammad knew Jews and Christian Arabs who scoffed at the idea of many gods.

One night while at prayer on a mountain outside Mecca, Muhammad believed he saw the angel Gabriel. Gabriel told Muhammad that God had chosen him to carry his message to the Arab people. Muhammad had not prepared himself to become a prophet, but the angel persisted. Wherever he looked, Muhammad saw Gabriel. Muhammad came down from the mountain aware that he had a new mission, to be God's prophet to the Arabs.

Not surprisingly, he was greeted with disbelief. Only a few Meccans, including his wife Khadijah, believed him. Opponents arose who disputed his claims to speak for God. Mecca's merchants and innkeepers feared Muhammad's teaching would ruin their businesses. Life became so difficult that Muhammad dispatched some of his disciples to the Ethiopian kingdom of Axum. While he had the protection of his clan, he was safe. Later his clan chieftain withdrew this protection, forcing Muhammad to leave Mecca.

While in exile, the Prophet received a small delegation from Yathrib (now Medina), a town and farming oasis to the north of Mecca. Having learned of Muhammad, the chiefs of Medina's tribes delegated their ambassadors to invite him to their city to arbitrate differences between the Jewish and Arab tribes living there. Muhammad agreed, and in the year A.D. 622 he departed for Medina. Muhammad's relocation to Medina is known as the **hijra**. This event marks the first year in the Muslim calendar, abbreviated A.H.

Over the next few years Muhammad's followers grew more numerous. They included Medinan converts and his followers who now returned from Axum. Those who professed Islam became known as Muslims.

Muhammad continued to receive messages from God (*Allah* in Arabic). These revelations were written down so that they might be preserved; after his death they were collected in a book called the **Qur'an.** According to Muslim belief, the Qur'an is the word of God, and Muhammad was acting only as God's intermediary. The content of the revelation was easily summarized: There is one God, and Muhammad is God's prophet. This is the essence of the religion known as **Islam**, that takes its name from *submission* to the divine will.

The Qur'an taught that there had been many prophets before Muhammad. Adam was the first, followed later by Abraham and his son Ishmael. Together they built the first Ka'bah of Mecca. Moses and Jesus were also numbered among the prophets, and Muhammad was the last. Muhammad predicted that at the terrible final judgment God would save those who believed his message, but nonbelievers who rejected it would suffer because they had rejected God's revelation.

The Ka'bah was a place of pilgrimage before Muhammad's time. After he purified it of idols, it continued to be a focus of Islamic veneration.

Muhammad directed his communication to his fellow Arabs who were still polytheists. The message was also aimed at the Jews of Yathrib whom Muhammad hoped to win over. The Prophet asserted that both Jews and Christians had once been given God's message, but over the years Jews and Christians either misunderstood God's word or altered the original message. Jews had rejected Jesus, whom Muhammad believed to be a true prophet. Christians erred when they said that there were three persons in the one God. In Muhammad's view, this doctrine destroyed the oneness of God.

To the disappointment of Muhammad, most Arab Christians and Jews did not become believers in his lifetime. Nevertheless, he made a place for them in the Muslim world, for he believed that they once had served the true God. The Hebrew scriptures and the New Testament made them "people of the book." Muslims had a duty to tolerate Christians and Jews, even to protect them, as long as they accepted Islamic political and military leadership.

The Qur'an, containing the messages Muhammad believed to be given to him by God, did much to replace the tribal loyalties of the Bedouin. In place of allegiance to the clan or the tribe, people now looked to the larger community of Islam.

The Qur'an also set up a more demanding ethical system. It forbade Muslims to drink wine or any other alcoholic beverage. Gambling was also forbidden. Infants that were once left to die were now protected. Orphans and widows, formerly so frequently exploited, received special care. A special tax provided for them and all the poor. Polygamy was limited, for the Qur'an ruled that a man could marry no more than four women, provided he could care for them all and love them equally.

There was no priesthood in Islam nor were there any monasteries. Each person stood before God on his or her own merits, obedient to a God who was forgiving and merciful to those who believed.

Most of the information about Muhammad is found in the Qur'an. But additional knowledge of his life and teaching was written in accounts orally transmitted about the Prophet called **hadiths.** The hadiths tell what Muhammad said or did on a particular occasion. Although not as important or authentic as the Qur'an's words, the hadiths provided a model or guide to Muslims about human behavior. Literally thousands of hadiths exist; some are fictitious, but others are authentic. For this reason, every hadith has a chain of witnesses to provide verification.

Genealogy became a very important study within Islam since it would or would not confirm the authority of a hadith. The scholar Abd Allah al-Bukhari in the ninth century published 3,000 hadiths that he believed to be truthful. After the Qur'an Muslims revere his collection.

Toward the end of his life Muhammad's followers were strong enough to force the Meccans to allow the Prophet to return to his native city. There he purified the Ka'bah of its idols. Once this was done, Muhammad made the Ka'bah the center of pilgrimage for the Islamic faith. The Qur'an demanded that Muslims must face toward it whenever they prayed.

The essentials of Islam are found in five pillars that every Muslim was required to follow:

1. A Muslim must confess, "There is no God but God and Muhammad is his prophet."
2. A Muslim should pray five times each day: at dawn, noon, mid-afternoon, before sunset, and before going to bed.
3. A Muslim should give contributions to the poor.
4. A Muslim should fast during the month of Ramadan. Muhammad's first revelation had come during Ramadan.
5. A Muslim, once in his or her lifetime, should make a pilgrimage to Mecca to pray at the Ka'bah, if he or she can afford to do so.

Muslims pray in a mosque. The Friday noon prayer is the most important of the week, when all men who are able attend the service.

After Muhammad

Before Muhammad's death in A.D. 632, most of the tribes of the Arabian peninsula had become converts to Islam. Since Muhammad died rather suddenly, his community had no clear instructions on how his successor should be chosen. One group, the **Sunnites**, concluded that any male Muslim could represent the Prophet. Another party, the **Shi'ites**, believed that the leader of the Muslim community must be one of Muhammad's descendants.

Muhammad had only one daughter, Fatimah, who outlived him. Her husband was Ali. The Shi'ites argued that only Ali had the right to succeed Muhammad. When a decision was made, however, Ali lost out. He was passed over for Abu-Bakr. Abu-Bakr was an early follower of Muhammad and the father of Muhammad's favorite wife, A'ishah.

Abu-Bakr proved to be an excellent choice. He was an able administrator and prepared for an expected Bedouin revolt on news of the Prophet's death. Thanks to his skills, Muslim armies soon suppressed the revolutionaries and restored the preeminence of Islam over Arabia.

Byzantine–Persian Conflict

When Muhammad was living in Arabia, the two major powers of Southwest Asia once again took to the battlefield. In Constantinople Emperor Heraklios was determined to regain the territory lost to the Sasanian kings because of the incompetence of his predecessors. In the early sixth century the Persians were in control of Syria, Palestine, and Egypt, the three richest provinces that were once Byzantine lands. Heraklios was especially angry that when the Persian king, Khosrow II Parviz, burned down the Church of the Holy Sepulchre in Jerusalem, he gave the relic of Jesus' cross to the head of the Persian Christian church.

In A.D. 623 Heraklios marched against the Persians, an expedition that kept him in the field for the next 5 years. At the war's conclusion the Byzantine emperor had regained the lost provinces and restored the cross to Jerusalem. Both the Byzantines and the Persians, now exhausted, did not foresee the danger of a challenge from the Muslim Arabs.

Arab Conquests

After the Arabian peninsula was regained, the Muslim armies began to look farther afield. Palestine, Syria, Iraq, and Egypt were added to the Islamic world within 10 years of the Prophet's death.

Many reasons are given for the rapid expansion of the Arab people over the following centuries. One is based on economics. This opinion holds that the population of the peninsula had grown to the point where it could no longer support so many people.

A second reason was military. The Bedouin were excellent fighters, for they could cross the desert as a sailor used the sea. Riding their camels in secret, they easily took by surprise the forts of their enemies on the edge of the desert. In the past many Bedouin tribes lived by raiding, but Muhammad forbade Muslims to attack other Muslims. Therefore, raids had to be directed outside the Arabian peninsula.

Finally, Islam was a powerful religious driving force. Muhammad taught his followers that they had a duty to spread Islam and defend it against its enemies. Religions that worshipped false gods had no right to exist. A soldier who died in battle defending Islam was to be admitted into heaven at once.

When the Arab armies invaded Palestine and Syria, Heraklios made only a half-hearted response. His long wars against the Persians had sapped all his strength. Everything he gained was now lost, and only Anatolia remained secure. Syrians and Palestinians, once Byzantine citizens and Christians, became part of the Arab, Islamic world.

In A.D. 658 Ali was at last chosen to be **caliph,** the head of all the Islamic community. This title meant that he represented the Prophet to the Muslims. Of course the Shi'ites, who had always supported Ali now felt confirmed in their view that he should have been chosen from the beginning. Among some Sunnites, he received no welcome.

Muhammad's widow, A'ishah, was among his opponents. She tried, but failed, to rally support against him. The governor of Damascus, Mu'awiyah, was more successful in resisting his claims. He led an army against Ali, and although the battle ended in a truce, Ali kept his title. When in A.D. 661 Ali was killed, Mu'awiyah's party proclaimed him caliph in Jerusalem. To make certain that Ali's sons, Hussein and Husayn, would not challenge him, he ordered them to stay in Arabia.

Umayyad Caliphate

Mu'awiyah moved the Islamic capital to Damascus, beginning the Umayyad Caliphate, which was to last about 100 years. Under his direction Muslim armies occupied the islands of Cyprus and Rhodes as well as Armenia. His military forces, made up of seasoned Bedouin, pushed along the coast of northern Africa and deep into Persian provinces. The caliph had only one serious setback, when the fleet he dispatched to take Constantinople failed.

In A.D. 680 Mu'awiyah died. He had already appointed his son to succeed him, but in Yathrib the Shi'ite supporters of Ali's son Husayn rallied around him, urging him to declare himself caliph. On the way to Iraq, a battle took place at Karbala and the Umayyad army killed Husayn. Among the Shi'ites, Husayn's death made him a martyr, and they pledged never to forget Karbala. Each year there is still a ceremony held there and in other places of the Shi'ite world to commemorate Husayn's death.

During the rule of the Umayyad caliphs, Damascus was the center of the Islamic world. A great **mosque** was built for the capital, and the **bazaar,** or marketplace, of Damascus was the destination of merchants from all over southwestern Asia.

Islamic armies continued their advance. In the east the caliph's sovereignty extended over many famous cities of Inner Asia: Bukhara, Samarkand, and

The Umayyad mosque of Damascus became one of the most important of the Islamic world.

Tashkent. Because several Turkish and Mongolian tribes converted to Islam, the Chinese influence on the peoples of Inner Asia was limited.

The Muslims then crossed into the Punjab and the Sind, regions of northwestern India (now Pakistan). In A.D. 713 the Muslims took Multan, an ancient city holding both Hindu and Buddhist temples, winning many people over to their faith.

Two years before the fall of Multan, in A.D. 711, a Muslim force crossed the straits that separate Morocco from Spain. The Muslim general, Tariq, landed near a great cliff, which was named Gibraltar after him. Gibraltar means the mountain of Tariq. From there the Muslims spread throughout Spain capturing Toledo, the Visigothic capital. All of Spain except the far northwestern corner fell to the Muslims. In that region Christian princes were strong enough to keep their independence.

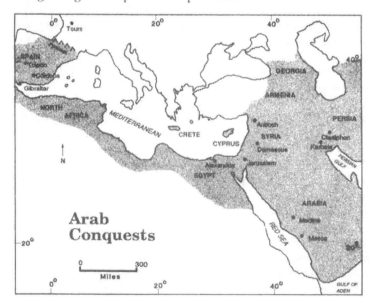

Arab Conquests

From Spain the Muslims crossed the Pyrenees mountains to reach the Frankish lands. In A.D. 733 Charles Martel, the Frankish king's Mayor of the Palace, turned them back at Tours, so Muslim rule never extended into western Europe beyond Spain.

Life Under the Caliphate

The Umayyad Caliphate brought many changes to the world that its armies occupied. The language of most of the native peoples slowly changed to Arabic. Syrians who once spoke Syriac, Egyptians who spoke Coptic, and Spaniards who once spoken Latin now adopted Arabic, learning to read and write in its script. An exception were the native Persians who adopted the Arabic script, but not the language. Many of the former upper class of Sasanian Persia found a place in the Muslim administration.

There was an economic boom during Umayyad times in Southwest Asia. The caliphs minted both gold and silver coins, making trading easier. They ordered canals dug and reservoirs repaired in order to increase the amount of farmland. Plants from India began moving westward across the Islamic world, increasing food production.

In Jerusalem, Caliph Abd al-Malik commissioned the famous Dome of the Rock on the site where the Jewish temple once stood. The great golden roof over the Dome of the Rock soared over the city's mud brick houses. The caliphs covered the Islamic world with mosques. On Fridays at noon, businesses closed so that the men of the town might attend prayer. Inside the front of each mosque a special niche, the **mirhab,** showed the direction to Mecca. A fountain for washing before prayer was located outside the mosque door that was always kept unlocked so that people could pray.

Jerusalem's Dome of the Rock is located where tradition holds that Muhammad made an ascent to heaven.

The Qur'an did not permit art that pictured any living thing. This law was meant to prohibit idolatry, which was still a temptation in the eighth century for new converts. Therefore, Islamic art depended on geometric forms and the beauty that comes from architectural shape. Another artistic medium of the Islamic world was calligraphy. Because copying the Qur'an was one of the most meritorious acts a person could do, a scribe who wrote beautiful letters was highly honored.

The four great cities of Islam were Mecca, Medina, Jerusalem, and Damascus. These cities were specially adorned with mosques, hotels for travelers, hospitals, and schools. Because Muslims were still a minority in the world they occupied, they usually lived together in their own section of these towns.

Women enjoyed a special place in the Islamic religion. Muhammad's wives, Khadijah and A'ishah, were very active in the history of early Islam. Later tradition presumed that upper-class Muslim women should spend most of their time within the home. Many of these women went veiled, a custom not found in the Qur'an, but introduced into Islam out of the Persian tradition.

A major development within Islam occurred when the **Sufi** movement came to accentuate more emotion in their prayer than devotion in the mosques permitted. The Sufis became known as mystics, believers who not only prayed to God on formal occasions but who also wanted to feel close to God through personal experience and communal services. The Sufis quoted the Qur'an: "God is closer to man than the vein of his neck," finding in this verse ample justification for their devotions.

Many Sufis did not care about the rule of the caliph or about the laws that Muslim judges thought important. They met in groups and prayed outside the mosque. In their assemblies they used chants, songs, and dances to help them come closer to God.

By the mid-eighth century many Muslims, many of them Sufis, believed that the wealth and luxury of the Umayyad court distracted the caliphs from their responsibilities in leading the Islamic community. The caliphs lived in great palaces where hundreds of slaves and civil and military officials served them. Their palace walls were adorned with pictures, contrary to Muslim law, for the caliphs began to act much as Byzantine emperors or Persian kings.

Dissatisfaction with the Umayyad kingdom resulted in a rebellion. It first emerged in eastern Persia and then spread to other parts of Southwest Asia under the leadership of Abu al-Abbas, a descendant of an uncle of Muhammad. In A.D. 750 his army, the Abbasids, conquered Damascus. The last Umayyad caliph died while fleeing to Egypt, and most of his relatives were put to death. Abu al-Abbas came to power creating the second Muslim dynasty.

Abbasid Caliphs

The fall of the Umayyads meant that Persian customs and culture became even more prominent. Persian converts became the civil officials and the caliphs' bodyguards. Damascus was no longer the capital, which was now located at Kufa in Iraq.

The Abbasid Caliphate lasted a long time, from A.D. 750 to 1258. During this time the descendants of Abu al-Abbas were the caliphs. Abu al-Abbas claimed that he was restoring a purer form of Islam and had no intention of living in the luxury of the Umayyad caliphs. At Friday prayer the caliph wore the coat of the Prophet Muhammad as a symbol of his legitimacy. The Abbasids promised that they would rule the Muslim world until Jesus (*Isa* in Arabic) returned to earth at his Second Coming.

Caliph al-Mansur, who governed from A.D. 754 to 775, was intent upon building a capital that would reflect the glory of the Islamic world. He had little interest in preserving the simplicity of Abu al-Abbas and laid the first foundation stone for Baghdad, the name of his new capital on the Tigris River in Iraq, close to the site of the old Persian capital of Ctesiphon. He called it the city of peace. It is estimated that he commissioned as many as 100,000 workmen to build its three great walls and palaces, gardens, and streets. A great mosque was placed next to the caliph's palace.

The style of Baghdad was distinctly Persian, built in a circle according to a prepared plan. In many ways Baghdad's culture recaptured the age of the ancient Persian kings. A large bureaucracy carried out the wishes of the caliphs, whose most important official was the **wazir**. He headed the caliph's administration and the **diwan,** the council that carried out his wishes.

The Abbasid caliphs built a minaret at the mosque of Samara in traditional Mesopotamian style.

The golden age of the Abbasids appeared during the rule of Harun ar-Rashid who headed the Muslim world from A.D. 786 to 809. Harun lived at the same time as Charlemagne ruled in Europe. The two leaders exchanged gifts as a sign of mutual respect.

Harun embellished the Baghdad palace with even more rooms and halls. Poets, musicians, singers, dancers, and falconers were always in demand to provide entertainment. Harun and his queen ate only from gold and silver plates. The queen's clothes were the finest with precious jewels sewn on them. At the wedding of a favorite couple, a thousand pearls were poured from a golden dish over the bride and groom.

On the palace grounds the caliph kept chained lions in a magnificent garden with trees and plants that made the palace a marvel to all who saw it. This was the Baghdad of a *Thousand and One Nights,* the great story book that has come down from the Abbasid period.

Baghdad was more than just a place for the Abbasid administration. It also became a city of teachers and scholars. The focus, of course, was on Islamic learning. In addition, however, the great classics of the Greek world were translated and copied so that they would not be lost. Aristotle's work was well known in Baghdad. Besides Greek, translators worked in Persian, Sanskrit, and Syrian literature.

From India came the numerals which, when they later came into Europe, were known as Arabic numerals. Significant advances were also made in geography and astronomy, for every Muslim needed to know the direction of the Ka'bah in Mecca for saying prayers. Chemistry made great strides as all the terms that begin with *al*, the Arabic word for *the* give evidence.

The glory of Baghdad eventually was threatened by revolts in the distant provinces of the Abbasid Caliphate. At the edges of the empire, Muslim rulers in Spain and Tunisia declared their independence and refused to pay tribute to Baghdad. In the tenth century strong wazirs, some of them Turks in origin, pushed the caliphs out of administration, limiting their activities to religious matters.

The Great Mosque at Kairouan served the Berber and Arab populations of Tunisia.

A number of Shi'ite sects also troubled the caliphate. One was the **Isma'ili**, many of whom lived on the island of Bahrain in the Persian Gulf, named for Isma'il, the seventh successor to Ali. His followers believed that for a time Isma'il's descendants had gone into hiding but had reappeared. Their dynasty was called Fatimid, after Muhammad's daughter.

Another violent faction of Shi'ites was the **Assassins**, a word that has come to be associated with murder. In the late eleventh century an Assassin, the Persian Shi'ite Hassan e-Sabbah, seized a Syrian fortress and announced that he was the deputy of a hidden **imam**, a Shi'ite religious leader who was considered more powerful than the caliph. Hassan declared that all leading Muslims who rejected him were deserving of death. Throughout the Muslim world governors, generals, and all office holders became targets for assassination.

Turks Enter the Muslim World

In the sixth century the Turkish world began to stir. These were the people who lived in the steppe lands of Inner Asia, west of the Mongols and extending to the Caspian Sea. There were many tribes of Turks, but all spoke a similar language.

Most Turks were nomads who herded horses and sheep on the grasslands of the steppes. Life here was harsh, but the Turks were taught to cope with hardship. Young people grew up in large families with plenty of brothers and sisters. The father was the patriarch, who made the decisions for all the family. When he died the eldest son inherited all the father's wealth, property, and even the father's wives except for his own mother. This gave the Turkish family strong and cohesive leadership.

Several families who lived together in the winter time were led by a chieftain. His title was **beg.** Ordinary people made payments to him, making him richer than everyone else. When a matter of importance to the tribe appeared, the chieftain took counsel with other begs. All had a chance to give an opinion, but after a decision was reached, there was no turning back.

In times of crisis and war, the begs chose someone from their group to be **khan.** Everyone then owed him allegiance. There was no formal administration or civil service in the Turkish world, for political authority was built upon personal charisma. People paid tribute to the khan because they feared him. When he died, or the crisis passed, authority returned to the begs. This is what made Turkish empires of this period quick to rise and quick to fall. Only a very strong khan could start a lasting dynasty.

The Turks began to move into the Muslim world in the ninth century. The Abbasid caliphs welcomed them and offered them positions in their army. After a few years Turkish officers began to wonder why they should not share rule with the caliphs. Their leader took the title **sultan,** which means a person who has authority to lead the caliph's armies.

In the tenth century the Turks within the Abbasid Caliphate began to convert to Islam. One of their leaders, Seljuk Beg, organized his people into a strong nation of warriors. In A.D. 1055 his grandson captured Baghdad, and it was now the turn of the Seljuk Turks to take up the cause of Islam. The Seljuks crushed a Byzantine army in Anatolia that allowed the Turks to move into a part of the world that had held off Muslim armies for centuries. Christian Greeks and Armenians now became the subjects of the Turks.

Modern pilgrims to Mecca wear the traditional white garb for their visit.

The Turkish sultans wanted the cultural tradition of Baghdad kept alive. The Wazir Nizam al-Mulk, a Persian, was appointed to serve the Seljuk sultan, Alp Arslan. Nizam established a center for study to which he gave his name, the **Nizamiyah.** Nizam enjoyed poetry so much that he became the patron of the Muslim world's most important poet, Umar Khayyam. Assassins later struck down Nizam, who fell victim to their terrorism.

Another great Muslim teacher was Abu Hamid al-Ghazzali. Al-Ghazzali was born in the middle of the eleventh century in northeastern Persia. His talent earned him an appointment to the Nizamiyah in Baghdad. Here he combined the teachings of the Qur'an with those presented by the ancient Greek philosophers.

Al-Ghazzali accepted much that the ancient philosophers said, but nothing that contradicted Islam. For a while he gave up on thinking about God and simply turned his attention to the practice of Sufism. Once satisfied that orthodox Islam and Sufism were compatible, he wrote a book on how best to practice the Muslim faith, *The Revival of the Religious Sciences.* It remains the most important book ever written on the subject.

While scholarship flourished in Baghdad, Turkish arms continued to win victories far from the capital. Seljuk forces occupied Antioch and then Jerusalem, taking it from the Fatimids. Even though the Egyptians were tolerant of Christians, the Turks, new converts, were not. Their treatment of European Christian pilgrims to Jerusalem was to become a major cause of the Crusades.

Conclusion

The rise of Islam not only changed Southwest Asia but also much of Africa and South Asia. The Arabs, once a people with little claim to attention, burst on the world, bringing their religion and their language to millions of other peoples. Muslims created a civilization that brought new life into the world in the arts, scholarship, and the sciences.

CHAPTER 18 REVIEW
THE ISLAMIC WORLD OF SOUTHWEST ASIA

Summary
- The Arabian peninsula is a hot dry land with no rivers.
- Towns grew in oases, where water was available. One of these towns was Mecca where there was also a religious shrine called the Ka'bah.
- In the seventh century, Muhammad, a citizen of Mecca, believed that he had received a revelation from God to start a new religion called Islam.
- Inspired by this new faith, Muslim armies spread out from Arabia into Southwest Asia, North Africa, and Spain.
- Under the Umayyad and Abbasid caliphates, southwestern Asia reached a high level of civilization.
- Seljuk Turks settled in Anatolia and became vigorous Muslims.

Identify
People: Muhammad; Bedouin; Sunnites; Shi'ites; Khadijah; sufis; Seljuks; Assassins; Mu'awiyah; Fatimah; Heraklios; Ali; Husayn; al-Mansur; al-Ghazzali
Places: Mecca; Yathrib; Damascus; Kufa; Karbala; Baghdad; Yemen
Events: Muhammad's message to the Arabs; coming of the Seljuk Turks; Arab conquests in southwestern Asia and the cultural assimilation of people living there

Define

Islam	hadiths	Qur'an	Ka'bah	hijra
imam	caliphate	khan	mosque	Shi'ites
Bedouin	Assassins	Isma'ili	Sunnites	Sufi
caliph	diwan	bazaar	mirhab	
beg	sultan	Nizamiyah	wazir	

Multiple Choice
1. To the west of the Arabian peninsula is
    (a) the Persian Gulf.
    (b) the Mediterranean Sea.
    (c) the Red Sea.
    (d) the Indian Ocean.

2. A Bedouin was someone
    (a) who lived in an oasis.
    (b) who herded camels.
    (c) who sailed ships on the Red Sea.
    (d) who herded sheep and cattle.

3. During the time of pilgrimage, it was not allowed for desert tribes
    (a) to eat meat.
    (b) to shave one's hair.
    (c) to bathe.
    (d) to fight among themselves.

4. The Ka'bah was a sacred building of
   (a) Mecca.
   (b) Medina.
   (c) Damascus.
   (d) Jerusalem.

5. The hijra refers to the time
   (a) when Muhammad received the Qur'an.
   (b) when Muhammad began to preach.
   (c) when Muhammad left Mecca for Medina.
   (d) when the Angel Gabriel appeared to Muhammad.

6. The Qur'an taught that there had been prophets sent by God that included
   (a) Abraham.
   (b) Jesus.
   (c) Moses.
   (d) all of the above.

7. Muhammad's teachings are contained in the Qur'an and
   (a) the hadiths.
   (b) the Bible.
   (c) the Vedas.
   (d) the New Testament.

8. Muhammad's daughter was
   (a) Khadijah.
   (b) Fatimah.
   (c) A'ishah.
   (d) Helen.

9. Shi'ites believe that
   (a) Muhammad should have no successor.
   (b) any Muslim could be the leader of the community.
   (c) a successor to Muhammad should be elected every 5 years.
   (d) only a blood relative of Muhammad could succeed him.

10. Ramadan is
    (a) a month of fasting.
    (b) the payment of taxes.
    (c) the pilgrimage to Mecca.
    (d) prayer five times a day.

11. The building in which Muslims pray is called
    (a) a church.
    (b) a temple.
    (c) the Ka'bah.
    (d) a mosque.

12. Muslim armies first crossed into Europe at
    (a) Seville.
    (b) Gibraltar.
    (c) Gallipoli.
    (d) Segovia.

13. Mu'awiyah is the first caliph of
    (a) the Umayyads.
    (b) the Abbasids.
    (c) the Ismailis.
    (d) the Shi'ites.

14. In Jerusalem the great Muslim shrine is
    (a) the Ka'bah.
    (b) the hijra.
    (c) the Dome of the Rock.
    (d) the Umayyad mosque.

15. The famous capital of the Abbasids was
    (a) Damascus.
    (b) Jidda.
    (c) Jerusalem.
    (d) Baghdad.

16. The original home of the Seljuk Turks was
    (a) in India.
    (b) in Mongolia.
    (c) in Manchuria.
    (d) in Inner Asia.

Essay Questions
1. How do you explain the success of Muhammad?
2. Discuss how the pillars of Islam compare with the teachings of Christianity and Judaism.
3. What caused the split between Sunnites and Shi'ites?
4. What were the major achievements of the Abbasid caliphate?
5. What were the effects of the Seljuk Turk invasion of Anatolia?

Answers

1. c	5. c	9. d	13. a
2. b	6. d	10. a	14. c
3. d	7. a	11. d	15. d
4. a	8. b	12. b	16. d

The Early Middle Ages in India

The history of India from A.D. 500 to 1100 is one of foreign peoples moving into the subcontinent. In A.D. 500 the Gupta empire was now but a shadow of itself, inviting foreign invaders to fill in the vacuum created as strong central power deteriorated. The wealth of India was like a magnet that drew peoples of Inner Asia into the subcontinent. Far inferior in numbers and culture, the one advantage the invaders enjoyed was that of swift decisive cavalry charges that overwhelmed the native rulers in the north of India.

A Period of Migrations

The Xiong-nu, or Huns, were first to take advantage of India's fragmentation. By the middle of the sixth century, the Huns controlled much of the Ganges Valley as well as the Punjab. Their hold, however, did not last since their subjects were many, and they were few. The powerful weapon of the majority, assimilation, worked against their lasting presence. Much like the collapse of their Hunnic cousins who rode their horses west into Europe, the vigor of the Huns in India rapidly vanished once the chiefs who first led their attacks passed on leadership to sons and grandsons accustomed to lives of ease and wealth.

One brief period of culture was achieved in the seventh century. In A.D. 606 Harsha Vardhana sought to revive something of Gupta splendor. He was, himself, a relative of the imperial family, so that he held claims to legitimacy. The monarch was also a Buddhist, proving the enduring attraction of that belief. Harsha had no heirs, and hardly surprising, after he died, his empire collapsed.

A new Inner Asian people now passed through the Hindu Kush into northern India. The natives knew them as **Rajputs,** or the sons of kings. Like the Aryans before them, the Rajputs were a quarrelsome lot for whom war was a natural state. For good reason the Hindu brahmans sought to win them over to Hinduism, welcoming them into the warrior class.

The Rajput chieftains set up small kingdoms throughout the Indus and Ganges Valleys. Over the years they adopted Hinduism as their faith. The Rajputs also developed a code of honor to lessen the terror of their interminable wars, much as occurred later among the knights of western Europe and the samurai of Japan.

Developments Within Hinduism

While the political life of India during the early Middle Ages was turbulent, within Hinduism, the religion of India's majority, several major developments took place. It was at this time that Hindu devotional practices, **puja**, became formalized. The worshipper brought offerings to the images of the deities in the form of food specialties such as fruit or cakes. It was believed that the divinities then took the essence of these goods for their meals.

Dancing figures were often portrayed on the exteriors of Hindu temples.

In addition to a prescription for offerings, an emphasis was placed on close personal devotion, expressed with emotion to Shiva, Vishnu, Kali, or whatever divinity was the personal protector of the worshipper. This devotion, called **bhakti,** spread throughout the masses of India. The Hindu vedas, once exclusively in Sanskrit, were put into Hindi, the vernacular.

There was also a version of this devotion that expressed itself in tantric rituals. **Tantrism** was especially identified with Shiva, who was the god of fertility and whose symbolic image was the phallus. Fertility worship antedates the Aryan conquest of India and probably was never quite extinguished when the brahmans taught their religion to the indigenous Indian peoples. Devotees of Tantrism engaged in group sexual activity as a sign of their devotion to the female power in nature, **shakti.** Because most brahmans would have nothing to do with tantric ritual, its devotees met at night and kept their practices secret.

In southern India bhakti practices also flourished. **Yoga,** controlled breathing and bodily posture, became a part of religious activity. Such practices won converts from among the Jains and Buddhists.

Many of the Hindu rulers in the south commissioned the building of great temples, cut from rock, to their divinities. About A.D. 756 Krishna I, a ruler in the Deccan region, sponsored a temple to Shiva hollowed out from the interior of a mountain. Entering through a narrow passageway, the worshipper came into an open courtyard of startling images of the Hindu pantheon. This temple, at Mount Kailasa, is considered the apex of Hindu sculpture.

A Hindu temple in southern India is decorated with hundreds of exterior sculptures.

Muslim Invasions

Arab traders long had sailed their boats across the Indian Ocean to the ports of India. When Islam became the religion of most Arabs, these merchants were the first Muslims to come into India. An exploratory expedition out of Persia, however, informed the Umayyad caliph in Damascus that an attack on India was not worth the trouble.

In A.D. 713 this perspective changed. The first Muslim forces advanced against Multan and other cities of the Sind, the region in the far northwest of India. The army was made up of 12,000 soldiers, a cavalry, and a camel corps. Over the next few years a permanent occupation of the Sind took place, and the Umayyad caliphs made it another province of their state.

A small group of Indian converts to Islam joined the Arab immigrants who settled in the Sind. The egalitarian nature of Islam proved attractive to those people at the bottom of the caste system.

The religion of Islam and Hinduism offered stark contrasts. Of all faiths, Islam is most insistent on the oneness of God, a concept altogether foreign to the tolerant polytheism of most Hindus and Buddhists. Muslims are strictly a people of the book, the Qur'an, which is considered the exact word of God. On the other hand, the brahmans emphasized oral tradition and the memorization of texts. Most importantly, Islam had no hierarchy, no castes, and a rigid simplicity in its worship, in great contrast to the colorful festivities and emotional aspects of Hindu bhakti.

Unlike all other invaders of India since the Aryans, the Hindus and Buddhists discovered that the Muslims were going to be assimilated only with great difficulty. They were in India to stay as a distinct religious group.

The Muslim rulers in the Sind, after first plundering the temples and smashing the images, which they considered idolatrous, assigned the Hindus and Buddhists the status of **dhimmis.** They were people who enjoyed the protection of Muslim rulers but paid a poll tax for that assurance.

After the initial attacks passed, the remaining Indian Hindus and Buddhists rebuilt their temples and monasteries. The Sind Muslims were content to remain in this region and at this time curtailed any spread of Islam to other parts of the country.

In the tenth century the population of India discovered what aggressive Islam meant. By this time, the Muslim world was ruled from Baghdad, and Persian culture dominated the Abbasid caliphs. The fighting spirit of the Arab warrior had given way to the comfortable ways of the bureaucrat, necessitating a search for new warriors to be the driving force of Islam. These were found among the Turkic peoples of Inner Asia who embraced Islam and the expansionist drive that once was its motivating force. Many of the Turks were slaves, young men purchased to become mercenaries in Muslim armies.

In A.D. 962 a Turkish chieftain with his soldiers seized the Afghan fortress of Ghazni. Once in power, further additions to his territories left a rich heritage for his successors. His grandson was Mahmud, known to the Indians who felt his wrath as the Sword of Islam.

Beginning in A.D. 1001 Mahmud began the first of his attacks on India. Before his death he had made 17 expeditions. One was more devastating than the next. The army of Mahmud of Ghazni plundered the Hindu and Buddhist shrines and then burned them to the ground, taking thousands of prisoners and slaughtering thousands more. The Rajputs were at a disadvantage because they preferred to fight on elephants. Against the swift horsemen of Mahmud, this strategy proved unavailing. Never before had India encountered such destruction.

Mahmud and his followers brought so much plunder, gold, silver, and precious stones back to Ghazni that this remote city of southern Afghanistan became one of the major cities of the Islamic world. Its court attracted two eminent scholars to live there in the eleventh century, Abu ar-Rayhn al-Biruni, the philosopher, doctor, and historian, as well as the Persian writer, Abu ol-Qasam Firdawsi, author of the *Shah-nameh* (Book of Kings), the national epic of ancient Persia down to the Muslim conquest.

For native Indians, especially those Hindus in Gujarat and the Punjab that bore the brunt of Mahmud's attacks, his invasions would never be forgotten. Survivors harbored an intense hatred for what had happened, especially Mahmud's placing the remnants of the images of their deities at the entrance of mosques so that they might be stepped on by every passerby.

Indian women of Gujarat dress in elaborate costumes.

For two other communities of India, this period was one of growth. A group of Mazdaists moved from their Persian homeland to Gujarat, where they took refuge in a Hindu kingdom. They became farmers and merchants and kept a low profile so as to accommodate themselves to the Indian way of life. Among the Indians they were known as Parsees.

Temples at Palitana are a favorite pilgrimage site for the Jains.

The Jains also prospered. Rich tradespeople financed the construction of a great white marble temple on Mt. Abu, a major destination for Jain pilgrims.

Conclusion

The Muslim invasion of India was the major event to take place during this period of Indian history. The Muslims in the Sind were fairly passive, but the Turks of Afghanistan were expansionists and anxious to make India their source of wealth. Their presence left an indelible mark on India.

CHAPTER 19 REVIEW
THE EARLY MIDDLE AGES IN INDIA

Summary
- Many foreign people immigrated into India after A.D. 500.
- The Rajputs set up small kingdoms in the Indus and Ganges Valleys.
- Hinduism experienced several developments leading to a more intimate and emotional attachment to the deities.
- Muslim invaders appeared in the Sind, the western part of India.
- In the tenth century a Turkish chieftain, Mahmud of Ghazni, led his armies from Afghanistan into India.
- Ghazni became a center of Muslim culture.

Identify
People: Xiong-nu; Harsha Vardhana; Rajputs; Mahmud of Ghazni; Abu ol-Qasam Firdawsi

Places: Sind; Ghazni; Mount Abu

Events: new invaders; the Rajputs come to India; Muslim armies cross into India

Define
puja	yoga	bhakti	Tantrism
dhimmis	shakti	Rajputs	

Multiple Choice
1. The brahmans were able to deal with the Huns and Rajputs by
   - (a) destroying them.
   - (b) isolating them.
   - (c) assimilating them.
   - (d) driving them from India.

2. Puja requires
   - (a) using incense.
   - (b) singing chants from the *Mahabharata*.
   - (c) bringing food to the deities.
   - (d) offering animal sacrifices.

3. Yoga is a form of devotion that requires
   - (a) controlled breathing and bodily posture.
   - (b) reading aloud from a sacred book.
   - (c) eating only foods previously offered to the deities.
   - (d) going on pilgrimage.

4. The first Muslims came into India's region known as
   - (a) Punjab.
   - (b) the Sind.
   - (c) Rajastan.
   - (d) the Deccan plateau.

5. Hindus thought of Mahmud of Ghazni as
   (a) the Scourge of God.
   (b) the Sword of Islam.
   (c) the Avenger.
   (d) the Hidden Imam.

6. The *Shah-nameh* is a book of
   (a) early Arab history.
   (b) Hindu songs.
   (c) Muslim quotations.
   (d) early Persian history.

Essay Questions
1. How did Hindus and Muslims interact in India during the Middle Ages?
2. What devotional practices within Hinduism demonstrate its flexibility?

Answers
1. c   4. b
2. c   5. b
3. a   6. d

East Asian Traditions

Chinese civilization from the year A.D. 500 onward included more people than any other world society. China's isolation from other civilizations continued to allow it to develop independently with little outside influence. Left alone, its people produced a distinct government, religion, and society.

Chinese culture extended to an area much larger than the country itself. Japan, Korea, Manchuria, Tibet, and Vietnam were at one time or another dependent on China. All these nations, with the exception of Vietnam, continue to use modified Chinese characters when people write. Furthermore, the art, architecture, and traditional family values found in these cultures are the result of Chinese influence.

China's climate and fertile land explain the large population of China. Although famine at times wiped out large numbers of people, the Chinese always recouped these losses because of their high birthrate.

China Under the Sui Dynasty

About the year A.D. 500, the future of China was not a promising one. The former greatness of the Han dynasty, when China was a rich and prosperous empire, was gone. Due to the ambition of local families and office holders, the central government's orders fell on deaf ears. In the north, nomad chieftains broke through the Great Wall in order to seize the territories of the Chinese. They forced the peasants under their control to grow grain for them and to serve in a conscripted labor corps.

Something similar was happening in Europe at exactly the same time. The old Roman Empire had broken into small fragments. German warrior chieftains now ruled in place of Roman civilian governors. Europe was divided in such a way that it still lacks the unity that Rome once provided. In China, however, imperial unity was restored. A strong personality, quite willing to use force against any rivals, could bring the Chinese back together. Europe was like Humpty Dumpty; after Rome fell Europe could not be put back together again. It lacked the strong cultural uniformity of China.

For several generations the nomads held power in the Chinese North. Eventually his lieutenants declared their commander, General Yang Jian, to be emperor. Yang took the title Emperor Wen, or Wendi. He was the first ruler of the Sui dynasty.

Emperor Wen's first task was to war against Turkish tribes that had settled within northern China. Then he moved southward, pushing out all the local leaders and their followers. Emperor Wen did not hesitate to burn cities that resisted and to kill their leaders. He wanted no one in China to have any doubt that a unified empire should be restored under a single Chinese ruler.

When the bloodshed ended, the exhausted Chinese found their new ruler an energetic person. He promoted land reform so that poor peasants might have their own farms. He restored the examination system for civil service candidates and ordered architects and builders to put up new public structures in Qangan, the capital. Emperor Wen issued a new and improved law code and introduced it into southern China.

Upon his death, his son Yangdi moved the capital to Lioyang. He wanted to prove that he could accomplish even more than his father. Therefore on his orders surveyors commenced plans for a great canal to link northern China with the south.

China's Grand Canal is, like its Great Wall, a tribute to those who built it. Under very difficult conditions men and women shoveled the earth and carried it away in wheelbarrows and baskets. They worked for 5 years, from A.D. 605 to 610, in labor battalions. When it was finished the canal traversed 900 miles, all the way from Beijing to Hangzhou on the coast.

Yangdi traveled the length of the canal on an imperial barge when it opened. It was four stories tall. The emperor, from his throne atop the barge, watched the farmers in the fields of southern China growing the rice that the people of Lioyang would eat in the winter time.

The canal and Yangdi's building program was not enough for the emperor. He wanted to restore Chinese influence over the Vietnamese, Turks, and Tibetans. Yangdi's armies marched out of China to bring these nations back under imperial control. The Koreans resisted his forces, wiping out the Chinese army sent against them. The loss of his army and the enormous expenses that Yangdi placed on his nation at last forced him from office. In A.D. 618 Yangdi died while fleeing to the south.

There were only two Sui emperors, but their impact on restoring Chinese unity was important. They prepared the way for a Golden Age, the dynasty of the Tang emperors.

Golden Age of the Tangs

This period in Chinese history lasted about 300 years, from A.D. 618 to 907. The Tang emperors are thought of so highly because they offered the Chinese people a long period of peace and prosperity. Most of all, they presented a period of stability to a people whose rulers during the Sui period had exhausted them in the pursuit of fame and conquests.

The first great ruler of the Tang was Emperor Taizong, whose name means great ancestor. For 23 years he wore the yellow silk robe that identified him as emperor. Taizong ruled over the largest amount of territory held by any other monarch in the world. No other ruler commanded so many servants or lived in such luxury.

Taizong moved the capital back to Qangan. Each day at his capital he met with the officials who carried out his orders. These officials formed a council that reported all that was happening in their offices so that the emperor could make his decisions. He also had hundreds of aides to assist him headed by a chancellor and six other major ministers. One was in charge of finances, another was responsible for public works, and a third was the war minister. In addition, the emperor appointed an official in

The Emperor Taizong wore the costume of the Chinese emperors.

charge of the ceremonies required of the emperor, a head judge, and a supervisor of the civil service.

The emperor's lands were divided into **prefectures,** or provinces. Governors were in charge of the prefectures because they had passed all the required examinations, proving that they were the most capable of all the candidates. The governors' major duties were to gather the taxes and provide internal security. Each also had to organize the labor battalions for public works. The Chinese followed the advice of Confucius that government depended more on good men holding office than upon the laws by which a country is ruled. The idea that government depends on law rather than the people who hold office is a legacy of the Romans.

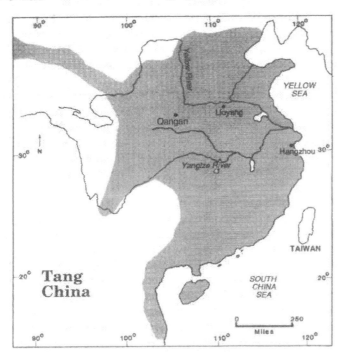

Emperor Taizong could not resist launching a few expeditions to bring him more territory. He certainly wanted to control the immensely profitable Silk Road. Therefore, Chinese forces moved against the Turks and Mongols who stood in the way and regained the Silk Road as far as the Caspian Sea. Taizong also overwhelmed the Koreans whom the Sui rulers had found so difficult. Tibet was linked to China by a royal marriage.

Taizong ruled during the same years as the Muslim expansion in Southwest Asia. As a result of the invasion of their country, Persian exiles sought refuge in China. They brought their religions, Mazdaism and Christianity, to Qangan where the emperor welcomed them. Even more welcome were the Persian horses and riders who could be put to use in Tang armies. The Persians also had a sport to teach the Chinese. This was polo, which the aristocrats of the court eagerly took up.

It had never happened before and it did not happen again, but for a few years at the close of the seventh century China had a woman ruler. This was the Empress Wu Zhao. Previously, some imperial wives were strong women and dominated their husbands. Wu's power began that way. Then in A.D. 690 she began to govern in her own name.

She started her rise to power as a woman in the harem of Emperor Taizong, but her beauty was such that everyone noticed her. When the emperor died, she and all the rest of the harem were shipped off to a Buddhist monastery. Her hair was cut off, and she began the life of a nun. One day the new emperor came to the monastery. He recognized her and took her as his wife. From that time forward Wu Zhao dominated the domestic and foreign affairs of China, a task she performed with skill. She made sure that the frontiers were safe and that China received the benefits of the silk trade. After her husband died, she dismissed the man appointed to become emperor and assumed the office herself.

During her rule, the empress showed great favoritism toward Buddhism. She found Confucius's teaching too narrow. Even though her predecessors were unhappy with Buddhist activities because so many Chinese enlisted in monasteries, Empress Wu was not. She found Buddhist teaching in line with the goals she had for China. She made it the official religion of the state.

In A.D. 705, when she was over 80 years old, a rebellion at court forced Wu Zhao from her throne. No one ever forgot her, however, for she had demonstrated that a woman could run the huge Chinese Empire.

For a while there was confusion over who would follow Wu Zhao on the throne. Then one more very capable ruler succeeded in gaining the imperial title. Xuanzong started a reign that lasted almost a half century.

The period of Xuanzong's rule, from A.D. 712 to 756, is considered the high point of the Tang dynasty. It deserves to be recalled in such a way because Xuanzong brought greater wealth to the country than ever before. He was a kind, tolerant man who loved books, music, and art. He welcomed new ideas and inventions and made Qangan the most beautiful city in eastern Asia.

At a time when many other cities of the world held fewer than 20,000 people, Qangan, the Chinese capital, had room for 2,000,000 people. It was built in the shape of a rectangle, 6 miles east to west, 5 miles north to south. Broad streets were laid out on a grid pattern. Several led to the two public markets that served the merchants bringing food and articles for sale to the capital. A canal allowed barges and ships to haul merchandise by water because the daily needs of the huge population of the capital were immense. In the far southeast a lake surrounded by gardens provided a place for enjoying leisure.

The western gate of Qangan admitted merchants and travellers into the city.

Most of the town was filled with apartments for housing its people. Religious buildings were also numerous, numbering 64 Buddhist monasteries for men and 27 for women, 16 Daoist monasteries, 4 Mazdaist temples, and a Christian church.

Built above the city and overlooking it was the Great Luminous Palace, the emperor's residence. It contained dozens of buildings housing the offices, archives, and headquarters of the emperor. No other governmental center in the world had a staff filled with so many educated civil servants.

Architecture and Arts

Architects of Tang China first developed the turned-up eaves on the edges of roofs that spread throughout East Asia as a sign of Chinese influence. Wood was the primary building material during the Tang period so the buildings constructed at that time, unfortunately, are no longer standing.

Houses of rich people had bathrooms with running water and fans to cool rooms in summer. Their homes, just as those of humble farmers, were built around a courtyard with an outside wall.

The Chinese value system, especially that promoted by Daoists, argued that nature was all important. To understand nature was to find serenity. Therefore, a painting of landscapes, showing pine-clad mountains and placid lakes, placed the viewer in the mood to appreciate a painter's work.

It took years of practice for a calligrapher or painter to develop a style considered artistic. The novice artist had to learn to perfect every detail. He copied earlier masters to learn how to hold the brush so that he could make fine, swift strokes that gave the painting its life. The final product had to be realistic and yet appeal to the personal impressions felt by the artist.

Choice of colors was important because each had a symbolic meaning. Artists used the primary colors of red, blue, and yellow to highlight their work. Some artists preferred to paint animals, which like landscapes, had a special charm for Tang aristocrats and the imperial court.

Sculptors worked in wood and stone with great skill. They made statues of the Buddha and fierce **Guardian Spirits** to protect the entrance of Buddhist temples. Artists also made statuettes of entertainers to be buried in tombs to accompany the deceased into the next life.

One of the Chinese artists' most advanced skills was making porcelain. Tang pottery became one of the most prized possessions of any well-off gentleman's family. Many potters specialized in shaping tea cups, for it was during the Tang dynasty that tea became China's national drink. Although the Chinese knew that tea leaves when brewed in water produced a pleasant drink, only after the seventh century was there enough grown to allow the Chinese to become a nation of tea drinkers. Some scholars believe that Chinese people lived longer because they boiled their water to make tea.

A lady of the Tang court is cast in porcelain.

Gardeners in Tang China were considered to be artists. They created the harmony found in a garden of flowers, shrubs, water, and rocks. The garden became a miniature painting of living plants. Chinese aristocrats found that they not only liked to view paintings and drink tea but to walk amid their camellias and magnolias, their ponds and weathered rocks at the end of a day.

Literature of the Tang Period

Many writers, especially poets, appeared in China after the seventh century. In translation their poems have made a major contribution to world literature. Two of the greatest poets were Li Bo and Du Fu. Li Bo enjoyed watching animals, while Du Fu was much more serious about his purpose in life after reaching old age.

> Li Bo's *Autumn Cove:*
> At Autumn Cove, so many white monkeys,
> bounding, leaping up like snowflakes in flight!
> They coax and pull their young ones down from the
> branches to drink and frolic with the water-borne moon.

Du Fu's *A Traveller at Night Writes His Thoughts:*
Delicate grasses, faint wind on the bank;
stark mast, a lone night boat:
stars hand down, over broad fields sweeping;
the moon boils up, on the great river flowing.
Fame—how can my writings win me that?
Office—age and sickness have brought it to an end.
Fluttering, fluttering—where is my likeness?
Sky and earth and one sandy gull.

Chinese literature included history, chronicles, fables, fairy tales, and songs. Certain themes ran through the literature. These included the love of a friend, the suffering of an exile, and a nostalgia for the past.

Even though works based on imagination were numerous, many Chinese scholars believed copying and commenting on the Confucian classics was much more rewarding. Boys studying to pass examinations had to memorize practically every detail of what was considered the ancient sage's writings. Why, asked government examiners, would anyone think they could improve on what Confucius wrote? Conservative Chinese believed that only Confucius's works had merit.

The costumes of wealthy Chinese men and women were quite elaborate in Tang times. People spent many hours arranging their hair and choosing their costume. Men's hair was worn long and tied or pinned in buns. Gauze caps stiffened with lacquer were placed on top of their hair. Silk robes covered their bodies.

Women dressed in long flowing gowns and many jewels. Their hair was swept to the back of their heads with tresses allowed to fall naturally in front of their ears. Gold crowns with pearls sat on top of their heads. They liberally applied cosmetics to their faces, with special concern given to eyebrows, shaped sometimes like mountains and other times like teardrops.

Astronomy and Inventions

During the Tang period there was an interest in discovery. Because the wise men of China believed that a person's fortune could be told in the movement of heavenly bodies, astronomy was the most important scientific study.

Chinese astronomers sought knowledge that would enable them to predict the future or give an answer to a problem. They were quick to seize on any extraordinary event in the heavens like an eclipse, the appearance of a new star (called a supernova today), or the passage of a comet to predict dire events. Emperors received reports of whether to expect a good day or a bad one. Probably it would be better to call the astronomers' study astrology rather than astronomy.

Because many officials at the court believed that knowledge of the stars gave people power, ordinary people were not allowed to study astronomy until the eighth century. A person might find him or herself under arrest for having any kind of astronomical instrument.

Astronomers provided the imperial court with an almanac to be sure that everyone knew when the New Year began. This was always a time of great celebration, a sign that new life had returned to the universe.

Several major inventions had their origins in Tang China. The most important of these was printing. It is impossible to know the exact year when a bright inventor got the idea to carve a wood block in the shape of a Chinese character. Apparently this happened early in the seventh century. He probably learned how to do it from watching people stamping textiles with patterns or from the custom of rubbing an engraved stone tablet so as to make an impression that could be read more easily. Whatever the case, the oldest existing printed book in the world is a scroll, *The Diamond Sutra*, written in A.D. 868.

The first books printed were the scriptures of Buddha. Soon a literature developed that included descriptions of the lives of Buddhist saints, almanacs, and dictionaries. An eager reading public awaited the printer's work, especially in the tenth century when Confucius's writings were first published.

It was fortunate that Chinese inventors had also come up with better ways to make paper on which books could be printed. Although paper-making existed as far back as the Han period in ancient China, making paper out of bark, hemp, or rags in large quantities only appeared in the eighth century. Tang papermakers enjoyed using stains in their products to make them more attractive.

Printing was a major step forward for the Chinese people. Soon books or scrolls became cheap enough that they spread all over China. Information could be stored and made available to millions instead of hundreds of people. The technique of printing expanded to other countries, but it did so slowly. Printing did not appear in Europe until 700 years later.

Several other inventions appeared in the Tang period. One was an iron bridge that was built over the Yellow River. A second was the compass. Gunpowder was also discovered in the seventh century. Court entertainers used it for fireworks displays.

Religion

The Tang era was dominated by Buddhism. Yet this was not one single faith. Different interpretations of the meaning attached to Buddha's teaching were common. Chinese monks went to India, often at great risk, to obtain the Sanskrit writings of Buddha. They translated them and then brought them back to China. The Emperor Taizong tried to slow down the growth of Buddhism, but little could be done given the hope for salvation that this religion gave to everyone who believed in it.

The Chinese interpreted Buddhism to make it fit their own view of life. One group, known as **Pure Land** Buddhists, promised that those who believed would reach the Pure Land in eternity where they would always be happy. Followers of **Qan** Buddhism were more inward looking. They believed people should find peace and harmony within themselves. When Qan Buddhism reached Japan, it became known as Zen.

In addition to the various forms of Buddhism, other religions could be found in China. Daoism, easily mixed with the beliefs of some groups of

Buddhists. Mazdaists and Christians existed in very small numbers. Muslims were more numerous. They appeared as traders in southern Chinese ports and converted some natives to Islam. In the ninth century a Tang emperor persecuted the members of all the religions brought into China from abroad except Buddhism.

Later Tang Emperors

Conversion of some Turks and Mongols to Islam and a defeat by a Muslim army on the banks of the Talas River in A.D. 751 presented a major setback to the Tang emperors. Much of this area, long under Chinese influence because the Silk Road passed through it, now became part of the Islamic world.

Soon afterward rebellion and civil war rolled over the countryside. The Tibetans, neighbors of the Chinese, took advantage of the weakness of the empire and occupied Qangan for a time. It seemed as if nothing went right for the later Tang rulers. Droughts alternated with floods to destroy the peasants' confidence in gaining anything from hard work. Officials sent out to collect taxes paid no attention to the emperors once they were far from the capital. The revenues coming to Qangan became less and less at a time when the emperor could not pay his army.

At a festival in the spring of A.D. 905, rebellious officers took the emperor's brothers and hanged them. The emperor could do nothing to save members of his own family. A year later the last Tang emperor resigned and later was put to death.

For the next 50 years there was chaos. Marauders pillaged Qangan and then burned it down. Once more China appeared on the point of collapse. Many a general declared that he was establishing a capital and intended to rule "forever," only to learn that an army of another commander was at the gate challenging his claim.

Song China

At last in A.D. 960, a general who was able to dominate all his rivals appeared. His descendants, in the Song dynasty, would rule parts of China until A.D. 1279. The Songs never had as much territory under their command as the Tangs. This was because just prior to their rule a group of people from the north, the Khitans, occupied the area south of the Great Wall. In order to keep these "barbarians" quiet, the Song emperors gave the Khitans gifts of silver and silk. To compound their problems, both Vietnam and Tibet broke away from China and established their independence.

In spite of the smaller size of the empire, the Songs had a magnificent capital at Kaifeng. The city proved to be a worthy successor to Qangan. It grew into a large metropolis holding nearly a million people. From all over the world, sometimes by caravan, other times on the excellent canal network, the goods of many nations poured into the Song capital. Merchants loaded their shops with groceries, leather, and metal goods. Kaifeng had dozens of restaurants for dining out, with specialities of every kind. Chinese cooking is one of the gifts of Song China to the rest of the world.

At the center of Kaifeng's life was the imperial palace. It was always a busy place because the emperor had to make every major decision. Messengers arrived daily at Kaifeng to inform him of events.

An artist has sketched the busy life of Kaifeng, the imperial capital of Song China.

The emperor's subjects depended on him to bring good weather and prosperity to the country; therefore, a good part of the day involved ceremonies to the gods. After he finished his religious duties, the emperor could spend the rest of the day hunting, practicing archery, or playing polo. In the evening actors, acrobats, and musicians entertained him.

Many women lived in the palace with the emperor. Every ruler kept many wives, who had to be very careful not to bother him. They could not appear in his presence unless requested. The emperor's many children were also kept out of sight unless he was in the mood to see them. Tutors instructed his sons, but his daughters were given little or no education. They were only instructed in how to dress beautifully and arrange their hair. Sometimes a princess might be sent off to a foreign country as part of a treaty with China. Women, especially those in the court, had little to say about how they should lead their lives.

When the emperor traveled, he was carried by porters in a chair. His officials had their chairs as well. Behind the court hundreds of donkey carts brought the baggage necessary for the imperial party. If making a journey on one of China's canals, hundreds of boats made a train behind the imperial barge.

Song emperors continued to wear a yellow silk robe tied at the waist. Its decoration was considered very important for the tailors who took on the task. The emperor's hat looked very much like the mortarboard that students wear at graduation ceremonies today.

Economic Activity in Song China

Agriculture in Song China provided a surplus of food that allowed its cities to grow. People lived longer because they ate more regularly. In the eleventh century a new kind of rice was brought to China from southern Vietnam. It grew so quickly that farmers could get two crops a year from the same field.

There was an important iron industry in Song times that employed several thousand people. Lumber production expanded as the need for houses and public buildings increased. Papermaking and silk-weaving were other important crafts. The army had to have harnesses for its horses and armaments for its soldiers.

Chinese silk continued to be the country's largest export to Europe and Southwest Asia.

Despite this progress in trade, Chinese currency was made only from copper rather than gold or silver. Each coin had a hole in it because many coins, tied together on a string, were needed to buy something. A thousand coins weighed up to 1.5 pounds and were difficult to carry around. So what happened? Merchants wrote how much they owed on a piece of paper. This could be exchanged at another destination by a relative or friend with whom they had made a deposit. These certificates were the world's first paper money.

Despite the profits that could be made from business, the Song aristocrats believed, as Confucius taught, that a gentleman should not be a merchant. A gentleman could serve as a government official, an army commander, a landowner, a poet, or a painter, but to buy and sell articles at a market was an embarrassment. The examination system that was required of candidates for offices in the empire reinforced the prejudice against private business.

For this reason, the imperial government of the Song period remained indifferent to the thriving merchant communities along the Chinese coast. Officials still thought tax revenue should come from the land, even when it did not always meet Kaifeng's needs.

Another way for the emperors to collect money was by holding monopolies on certain products. The emperor got all the profits from the sale of arms, salt, iron utensils, wine, leather, silk, and clay pottery. Although the monopoly of the emperor cost consumers, few were aware of it.

In the middle of the eleventh century, the emperors experienced a very difficult time making ends meet. The government was in debt, and tax revenues were low. Too many officials allowed the landowners, who might be relatives, to escape paying taxes. In A.D. 1069 Wang Anshih, a reforming emperor, announced the **New Policies.** He cut the number of soldiers in half to save money and raised the salaries of officials so that they would not take bribes. Wang sold grain cheaply from government warehouses and charged only 2% on loans. In this way, peasants could have enough to eat and pay off their loans from state banks; they would not need to borrow from individual lenders who charged high interest rates.

The New Policies program was not permanent. Too many landowners were outraged at the decline of their income. They saw to it that the emperor stopped interfering in the economy against their interests.

Cultural Life

The greatest invention of the Song period was an astronomical clock. An inventor, Su Song, took the 4 years from A.D. 1088 to 1092 to construct it in Kaifeng. This clock was run by water that fell into 36 scoops at a constant rate. When one scoop filled with water, it dropped, and the next empty scoop appeared. At the top of the clock, a sphere measured the motion of sun, moon, and planets.

With the exception of Kaifeng's great clock, the Song period was not as inventive as the Tang. However, there were several important accomplishments. The use of the compass for navigation became more widespread. Gunpowder was now used to propel arrows and thus ushered in the potential for weapons that were much more deadly.

Chinese women are shown at work processing silk, the country's major export.

The variety of books increased considerably in Song China. Literacy became more common, not only in the capitals of the provinces but also in the country homes of the Chinese aristocrats. The emperor's library at Kaifeng held 80,000 scrolls.

Official histories of the dynasties appeared in print. They were added to the dictionaries, almanacs, and encyclopedias that already delighted the reading public. Religious texts continued in high favor. At the end of the tenth century, 500,000 copies of Buddhist scriptures were in circulation.

The work of artists during the Song period showed a change in style and taste. The bright colors of the Tang period were replaced by black and white ink drawings, notable for their simplicity. The Song painters stressed composition. As the viewer looked at the scroll, the landscape "moved." Its mountains, trees, and rivers, the usual parts of traditional landscapes, were painted in such a way as to bring the viewer into the composition itself.

Chinese Influences Reach Japan

After the fifth century, Japan was increasingly drawn under the influence of China. At this time Buddhism appeared as a friendly rival to the national faith of Shinto.

Mt. Fuji has always been a symbol of the Japanese homeland.

Japanese indigenous religion is known as **Shinto,** which means the way of the gods. For the early Japanese everything had a spirit in it: mountains, trees, rivers, bridges, and even ordinary household objects. These spirits were the **kami.** To keep the kami contented, the Japanese people had to offer prayers and sacrifices. If the kami were unhappy, the harvest would fail, or the fish would not be brought up in the nets.

Shintoism was a religion that rejoiced in life. Everything about nature was considered good, yet evil existed as a result of doing something unclean. Therefore there was always great concern to avoid pollution. This could be a dead body, a sore on the skin, or a wound suffered in battle. Shinto priests could get rid of anything considered unclean through a purification ceremony.

Shinto shrines were very simple and plain. There were no images or pictures inside. Located in places of natural beauty, the buildings were made of wood and had thatched roofs.

The shrine to the sun goddess Amaterasu was at Ise, where the presence of the goddess was represented by an ancient mirror in a cabinet. Every 20 years the shrine at Ise was torn down, and a new one, built exactly like the old, was put up. Tradition allowed only the emperor and empress to enter the shrine.

The simplicity of the Ise shrine reflects the values of Shinto.

Introduction of Buddhism into Japan

In the middle of the sixth century, one of the Korean kingdoms was at war with another. Its ruler sent an embassy to Japan to ask the emperor for assistance. Monks were in the group and brought a gift, a statue of the Buddha, from the Korean king.

The Japanese court was uncertain about accepting the gift. It was decided by one group of court officials to have nothing to do with Buddhism, so the statue was thrown into a canal. The prime minister Iname, however, was very interested in Buddhism. Iname and his son and successor Umako prevailed, and Buddhism found a place in Japan. Shintoism, however, was not displaced. For the Japanese it was quite possible to be both a believer in Shinto and Buddhism.

Prime Minister Umako sent Japanese students to China to learn the teachings of Buddhism first hand. He ordered temples to be built and installed monks whose ritual chants and use of incense, gongs, and drums added color to Japanese religion. Buddhism was also attractive because of its speculative nature, for Shintoism lacked any theology.

One further step in bringing Buddhism to Japan occurred when Umako nominated Prince Shotoku Taishi to the imperial throne. Shotoku liked everything Chinese, including Buddhism and Confucianism. During the years he ruled, from A.D. 593 to 622, Emperor Shotoku encouraged Buddhism in every possible way, from building temples to copying Buddhist scriptures. Shotoku issued a decree of 17 articles that introduced Confucianist principles into imperial administration.

Many aristocrats, following the lead of the court, were anxious to show their support for Buddhism. They offered funds for temples and monasteries. One of them, the Golden Hall of the Honji Monastery, still stands on the Yamato Plain.

Zen, one of the more mystical sides of Buddhism, confirmed the Japanese love for beauty in a small place. A carefully tended garden was a place that was bound to inspire inward thought for Zen Buddhists. The garden was constructed of rocks, sand, and water ponds with plants such as mosses, chrysanthemums, and azaleas placed in just the right spot. The garden became the universe with mountains, rivers, forests, and oceans, all in miniature. To the viewer the garden opened a door to his or her own universe within.

Buddhist temples are always situated in places of natural beauty.

The Great Reform

For a long time China was the model for all East Asian societies. The large number of its people, the size of its cities, and the organization of its government had a profound impact on all neighboring peoples.

In the seventh century Emperor Kotoku, under the influence of a Fujiwara prime minister, summoned the nobles to announce a series of changes he was going to make. One change involved putting all the land of the country under the control of the emperor. As in China, officials, who were appointees of the emperor, were to govern the country. The landowners might also become court officials because "Under the heavens there is no land that is not the king's land. Among holders of land there is none that is not the king's vassal." This centralization of authority is known as the **Great Reform**.

Clan chieftains were assigned ranks that allowed them to wear special clothes and serve at certain ceremonies. Men in the top five ranks were free from all taxation. In this arrangement the Chinese model was followed, but, unlike China, every official held his position because of his ancestry. State offices were passed from father to son. As so often happened in world history, a small group in society lived very well, while the mass of people worked to support them.

Building the Capital at Nara

Before the Great Reform, and several decades afterward, no cities were large enough to become a capital. When Japanese travelers returned from China, they insisted that, to be a true nation, Japan needed a capital. Therefore, in A.D. 710 a site at Nara, not very far from where the emperor lived on the Yamato Plain, was chosen for the honor.

By this time, Buddhist monks and monasteries were all over the Yamato Plain. The new capital gave them a chance to move into the city where wealthy officials gave the funds needed for the construction, decoration, and maintenance of temples. Images of Buddha multiplied because each monastery sought to have a more striking statue than its neighbor. Ordinary Japanese still preferred Shinto, the national religion, but at the court only Buddhism would do.

Nara also became a center for libraries that held books and scrolls of the Chinese classics. Japanese poets wrote their verses in Chinese because this was considered proper. The large number of Buddhist monks, some of whom had political ambitions, began to irritate government officials.

While Emperor Kammu ruled, the court made the decision that Nara had too many monasteries and too many monks. He sought and received permission from the Fujiwara prime minister to leave the town. In a new capital he intended to place a strict limit on how many monks could settle there.

Heian Japan, A World at Peace

In A.D. 794 Emperor Kammu found the place he wanted for his city. He called his new capital Heian-Kyo, or the capital of peace and tranquility. For a long time it lived up to its name. Today it is the city of Kyoto, or the capital.

The founding of the Heian capital meant that there was now less dependence on Chinese models, as well as Buddhism, which, after all, was a Chinese import. For the first time daring poets composed in Japanese.

The first few centuries in Heian-Kyo were very pleasant. The emperor was surrounded by courtiers and aristocrats who had little to do except enjoy themselves. People spoke of themselves as dwellers among the clouds. Emperors had only one responsibility: to father children to be sure that the dynasty continued. There was such security that a thin wall around Heian soon collapsed, and no one thought to rebuild it.

This life of ease is portrayed in the literature of the time. Much of it was written by women authors who were allowed to use a simplified Japanese script. Men were required to write in Chinese. Women authors composed letters, diaries, poems, and, most important of all, novels.

The world's first novel was produced in the eleventh century by a Japanese woman, Lady Murasaki Shikubu. Her story is called *The Tale of Genji*. It tells of the events of Prince Genji's life, principally the times he fell in love with the beautiful women of Heian-Kyo. It became the great classic of Japan, similar to the Greek works of Homer.

The society of Heian-Kyo was deeply concerned about how to make life more beautiful. Much attention was given on how to fold a letter or what perfume should be used. Aristocratic women talked to men while hidden behind a curtain seated on a cushioned platform, the **kicho.**

The palace of Heian-Kyo was the residence of the Japanese emperors.

Fashion experts dictated the costume of the people. Men wore short beards and hats that looked like a quail's head. Both women and men put white powder on their faces. Women shaved off their eyebrows and then painted others on, much larger and higher on the forehead; they allowed their hair to grow as long as possible. One aspect of Heian beauty seems very strange. People thought having white teeth was vulgar, so they painted them black.

In this atmosphere of elegance, it is a wonder that any business got done. Government officials under Fujiwara direction did carry on in the emperor's name, doing everything they could to support the way of life enjoyed by the Heian aristocrats. As the years passed, this became more difficult.

A pagoda of Heian-Kyo was constructed to hold relics and images of the Buddha. The origin of the pagoda was in India where it covered the burial mounds of Buddhists.

In the countryside a class of tough clan chieftains used official indifference to build support for themselves. They had no use for the soft life of the capital. Frequently they sent imperial tax collectors back to the capital without their mission accomplished. Instead of an army coming to punish them, their lack of cooperation was ignored in Heian-Kyo. The days of quiet living in the capital were approaching an end.

Asian Neighbors of China

The three kingdoms of Korea lived in uneasy proximity until the Tang emperors of China intervened in the peninsula. The Korean kingdom of Silla led the defense against the Chinese. The military aristocrats who organized the Korean armies had no intention of accepting direct rule over Silla, and as long as tribute to the Tang emperors was forthcoming, Korea kept its independence. This was an age of fine pottery making in Korea, and artistic creativity flourished.

The major event in the history of Vietnam during these years was a continuous migration from the Red River valley southward. Vietnamese people continued to move for every effort was made to keep free of Chinese political control.

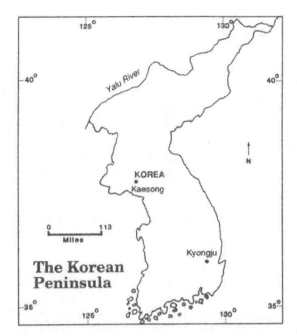

The Korean Peninsula

About A.D. 800, the Burmese people first enter history in what is now their homeland, displacing the original inhabitants. These tribal people could not be assimilated, with the result that they kept their own culture. The Burmese established their capital at Pagan, in the Irrawaddy Valley. Here they came under the influence of the Indian Buddhists, linking them to their western neighbors.

The people who have left the region's most lasting monument were the Khmers. The king of the Khmers, Yasovarman I, in the late ninth century planned a new capital, which was to be the largest in Southeast Asia. He assembled thousands of workers, on a scale matching the pharaohs of Egypt, to work on his project, the city of Angkor Thom.

Conclusion

After its sixth century reunification, China entered a golden age under the Tang and Song emperors. It became the state with not only the largest number of people but also its richest. The inventions of these times still affect the world. Japan also witnessed major events in its development as a people under Chinese influence, by adapting what its large neighbor offered to its own culture.

CHAPTER 20 REVIEW
EAST ASIAN TRADITIONS

Summary
- Each dynasty of China in the Middle Ages had its own distinctive characteristics.
- The Sui dynasty reunified China after a period of regional kingdoms.
- The Tang dynasty is considered China's Golden Age, noted for its arts, literature, and inventions.
- Buddhism continued its progress in Tang China.
- The Song dynasty replaced the Tang, its capital at Kaifeng.
- Buddhism entered Japan.
- Japanese capitals were at Nara and Heian-Kyo.
- Southeast Asia was shared among Vietnamese, Khmers, and Burmese.

Identify
People: Wendi; Yangdi; Taizong; Wu Zhao; Xuanzong; Daoists; Vietnamese; Wang Anshih; Su Song; Khmers; Shotoku Taishi; Murasaki Shikubu
Places: Lioyang; Hangzhou; Qangan; Kaifeng; Nara; Pagan; Heian-Kyo
Events: building the Grand Canal; artistic accomplishments of the Tang period; printing the first books; arrival of Buddhism in Japan

Define

prefectures	Pure Land	kicho
Guardian Spirits	New Policies	kami
The Diamond Sutra	The Great Reform	
Shinto	Qan Buddhism	

Multiple Choice

1. One major reason for the distinctive culture of China was
   (a) its government.
   (b) its isolation from other civilizations.
   (c) its geography.
   (d) its acceptance of Buddhism.

2. Besides the Chinese, other people who have adopted a writing system with characters, rather than an alphabet are
   (a) the Japanese.
   (b) the Koreans.
   (c) the Tibetans.
   (d) all the above.

3. The large Chinese population can be attributed to the country's
   (a) imperial government.
   (b) access to the Pacific Ocean.
   (c) low birth rate.
   (d) climate and fertile soil.

4. The recovery of Chinese unity in the sixth century A.D. was due to the policies of the Sui emperor
   (a) Wendi.
   (b) Taizong.
   (c) Wang Mang.
   (d) Wu Zhao.

5. China's Grand Canal ran from
   (a) Beijing to Kaifeng.
   (b) Kaifeng to Hangzhou.
   (c) Qangan to Anyang.
   (d) Beijing to Hangzhou.

6. The title of the Chinese emperor was
   (a) first citizen.
   (b) son of heaven.
   (c) king of kings.
   (d) universal ruler.

7. The most important Tang ruler was
   (a) Wendi.
   (b) Yangdi.
   (c) Wang Mang.
   (d) Taizong.

8. Confucius taught that good government principally depended on
   (a) law.
   (b) who held office.
   (c) who directed religious policies.
   (d) God.

9. China's famous empress during Tang times was
   (a) Wu Zhao.
   (b) Lu Wang.
   (c) Xing Lain.
   (d) Wu Di.

10. The importance of Qangan came from its
    (a) economic activity.
    (b) position as China's capital in Tang times.
    (c) location on the Yangtze River.
    (d) role as the Chinese capital under the Mongols.

11. The New Policies of Wang Anshih were meant to aid
    (a) the imperial court.
    (b) peasant farmers.
    (c) merchants.
    (d) landowners.

12. In order to know the future, the Chinese studied
    (a) tea leaves.
    (b) the flight of birds.
    (c) astronomy.
    (d) geology.

13. The *Diamond Sutra* is
    (a) a jewel.
    (b) a prayer.
    (c) the imperial crown.
    (d) the world's oldest known printed book.

14. The Chinese were the first to use
    (a) paper.
    (b) forks.
    (c) concrete.
    (d) wood.

15. Chinese coins were always made of
    (a) gold.
    (b) silver.
    (c) bronze.
    (d) none of the above.

16. In Shinto, evil is considered to be
    (a) the result of ignorance.
    (b) a failure of will.
    (c) believing in another religion.
    (d) doing something which makes a person unclean.

17. This emperor was anxious to bring Buddhism into Japan:
    (a) Jimmu Tenno.
    (b) Kotoku.
    (c) Hirohito.
    (d) Shotoku Taishi.

18. Japanese Buddhism promoted
    (a) a single religion.
    (b) many sects.
    (c) only two sects.
    (d) conflicts between Shinto and Buddhism.

19. The Great Reform in Japan referred to
    (a) centralization of imperial power.
    (b) redistribution of land.
    (c) changing the imperial dynasty.
    (d) changing the prime ministers.

20. Women authors first appeared in Japan during
    (a) the Great Reform.
    (b) the eighth century.
    (c) Heian Japan.
    (d) the ninth century.

Essay Questions
1. How does the early history of Japan differ from that of China?
2. From the two poems in this chapter, what can you learn of Chinese values?
3. What accounted for Buddhism's acceptance in Japan?
4. Contrast the world of Nara in Japan with Kaifeng in China.

Answers

1. b	6. b	11. b	16. d
2. d	7. d	12. c	17. d
3. d	8. b	13. d	18. b
4. a	9. a	14. a	19. a
5. d	10. b	15. d	20. c

CHAPTER 21

African Kingdoms

The arrival of Islam in Egypt and North Africa in the seventh century changed the course of this region in a dramatic way. The Byzantine rule of these areas quickly perished as resistance to the energetic forces of Islam swept it away. The Muslims of northern Africa then turned their attention south of the Sahara for trade, and at one of its centers the first western African state was born.

Muslims in Egypt

After conquering Syria and Palestine, the Arab general Amr Ibn al-As sought permission from the caliph to lead an army into Egypt. Knowing how well the Byzantines fortified the country, the campaign was considered risky. Nevertheless, the caliph agreed, and in A.D. 640 Ibn al-As marched into Egypt, putting the fortress of Babylon, close to ancient Memphis, under siege. When it fell, Ibn al-As turned toward Alexandria.

Cyrus, the pope of Alexandria, in charge of the city's defense, agreed to turn the city over to the Arabs without a fight. He apparently thought his surrender would allow him a kingship under the Arabs. The Byzantine army evacuated the city, and the Arabs took it over. They were dazzled by its wealth and rich palaces.

Because Alexandria's riches could well have sapped the fighting spirit of the Muslims, Ibn al-As set up a military camp outside Babylon, at al-Fustat. Here he commissioned the building of Egypt's first mosque. His successors laid plans to move farther west at Byzantine expense. Tripoli, Carthage, and then Tangier fell to the Arabs and opened the door to Bedouin migration from the Arabian peninsula.

The Umayyad caliphs ruled when the conquests occurred, and the Abbasids governed when the task of preserving the territories arose. This responsibility was more than they could handle. First, a state based on Fez in Morocco broke free. Next, the area of modern Tunisia, the Arab Ifriquiya, was transferred to an independent dynasty. Finally a Turkish soldier-of-fortune took Egypt out of Abbasid rule.

The most successful leader of revolutionaries to proclaim independence from Baghdad was Abu Abdallah al-Shi'i. Beginning in Yemen, this leader represented an Isma'ili party of Shi'ites. Moving to North Africa, in A.D. 909 he announced the discovery of the Hidden Imam, whom all Shi'ites awaited. The Hidden Imam, a supposed descendant of Muhammad's daughter, Fatimah, gave the name **Fatimid** to his dynasty.

In A.D. 969, after Fatimid armies captured Egypt, the Fatimid caliph, al-Mu'izz, created a new capital in Egypt, calling it al-Kahira, the victorious, a city westerners recognize as Cairo. In his new capital he founded a school, **al-Azhar,** which remains to this day preeminent in all Muslim studies.

During the days of Fatimid rule, Egypt again prospered under a succession of tolerant and able caliphs. The palace of the caliphs was as opulent as that of the Abbasid caliph of Baghdad. Coptic Christians, for a time, served on an equal basis in the government of Cairo.

A dramatic change then occurred in A.D. 996, when Abu Ali al-Mansur al-Hakim assumed the caliphate. Possibly insane, he ordered all the dogs of Cairo killed, shops to open only at night, and women not to leave their houses. Contrary to Islamic law, he ordered the destruction of churches and synagogues and on the list was the church of the Holy Sepulchre in Jerusalem.

Two Isma'ili teachers convinced al-Hakim that he had a divine spirit in him. When this was proclaimed, riots broke out in Cairo. One of the Isma'ili scholars fled to Mt. Lebanon, where his followers, the Druzes, still remain to this day. Al-Hakim later disappeared while on a journey outside the capital.

The Fatimids were now troubled by the rise of the Seljuk Turks, who contested Jerusalem with them. The Fatimids were in charge of the city at the time the Crusaders approached Jerusalem in A.D. 1095.

South of the Sahara

At the beginning of this period the Axumites of Ethiopia were the only people below the Sahara Desert to have writing. Africans memorized their history and often sang about their great heroes of the past at festivals.

Written records about the people in West Africa only start when Arab travelers journeyed into the region in the eighth century. For those places the Arabs did not reach, information appears much later, sometimes as late as the nineteenth century.

African history can best be studied by looking at one region at a time. During the years from the sixth through the tenth centuries, several cultural areas appeared: the northern sahel, Guinea or the coast of western Africa, Ethiopia, East Africa, and South Africa. There were no "Middle Ages" in Africa as there were in Europe. A better division of the African past is to follow the continent's history from before and after Islam and then to look at the period of European contact.

Ghana, The First West African Kingdom

Ghana was the oldest of West African kingdoms. (It should not be confused with the modern state of the same name. Today's Ghana is located far from the original kingdom.) Ghana was probably the title of the ruler of this state who gave his name to the nation, much like the Inca of Peru.

The origins of Ghana may be traced back to the introduction of the Arabian camel to North Africa, some time about A.D. 200. The dromedary made it possible for Berber traders to cross the desert again. Many Berbers abandoned farming or sheep herding to take up a life of raising camels on

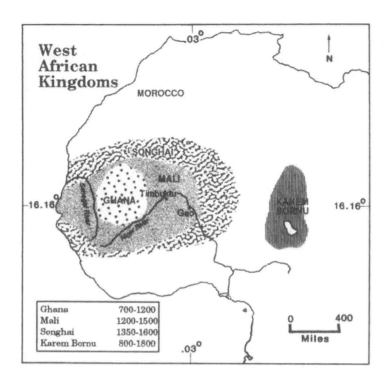

West African Kingdoms

MOROCCO

SONGHAI

MALI

GHANA

Timbuktu

Gao

KANEM BORNU

N

Ghana	700-1200
Mali	1200-1500
Songhai	1350-1600
Karem Bornu	800-1800

0   400
Miles

the steppes bordering the desert. Soon they began outfitting caravans to travel to the south, the region of the **sahel.**

By A.D. 500 the Berbers that were engaged in the commerce of the Sahara were the Tuareg. After the Islamic invasion of North Africa, the Tuareg, nominal Christians, converted to a sect of Islam.

The Tuareg caravans brought salt to the black people of the sahel. The Tuareg controlled the oases and the salt pans where the salt was manufactured in Morocco. One way to get it was to dig holes in the earth that had a high salt content. The holes were filled with water which, when it evaporated, left rims of salt. When this process was done often enough, blocks of salt formed. These blocks were then loaded on camels to be taken to the south, making the **salt trade** very lucrative.

African women tend the pools that produce salt.

After unloading their salt and other products, like metals, cloth, and swords, the camels were reloaded with products of the sahel—gold, ivory, kola nuts, and animal hides. The Berbers also took slaves with them back to the Mediterranean for sale as domestic servants.

There were several major routes across the Sahara. Some began in Morocco; others started in Algeria or Ifriqiya. Caravans tried to follow the same routes because sand storms that lasted for days could cause them to lose their way. Tuareg tribesmen patrolled the routes, charging considerable tolls for their protection. The important caravan stations in Morocco were at Sijilmasa and Tahret.

On the south side of the Sahara, the caravans unloaded their wares at marketplaces in the sahel. As in other world societies, a political organization was needed to police a trading center once it became a market.

At some centers the exchange of salt for forest products was done without speaking a word. The Tuareg piled the salt on the ground. Then Negro merchants from the forest regions placed a quantity of goods nearby. If the Tuareg were not satisfied, they took away some of the salt. At last a silent bargain was struck that satisfied both parties.

No one knows exactly when Ghana became a city and then an empire. It lay at the end of the caravan route that passed through the region of the Upper Niger and Senegal Rivers. Ghana's capital, now destroyed, was within the boundaries of modern Mauritania.

The people who formed the empire of Ghana at first were possibly a colony of Tuareg who settled there. In a short time the Negro peoples, the Soninke, absorbed the Tuareg and provided the leadership in the Sahara trade. From among their prominent chieftains, they chose a king.

Ghana's kings grew wealthy because they controlled the production of gold and put a heavy tax on commodities that were brought to their capital for export. Their area of control increased or declined depending on the strength of their armies. Sometimes they raided other people to get slaves or gold to sell to the Tuareg.

Al-Bahri, an Arab traveler from Spain, visited Ghana in the eleventh century. In his report he wrote of Ghana's wealth and its king whose army numbered 200,000 men. While his count was an exaggeration, his report shows the impression that Ghana made on travelers.

Al-Bahri described the Ghanian capital saying that it was actually two towns. In one lived Muslim merchants with 12 mosques and schools established for the study of the Qur'an. The king of Ghana's castle was 6 miles away "with a number of dome-shaped dwellings, the whole surrounded by an enclosure like the defensive wall of a city."

The wealth of Ghana became so well known that in A.D. 1076 the Almoravids, a fanatical sect of Moroccan Berbers, attacked Ghana and destroyed it after robbing its wealth. Ibn Khaldun, another Arab traveler, gives this account of Ghana's last days:

> [The Almoravids] spread their dominion over the Negroes, devastated their territory and plundered their property. Having submitted them to poll-tax, they imposed on them a tribute and compelled a great number of them to become Muslims.

Axum

Axum, the first African state south of the Sahara to become Christian, was very dependent on the leadership of the Coptic church of Alexandria. The head of their church traveled to Alexandria to receive his consecration as bishop. Later the pope of the Coptic church sent one of his own bishops to Axum, when a vacancy occurred. Egypt supplied many of the books and ceremonies that were a part of Axumite Christianity. In the fifth century, when the Egyptian church broke with the Greek and Latin churches over a matter of doctrine, the Axumites, now better known as Ethiopians, followed along.

The Ethiopian church remained closely tied to the political life of the country. Christianity was promoted by the kings since it helped them to unite their people to the throne. Among the Ethiopians there was a great interest in monasticism. On islands in the lake country and on remote mountain sides, Ethiopian monks sought to find God. The monks inspired the people to do the same.

An Ethiopian bishop carries a cross he uses for blessings.

When the Muslims conquered Egypt in the seventh century, the Islamic armies did not go farther than the first cataract of the Nile. Here, in Nubia, there was another Christian kingdom, and it was agreed between Muslims and Christians that they would respect each other's borders. Nubia promised to supply gold and slaves to Egypt, and Egypt would export horses and cloth to Nubia. Peace between Ethiopia and the Muslims of Egypt was also guaranteed.

Each year thousands of Ethiopian pilgrims trekked through Egypt to worship in Jerusalem. The truce with the Muslim Egyptians also allowed the Ethiopians to continue to control the traffic of the Red Sea.

Not much is known of Ethiopia during these years. The country was too isolated from the Mediterranean world for news to get in or get out of the country. The Sudd, a vast swamp on the upper Nile, made communication almost impossible. More native customs appeared in worship, which gave Ethiopian Christianity a unique character.

Conclusion

African cultures were remarkably diverse, from the Muslim North and Egypt to the continent's southern tip where hunters and gatherers still followed a very satisfactory way of life. The introduction of the dromedary once more opened the Sahara to trade and, with it, allowed the founding of Ghana, the first western African kingdom. Ethiopia produced a unique form of the Christian religion in eastern Africa that was remarkably vital, despite its isolation.

CHAPTER 21 REVIEW
AFRICAN KINGDOMS

Summary
- The Muslims came to Egypt, taking it away from the Byzantine ruler.
- The Fatimid caliphs, a Shi'ite group, built a capital at Cairo.
- Ghana was the first western African kingdom, growing out of a trading center on the sahel.
- Axum continued its close relationship with Alexandria in Egypt.

Identify
People: Amr Ibn al-As; Abu Abdallah al-Shi'i; Tuareg; Abu Ali al-Hakim; Almoravids
Places: Babylon in Egypt; Tangier; Infriquiya; Ghana
Events: Arab conquest of Egypt; founding of Ghana; the Fatimids building Cairo

Define

Fatimids   al-Azhar   salt trade   Druzes

Multiple Choice
1. Amr Ibn al-As, after his conquest of Egypt, placed his soldiers in
   (a) Alexandria.
   (b) Suez.
   (c) Babylon.
   (d) the military camp of al-Fustat.

2. The great Muslim university of Cairo is
   (a) the al-Bakkri.
   (b) the al-Azhar.
   (c) the Jebal Tariq.
   (d) the al-Bazzar.

3. The first West African kingdoms arose in
   (a) the sahel.
   (b) the rain forest.
   (c) the savannahs.
   (d) the Sudan.

4. The Tuareg were
   (a) people of the rain forest.
   (b) traders of the desert.
   (c) explorers of the eastern coast of Africa.
   (d) explorers of the western coast of Africa.

5. The major commodity needed by Africans south of the Sahara was
   (a) ivory.
   (b) iron.
   (c) bronze.
   (d) salt.

6. The wealth of Ghana's kings came from
    (a) iron mines.
    (b) gold mines.
    (c) copper mines.
    (d) horses.

Essay Questions
   1. Discuss the importance of the Fatimids to Egyptian history.
   2. Explain the importance of the dromedary to African trade.
   3. Discuss the relationship between North Africa and Ghana.

Answers
1. d   4. b
2. b   5. d
3. a   6. b

The Early Middle Ages in Europe

The Early Middle Ages is that period of European history from the sixth century to the reign of Charlemagne. A number of Germanic kingdoms occupied western Europe during this era. Much of what had been Roman and Christian civilization was taken over by the Germans, but they added new elements of their own.

In eastern Europe south of the Danube, the situation was very different. At the beginning of the sixth century, town life and economic prosperity continued to function. A Roman emperor still lived in Constantinople, the richest city in Europe.

Byzantine World

It is difficult to know exactly when the Late Roman Empire became the Byzantine Empire. It is simply convenient to speak of this time as the Byzantine Empire so that it will not be confused with other periods of Roman history. It must be remembered that the Byzantines, even though nearly everyone spoke Greek, still called themselves Romans as long as the empire lasted.

At the core of the Byzantine Empire were the Greek people, who were a majority in Constantinople, in the southern Balkans, on the Aegean Islands, and the island of Cyprus. Other Greek communities were scattered throughout all the major cities of the eastern Mediterranean. They were very proud of their language, which all educated people in the eastern Mediterranean read and spoke. Their skills in administration gave them access to the major positions of influence in both the church and government.

The empire may have contained many different people, but they all looked to Constantinople as long as it provided good government. For the Greeks loyalty to the emperors came easy. But Armenians, Syrians, and Egyptians, the other three large populations of the empire, resented Constantinople's high taxation, haughty governors, and demands for religious conformity.

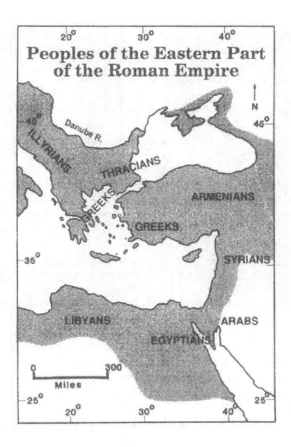

Peoples of the Eastern Part of the Roman Empire

Justinian and Theodora

In A.D. 527 two very able people ruled the Byzantine world, Emperor Justinian and Empress Theodora. Their rule is considered to be the most notable in Byzantine history. Living in a magnificent palace overlooking the Bosporus Straits, they employed thousands of household servants, civil officials, army personnel, and churchmen to carry out their wishes.

Justinian had come to office because he was the nephew of the previous emperor. He married Theodora against the wishes of many at the court, for she was not an aristocrat and once was an actress in the circus. Both Justinian and Theodora were extremely ambitious and looked to recreate the imperial past of Rome's days of glory. This plan demanded that they win back the lands that had been lost to the Germans a century earlier. A second goal was to make the administration in Constantinople more efficient.

Justinian first took on the task of reforming the Roman law. The Romans always boasted of their legal system, but over the centuries so many imperial decrees and edicts accumulated that judges could no longer chart a course through them. Someone needed to sort things out. Therefore Justinian appointed a jurist friend to lead a committee to go through all the laws, put them in order, and get rid of those that were obsolete or contradictory.

A mosaic in Ravenna pictures Emperor Justinian and his court presenting the bread for the Liturgy to Archbishop Maximianus.

By A.D. 529 the committee finished its work and issued a new code. Later it provided a commentary on the code that was called the *Digest*. Finally the committee put together a handbook for law students, the *Institutes*. When the **Code of Justinian,** the *Digest,* and the *Institutes* were put together, supplemented by Justinian's own decrees, the collection became the official law of the Empire.

As long as the empire lasted, the Code of Justinian was the basis of Byzantine law. Eventually the Code also passed into western Europe to provide the legal structure for continental states in the Middle Ages.

In order to pursue the dream of a reconstructed empire, Justinian first had to make sure that the Persians would be quiet on his eastern frontier. He told his general in the East to make peace with the Persian king, Khosrow I, so that the army could move to the west. The Persians agreed to an "endless peace," and Justinian pursued his plan to win back the former Byzantine provinces.

The first Byzantine offensive struck the Vandal kingdom of North Africa. The Vandals collapsed, and Justinian once more ruled here. The Vandal king was returned in chains to Constantinople to be paraded through the town in the emperor's triumph.

The next part of Justinian's plan was to attack Italy. There were no easy victories here, for the Ostrogoths who ruled the peninsula had not let their swords go rusty. It was a long and difficult campaign that stretched over years, not months. Eventually Rome and then Ravenna, where the Ostrogothic king kept his residence, fell to the Byzantine forces. Elsewhere Justinian's army regained parts of Spain from the Visigoths and several of the larger Mediterranean islands.

This was as far as the Byzantine army was ever to go. Its strength was exhausted. The Persians, learning of its overextension, did not let the opportunity pass to make trouble again in the east. The Persian army captured Antioch, the largest city of Syria, and looted it.

In addition to this setback, disease took a heavy toll on the population. A terrible plague struck the empire causing a severe loss of life. It continued to come back afterward with discouraging regularity. Towns were emptied, farms abandoned, and government revenues disappeared in the stricken regions.

Justinian and Theodora hoped to win back the old Roman world, but they failed. Certain territories of the West were regained, but at a very high price. The emperor and empress had consumed much of the empire's wealth and manpower but had little to show for all the effort. For the men and women of Italy, it took centuries to recover from the war between the Byzantines and Ostrogoths.

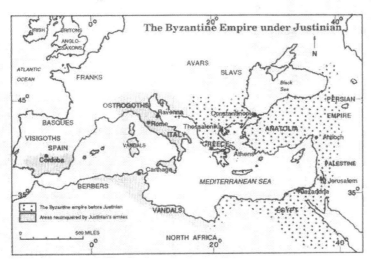

A much more lasting monument to the two rulers, in addition to the Code, was the many great buildings erected on imperial orders throughout the Byzantine world. After a city riot destroyed much of Constantinople, the ground was cleared for several new churches. One was the Church of the Holy Peace; another was Constantinople's cathedral, the **Church of the Holy Wisdom**. Both buildings still stand in downtown Istanbul.

For the following six centuries the Church of the Holy Wisdom was the largest building in Europe. Its length was 270 feet, its width 240 feet, and its great round dome 180 feet high. The interior was covered with rich marble and mosaics. Thousands of oil lamps hung from the ceiling casting light and shadow reflections. Visitors to the capital were in awe at the sight.

The Church of the Holy Wisdom (Hagia Sophia) was the cathedral of Constantinople in Justinian's day. The Ottomans added the minarets when the building became a mosque.

In Italy Ravenna had three great churches that testified to the imperial reconquest. They were begun while the Ostrogoths still ruled, but Justinian's artists completed the design. One, San Vitale, contains two famous mosaics of the emperor and empress, which have greeted visitors to the church for the past 1,400 years. The Ravenna churches are the best examples of the architecture and art of the sixth century in the West.

One of Ravenna's churches of the sixth century demonstrates the importance of the city as the residence of the Byzantine governor of Italy.

Upon Justinian's death, imperial fortunes declined in a serious way. The emperor's constant wars and his immense building program bankrupted the treasury. There was little money left to squeeze out of the taxpayers of the empire. Within a decade most of the gains made in Italy were lost when a new Germanic people, the Lombards, entered the peninsula. By A.D. 600 Spain was abandoned once more to the Visigoths.

Struggle Over the Balkans

In the late sixth century attacks mounted on the Danube frontier became more intense. The Avars, fierce horsemen from Inner Asia, swept into Europe and across the Danube. They were Turkic nomads who had little appreciation of the civilized ways of the Byzantine population. The Avars learned that plundering people was more profitable than herding animals.

In the wake of the Avars came Slavic-speaking people from eastern Europe, farmers who occupied the wasted land after the Avars passed over it. The largest city of the Balkans, Thessaloniki, filled with refugees. One of the Byzantine emperors invited the Serbs and Croatians to settle in the Balkans as allies of Constantinople. They agreed to accept the offer and what once was the Roman province of Illyricum became the land of the South Slavs.

In the eastern Balkans the mixed population of Dacia took refuge in the mountains nearby to avoid the Avar and Slavic invaders. They went into hiding for a full 500 years, reappearing as the Romanians. Another Balkan people, the Albanians, also disappeared into the mountains to avoid the harshness of Avar rule.

The Balkan invasions did not conclude until late in the seventh century when another people, the Bulgarians, immigrated into the provinces north of Constantinople. The emperors tried hard to push them back across the Danube River, but they were too numerous. The Bulgarian invasion proved to be a permanent one. The modern Balkan state of Bulgaria dates from this period.

Almost all the Byzantine Balkans except the coastal cities were lost to foreign peoples during the difficult years of the Early Middle Ages. The emperors might still rule the cities of the coastline, safe behind their walls and with access to the sea, but the interior towns disappeared or became small villages with a population that had never experienced the civilizing role of Greek or Roman culture.

Early in the seventh century one more series of invaders racked the Byzantine territories in Asia and Egypt. First had come the Persians and then the Muslim Arabs. Emperor Heraklios sought to hold the frontiers, but the task was beyond him. Byzantium permanently lost its Asian provinces and Egypt, retaining only Anatolia.

All the emperors who followed Heraklios lived in the shadow of the Arabs who constantly threatened the existence of the empire. Twice fleets sailed against Constantinople, in A.D. 674 and again in 717. Each time the Byzantines held out, and the Muslim fleets had to return without a victory. The capital's walls and a secret weapon, **Greek fire**, an inflammable liquid that could burn on water, saved the day. In the opinion of the Byzantines, it was proof that Constantinople was a city still protected by God.

A drawing based on an illustration of a contemporary manuscript shows the Byzantine navy using Greek fire against its enemies.

Daily Life in Byzantine Times

The vast majority of the people in Byzantium were farmers. A major division was present among them between those who were free peasants and those who were not. A free peasant family owned the land it farmed and its members could sell their produce in the towns for whatever price they could get. Unfree peasants, the **coloni,** were tenants who worked on the large estates of aristocrats, the government, or the church. They were not free to leave the estates on which they were born or to change jobs. The officials of the empire wanted to be sure that every farmer was working and easy to locate. This made gathering taxes much easier and the food supply more dependable.

The main task of Byzantine farmers was to cope with the Mediterranean climate. During the summer months, when no rain fell and strong winds blew for days, the soil became parched. Every effort had to be made to see to it that the fields should get enough water through irrigation.

In some provinces a two-field system was used. This meant that in alternate years half of the farmland was planted, while the other half was left fallow. In some places the soil was fertile enough to plant every year. Cereal grains were sown in the fall and harvested in the spring. Kitchen gardens, vineyards, fruit orchards, and olive groves were carefully tended to make each village as self-sufficient as possible.

Agricultural implements were few. Farmers had only a simple plow, called an **ard,** which was pulled by oxen to prepare the field. Seed was not planted in rows but broadcast across the field. Hand sickles were used to harvest the grain. Two years of drought in a row resulted in famine.

The most common domestic animals were pigs and chickens. Sheep, goats, and cattle grazed on the large estates or were herded by shepherds in the mountains. Sheep provided the wool that was used for making clothes. Landowners bred horses for the army cavalry, for racing, and for pulling carts and carriages. Mules and donkeys were everywhere in the rural areas, where they were employed for riding and pack animals. Medieval people owed more to the patient donkey than any other animal for getting about.

The cities of the Byzantine Empire were busy places where people of every nation were to be found. Many were engaged in trade and manufacturing. Others were government employees, soldiers, and clerics. All day long the narrow streets of the towns filled with buyers and sellers, travelers and bureaucrats, construction workers and shipbuilders.

Foreign trade was always brisk. Precious stones, pigments, dyes, spices, and medicinal herbs came from China, India, and Persia. The most sought after import was silk cloth. Since the days of the Roman Republic, this cloth was brought across the long Silk Road that ran from China, passed through Inner Asia, and then to Antioch or Alexandria where it was shipped to all the Mediterranean cities.

In Justinian's time welcome news arrived in Constantinople. Monks on a visit to China had smuggled silkworms out of the country and brought them to the Byzantine capital. Now the Byzantines could produce their own silk. The emperor saw to it that its production should be a government monopoly.

Byzantine merchants exported glass, ceramics, papyrus, jewelry, and textiles to the Orient. They had to pay in gold coins for their purchases in the East, but were forbidden to send out gold bars from which the coins were made. Most domestic trade was in food products: timber, cheap pottery, and construction materials. The cost of transporting bulky materials was too high for them to be carried overland for long distances.

Byzantine craftsmen fashioned this medallion of Christ.

Because the government fixed prices, it was difficult for merchants to become rich. They had to be content with moderate profits. Byzantine aristocrats thought that buying and selling was dishonorable, continuing a prejudice that started in ancient Rome.

The Byzantine family was a closely knit unit in which both law and tradition put the father at the head of the household. Divorce and remarriage was made very difficult for both husbands and wives, which helped to make families stable.

Marriage involved joining families as well as individuals. Therefore marriages were arranged by parents who tried to find mates for their children among those of their own social class. Girls were eligible for matrimony around 13 years of age. Boys were older before they were married. Engagement involved a solemn signing of a contract between the parties and an exchange of gifts. The boy offered the girl a ring, and her family transferred a dowry to him. The dowry, which might be a gift of lands, a house, or even coins, was meant to provide a financial start for the young couple.

The wedding took place several months or even years after the boy and girl were engaged. On the wedding day the families of the bride and groom came to church where they exchanged vows before their bishop or priest. The priest blessed them and placed a garland on their heads. The husband then took his wife home where a party with guests among relatives and friends lasted the rest of the day.

A wealthy Byzantine wife had many responsibilities. She was in charge of the household overseeing the preparation of meals, washing, cleaning, and weaving. Generally servants or slaves did this work, but without her supervision not much would get done. Mothers taught their daughters the same skills so that they would be good wives when they grew older.

Rich women in Constantinople dressed elegantly in expensive dresses and jewelry. They enjoyed visiting friends, going to the baths, and cheering the charioteers at the Hippodrome. In the churches they had their own places upstairs in the balcony, while men worshipped in the body of the church.

The life of poor women was less restricted than that of the wives of aristocrats. Necessity forced them to work outside the home with their husbands. Wives of farmers, shopkeepers, and artisans, often with their children beside them, contributed to the income of the family by working. These women had little education and, except for Sundays and holy days, did not have much time for relaxation.

The Byzantine upper classes paid great attention to the education of their children. Both boys and girls were taught at home while they were still young. Generally only boys, when they were older, went out to school. Grammar was stressed since writing and speaking skills were essential for public careers. The study of the Greek classics, the Bible, and Christian authors made up the texts that were used in the schools. At a time when only the clergy in western Europe were literate, the Byzantine urban aristocrats, both men and women, prized their ability to write and speak well.

Among the rural people, except for the village priest, literacy was unknown. The world here was shaped by custom, and reading was not needed to get along. Despite the fact that they were Christians, nearly everyone believed in magic, astrology, and dreams. Angels and demons, the unseen world, were thought to intervene in the ordinary affairs of the day. People believed that miracles happened all about them and saw God's hand in every event that did not have a simple explanation.

The Byzantine view of the world did not provide that equal opportunity should be provided everyone. It held that men were superior to women and that rich people were better than the poor. Tradition asserted that everyone had a certain position when they were born into the world and nothing could be done to change that position.

The Byzantine Church

Christianity shaped the beliefs and values that the majority of people in Byzantium shared. Sunday worship, the Eucharist, was offered by the bishops and priests throughout the whole of the empire. This worship followed a structure that provided an experience to people in song, ceremony, light, and color. Clouds of incense filled the churches with sweet smells, and hundreds of candles burned before the pictures of Jesus, Mary his mother, and the saints. These pictures were called **icons** and were painted on wood by monastic artists. Mosaics of brilliant colored marble pieces covered the interiors of churches. The Eucharist brought culture to townspeople and farmers, rich and poor, alike.

A Byzantine church of Cyprus gathered the men and women of Kiti to worship. Cyprus was the first autocephalous church, independent of any patriarchate, in Christendom.

Byzantine people held the relics of the saints in great honor. These relics might be a piece of bone or a patch of a garment that once belonged to a holy person. The relics were thought to hold power that could heal people.

The emperor, as in the Later Roman Empire, was considered to be the head of the church. He continued to build and maintain its churches. He also had an obligation to protect the church from its enemies. Many emperors also felt themselves competent to interpret church doctrine for their subjects. At times like that, the patriarch of Constantinople, the pope of Rome, or a council of bishops usually stepped in to assert their authority.

Monks and nuns were everywhere in the Byzantine world. There were over 100 monasteries in Constantinople alone. Others were found in every major town and scattered as well in remote deserts or on the sides of rugged mountains. The monasteries were supported by the Byzantine people because it was believed that the prayers of the monastics were essential to the well-being of the Empire. Monks and nuns were the ideal Christians.

The monasteries were often called upon to serve as hospitals for the sick, homes for the poor and aged, and schools for clerical candidates. Nearly all the social tasks performed today by public social agencies were then undertaken freely by monks and nuns.

One group of monks lived very difficult lives. They put up pillars, climbed up, and sat on them. No matter whether the weather was hot or cold, in the rain or snow, they stayed on top of their pillars without any shelter. People from neighboring areas were always happy to have a pillar saint in their midst because anyone with a problem could climb up a ladder to talk to the holy man to ask his advice.

The emperors always entered Constantinople through the Golden Gate for a triumph after a successful campaign. Today it is bricked up.

The Byzantine world was made up of three elements: Roman political forms, Greek culture, and the Christian faith. These three forces shaped Byzantium for the thousand years of its history.

Ireland

In western Europe the sixth century was the golden age of the Irish. Spared the destruction of the Germanic invasions of Britain and the continent, Ireland, drawing upon its Celtic heritage, came to dominate the cultural life of the West.

The centers of intellectual activity were in monasteries scattered across the countryside. Every major clan supported one. Because Ireland had no towns, the monasteries provided the focus of clan life, where men and women came for religious and social events.

A large cross with scenes taken from the Bible was at the entrance of every Irish monastery.

These early monasteries were wooden buildings. Stone was used only in places where trees did not grow. Inside a circular earthwork the monks put up their cells, an oratory, a church, and a kitchen. The stone cells that survive show remarkable skill, built without mortar, one layer of stone placed over another so as to provide a beehive shape. Stone crosses were placed both inside and outside so as to identify the enclosure. The largest monasteries were at Clonmacnoise, Durrow, Bangor, and Glendalough. Powerful abbots and abbesses directed the life of the monks and nuns in the ways of asceticism that the Irish embraced with fervent enthusiasm.

Monastic education consisted of a study of both Christian and classical authors, both Latin and Greek. Great attention was given to grammar. Celtic literature was also treasured and put to memory. Besides the monastic schools, there were institutions that harked back to pre-Christian times for the study of poetry and law. The graduates of the former provided entertainment by reciting stories of the great heroes of the past. The schools of law required young men to memorize the traditions of their people and their genealogies so as to settle disputes over property.

Artists and artisans were busy providing gold- and silver-embossed sacred vessels for use in the Liturgy. Scribes copied manuscripts and illuminated them with Celtic spirals, swirls, and scroll patterns.

One quality of the Irish monks was a roving spirit. It was considered a great sacrifice to leave friends and family, so many monks took to the sea, landing in Wales, Scotland, northern England, and the continent. Associated with this missionary movement was St. Colum Cille and St. Columbanus, both monks of the sixth century, and St. Aidan of the seventh. They and their fellows "journeyed for God," setting up **monasteries**

Irish silversmiths fashioned this chalice for use at Mass.

wherever they went. The ascetic life was practiced with such devotion in the monasteries that the local population was filled with admiration.

Columbanus wrote a rule for his monks, which in its simplicity urged, "Pray each day, fast, study, and work." Columbanus, who lived among the Franks and Lombards, was not always welcome because he denounced the immoral life of the upper classes. His major foundations flourished at Luxeuil in Gaul and at Bobbio in northern Italy. He proudly told his listeners, "We Irish, living at the end of the world, followers of St. Peter and Paul, there has never been a schismatic or heretic among us."

England

The Germanic invasions of the fifth century smothered Roman Britain. After a hundred years of migrations, small principalities of Saxons, Angles, and Jutes emerged, sharing the island with a Briton kingdom known as Strathclyde. In modern Wales, the Britons formed still another nation where Celtic culture survived.

Urban life and Christianity had all but disappeared in those areas where the Germanic peoples settled, so that a new effort had to be made in the late sixth century to restore Britain to Christendom. The initiative was taken by Pope Gregory I, the Great, who commissioned monks from his own Roman monastery to go to England. At the head of the missionaries was Augustine. He landed with his monks in the kingdom of Kent where King Ethelbert and his Christian Frankish queen Bertha welcomed them.

Augustine was allowed to build a monastery and church and to preach freely to the citizens of the kingdom. Canterbury became the archiepiscopal residence of the Anglo-Saxons. Gregory wisely directed Augustine to allow the customs of the population to be retained as long as they did not conflict with Christian teaching. Pagan shrines were to be transformed into Christian churches and pagan holidays into Christian saints' days. It was an astute policy that greatly facilitated the conversion of the English.

Hardly three generations of Christians passed in England before the island was dotted with churches and dozens of monasteries, rivaling those of Ireland. The Celtic monks of Northumbria, centered in the monastery of Lindisfarne, proved too limited in vision for the English. In A.D. 644 the Anglo-Saxon church transferred its allegiance to the broader world of the Catholic church on the continent after a synod held at Whitby. The Irish monks packed their few belongings and returned home.

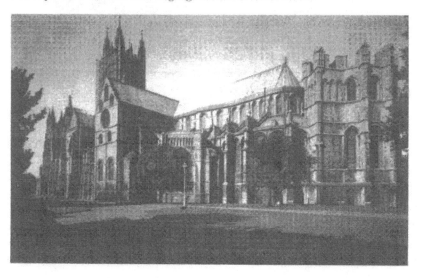

Canterbury cathedral, since the time of Augustine, has been the residence of England's archbishop.

In the north of England, where several important monasteries were located, the success of Christianity was remarkable. At one of these monasteries, late in the seventh century, a monk named Bede took his vows. Although he hardly ever left the cloister, Bede became the outstanding scholar of his age. He commented on many books of the Bible, wrote sermons, essays and grammatical works, and the first work of the island's past, *The History of the English Church and People.* Bede usually wrote in Latin, but he also composed books in Anglo-Saxon, the first author to do so.

Nature and chronology were also among Bede's interests. He noted that measuring tides required various locations and commented on planetary motion with remarkable insight. His work on chronology is important because he promoted dating with the birth of Christ rather than with the founding of Rome.

English Missions to the Continent

The English monasteries rivaled those of Ireland in exporting members to the continent. Two of these deserve mention. One was Willibrord who worked to Christianize the people of the Netherlands and Luxembourg. Another was Wynfrith whom history recognizes as Boniface, a Latin name given him in Rome. Boniface spent his life among the Franks and the other German tribes of the Rhineland. The pope allowed him to be bishop of that area with no fixed residence such as was required of other episcopal appointees. Boniface passed up and down the Rhine Valley on many occasions, planting monasteries and convents to continue his work and preaching and baptizing hundreds of people. He died a martyr while trying to evangelize the Frisians of the northern Netherlands.

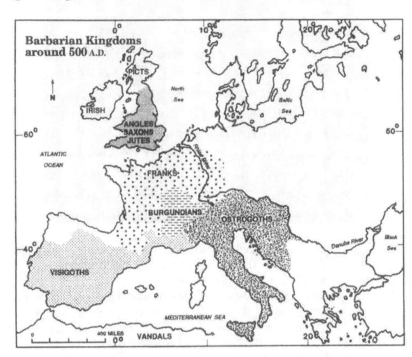

Merovingian France

The Frankish kingdom, nominally Christian since King Clovis was baptized a Catholic in A.D. 496, had made little progress in assimilating Christian values. Murder, extortion, and robbery were everyday occurrences, and marital fidelity was practically unknown. The Frankish nobility were especially notorious for their dissolute way of life. Both Irish and English monks attempted to change these attitudes, preaching that Christians should follow a moral code based upon honesty and fidelity, but to little avail.

Frankish tradition held that the kings, belonging to the Merovingian dynasty, owned all the land. Lawmaking, administration, and judicial affairs were under their authority. What was held to be true in theory, was not so in practice. The local chieftains held the power; the **counts** and **dukes** commanded the militia. The difference between the two titles, both borrowed from Roman usage, was that counts administered the interior and dukes, the frontiers. Rents from their estates supported the Frankish nobles and allowed them to raise warriors for their militias. Their estates, known as villas, were later to become the nuclei of many French towns.

The church brought the Frankish and Roman populations together and provided the small educated class who served the king and magnates. Latin, the church language, was also the language of the official documents

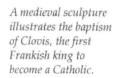

A medieval sculpture illustrates the baptism of Clovis, the first Frankish king to become a Catholic.

of the king, and in time the spoken language of the population developed from Latin into Old French. The bishop's cathedral and residence were the only significant buildings in Frankish towns.

The Merovingian kings, in response to the power of the local aristocracy, depended increasingly upon their ministers, especially the principal one, who bore the title mayor of the palace. In A.D. 733 Charles Martel, mayor of the palace, raised the army that battled and defeated the Muslim army outside Tours. He dominated the king in whose name he fought. Martel's son Pepin succeeded him. Pepin decided that it was time for a change in dynasties. Following the principle that a king who did not rule effectively could be removed from office, Pepin requested and received from Pope Zacharias in Rome permission to dismiss the Merovingian incumbent. In A.D. 752, St. Boniface officiated at his coronation, which made him king of the Franks as Pepin III.

Italy and the Papacy

The pope was wise to have placed the Frankish monarch in debt to the papacy. For decades Italy suffered from perennial unrest at the hands of the Lombards, who had descended into the peninsula shortly after Justinian's Gothic Wars. The Lombards were a Germanic people with a veneer of Arian Christianity. They proved to be as troublesome to the Italian people as the Ostrogoths who preceded them. Whatever lands attracted them, the Lombards confiscated. Their kings unmercifully taxed both the rural and urban populations of Italy.

Pope Gregory the Great won some of them to Catholic Christianity and obtained an assurance that they would not attack Rome, but this promise did not change their predatory habits. Therefore, Pope Stephen II, acting as protector of Italy, called in the debt Pepin owed the papacy. For the first time in history, a pope crossed the Alps to seek Pepin's aid against the Lombards. Pepin accepted the pope's invitation and with his Frankish army defeated the Lombards. He then retired from Italy, but only after donating the captured Lombard lands to the pope. This area became the Patrimony of St. Peter thanks to Pepin's donation, the core of which later became the Papal States.

Gregory the Great was also active in contacting the Visigoths of Spain and convincing them to abandon their heretical Arian beliefs. From the time they became Catholic until the Muslim invasion, the Visigothic kings struggled with the rule of their subjects.

Western Monasticism

By the sixth century the pope of Rome was the undisputed head of the Western church. Papal authority was exercised throughout both the Latin-speaking West and the Greek Balkans through letters and legates sent out from Rome to the various churches. None of the popes took his position more seriously than Gregory the Great who intervened in church life all over Europe. In addition the pope sponsored a number of liturgical reforms and enlisted musicians to write out the plainsong melodies of the Mass, which ever since have held the name **Gregorian chant.**

One of Gregory's literary works is a biography of a remarkable man, Benedict of Nursia, who lived in the days of Ostrogothic Italy. According to Gregory, Benedict was a rich Roman who gave up his wealth to lead the hermetical and later the cenobitic monastic life at Monte Cassino. Tradition holds that Benedict composed a **Rule** that provided a monastic constitution in such a way that allowed even the moderately motivated Christian to follow the monastic life. The rule allowed two meals a day, a nap after lunch in summer, and meat for those who were ill. The monks were to have sufficient sleep and leisure for private reading after hours of public prayer and labor. The rule had no room for the austerities that were so much a part of Eastern and Celtic monasticism. All were to work and pray together under the leadership of the abbot who, once elected, held office for life.

It was not Benedict's idea that the monastery should be a center of learning. Most of his monks were peasants and had little education. However, because the rule required that each brother read a book during the Lenten season, each monastery needed a library and every monk had to be literate. The importance given to the **scriptorium,** the room used for copying manuscripts, was a feature borrowed from the monastic foundation of his countryman, Cassiodorus.

The monastery, according to Benedict's way of thinking, was to be a haven for those who sought to serve God and man in a life marked by discipline. It was to be an oasis of peace at a time when violence dominated the outside world.

An artist of later times has pictured St. Benedict with his rule.

Conclusion

The Early Middle Ages was a time of transition in both the East and West. Roman civilization was no longer predominant in western Europe, being replaced by a Germanic model. In eastern Europe, Roman culture was still alive but modified by Hellenistic values. The Islamic possession of many lands in the East was much more serious for Constantinople's rulers than it was in the West where only Spain experienced a prolonged occupation.

A synthesis developing in the West brought the pope and the Latin Catholic church to the fore in alliance with the vigorous rulers of the Frankish state. Together they would dominate western Christendom in the following centuries.

CHAPTER 22 REVIEW
THE EARLY MIDDLE AGES IN EUROPE

Summary
- The Byzantine world, successor to Rome, extended over the whole of the eastern Mediterranean.
- Justinian and Theodora were the outstanding rulers of sixth century Byzantium.
- New invaders, the Avars and Slavs, came into the Balkans in the late sixth century, while the Muslim Arabs attacked Byzantium from the south.
- The Byzantine family was a closely knit unit where husband and wife combined duties.
- The religious life of Byzantium was based on an Eastern form of Christianity.
- In the Early Middle Ages, Ireland became a major center of western civilization.
- Over the centuries the Germans became Christians and settled into a new way of life.
- Augustine of Canterbury brought Christianity to Anglo-Saxon England.
- Merovingian France was a society known for violence.
- A rule ascribed to Benedict of Nursia became a norm for monasticism in western Europe.

Identify
People: Avars; Slavs; Justinian and Theodora; Bede; Colum Cille; Augustine of Canterbury; Heraklios; Gregory the Great; Romanians; Bulgarians
Places: Balkans; Ravenna; Monte Cassino
Events: revival of the Roman world; Ireland and England influence continental Europe; Slavs settle in the Balkans

Define

Rule of St. Benedict	ard	coloni
Church of the Holy Wisdom	Code of Justinian	scriptorium
mosaics	Gregorian chant	villas
Greek fire	monasteries	
counts	dukes	

Multiple Choice
1. One of the Byzantine Empire's most important contributions was in the production of
   (a) law codes.
   (b) economic plans.
   (c) scientific treatises.
   (d) all the above.

2. The long-range effect of Justinian's conquest was that
   (a) the Arabs were pushed back into Southwest Asia.
   (b) the capital was returned to Rome.
   (c) Gaul was regained from the Franks.
   (d) the Empire was exhausted.

3. The great church of Constantinople was
   (a) St. Peter's.
   (b) St. Paul's.
   (c) St. Andrew's.
   (d) Holy Wisdom.

4. To see the best remaining mosaics of Justinian and Theodora, one must travel to
   (a) Constantinople.
   (b) Rome.
   (c) Ravenna.
   (d) Alexandria.

5. The Avars and Slavs directed their attacks into
   (a) the Balkans.
   (b) the Mediterranean islands.
   (c) Southwest Asia.
   (d) Italy.

6. After Constantinople the largest Balkan city of the Byzantine Empire was
   (a) Athens.
   (b) Belgrade.
   (c) Thessaloniki.
   (d) Adrianople.

7. Much of the successful defense of Constantinople after the seventh century was due to
   (a) the invention of gunpowder.
   (b) Greek fire.
   (c) the invention of the crossbow.
   (d) Venetian seamen.

8. The simple plow of the Byzantine farmer
   (a) was called an ard.
   (b) was pulled by oxen.
   (c) made a furrow in the field.
   (d) all the above.

9. The silk imported into Constantinople before the sixth century was produced in
   (a) China.
   (b) Japan.
   (c) India.
   (d) Sri Lanka.

10. Men and women in Byzantium married after
    (a) their families made the arrangements.
    (b) they were in love.
    (c) boys and girls went to the same school.
    (d) all the above.

11. One of the effects of Eastern Christian worship was
    (a) to entertain.
    (b) to promote the emperor's wars.
    (c) to bring culture to everyone.
    (d) to promote the education of all citizens.

12. A sacred picture on wood in the Byzantine church was known as
    (a) an icon.
    (b) a mosaic.
    (c) a graven image.
    (d) an iconostasis.

13. Byzantium overall was
    (a) a democratic society.
    (b) a very creative society.
    (c) a society concerned about economic progress.
    (d) a very conservative society.

14. The first archbishopric of Anglo-Saxon England was placed in
    (a) London.
    (b) Bath.
    (c) York.
    (d) Canterbury.

15. The Franks became Christian under their king
    (a) Clovis.
    (b) Pepin.
    (c) Charles Martel.
    (d) Wynfrith.

Essay Questions
1. Discuss the building program of Justinian.
2. What made Roman law so important?
3. How do you explain the growth of culture in Ireland and England in the Early Middle Ages?
4. How did the Merovingian kings of France govern?
5. Why was the monastic life held in such high esteem in the Early Middle Ages?

Answers

1. a	6. c	11. c
2. d	7. b	12. a
3. d	8. d	13. d
4. c	9. a	14. d
5. a	10. a	15. a

The Age of Charlemagne

Of all the Germanic nations established in western Europe during the Middle Ages, the Franks showed the most promise. Because Pepin III, known as the Short, had revived the authority of the Frankish monarchy, he laid the groundwork for his son, Charlemagne, to become the strongest king of the age. Under Charlemagne continental Europe north of the Alps, for the first time in history, entered into a period of cultural and intellectual activity.

Meanwhile in Scandinavia the Vikings were preparing to launch their expeditions in what proved to be the last Germanic invasion into the lands of western Europe. Viking attacks gave birth to a new social order known as **feudalism** and set a pattern for centuries to come. One country that escaped Viking settlement was Islamic Spain, which became a channel for Muslim culture, both material and intellectual, to enter European civilization.

In the Byzantine world an important outreach was made to the Slavic peoples of Europe. It had a lasting effect on the subsequent history of eastern Europe as the peoples there accepted the institutions that had taken shape in Constantinople.

Charlemagne

Upon the death of Pepin the Short in A.D. 768, the kingdom of the Franks passed to his two sons, but after only 3 years one died, leaving Charles to rule alone. For the next half century Charles the Great, Charlemagne, dominated European history. Like his father, he promoted the idea that he was God's representative on earth. Just as King David was anointed to become king of the Israelites, so Pepin and now Charlemagne began his rule with a sacred unction. Apparently this had a powerful influence on his subjects, promoting the monarchical ideal. To obey the king was a religious duty that came to be taken very seriously.

The king had resources to reward those who served him in a military or civil capacity. Through wars and confiscation, the pool of lands at Charlemagne's disposal was quite large so that the counts and dukes who governed in his name were handsomely compensated for their services. The king chose them with great care because the counts were responsible for issuing Charlemagne's orders, collecting taxes, keeping the peace, holding court, leading the militia of their districts, and receiving the oath of allegiance demanded of all the king's male subjects at 12 years of age.

Charlemagne sits astride his horse. The emperor was always on the move since the castles and monasteries where he and his court stayed soon ran out of provisions.

It was in the tradition of his father Pepin that Charles fell heir to the responsibilities of defending the Roman papacy. In A.D. 773 Charles marched into Italy and fought the Lombards who had once again violated the pope's territory. He defeated them decisively, sent the Lombard monarch off to a monastery, and assumed the title King of the Lombards. He then confirmed his father's donation with Pope Hadrian I.

Charlemagne believed it was his obligation to expand his territories in all directions. Motivated by a strong conviction that the pagan Germans should be made Christian, Charlemagne commenced a series of wars against his neighbors that did not end until his death. By that time he doubled the area under direct Frankish control. Pagan Germans, especially the Saxons, were worn down by a series of 18 campaigns lasting over three brutal decades.

Charlemagne also took part in a campaign against the Muslims of Spain. Here he met opposition both from the Arabs and the Christian Basques who resisted the presence of a Frankish army on their land. A story told of one of the battles between Franks and Basques was later to become the basis for the *Song of Roland*, the first epic poem written in French.

When Leo III succeeded to the papacy, the new pope recognized that Charlemagne was the acknowledged master of western Europe. The pope desperately needed Charlemagne's help, especially after Leo was attacked by a group of conspirators, who almost beat him to death and nearly blinded him. After the pope had at last been rescued, he made his way north to ask Charlemagne to sit in judgment on accusations brought against him by his enemies. Charles ordered the pope returned to Rome with a Frankish escort and promised to come to the Eternal City in person to pass judgment.

In A.D. 800 at the beginning of Christmas Mass in St. Peter's, the Frankish king was at prayer when the pope placed a crown on his head

while the well-rehearsed congregation shouted the imperial acclamation, "To Charles, the most pious Augustus, crowned of God, the great and peace-giving emperor, be life and victory." There are conflicting reports on whether Charlemagne was aware beforehand of his "spontaneous" coronation.

Afterward Charlemagne spoke of himself as governing the Roman Empire, but upon leaving the Eternal City, he never returned and apparently regarded his coronation a personal honor.

An artist, centuries later, portrays the coronation of Charlemagne on a manuscript.

The imperial coronation was important for several reasons. First of all, it showed that the papacy had abandoned any idea of further dependence on the Byzantine emperors in Constantinople. The popes, however, wanted still to be considered Romans, so they found a solution by creating a Roman Empire in the West. Secondly, it dramatically demonstrated that Pope Leo thought that he had no choice but to transfer the empire from the Greeks to the Franks, because they were the only nation strong enough to keep order in Italy.

Roman primacy also gained from the coronation. Popes could now claim that they were arbiters of European affairs. The question of church-state relations became more complex than ever before, for Charlemagne and his successors, although crowned by the popes, never for a moment thought that their powers were dependent on Roman confirmation.

Carolingian Renaissance

Significant cultural progress occurred during Charlemagne's lifetime. His favorite residence at Aachen in the Rhineland could not make much pretense as a capital until Charlemagne commissioned a number of important public buildings. These included his palace, a cathedral, and a number of other civil and ecclesiastical structures. Because no builders with sufficient skills were available in the West, the Frankish sovereign hired Byzantine architects for their construction.

Charlemagne was eager to raise the educational level of his subjects. If the strong kingship he inaugurated was to last beyond his own lifetime, his successors would require the services of civil servants to fill these posts. Therefore he invited scholars to come from all over Europe to teach in his palace school.

Scholars brought their manuscripts and purchased others so as to form an impressive royal library and school where they gave the study of Latin great prominence. In addition monks of the palace school developed a style of letters known as **Carolingian minuscule**. This is the origin of the printed letters in the book you are now reading.

Charles left a legacy to Europe that no one could equal for centuries. The size of his state, its administration and laws, and the churches, monasteries, and schools he founded gave European life a new direction, a breath of fresh air. Even though many of Charlemagne's accomplishments were not lasting, European civilization made a giant step forward during his lifetime.

Empire Divided

There were many reasons for the decline of the Carolingian Empire. Both internal and external forces were at work. The empire depended too much on the personal loyalty the Franks gave to Charlemagne. By dint of his own character, he was able to hold the various lands together, but his successors possessed too few of his qualities.

In A.D. 814, after his death, the crown passed into the hands of a sole surviving son, Louis the Pious. Three years later Louis divided the empire among his three sons and named Lothair, the eldest, as co-ruler. This arrangement was upset when Louis married a second time and he had to provide for a new son.

The next few years were filled with bloodshed as the brothers warred against their father and with each other. After Louis the Pious's death, Lothair claimed that he alone should succeed, opening a new series of conflicts with his jealous brothers. When peace finally ended their wars, the brothers agreed to divide the Carolingian territories marking the first step in the creation of modern France and Germany.

Northmen

While Charlemagne ruled the Franks, Europeans in central and southern Europe first became aware of the Northmen. The people who lived in Scandinavia until that time had few contacts with the rest of Europe. Speaking a Germanic language that is the common ancestor of modern Norwegian, Swedish, and Danish, the inhabitants were apparently too few and their struggle with the elements too difficult for them to play a role in the course of European civilization until the Early Middle Ages.

The Northmen were organized into clans who recognized a chieftain as their leader. Until the late eighth century, it appears that kings did not count for much. Then a process of centralization began, first in Sweden and then Denmark.

Despite the growth of monarchical authority, egalitarianism remained strong. Adam of Bremen, an early chronicler writes, "The Swedes have kings from an old family, but their power depends upon what the people think. The king must accept what the people have jointly decided, unless his opinion seems better. Then they follow him even though hesitatingly." It was at national assemblies, called **things,** that the king had a chance to hear from his subjects so as to chart his policies.

The families of the Northmen's upper classes loved ostentation following Europeans' long-standing tradition of accumulating prestige goods. If one had wealth, it was considered quite proper to flaunt it. Therefore men dressed in rich textiles, sometimes even imported silks for their cloaks and trousers, and tied ribbons around their foreheads. Scandinavian women wore a sleeveless dress over a chemise ornamented by bronze buckles at the breast. On a chain around their necks they carried household tools: a knife, keys, scissors, and sewing needles.

The Scandinavian home held a large group of people. In addition to his wife, a landowner might have had several concubines from among slave women, so that numerous children, as well as servants, were always about. People lived in long rectangular houses built of logs. A paved fireplace held a fire that was always burning. In a custom that extended back to the Bronze Age, lavish hospitality was required for all guests. Drinking horns with pointed bottoms, used by the Northmen, had to be emptied before they could be put down.

An excavated Viking ship, built in the ninth century, allows a minute inspection of its construction.

For the Northmen, their ships were their first loves. They lavished every attention and skill upon their ships, for they traveled upon the sea more than all other Europeans. Their long ships with their brightly colored square sails unfurled could race across the waves at close to 11 miles per hour. The boats had no decks. Each held seats for the crew, numbering about 34. When the winds were calm or when navigating rivers against the current, the crew's rowing propelled the vessels.

The religion of the Northmen contained the gods that once were common to all Germanic peoples. Woden was the god of battle and of wisdom, who guided the warrior in battle. He lived in **Valhalla,** a great hall that held 640 doors. Here **valkyries,** in the form of beautiful girls, brought the souls of fallen warriors before his court. Thor was also popular. As he rode through the sky, he threw his hammer into the clouds to make thunder. Freyr was the god of sunshine and fertility. In spring a cart with his statue surrounded by flowers toured the villages in order to ensure a successful farming season. Sweden's most sacred shrine was at Uppsala. According to Adam of Bremen, it was a fearful place where both human and animal sacrifices were offered to the gods and the dead bodies of the sacrifices hanged on trees.

Viking Raiders

Late in the eighth century the Scandinavians grew restless for adventure. The prospect of expansion beckoned when overpopulation made life more difficult in their homeland. Second sons were unable to inherit their fathers' properties; hence, they had to make their own fortunes. The riches that came as a result of piracy and trade among other Europeans acted as a powerful magnet to draw Scandinavians southward and eastward.

Swedish merchants from Uppland and the island of Gotland were active well before the eighth century in the eastern Baltic, settling along the rivers where they traded furs, hides, amber, walrus tusks (for ivory), and slaves.

Upplanders made their voyages along the North Way, giving the west coast of Scandinavia its name, Norway.

Late in the eighth century Danes and Norwegians commenced their first attack on Anglo-Saxon England. At the time the several kingdoms on the island were ill-prepared to resist the invaders, whom they knew as Vikings. According to the *Anglo-Saxon Chronicle*, "In the year 787 came three ships to the West Saxon shores and they slew folk. These were the first ships of Danish men that sought land of Angle folk."

The Viking warrior on land fought both as an infantryman and a horseman. His weapons were a highly ornamented, two-edged iron sword and a battle ax. He carried a round, wooden shield and wore a coat of mail and a helmet of leather bordered with iron strips. In the excitement of battle, some individuals, inspired by the god Woden, cast off their armor and wearing only a bear shirt (in Danish, *bare serk*) fought as if mad. Our English word *berserk* testifies to the impression such a warrior made.

In the mid-ninth century both Canterbury and London were pillaged and burned. Danish warriors roamed at will over England north of the Thames.

Following the first invaders, whose practice was to return home after plundering the countryside, Vikings made permanent settlements. Only in the south of England was the army of Wessex sufficiently strong to hold the line against their occupation, but they were not powerful enough to avoid paying tribute, the **Danegeld,** to fend off Viking raids.

The Celtic peoples also felt the might of the Vikings. Their great cultural centers—the churches and monasteries, which were most likely to hold treasure than anywhere else—were looted and burned. Many were never rebuilt. In A.D. 794 raiders struck Iona, the monastery of Colum Cille, for the first time and returned several times later in case anything had been overlooked. Fortunately, Vikings overlooked the **Book of Kells,** one of Ireland's most precious manuscripts and perhaps the world's most beautiful book. It escaped the general destruction and was preserved for future generations.

About A.D. 830 the Norwegian chieftain Turgeis descended upon the Irish, seeking out their monasteries and the graves of Celtic rulers for gold and silver. Because Ireland was so politically divided, no single leader appeared to repel the invaders. The reaction of the frightened monks along the River Shannon was to build stone towers that enabled watchmen to sound the alarm. When Viking ships were sighted, everyone hurried into the tower entrance built some 10 feet off the ground and pulled up the ladder behind them.

Turgeis and the Vikings who came after him placed their bases at the mouth of Irish rivers, which gave them an excellent position between the sea and the interior. These forts attracted colonists from Norway and Denmark in sufficient numbers to give Ireland its first towns: Dublin (founded by Turgeis himself), Waterford, Cork, and Limerick. The Norse attacks meant the destruction of the rich culture that had characterized Ireland in the seventh and eighth centuries.

Toward the end of the ninth century in England, Anglo-Saxon resistance stiffened when a remarkable ruler, King Alfred, came to the throne in Wessex. Alfred was able to reorganize the defenses of the country so that

The round tower at Cloyne, Ireland, offered security when a Viking attack threatened.

he could launch a counterattack upon the Vikings. After Alfred won several victories, the Danes agreed on a division of the island: Wessex should hold the south while the north, the **Danelaw,** was theirs.

This able Saxon king was a warrior and a devout Christian who promoted learning. At his palace school at Winchester, he translated Latin books into Anglo-Saxon for his people.

Charlemagne was well aware of attacks on the British Isles and began, as a precaution, building forts and garrisoning troops along the Frisian coast. The attack came sooner than expected. In A.D. 810 King Godfred of Denmark led a flotilla of 200 vessels against Friesland.

Over the next decades no one living along the Frankish coast was safe. Success spurred the Vikings still further, to Spanish ports and on to Italy where they landed at Pisa. The situation changed dramatically but a few years later. More peaceful ways replaced the predatory instincts of the early Vikings. Intermarriage with Frankish women assisted this process, as did the diminishing returns reaped by continuously plundering a land already denuded of its wealth.

About A.D. 911, after a life of raiding, a Norwegian chieftain named Hrolf (Rollo) suffered a defeat at the hands of the west Frankish King, Charles III. As a result, he agreed to a truce with Charles who, in return, allowed him to govern a province of the western Frankish lands that soon came to bear the name Normandy after its new inhabitants. In a very short time the Normans adopted Christianity, the farming techniques of the Franks, and the French language.

Feudal Order

All over Europe in the ninth century fear of a Viking raid made life so tenuous that it produced a new political and social system that bears the name of feudalism.

There was little that the Frankish kings after Charlemagne could do to prevent the swift and sudden attacks of the Vikings. Before they were aware of a landing, the Northmen were long gone. In addition, raising a royal army was time-consuming and expensive. Despaired of receiving protection from their monarch, the people of the Frankish lands turned to their local lord for whatever security might be had. A leadership vacuum existed at the top of society that left them no choice.

This decentralization of political authority in Medieval Europe stands in sharp contrast to the conditions of the late Roman period or even in Charlemagne's time, for now the local nobility became the political, judicial, and military authorities. A complex interlocking web of personal relationships based upon oaths of loyalty determined society's structure.

Already in Charlemagne's day the free peasant was hard-pressed to provide for himself and his family because of the 3 months of military service each year that were required of him. The civil wars and Viking invasions that followed were as onerous. To make ends meet, men as individuals or as village communities, transferred title to their lands to the large landowners of the region in which they lived. The nobles then returned the lands given them for the use of the peasants but exacted rents in kind or in service.

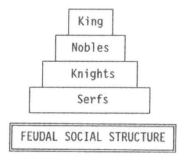

The free peasant, who became a **serf**, was permanently attached to his lord's lands. As a serf, he enjoyed the protection offered by the lord and his knights in time of war and civil strife, but he and his family had heavy obligations toward the landowner. The principal one was to spend 2 or 3 days a week working on his master's farm. Fees were placed on many of his activities: at his marriage, upon grinding grain at the mill, or upon using the lord's ovens or wine press. He could not leave his master's service, and he and his family had little hope of ever bettering their condition.

A few free men who were better suited to be soldiers than farmers became **vassals** of the lord. In a ceremony known as **homage** a vassal placed his hands in those of his lord and took a solemn oath that he would always be loyal to him. Some of the vassals made their residence with the lord where, in return for military service as knights, they were provided with clothes, food, and lodging. More frequently the lord gave his vassals a small estate, at first called a **beneficium**, later a **feodum**, or **fief**, for their support. Vassals often sought to increase their revenues and fiefs by pledging service to several lords. Theoretically, the fief was not an hereditary possession, but, as might be expected, a person who held it tried to make it such.

According to the feudal system, the landowning aristocracy of the whole nation were vassals of the king and were supposed to perform services for him, just as their vassals were obligated to them. These services included hospitality when the court traveled, various financial payments known as **aids,** and the reservation of a specific number of days, usually about 40 each year, when the king could call upon them to fight in his army.

The feudal system had a hundred different variations as local circumstances dictated and as the parties who entered into the arrangements made individual decisions on what their contract should contain. Feudalism was important for subsequent political development because it demanded cooperation within the ruling class. Both kings and nobles shared in governing, and this checked any tendency toward royal absolutism.

Farmers and Merchants in Carolingian Europe

In Charlemagne's day Europe's countryside remained covered by forests pierced now and then by horse and mule paths that allowed communication between farming villages and feudal estates. Few bridges existed so that crossing rivers required a ferry. The forests were fearful places to Europeans of this time, the home of felons and highwaymen, wild animals and evil spirits unseen by the human eye.

After an interlude of several centuries when much of the land farmed in Roman times had reverted to woods, Europe's farmers again began to chop away at forests and drain marshes in earnest. Mountains were cleared up to an elevation of 2,000 feet, the limit of tolerance for rye production.

A manuscript illustration depicts a medieval farming scene.

Families shared in the tasks of the farming cycles from planting to reaping. Grains, principally rye as well as wheat and barley, provided bread, the staple upon which most Europeans depended for daily nourishment. Vegetables and fruits were had in season, while meat was a rare luxury in the fall when animals born in the spring were killed. There would not be enough food for them to get through the winter. Fish was often on the table thanks to Europe's abundant rivers and streams. The ordinary drink was wine in the south and beer and cider in the north.

After the year A.D. 1000, people lived in villages clustered around the landlord's house, his **manor**. The villages had to be located at some distance from one another, since a considerable amount of land was needed to produce decent harvests. Every effort was made for the villages to be self-sufficient, for none could really depend on outside food supplies.

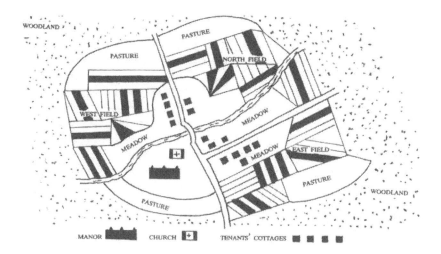

A graphic representation of a medieval manor divided the land between cultivated strips and pasture.

The villagers dwelt in houses of wood logs or branches with mud placed in the crevices to hold out the wind and rain. No windows brought in light so that the fire, used for cooking and heating, also had to serve for illumination when the door was closed. Smoke from the ever-burning fire was usually allowed to find its own way out through the thatched roof without benefit of a chimney. Wood and charcoal were the only fuels.

Men, women, and children lived in one large room where all the activities of both day and night occurred. This room was furnished with tables, chairs, and storage facilities for food. More prosperous farmers had beds, while the poor slept on straw on the floor. There was no privacy. The few possessions a family owned were stored in chests, as were tools used for repairs or farming. All clothes were made of either hemp or wool, and weaving them was one of the major tasks for women in the household.

There was no running water inside the houses, and the village well had to serve everyone for water. No refrigeration meant that food such as fruits, meat, and milk had to be consumed in a hurry. It was more sensible to make cheese, which could be preserved, rather than to try to keep milk from spoiling. Meats like ham and sausage could be dried and smoked and consumed later.

The nobility lived in the more spacious quarters of the manor, but their comforts were also limited. The site of the manor was chosen with regard to its defense, not its comfort. Once it was fortified, it became a castle. The medieval manor was a far cry from the comfortable Roman villa, its immediate predecessor.

The clothes of noblemen were of better quality, sometimes made of linen or silk, and their diets provided more variety. They lived from the labor of others, so that they might be warriors. In times of peace they could divert themselves with hunting rather than plowing or weeding.

Despite the dangers associated with travel, merchants journeying in groups found it worthwhile to move from one village to the next, making a living by selling their wares. The peddlers, from a word meaning dusty foot, were always a part of the medieval scene. They moved slowly along determined routes, for this was a world where the pace of travel depended upon the maximum speed of horse or mule trains.

Many of the merchants were Jews, for feudal law and custom effectively barred them from farming. Because Jews were not considered citizens of any particular state, but were dependent on whomever might be their "protectors," they enjoyed greater freedom of movement than other Europeans. During the constant strife of the European Middle Ages, this freedom was a decided advantage. In an age when Muslims and Christians were often at war, Jews provided a link between Europe and the Arab world. In their baggage Jewish merchants carried ornaments, household wares, arms, spices and salt, and medicines. Other Europeans who took to commerce in the Early Middle Ages were people located near the sea: Frisians, Italians, and Scandinavians.

A merchant pours grain into a buyer's sack.

Merchants were always welcome because they brought news of the outside world to the towns and villages of Europe. Traveling clerics and pilgrims supplemented these accounts. Because western Europe provided no post offices, it was principally merchants who carried letters between towns.

In southeastern Europe and Italy towns were more densely populated and commerce played a greater role in people's lives. In the tenth century several fairs were held in Byzantine cities; the largest fair was held at Thessaloniki. Merchants in the Byzantine world had an advantage over those in the west because the gold **solidus,** the coin minted by the emperors, was in ample supply and retained its value throughout the Early Middle Ages. In the west there was a serious shortage of coinage, inhibiting the flow of trade. Silver coins called **denarii** were minted by Charlemagne and other Frankish monarchs, but their value was never certain. There was little for people with money to do with their wealth except to invest in more land.

Islamic Spain

The Muslims of Spain called their land al-Andalus, a term picked up during the Vandal occupation, and were delighted to compare its productivity to North Africa and Southwest Asia where aridity made life so much more difficult. Poets spoke of the country as a garden, and, in fact, throughout Spain, Muslims planted flowers and shrubs to make their homeland live up to its reputation. Fountains, canals, and wells were built and carefully tended to irrigate both the city-dwellers' small plots of ground and the large farmers' estates.

The sophisticated irrigation technology that was learned over the centuries in arid Yemen and Iran was now imported into Spain. Olives, grapes, and figs were grown in such abundance that Andalusia was no longer subject to periodic famines that were to be expected in Europe north of the Pyrenees.

Commercial activity kept pace with farm production. The Muslim conquest of the Iberian peninsula, far from interrupting business and shipping, had exactly the opposite effect, for al-Andalus was now linked to markets in Africa and Asia. Muslim Spain experienced a rapid increase in population as a result, and old Roman towns that had stagnated in Visigothic times now burgeoned with new life and energy.

Most of the Andalusian towns were located along the road system that the Romans had built. Despite urbanization, the Muslims made no effort to keep up the highways because the Islamic world did not use wheeled vehicles for transportation. Betraying their nomadic past, Muslims in Spain preferred horse, camel, or mule trains to transport the country's goods to town markets or Mediterranean ports.

The Muslims were never unified in the Iberian peninsula. A major ethnic division existed between the Berbers who came from northern Africa and the Arabs who were further distinguished by loyalties to either Syria or Yemen. Tribal allegiances were fiercely maintained even after living for decades in Spain. The Arabs, although a minority among the Muslims, held the best lands and, hence, were more wealthy and displayed a superior attitude toward the Berbers. Moreover Arabic was the preferred spoken and the only written language of Muslim Andalusians. The Berbers were often influenced by **marabouts,** holy men, whom the Arabs thought to be quite outside orthodox Islam.

In the eighth century Christian descendants of Roman-Hispanic origin, as well as the Visigoths, counted perhaps 6,000,000 people in al-Andalus, a number that far surpassed that of their conquerors. While guaranteed freedom in their personal life, they held a second-class status in political and social matters, and each male of military age, except clergy, had to pay the **jizyeh,** the poll tax. Christians had their own courts and followed their own laws in internal community matters. Jewish citizens held the same privileges.

A remarkable event intervened in A.D. 756 when Abd ar-Rahman, a member of the Umayyad dynasty arrived in Córdoba. The Abbasids had eliminated his relatives in a bloodbath in Damascus, but he had escaped. After numerous adventures crossing Egypt and North Africa before reaching Córdoba, Abd ar-Rahman found a welcome from his fellow Syrians in Spain.

His presence infuriated the Abbasids who sent an army against him. In a display of defiance ar-Rahman and his closest followers burned their scabbards to demonstrate that they would never sheath their swords until the Abbasid loyalists were driven from the Iberian peninsula. This bravado had the desired effect. The Abbasids were overwhelmed. Ar-Raham sent the severed heads of the commanders wrapped in the black flag of the Abbasids to the caliph with labels on their ears for identification.

Abd ar-Rahman did everything possible to make Córdoba the equal of the other important Islamic cities. He built a large palace for himself, public buildings, and mosques for his subjects. During the last year of his rule, the Great Mosque of Córdoba came under construction. It was a huge building with multiple arcades decorated with contrasting green and red marble. Oil lamps, numbering 8,000, hung from 200 chandeliers to furnish light in the building.

The Great Mosque of Córdoba was the pride of Islamic Spain. It is now a church.

The successors of Abd ar-Rahman gave the Andalusians good government and economic stability. New plants were introduced into the Spanish countryside: palm trees, sorghum, cotton, hard wheat, and sugar cane. The Berbers who settled in the region of Oporto were expert sheep and cattle herders and cultivated the olive with improved techniques. Along with plants came other contributions to the future of European scholarship: medical treatises and Hellenistic scientific texts. Arabic numbers and algebra appeared in Andalusia, the work of Muhammad al-Khwarizmi, an Arab mathematician. The zero, from the Arabic **sifr** or void, appeared first in Spain before spreading throughout the rest of Europe.

In the small Christian principalities that escaped the Muslim conquest, Visigothic princes held onto their independence, refusing to pay tribute to the Arab emirs. In A.D. 739 the Prince of Oviedo, Alfonso I, organized the small territory of Asturias to become a bastion of resistance. Other principalities appeared in León, Navarre, and Catalonia. All were poor and isolated in the beginning, hardly a match for Muslim Spain, which was the most prosperous region of western Europe in the ninth and tenth centuries.

Byzantine Culture and the Slavs

In the eighth century the Byzantines focused on affairs in the Balkans, a region they considered to be part of their empire, despite its occupation by Slavs and Bulgarians. A constant state of war existed between the Bulgarians and the Byzantines. Constantinople could win the battles but not the war, for there were simply too many Bulgarians for the Greeks to rule.

Around A.D. 750 the Byzantine empire held only the coastal walled cities of Greece: Corinth, Thessaloniki, and Monemvasia. Slavic peoples occupied the interior of the country, although they organized no single state. This allowed the Byzantines to reconquer Greece piecemeal. As their armies brought in more territory, **themes,** military districts, were created to hold it. About A.D. 810 both Patras and Athens were reconstituted as Christian bishoprics testifying to the success of Byzantine arms. By the close of the century, the Greek reconquest was complete. All the major cities of the peninsula were in imperial hands, the majority of Slavs had accepted Christianity, and those who did not were isolated in the Peloponnesian mountains.

The expansion of the Byzantines into the Balkans and the Slavic world had lasting consequences. The architecture and art of the region testify to the abiding presence of the Greek world. It is hard to overestimate the importance of the Byzantine imprint upon the Slavic mentality.

Although the pope's coronation of Charlemagne as Roman emperor was welcomed by western Europeans, the court officials of the Byzantine Empire viewed it as an outrage. Among those who considered the matter, there was one possible explanation. At the time of Charlemagne's coronation, a woman was governing the empire for the first time in its history. This was Empress Irene, wife of Leo IV, whose ambition to hold the throne of Byzantium led her to blind her son, Constantine IV, for whom she first served as regent. Although no constitutional prohibition existed for a woman to hold the sovereignty, there were misgivings over the responsibility the empress had in leading armies. There was, therefore, a possible excuse for the pope to act, arguing that the Roman throne was vacant.

Irene proved to be quite inept at governing her realm, and this did not help her cause. Irene's support came from the **Iconodules,** especially the monks of St. John of Stoudios whose abbot Theodore strongly supported the empress. The Iconodules formed a party that insisted that icons should have a place in the churches and in the worship of the church. Their opponents, the **Iconoclasts,** argued that the icons promoted idolatry and the First Commandment of the Bible forbade their use. However, the abbot's support was not sufficient to keep Irene in power for long, and she was deposed. Her fall meant a temporary revival of iconoclast sentiment and exile for Theodore.

Missions to the Slavs

During the ninth century the Byzantine world took up the civilizing mission of the Slavs. With the Avars out of the way thanks to Charlemagne, conditions were right for Constantinople to make a significant contribution to European civilization by interacting with the many Slavic peoples who lived to the north and east of Constantinople.

The Slavic people today are the most numerous of Europeans. It may well be that they were also a plurality of Indo-European peoples in the ancient world, but little is known of their past. It is only in the fifth and sixth centuries that they come into history when records report how they moved westward to the Elbe and southward into the Balkans once the Avars had destroyed the Byzantine population.

The political structure of the Slavs was very simple. They had no kings, no central authority, no confederations, but only chieftains who headed individual tribes. Tradition ruled more than the leaders who were not allowed to make any decisions without obtaining the universal consent of their council of advisors. The early Slavs were farmers and herdsmen, supplementing their diets with hunting and fishing.

As late as the tenth century, all Slavic peoples spoke the same language with only minor differences in vocabulary. Then as a result of emigration from their common homeland southern, western, and eastern Slavic languages developed.

In the ninth century the people of Great Moravia, a principality occupying the central part of the modern Czech Republic and extending southward into Croatia, sought to break out of their isolation. Great Moravia's population was of Slavic origin, surrounded on three sides by Germanic Franks and fearful of possible absorbtion. A ready excuse for hostilities against the Moravians was present as long as they held to their non-Christian beliefs.

In A.D. 862, to head off possible German incursions, the ruler of Great Moravia, Rastislav, sent a delegation to Constantinople requesting Patriarch Photios to dispatch missionaries to his nation. By requesting Greek missionaries, the Moravians could avoid accepting Frankish sovereignty and at the same time, by converting to Christianity, remove the excuse Frankish kings had for an attack upon them.

Photios was delighted to honor their request and commissioned two veteran missionaries, Cyril and Methodios, to lead a party to Moravia. Before leaving for their destination, the brothers put together an alphabet for the Slavic language. This alphabet is known as **Glagolitic** and made use of newly invented letters to reproduce the Slavic sounds. The Liturgy and part of the Scriptures were then translated into Slavic.

Welcomed to Moravia, the brothers offered instruction and then baptism to thousands. The success they enjoyed, however, was resented by the Franks who regarded the Greeks as trespassers engaged in perverting the Eucharist by using the vernacular, rather than Latin. To silence their critics, the brothers left for Rome, taking some of their converts along to convince the pope of the value of their effort.

The pope gave his approval and consecrated Methodios, bishop of Sirmium, a vacant see (jurisdiction), once an important town of Roman Illyricum. He returned alone to Moravia after the death of his brother Cyril in Rome but was imprisoned on the way by the Latin bishop of Salzburg. Upon his release Methodios's missionary work gained new Slavic communities for Christianity, but following his death the Frankish bishops had their way. The leaders of the mission were expelled, and Latin Catholicism was imposed upon both the Moravians and the Bohemians, their cousins further to the west.

The disciples of Methodios, thrown out of their homeland, made their way into Poland and Croatia, everywhere continuing to proselytize among the Slavs. Some of his disciples were sold into slavery where Byzantine merchants purchased them and sent them to Constantinople. Later a number of these settled at Ohrid in the Bulgarian khanate. The Glagolitic was modified at a monastery here so as to become the **Cyrillic alphabet,** named in honor of Cyril who had devoted himself to the education of the Slavs of Moravia.

Literature written in Cyrillic became common among all the eastern Slavic peoples and remains in use among them to the present. That a Christian school could be founded in Bulgaria in the late ninth century testifies to the conversion of the Bulgarian khan some decades earlier. Khan Boris, after considering both Latin and Greek forms of the faith and hoping to obtain his own patriarch, finally opted for the latter. About A.D. 860 the Serbians also became eastern Christian.

The people of what is now Slovenia and Croatia did not fall within the orbit of the Byzantine church. Both the Slovenes and Croatians, under Frankish influence, received Christianity from clerics of the Latin church.

In the Early Middle Ages the ancestors of the modern Russians lived in the great forests of eastern Europe. They were farmers, hunters, and fishermen, speaking a Slavic language. Between them and the Black and Caspian Seas, Turkic-speaking people kept their nomadic way of life on the great steppes of Ukraine and beyond. The most important of these were the Khazars, whose capital was at Itil on the delta of the Volga River. The Khazars, whose upper class had adopted Judaism, were strong enough to keep the Muslim Arabs at bay.

A new element was added to the mosaic of peoples already in the Russian lands when the Swedes settled along the Baltic coast and then moved into the interior. Here they encountered the great rivers of Russia: the Volkhov, Neva, and Dvina in the north and the Dnieper and Dniester in the south. By following them, they reached the Black Sea.

According to the *Primary Chronicle*, the first written source on Russian history, the people of Novgorod, troubled by warring factions and civil unrest within their city, invited the Rus, a Swedish tribe, and its chief Rurik to come and rule over them. Rurik and his relatives willingly accepted this invitation around A.D. 860 and took up residence in Novgorod and Kiev in Ukraine, the most prominent town of the Dnieper valley. Kiev was soon to outdistance all other towns of the Russian lands after the Novgorod prince, Oleg, late in the ninth century captured it, making it his residence.

Novgorod became the most important city of northern Russia.

Magyars

The last people to enter the European community were the Magyars or Hungarians, who, until the tenth century, made their home deep inside the steppe land of Ukraine. They made up a federation of ten tribes that lived through herding. Their language was Uralic-Altaic, native to the peoples who live in Inner Asia. The Magyars were expert horsemen and able marksmen but were not powerful enough to ward off the attack of still another steppe people, the Patzinaks or Cumans. Depredations by the Patzinaks caused one group of Magyars to move westward until they settled on the great plain of the middle Danube where they found ample pasture for their herds.

While there, they received an invitation from the king of the East Franks to help him in an attack upon Great Moravia. Under the combined German-Magyar onslaught, Great Moravia, the first of the Slavic states, was destroyed in A.D. 895. Victory whetted the appetite of the Magyars to push even deeper into central and western Europe.

Their horsemen penetrated Italy and as far as Burgundy at a time when the Vikings were striking the western coasts of Europe and Muslim pirates pillaged indiscriminantly along the Mediterranean shore. For the peoples of central Europe, the Magyars were a scourge that they feared would never end. What they did not foresee was a peaceful nation a hundred years in the future.

Orthodox and Catholics

The man who dominated the Byzantine religious scene in the mid-ninth century was Patriarch Photios of Constantinople, who first held office from A.D. 858 to 867 and again from 877 to 886. He was an active prelate who contested with the Roman papacy the right to send missionaries to the Slavs and Bulgarians. He also accused the papacy of heresy for allowing an addition to the Nicene Creed to be used by the Catholic clergy in Bulgaria: this was but a single word, *filioque* in Latin ("and the Son" in English), which had been inserted after the creedal phrase declaring that the "Holy Spirit proceeds from the Father."

Photios broke relations with Rome and accused Pope Nicholas I of tolerating an erroneous view of the Trinity. The *filioque* issue did not die, since the Roman church began to use it in its own creed in the eleventh century. It remains to this day the single most important theological issue dividing the eastern Christian or Orthodox and the western Christian or Catholic churches.

During this period, with the single exception of Nicholas I, pope from A.D. 858 to 867, the papacy was filled with men of mediocre ability. Nicholas proved to be a staunch advocate of papal powers. His actions were based upon his opinion that God gave the pope the right to intervene whenever morality was involved. However, at that time Italy was torn by struggles between Frankish and Muslim armies, and the papacy was at the mercy of whichever group was temporarily ascendent. What little spiritual leadership remained was found in the monasteries and convents of western Europe.

Unfortunately, too many monasteries lacked enough monks to carry out the order of public prayer. Too many were poor because of the pillaging of ninth century invaders and the local landowner's taxation and interference. Contrary to common belief, poverty has always been a greater problem for monasteries than too much wealth.

Conclusion

In the Early Middle Ages the worldview of most Europeans was very limited. What they knew of the outside world they did not like. It was foreign and strange. Once accepted, Christianity provided them with a value system that they found agreeable. Life was difficult; violence was omnipresent. The voice of the oppressed, except in Charlemagne's day, was drowned by those who believed that might was right. The church was the single place that offered a bit of beauty in this world. Its ceremonies transported people beyond their earthly existence and promised them that this life was only an introduction to a better one to follow.

By the middle of the tenth century invasions had slackened, and European society began to reshape itself. The peoples of Europe were at the dawn of a better day.

CHAPTER 23 REVIEW
THE AGE OF CHARLEMAGNE

Summary
- Charlemagne was Europe's most important monarch of the eighth century.
- During his rule there was a modest renaissance in European intellectual life.
- After Charlemagne's death, his empire divided into east and west, the origins of modern Germany and France.
- The coming of the Northmen was the last great Germanic invasion of Europe.
- In western Europe feudalism became the social and economic system during the Middle Ages.
- The peoples of eastern Europe became a part of the European community in the Middle Ages.
- Christians in the Middle Ages were either Latin Catholic or Greek Orthodox, while Jews and Muslims were smaller groups.
- Islamic Spain was a center of culture with Muslim, Jewish, and Christian contributors.

Identify
People: Vikings; Lombards; Photios; Abd ar-Rahman; Cyril and Methodius, Magyars; Empress Irene; Iconoclasts
Places: Aachen; Scandinavia; Uppsala; al-Andalus; Novgorod; Great Moravia
Events: coronation of Charlemagne; Viking raids; feudalism

Define

knight	Cyrillic alphabet	Carolingian minuscule	things
vassal	feudalism	Valhalla	Iconoclasts
serf	Danegeld	fief	Book of Kells
Glagolitic	valkyries	jizyeh	manor
themes	feodum	beneficium	Iconodules
Danelaw	homage	aids	
marabouts	denarii	solidus	

Multiple Choice
1. Charlemagne's empire failed because
   (a) it was too large.
   (b) his grandsons fought over the succession.
   (c) it needed a very strong ruler to keep it intact.
   (d) all the above.

2. The Vikings came from
   (a) England.
   (b) France.
   (c) Scotland.
   (d) Scandinavia.

3. In England the Norse were stopped north of the Thames River by
   (a) William the Conqueror.
   (b) Otto II.
   (c) Arthur and the Knights of the Round Table.
   (d) Alfred the Great.

4. Feudalism requires
   (a) a strong king.
   (b) a large army under a king.
   (c) many armies made up of knights.
   (d) strong central government.

5. A peasant required to work on the farm of a landowner is known as a
   (a) fief.
   (b) serf.
   (c) slave.
   (d) indentured servant.

6. Great Moravia received these missionaries in the ninth century:
   (a) St. Patrick and Bridget.
   (b) St. Francis and St. Dominic.
   (c) St. Cyril and St. Methodius.
   (d) St. John and Philip.

7. This alphabet is used by eastern Slavic peoples:
   (a) Latin.
   (b) Greek.
   (c) Phoenician.
   (d) Cyrillic.

8. The earliest Russian cities were
   (a) Moscow and Archangel.
   (b) Novgorod and Kiev.
   (c) St. Petersburg and Moscow.
   (d) Odessa and Moscow.

9. Northmen assemblies were known as
   (a) parliaments.
   (b) councils.
   (c) things.
   (d) congresses.

10. Thor was the Northmen's god responsible for
    (a) Valhalla.
    (b) fertility.
    (c) thunder.
    (d) rain.

11. The Book of Kells was rescued from a monastery of
    (a) Germany.
    (b) Trier.
    (c) Monte Cassino.
    (d) Ireland.

12. Dublin was one of Ireland's first cities, founded by
    (a) Harold Blue Tooth.
    (b) Leif Erikson.
    (c) Turgeis.
    (d) St. Patrick.

13. Normandy is a province of
    (a) England.
    (b) Roman Empire.
    (c) Italy.
    (d) France.

14. Feudal social life depended on
    (a) a money economy.
    (b) strong central control.
    (c) oaths of loyalty.
    (d) none of the above.

15. Knights in the Middle Ages received their income from
    (a) commerce.
    (b) fiefs.
    (c) government office.
    (d) the king.

16. In Muslim Spain people traveled
    (a) on animals.
    (b) in wagons.
    (c) on boats.
    (d) on barges.

17. Bulgarians settled
    (a) south of Constantinople.
    (b) in the Peloponnesus.
    (c) north of Constantinople.
    (d) in Anatolia.

18. Magyars are people known today as
    (a) Hungarians.
    (b) Bohemians.
    (c) Gypsies.
    (d) Romanians.

19. Modern Moravia is in
    (a) the Czech Republic.
    (b) the Slovak Republic.
    (c) Croatia.
    (d) Hungary.

20. Photios was the chief bishop of
    (a) Rome.
    (b) Antioch.
    (c) Alexandria.
    (d) Constantinople.

Essay Questions
1. What were the accomplishments of Charlemagne?
2. How do you explain the raids of the Northmen?
3. What was the structure of feudalism?
4. Describe the life of a farmer in Carolingian empire.
5. What was the significance of the papal coronation of Charlemagne?

Answers

1. d	6. c	11. d	16. a
2. d	7. d	12. c	17. c
3. d	8. b	13. d	18. a
4. c	9. c	14. c	19. a
5. b	10. c	15. b	20. d

Western Recovery and East European Awakening

The raids of Vikings, Magyars, and Muslims, which destroyed much of Western society in the ninth century, became less frequent as decades passed. The invaders settled down to more peaceful ways, and some, but not all, gave up their old way of life. This was especially true of the Normans who occupied their Frankish province. They were now assimilated into the feudal system, had adopted French ways, and were contemplating expanding beyond Normandy.

The Normans were not the only people of Europe bent on enlarging their borders in the Middle Ages. The Germans, united around a Roman Emperor and the missionaries of the Catholic church, pushed eastward against the Slavic population of central Europe. Only those Slavic people who were more numerous and more cohesive like the Poles and Bohemians organized kingdoms strong enough to accept the new religion while resisting the emperor's sovereignty.

People who lived in the Middle Ages still thought of themselves first in terms of where they lived and then in religious terms. Were they from Cologne, Aachen, or Mainz? Were they Christians, Jews, or Muslims? Latin, Greek, Hebrew, and Arabic, the sacred languages, were powerful agents promoting unity within their communities. Nevertheless, national vernaculars were already developing in geographically separated regions. In time they would form a foundation for the nationalism that appeared in the Late Middle Ages.

Holy Roman Empire of the German Nation

The vision of the Later Roman Empire appeared once more in the Middle Ages urging that all Christian peoples of Europe should be governed by two authorities: the emperor, in charge of secular matters, and the pope, in charge of spiritual concerns. All the larger European nations should have their own royal house and internal autonomy but acknowledge that the emperor and pope had the right to intervene, if necessary, when issues arose that could not be settled on the national level.

The imperial ideal won over the best minds of Europe for many centuries, but in practice it did not function as intended. The attention of Europe's princes to the maintenance of their own interests necessarily limited their concern with outside affairs. The rulers of England, France, and the Spanish Christian kingdoms did not welcome any diminution of their sovereignty by an Italian pope or a German emperor. The close cooperation between church and state envisaged in this model was doomed to founder on hard reality as the diverse goals of popes and emperors became apparent.

The Holy Roman Empire of the German nation began with the dynasty of the Saxon duke, Otto I. He proved to be the most important person to appear in western Europe since Charlemagne. Otto came to power in A.D. 936 convinced that he could reconstruct the empire of his illustrious predecessor. Everything depended on his own personality, for there was still little consciousness of a common nationality among the Germans who thought of themselves as Saxons, Franks, Bavarians, or Swabians. Otto found that it was no easy task to wean them away from local interests and attach them to his crown.

Otto's first move was to have himself crowned and anointed king of the East Franks at Aachen. The Archbishop of Mainz presided at a ceremony that recalled Charlemagne's accession. The other great Frankish dukes acknowledged his sovereignty on that occasion by serving at his table. Later, when some forgot their promise of allegiance, Otto occupied their territories, ousted them from office, and installed trustworthy members of his own family in their places.

Otto gained the gratitude of all Europe when he defeated the Magyars whose devastating raids had troubled the countryside for the past half century and threatened to submerge the German settlements along the frontier. The bishop of Augsburg delayed a Magyar raid into southern German lands until Otto arrived with his forces. The king hemmed in their army with the Lech River at their backs preventing their usual hit-and-run tactics. Frankish cavalrymen assisted by Bohemian troops engaged in close combat with the encircled Magyars until the latter were exhausted. When the battle of Lechfeld ended, only a few survivors were left. The victory of Lechfeld in A.D. 955 proved to be a decisive one. There were no more Magyar raids.

It was now time for Otto to take action on his imperial plan. His wife Adelaide was Italian and had claims to a variety of territories in the peninsula. Moreover, Pope John XII extended an invitation to the Frankish king to come to Rome for anointing and coronation. This was done with great ceremony. Adelaide at Otto's side was crowned empress. Otto's original vision had at last become a reality, for the Roman Empire was reborn among the German peoples. Later, in the twelfth century, the word *Holy* was added to distinguish it from its earlier predecessors.

Otto's remaining years as ruler were marked by a strengthening of his alliance with the church. He personally intervened in overseeing episcopal elections and generously endowed churches and monasteries. The emperor invested churchmen in their office, and in return bishops and abbots promised him homage and loyalty. He also brought churchwomen into positions of authority. Matilde, abbess of Quedlinberg, often served as his deputy and summoned episcopal conferences in her own name. The obligation of clerical celibacy served Otto well, for the powerful bishops and abbots could have no legitimate children to inherit their position or lands.

Pope John XII placed this crown on the head of Emperor Otto I, beginning the Holy Roman Empire.

When the first Otto died, the second was but 18 years old, untried and lacking the support his subjects gave his father. A unified kingdom collapsed as did the empire because of dissension among the Germans themselves and foreign invaders who took advantage of Otto II's lack of experience. The Slavic frontier between the Oder and Elbe went up in flames. Danes poured in from the north, and Bavaria royal officials could not prevent rebellion. For years Otto II had time for little besides repressing these challenges to his rule.

Otto II's untimely death after only 10 years' reign left his heir, 3-year-old Otto III, in the hands of his mother Theophano and his grandmother Adelaide. They saw to it that the boy was taught his responsibilities early in life and when only 16 he moved to Rome fired by his grandfather's imperial plan. Subsequently, he made the acquaintance of a French cleric, Gerbert of Aurillac, one of Europe's most prominent scholars and a man who shared Otto's universalist vision. At his court in Rome, Otto gave his officials Greek titles and on his seal portrayed a figure symbolizing Rome on one side and Charlemagne on the other with the caption, "Emperor of the Romans." Otto named Gerbert to the papacy, where he assumed the name Silvester II.

In Rome, however, angry citizens resented the Germans and threw out the imperial officials. Otto died without fulfilling his goal. Like his father, he was too ambitious, and the tasks he set for himself were beyond his capacities. Pope Silvester lived only a year after Otto's death, closing the alliance between pope and emperor. The imperial ideal was, for the moment, buried with them.

The Empire survived, however, even if weakened due to the accident of the early deaths of Otto II and Otto III. It served to give central Europe stability, which was confirmed whenever strong personalities arose to hold the imperial throne. On the negative side, the emperors' involvement in Italian affairs often distracted them from their true interests, a pattern discernible from the very beginning of the Roman Empire created by the Frankish rulers.

A manuscript illustration pictures Otto III holding his symbols of office.

Because the third Otto was without an heir, the emperors were chosen from the ducal house of Franconia after his death. Some were men of ability, but they constantly had to ward off the efforts of the great nobles to limit their power. Otto III's inattention to German affairs gave the nobles a taste for independence that they were reluctant to yield. Only the physical presence of the rulers guaranteed that imperial authority would be acknowledged by the powerful German aristocrats.

Cluny and Church Reformation

In A.D. 909 Prince William of Aquitaine endowed a monastery on his property at Cluny that followed St. Benedict's rule. He not only provided sufficient funds to take care of the monks comfortably but also promised that neither he nor his heirs would ever interfere in the monastery's internal life. Within a short time Cluny attracted a large number of novices interested in joining a community that enjoyed such privileges. Kings and nobles throughout Europe eagerly donated lands for Cluniac establishments.

From Cluny and other monasteries to the north, a rebirth of monastic devotion soon spilled over into the life of the church. In the eleventh century the number of monks and monasteries affiliated with Cluny grew until over 300 institutions were part of its federation.

The life of the medieval monk required daily commitment. Those noblemen who entered religious life had to give up their homes and family as well as their properties. In some communities they had to work and pray alongside peasants, giving a dignity to labor never before accepted by upper-class Europeans. Social, national, and economic barriers dissolved in monastic life to the great advantage of Western culture.

Cluny produced a succession of remarkable abbots, genuine spiritual leaders, who were highly visible in the courts of Europe advising, mediating, and consulting. The abbot of Cluny was its single head. All other monasteries within the federation were governed by **priors** who had to visit Cluny annually for an audit of their affairs and for direction in the business of their monasteries. This arrangement kept the spiritual tone of the Cluniacs very high, and the reforms begun at Cluny soon were reflected in the entire church.

A single tower remains from the church of the monastery of Cluny. The monks there began a spiritual reform that spread across Western Europe.

In spite of Cluny's reforms, the Catholic church's general condition demonstrated the problems of operating within the feudal system. Bishops were also princes and expected to provide military service every bit as much as the secular nobility. Because they were the chief officials of the towns, many showed themselves to be as violent as their peers.

Germanic law made no provisions for corporate ownership of property. Everything had to be owned by some individual. Therefore, churches were the personal possession of those who endowed them and their heirs. Parish priests who served those churches had to please the local lord and his family or lose their **benefice**, their appointment, along with the revenue that provided for their support. Despite church and imperial legislation forbidding it, clerics continued to marry so that the more lucrative benefices were passed on through generations as family inheritances.

Episcopal candidates in the Catholic church took office in a ceremony known as **consecration**, a service that demanded at least two bishops to be present for the laying on of hands that conferred the candidate's authority. Preceding inauguration, his secular lord invested the episcopal candidate in his office and lands, symbolized by conferring on him a staff and ring. In effect, this made churchmen vassals of their lord and his dependent.

It should not be thought that investiture was inherently corrupting. Many churchmen did perform adequately and took their responsibilities seriously. On the other hand, in an economy that offered few opportunities to increase one's wealth, the potential for mischief was high. Abbots and bishops were apt to incur debts upon assuming office and to repay them was a heavy burden. Even though payment for a church office was considered to be **simony**, a crime first attempted in New Testament times by one Simon Magus and hence the name, in a world where "everybody was doing it," most people did not consider lay investiture a serious problem.

On the other hand, the experiences of monasteries like Cluny in Burgundy and Gorze in Lorraine, institutions free of lay interference, could not be ignored. The abbots of these houses were effective propagandists for a change in the system.

It was only in the mid-eleventh century, when the reforming monks of France and Germany occupied the papacy, that there was a concerted effort to free the church from lay control. The reformers were convinced that the church must take the offensive against the general sentiment that allowed the nobility and kings so much power in the affairs of the church. They wanted clerics whose primary loyalty was to the church, not their sovereigns.

Pope Leo IX, although a relative of the imperial house, brought to Rome a plan for the church to rid itself of lay interference. He traveled all over Europe gathering support for his position, calling meetings of clergy to effect his reforms.

In A.D. 1059 one of Leo's successors ruled that only **cardinals**, pastors who served in Rome's parish churches, should elect the pope. This marked a great success for the reformers. Both the Roman emperor and the powerful aristocratic families living in the region about the Eternal City were thought to have at last been excluded from nominating their favorites to the highest church office.

A guiding spirit in the efforts to make the church independent was Leo's aide, a monk named Hildebrand. In A.D. 1073 his popularity was so great that he was chosen pope by acclamation and took the name Gregory VII. Gregory presided at meetings of the Roman clergy, called **synods,** in which he outlined his ideas for reform. Simony and clerical marriage were his targets, but to get at them he believed that lay investiture first had to be stopped. He believed that he now had the support of most clerics and some laymen.

Gregory issued a general prohibition against lay investiture. When the news reached the courts of Europe's kings and great nobles, there was shock and outrage. In a radical departure from past custom, Gregory was challenging all of western Europe's secular leaders for control of the church in their lands.

Although Gregory received protests from all sides, his most serious opponent was Emperor Henry IV. The emperor asserted that the administration of both church and empire was his right and responsibility and the wealthy German bishoprics and abbeys required his supervision. He called his own synod of imperial bishops whose support he could count on, accused Gregory of illegitimately holding office, and demanded his removal. Over the next few months, each side sought to strengthen its position. The pope had the greater success. He was able to persuade some of Henry's nobles, already disaffected, to announce their agreement with the papal view.

In February 1076 Gregory excommunicated Henry and forbade his subjects from recognizing him as emperor. Henry saw his defenses crumbling. At this critical moment he decided on a dramatic move. The emperor crossed the Alps to seek a personal conference with the pope. At Canossa in northern Italy, the two men came face to face, but not before Henry had to humble himself by waiting 3 days dressed as a penitent before the pope would see him. Gregory subsequently lifted the excommunication provided the emperor would no longer invest bishops. Henry agreed and returned to Germany with the pope's blessing, and the immediate crisis passed.

Henry soon returned to investing bishops and was again excommunicated. At length the emperor decided to be rid of the vexatious pope by appointing his own nominee to the office. The archbishop of Ravenna agreed to Henry's plan and, aided by German arms, was installed in Rome as Clement III while Gregory went into exile. Gregory died at this point apparently, but only on the surface, a failure, for his spirit was passed on to his successors. In A.D. 1088 a French Cluniac monk, a whole-hearted partisan of reform, became pope and took the name of Urban II. Henry may have thought Urban was Gregory's ghost.

The controversy over investiture continued to inflame relations between popes and emperors until a compromise known as the **Concordat of Worms** was reached between Pope Calixtus II and Emperor Henry V in A.D. 1122. It was agreed that kings and princes would abandon investiture but be given "due honor" at church elections and the right to veto candidates known to be inimical to their interests.

The investiture contest was an important one because it concerned who would actually rule in western Europe, emperor or pope. It also sought to determine the boundaries of national church development. How far could each nation go in setting up its own leadership? The fact that the investiture issue was settled by compromise meant that a creative tension between church and state was established in western Europe. This tension was to last for centuries. Neither institution was able to overwhelm the other. The realization that the secular arm of government was not holy marked a great step forward, a move never made in either Byzantium or Islam, and set Europe's western kingdoms on a separate course.

Peoples of the Iberian Peninsula

In the middle of the tenth century, one European nation exhibited a high degree of cultural and intellectual activity. This was the Spain of al-Andalus, ruled by the Muslim emir, Abd ar-Rahman III of the Umayyad dynasty. Córdoba, his capital with 100,000 people, was the largest city in western Europe and its most sophisticated.

In A.D. 929 Abd ar-Rahman declared himself caliph, thereby setting himself up as an independent religious leader and breaking whatever bonds remained between Córdoba and Baghdad. Peopled by Muslim Arabs and Berbers as well as Jews and Christians, the land he governed was enriched by talent from each community.

Scholars from all over Europe were drawn to Córdoba's schools where teachers of philosophy, science, art, and medicine were to be found in greater numbers than anywhere else in the west. Here translations were made so that the knowledge of ancient Greece might be stored in the city's libraries. Every mosque in Andalusia had its library. Thanks to the many copyists employed in this work, Christian Europe north of the Alps was later introduced to Greek learning principally by way of the manuscripts produced in Muslim Spain.

Abd ar-Rahman, in addition to his intellectual concerns, also encouraged agricultural pursuits. During the eleventh century several new vegetables from Asia and North Africa were first brought into Europe: spinach, water-melon, and eggplant. The acreage planted in sugar cane and cotton expanded because these crops admirably adapted to the Spanish climate.

Manufacturing was also an important part of Andalusian life. Thousands of people made their living through silk-weaving. Others worked at carpet-making with techniques brought from the East. Pottery of Majorca became famous for the gold luster baked onto it and was almost as renowned as the iron swords of Toledo's artisans. The caliph also built factories for manufacturing paper and minted gold dinars to facilitate trade between his country and western Europe. Andalusia was the major channel through which western Europe obtained products from Asia and Africa.

Several decades later hostility between Arabs and Berbers, between Christians and their Muslim leaders, as well as intrigues and conspiracies in the palace resulted in constant turbulence in al-Andalus. The Umayyad caliphate collapsed, overwhelmed by the factionalism in its territories.

The Spanish Christian kingdoms took advantage of the weakness of the Muslims. In A.D. 1085 one army recaptured Toledo and large parts of present day Portugal. The Muslims, fearing that their strength was too little to hold back the invaders, appealed to the Berber dynasty of the **Almoravids** of Morocco to send an army. The Almoravids turned back the Christian tide and in the process overran most of the emirates. More narrow in their interests and less cultured than the Umayyads, Almoravid rule meant a decline in the richness of Spanish life.

Normans

In A.D. 987 the last Carolingian king of the West Franks died, permitting the ascendancy of a new dynasty. Its first representative was Hugh Capet, a candidate whose support came from the bishops and abbots of the region about Paris. Capet's dynasty lasted for 300 years despite the fact that its beginnings were hardly impressive.

Capetian France presented a sharp contrast with Normandy, now a mature duchy with strong leadership. The Norman rulers easily dominated their barons. When they summoned their vassals into service, either they responded or faced the loss of their fiefs. The Norman knights were then the best soldiers in Europe, probably in the world. As expert horsemen, they had learned to ride their large horses at high speed with a lance held tightly between the upper arm and chest. Stirrups gave them strong support as they crouched low in the saddle.

There was no defense against this kind of attack. Infantrymen were powerless before them, for a mere dozen knights could put hundreds of bowmen to flight. The Normans were anxious to demonstrate their skills, and opportunities awaited them in the eleventh century.

Their first conquest was in southern Italy. Here there were Lombard principalities, regions belonging to the Byzantine Empire, as well as a number of city-states such as Salerno, Naples, and Amalfi that enjoyed a quasi-autonomous position. Early in the eleventh century Norman pilgrims on their way to Jerusalem stopped at these ports.

A local prince was eager to offer the Normans positions in his army because their reputation had preceded them to Italy. It is no wonder that when the pilgrimage was completed, many warriors were eager to trade residence in their cloudy homeland for sunny Italy. Robert, called Guiscard, came to offer his sword for hire, but he soon turned to carving out a kingdom for himself.

Guiscard swept the Byzantines from the field and then moved on to take Sicily from the Muslims. The Normans occupied Palermo and established it as the capital of their kingdom in the sun. The Norman occupation of Sicily caused the Muslim Mediterranean world to be cut in half, destroying the once flourishing trade between the Orient and Spain.

An invasion of greater consequence took the Normans to Anglo-Saxon England. A series of earlier events made such a project attractive. First there had been one more attack upon the island by the Danes under King Sweyn I. Sweyn and later his son Canute ruled over a northern empire that included England, Denmark, and Norway.

Upon Canute's death the kingship passed to his sons who proved unable to hold the empire together. Their incompetence and childlessness allowed the Anglo-Saxon pretender, Edward the Confessor, to return to England. The Earl of Wessex, Godwin, a powerful aristocrat, dominated the king, and when Edward died childless, Godwin's son Harold claimed the throne. At once Harold had two serious challenges to his rule. One was from Harald Hardraade, the king of Norway, who planned an invasion from the north. The other was from William, Duke of Normandy, who claimed that Edward the Confessor had promised him the succession.

Harold placed his army in the south awaiting the expected invasion from Normandy, but turbulent weather kept the Normans in port. On the news that the Norwegians had landed, the Saxons marched north, reaching York in 5 days. They won a decisive battle, Hardraade lay dead, and the battle's survivors melted away. While Harold was in Yorkshire, the wind changed to the west, and the Norman force of 7,000 crossed the channel, landing at Pevensey on the southern coast of England. William then moved his troops and ships to Hastings. Harold's forces, worn out by the long march across the country, proved no match for the Normans, and in October 1066 at the Battle of Hastings the English throne passed to William, afterward called the Conqueror.

William claimed that his conquest gave him all English land to dispose of as he saw fit. Those Normans who served in his army expected rewards and were not disappointed. The king gave them lands and houses but scattered them all over England lest power become concentrated in any single family. He introduced the feudal system to England, handing over the great Anglo-Saxon estates to Normans. To be sure of his finances, he commissioned a census of all real property in England to have an exact record of its worth and disposition. This was put into the *Domesday Book*, the only such compilation of the Middle Ages.

The Bayeux tapestry depicts the battle between William and his knights against the Saxon infantry.

For purposes of local administration, William retained the Anglo-Saxon organization of the country into large areas called **shires** and smaller units known as **hundreds.** Each shire had a **reeve** or sheriff who served as its chief official. His duties were to preside over the local court in both civil and criminal cases, to publicize and enforce royal decrees, to oversee the collection of taxes, and to captain the local militia. The king's laws were issued in **writs,** a peculiar form of administrative decree that is still found as a court order in American jurisprudence. Another Norman innovation was the introduction of trial juries that under oath heard cases and delivered verdicts brought before them, a predecessor of the modern Grand Jury.

The Norman invasion of England introduced the French language into England. Because French was the language of the conquerors, Anglo-Saxon lost its former importance and many new words of French origin, originally Latin, came to be spoken. As a literary medium, Anglo-Saxon disappeared, and English, a combination of Anglo-Saxon and French, replaced it. The Normans brought continental taste in food, entertainment, art, and dress into the country. The conquest also linked England much more closely to continental affairs because the Norman kings were always interested in events in France.

The Norman adventurers in both England and Italy made the eleventh century memorable for their people's activities. The soil of Normandy produced strong personalities, men who were ambitious, calculating, and cruel, who allowed nothing to stand in their way.

Meanwhile the Scandinavian homeland of the Normans was experiencing two major social changes: the emergence of strong monarchies and the advent of Christianity. The new religion based upon a hierarchical structure gave assertive national monarchs significant help in furthering their plans for centralization. Great monuments were erected in the tenth century by figures like Harald Bluetooth whose runic inscriptions announced to all who passed by that this was the Harald "who conquered all Denmark and Norway and Christianized the Danes."

King Olaf Tryggvason, a Dane, was the principal figure in bringing the Norwegians under a single monarch. Olaf dominated the other chieftains and actively proselytized on behalf of Christianity among the Norwegians. Many were forcibly converted to the faith. On the other hand, in Iceland the **Althing,** the national assembly, debated and then voted to accept Christianity. The conversion of the Swedes was first attempted by King Olof Skötkonung.

In all the Scandinavian lands, Christianity was little understood, and the acceptance of its values was no more than a gesture. However, the second generation of Christians was better than the first, and the third was an improvement on the second.

Only in Ireland did the Northmen suffer a reverse, an exception to their widespread success in other parts of Europe. Native Celtic chieftains rolled back the territory in Norse hands. The leader of the Irish resistance was Brian Boru who styled himself Emperor of the Irish. In A.D. 1014 Brian led his army to Clontarf where he met a force of Northmen. The battle went to the Irish, although Brian was killed. The defeat at Clontarf marked the end of Norse political influence in Ireland.

Italy Turns to Commerce

The extraordinary growth of wealth and population in northern Italy during the Middle Ages was the result of increased agricultural production in the Po Valley. This region was the most fertile of the entire northern Mediterranean, giving cities such as Pisa, Milan, Genoa, and Venice an ample and dependable food supply. The citizens of these towns provided a ready market not only for food but also for goods that could be had only by importing them from the Orient. Merchants capitalized on these demands, trading surplus grain for the products of the Muslim world. They also created a vigorous shipbuilding industry as investors sought even greater profits.

The Italian merchant marine equaled and then surpassed the fleets of the Muslim countries. No city was more responsive to the change in economic forces than Venice, the city built at the head of the Adriatic. Venice

The Venetian cathedral of St. Mark was built on a plan that used Constantinople's church of the Holy Apostles for its model.

enjoyed remarkable freedom for trade because it was nominally under Byzantine sovereignty rather than under the Roman Empire.

The people who made policy in Italian towns such as Venice were businessmen. Either directly or indirectly they controlled the city councils and in Venice elected its chief executive, the **doge**. Everyone in Italy understood that continued prosperity depended on harmony between the politicians and the business community. Nowhere else in Europe was this linkage so well understood. For 600 years northern Italy was the wealthiest and most cultivated area of all Europe.

Byzantine Empire and the First Crusade

Constantinople remained the largest city in Europe in the tenth and eleventh centuries. Although shorn of much of its territories by earlier Muslim invasions, it showed remarkable resistance to further losses once the Arab armies reached the Taurus Mountains of southern Anatolia.

Toward the end of the tenth century, the emperors were experienced military men who regained Antioch and the island of Cyprus from the Muslims. The strongest of these emperors was Basil II who ruled from A.D. 976 to 1025. Basil brought the administration of the Byzantine state and the conduct of its domestic and foreign affairs to new heights. His main adversary in the Balkans was the Bulgarian tsar, Samuel Kometopoulos, who resisted Basil's pretensions to expand northward. Time after time the forces of Basil and Samuel clashed until a decisive battle was fought at Balathista. According to the chroniclers, Basil won an overwhelming victory over the Bulgarians. It is said that out of every 100 prisoners taken, Basil blinded 99 before allowing the hundredth, one-eyed, to lead the others back to Bulgaria.

Basil's victory was complete when Samuel died that same year permitting Bulgaria, split into three provinces, to be absorbed into the empire. By the time of Basil's death, the Byzantine world stretched from Azerbaijan to the Adriatic. It would never reach such proportions again.

Basil had no sons. His heir was an incompetent brother, and the succession then passed to his brother's daughter, Zoe. Zoe had three husbands in the 22 years of her reign, each of whom was recognized as emperor because of the marriage.

The foundation of the eleventh century monastery of Kaisariani was due to the Byzantine revival after Basil II.

One of the husbands was Constantine IX Monomachos. While he and Zoe were jointly ruling, an attempt was made to patch up differences between the Roman and Greek churches. There were issues on both sides. The Byzantines were upset over the Normans in Italy who insisted that their Greek subjects should accept Latin bishops, while the pope was dismayed that the Greek patriarch, Michael Kerularios, was complaining about the Latin churches in Constantinople using unleavened bread (rather than the leavened bread of the Greek tradition), making their Eucharist invalid.

In A.D. 1054 Pope Leo IX commissioned a delegation to visit Constantinople to discuss these differences. When the delegates failed to get a hearing from Michael, they excommunicated the patriarch and two other churchmen. In turn, Kerularios excommunicated them, but not the pope whom they represented. The importance of this incident, which is not so much as mentioned by a single contemporary Byzantine historian, has become so exaggerated that 1054 is mistakenly considered the year when a final schism occurred between the Greek and Latin churches.

The Seljuk Turks were the most dangerous of Constantinople's enemies. In A.D. 1071 Emperor Romanos IV led the Byzantine army into eastern Anatolia to hold the frontier. The two armies met at Manzikert near Lake Van in one of history's truly decisive battles. The Christian army was utterly defeated, and the emperor was captured and held as a hostage.

Ten years after the battle of Manzikert, the Byzantine Empire once more had a soldier-emperor, Alexios I Komnenos. Alexios, a realist, judged he could not dispose of the Seljuks so easily, however, and decided on an appeal for aid from Western Christians. At the same time without a navy of his own, he had no choice but to allow Venice to assume the role of protector of the eastern Mediterranean.

Alexios dispatched a delegation to meet with Pope Urban II to seek help against the Turks. Urban welcomed the Byzantine request, turning it to his own advantage as he called upon Western Catholics to launch a holy war against Islam, a crusade to recover Jerusalem from its Muslim rulers. Still in their memory was the Fatimid caliph al-Hakim's order to destroy the Church of the Holy Sepulchre.

Urban could now pose as the leader of the West rather than the emperor. He could also use the crusade to turn the attention of Western nobles away from warfare at home by finding an outlet for their violent instincts abroad. The pope took the occasion of a synod held at Clermont in A.D. 1095 to proclaim the project to regain the Holy Land for Christendom. The pope's ringing appeal, which followed a listing of alleged Turkish atrocities against Christian pilgrims to Jerusalem, evoked an enthusiastic response. "God wills it" became the acclamation of the French knights whom he recruited for the crusade. To demonstrate their commitment, a red cross was sewn upon their tunics.

Before the official army set off, crusading fever swept the masses of France and the Holy Roman Empire. Numerous self-appointed generals rose up to lead ragtag armies of peasants to Constantinople. The astonished Alexios was happy to transport them to Anatolia where Turkish forces, as expected, easily disposed of them.

The feudal army of the pope's crusade was composed principally of French and Norman knights, loosely held together by a bishop appointed by the pope. None of the European monarchs participated. In fact, because of the investiture controversy, most were then excommunicated. When at last the official army of the crusaders reached Constantinople, the anxious Alexios sought to extract a promise from them that all the lands they won would be turned over to him.

Spanish crusaders visited the church of Santiago of Compostela before setting out for Jerusalem.

Religious enthusiasm, when out of control, can become a dangerous thing. This happened as a by-product of the First Crusade. A wave of intolerance spread throughout Europe. Jews who had lived quietly in the midst of Christians now became victimized by popular prejudice against anyone who was not a believer.

Eastern Europe

The tenth century saw the expansion of the European community of nations as new peoples from eastern Europe entered the course of history. These were the Poles, Hungarians (Magyars), and Russians. Their entry into written history was effected when they converted to Christianity that, along with religion, brought them both new skills and personnel from beyond the German eastern frontier.

The Polish people were then settled in the lands between and around the Vistula and Oder Rivers. Their homeland was remarkably flat with mountains only in the far south. Poland's lack of definable natural borders on the east and west was to determine much of its subsequent history.

Poland's first historic prince was Mieszko I whose territories were located near Poznan. In A.D. 966 he converted to Christianity and announced that Poland would place itself under the protection of the pope, a move meant to secure the boundary with the Roman Empire.

His son Boleslaw Chrobry was even more energetic than his father in promoting the interests of the nation. He established Gniezno as an important religious shrine where the body of St. Adalbert, who died a martyr in Prussia, should be kept. While on pilgrimage to Gniezno, he obtained a pledge from Otto III that Poland's existence would be recognized by the Roman Empire and Boleslaw acknowledged as a brother prince. To the east, Boleslaw led a Polish army into Ukraine and occupied Kiev. In A.D. 1025, a year before his death, Boleslaw was crowned king, an action that confirmed the full independence of Poland.

After Boleslaw, the Polish nation was beset by troubles. The sovereigns who ruled the country could not inspire sufficient loyalty to prevent the magnates, the great landowners, from ignoring them whenever it was convenient to do so. Moreover, Poland's neighbors chipped away at the borders of the country. The title of king was lost, and incumbents had to be content to call themselves prince.

After Great Moravia's destruction, Bohemia and its major city, Prague, prospered under the dukes who ruled the city. Their autonomy was effected by an arrangement between Duke Vaclav I and the Holy Roman emperors. In return for a promise of fealty, which in practice meant the acceptance of certain obligations to the German rulers, the Bohemians were permitted to manage their own affairs.

After their chastening at Lechfeld, the Hungarians were content to stay within their Danubian homeland. About A.D. 970 Bavarian missionaries made them Christians. Henceforth they were integrated into the mainstream of European history. Prince Geza was the first Hungarian prince to accept baptism.

Medieval Hungarian history is highlighted by the reign of Geza's son, Steven. In the year A.D. 1000, Steven was able to secure from Pope Silvester II a crown that provided his nation recognition as a sovereign Christian state. Steven is remembered for his wise administration and just enforcement of the laws. He confirmed the Magyar tradition that a nobleman should never pay taxes but rather fulfill his obligation to the crown by military service. As with Vaclav of Bohemia, the people acclaimed Steven a saint and patron of his nation after his death.

It was during the course of the tenth century that the Swedish or Varangian element in the Kievan population was absorbed by native Slavic peoples. Prince Igor and his wife, Olga, were the last to bear Scandinavian names. The population living in villages located in the great forests of the country was still divided into numerous tribes isolated from one another by vast stretches of land. The princes who lived in the towns extracted tribute from them only with difficulty.

When Vladimir became prince of Kiev, he was aware that it was time for the Russians to adopt one of the higher faiths and abandon the animism of his forefathers. According to Russian legend, he explored Judaism, Islam, and Christianity, both Latin and Greek.

In what was a momentous decision for Russia's future, Vladimir decided that Constantinople's tradition was best. He forged an alliance with Emperor Basil II, and he was promised a princess. Vladimir was then baptized late in A.D. 988 and upon his return ordered the Kievan population into the

Dnieper for baptism by the Greek clergy who came north to establish Christianity in the Russian lands.

The church became a strong ally of the prince, and by the time of Vladimir's death, seven Byzantine bishops were located about Kiev. Even though the **boyars,** the nobles loyal to the prince, accepted Christianity with no qualms, the peasantry long remained only half convinced. Although they were nominal Christians, they continued to perform the ceremonies that were designed to honor the gods of their ancestors.

Byzantine churches provided a model for those built in Russia.

The Byzantine contribution to Russia was great. With Christianity came literacy, law, art, and architecture. The Bible, in Old Church Slavonic and Cyrillic script, was brought from Ohrid in Bulgaria where a translation had been made. Literacy came easily to the Russians in a language closely akin to their own, unlike the Western Slavs and the Magyars who had to master Latin. They also received Christianity as a finished product, thus imitation was given priority. Conservative tendencies predominated, and the monastic life, as in the Byzantine world, became the ideal expression of Christianity.

The high point of Kievan Russia was reached while Yaroslav the Wise ruled in the eleventh century. Kiev's population reached 80,000 people, a city filled with public buildings, churches, and monasteries. Foreign contacts were so numerous and important that Yaroslav's daughters became the queens of France, Norway, and Hungary. In the eleventh century the peoples of the Russian lands were then more a part of Europe's family of nations than they would be again until the reign of Peter the Great late in the seventeenth century.

After the death of Yaroslav, once more another Turkic people, the Polovtsi, drove across the steppe lands, forcing the peasant population out of Ukraine. It was simply too dangerous for farmers when no one knew when a group of horsemen out for plunder might appear on the horizon. The steppe lands, a sea of grass, were beautiful and rich, but the flat terrain served as a carpet for invading horsemen out of the East.

The Polovtsi occupied the river banks of Ukraine, especially those regions where portages were created so as to avoid rapids. Only a few brave merchants were willing to make the trip from northern Russia to the Black Sea as long as the Polovtsi were there. The rich trade routes that once led from the Russian forests to Constantinople and to Baghdad were practically abandoned.

Society in Medieval Europe

In the tenth century the monogamous family was the basic structure of European society in which each member had his or her own role to play. Girls were still married very young, but some changes had developed in the marriage ceremony. In western Europe the wedding party first stood on the church porch where the husband accepted the dowry provided by the woman's family. If a transfer of land was to be made, the woman knelt before the man and acknowledged that he would be her protector and that of her possessions, a role formerly played by her father or brothers. A ring, blessed by the priest in the name of the Trinity, was placed upon the bride's finger. She might also receive token gifts of gold and silver while the groom recited, "With this ring I wed you, with this gold and silver, I honor you." It was only in the tenth century that this ritual became common.

The increased sophistication of European society did not portend an improvement in the condition of women. In fact, greater access to patristic literature allowed clergy in the West to become more familiar with the anti-feminist views of the fifth century Christian church fathers. Sex was therefore looked upon as dangerous, a distraction for the true Christian. While marriage was good to the extent that children came into the world through procreation, it was such only to the extent that both men and women were weak and unable to control their passions. Women were seen as temptations for men and were encouraged to hide their bodies lest they lure unsuspecting males into sin. Biblical quotations and philosophical speculation combined against granting women the same status as men.

By A.D. 1100 legislation on marriage was completely taken over by the church in the Latin West. Canon lawyers determined the marriageable age for women was 13 and required that the girl give her consent before a wedding was considered valid. Most young women, however, had no choice but to agree to their parents' choice of a mate. Outside of life in the convent for single, upper-class women, there was no alternative to matrimony. Among serf families, when a couple began living together, they were considered married. Such unions were fragile, and a man who sought to dismiss his spouse had little difficulty doing so.

In the Middle Ages divorce was accepted if one of the parties wanted to enter a monastery or if a husband was held in captivity for over 5 years. By the tenth century the church canceled the second of these exemptions. Nevertheless, it did allow separation from "bed and board" in cases of adultery, heresy, apostasy, or cruelty, but this condition did not allow either party to remarry.

Byzantine church law allowed divorce and remarriage for a grave cause if one was the innocent party. This could be done only three times. A fourth marriage, even for widowers or widows, was absolutely prohibited. Abortion and infanticide were strictly forbidden both by secular and church legislation, but again it happened.

There were very strict legal penalties against homosexuality among men where it was identified as sodomy or the "sin against nature." Nevertheless, it appears that authorities were willing to look the other way as long as public opinion did not force them to take action against known offenders. On the other hand, lesbianism was tolerated.

Within feudal society it made a great difference to women whether they were born into noble, peasant, or town families. Among upper-class women the code of chivalry required that they be treated with respect, but the demand for military service to be paid by a male served to lessen the women's role in society. The law gave a husband the right to control his wife's dowry. If he was a knight and predeceased her, the right of guardianship passed to his lord. As guardian, the lord controlled the family property, and before a widow could remarry, she had to obtain his permission.

In reality the noblewomen of these times had many important responsibilities. Since the men of this class were so frequently away, it was their task to keep the accounts of the manor and to manage its affairs. Wives had to care for the education of the children from a neighboring upper-class family, for it was a general custom for both young boys and girls to be exchanged among the feudal aristocracy. Tutors taught music, grammar, and martial arts to boys destined to become knights, while young girls learned how to sew, brew, and make medicines and cosmetics.

During the Middle Ages children were considered to be young adults. No special role was given to them. As soon as they were old enough to work, they did so, contributing as best they could to the welfare of the family, which was considered all important. Each individual had to sacrifice for the family to survive. No one questioned the right of parents to send their children to a monastery or convent if the family could not provide for them.

Most of the lucky few who received an education outside the upper class were boys destined for the clergy. Latin was the principal subject, and learning was by rote. The teacher read out a text or conjugated a verb, and the students answered aloud in unison so that eventually the lesson was memorized.

Women make noodles for a dish of pasta. The art of making noodles was imported from China.

Cathedrals and monasteries were the schools of this age. Exceptional pupils learned something of the liberal arts and music, especially at Paris and Chartres, which had the best reputations. A teacher, called the **scholasticus,** oversaw the curriculum and the students' progress. In western Europe few women attended school, but in contrast, thanks to private tutors, Byzantine girls were often as well or even better educated than boys.

Work in Medieval Europe

The vast majority of Europeans labored at agricultural pursuits much as their fathers before them and were highly dependent upon the cooperation of the weather. The amount of land under cultivation was considerably expanded by the close of the eleventh century. Forests were cleared, swamps and marshes were drained, and the plowman moved ever higher up the mountainside. Some of this marginal land was quickly eroded and, when prices fell, abandoned.

Farmers came to town on market days to shop.

Before A.D. 1100 the usual practice in all of Europe was to follow what was known as the **two-field system.** In one year the field would lay fallow so as to regain some of its fertility. In the next it would be planted. Between A.D. 1100 and 1200 some farmers in northern Europe discovered that a three-field system improved their output. This permitted them to plant one field with a fall crop and one with a spring crop and to leave only one third of the land fallow in any given year.

Rotating the fields increased production, but yields were very small for all the work put into farming. Almost half to one third of the grain harvested had to be used for seed the following year because of the poor quality of the cereal plants then found in Europe. Agricultural pests, especially locusts, could devastate a field in a matter of hours adding to the perils of farming. Woods, ponds, and waste lands were held in common, but the landlord reserved hunting wild animals for himself and his friends. Poaching was severely punished but never completely eradicated.

Spring plowing was arduous. As many as eight oxen yoked in pairs were needed to pull the plow through the heavy, clay soils of northern

Europe. The farmer had to force the plow into the ground, often rocky or full of weeds, making the task extremely difficult. The Germans were familiar with the use of a plow since ancient times, but it was only in the Middle Ages that inventive farmers made a significant improvement on it by placing a curved iron plate, the **moldboard,** behind the plowshare. When outfitted with a wheel, the **moldboard plow** made it possible to expand the amount of land that could be prepared in a single day, since the earth was turned over and furrowed in a single operation.

Another agricultural advance came from the use of horses for plowing. Horses were stronger and could work longer hours than oxen, but their use as draught animals awaited the invention of the padded horse collar. This placed the weight upon the animal's chest and shoulders rather than the harness around the neck, which strangled the animal when pulling. Horseshoes also came into use after the tenth century. They protected fragile hoofs that otherwise easily cracked in a damp climate. Oxen, however, remained the major draught animals in France until the fifteenth century and in the Netherlands until the seventeenth century, demonstrating how tenaciously most European farmers held to traditional ways.

After the twelfth century in England and then on the continent, it became usual for farmers, now serfs, to work in open, unfenced fields. Each family held several strips of land about the size of an acre, the amount of land that could efficiently be plowed in a day. In addition, the landowner, the lord, had his strips of land along with those of the serfs, and these had to be worked by the serfs 2, 3, or 4 days a week. The amount of time the laborers had to spend on the lord's property had been agreed upon when first the serf commended his land to the lord.

A steward or bailiff directed the serfs' work and represented their concerns to the landowner. The village kept its breeding stock, its bull and ram, and its farming equipment on the grounds of the church.

Wives and children tended the animals and cared for vegetable gardens while men were responsible for farming the large fields planted in grain. Heat exhaustion and aching backs during harvest time were frequent since reaping the grain was done with hand sickles.

Holding land was of great importance to Europeans of this age. Foremost among concerns of the landowning class was to be sure that the farms held in the family name should be passed on intact to the next generation. In England the law of **primogeniture** held that the oldest son had the right to inherit the whole of his father's properties. Even in France and Germany, where the inheritance might be divided, the eldest son enjoyed certain prerogatives. Younger brothers often remained unmarried since there was simply not enough land to go around.

Entertainment was rugged in these times. Boxing, wrestling, archery, and feats of individual strength were all a part of life, and those who competed best were much admired. There were various kinds of ball games as well as cock fighting and bear baiting. Everyone enjoyed singing and dancing. Even monks and nuns joined in the village celebrations on the holy days of the year. Hrotswitha, a nun of Gandersheim convent located in Saxony, wrote stories based on the lives of the saints, but she was more famous for her plays modeled on those of the Roman author Terence. These were performed in the convent with the nuns assuming the various actors' parts, the first drama of the Middle Ages.

Despite the advances made in the European diet, the promise of a longer life for most people was still distant. Disease was omnipresent. Malaria, tuberculosis, measles, chickenpox, smallpox, and mumps, illnesses that now usually attack children in a mild form, were devastating for the adult population of medieval Europe. The medical profession, nonexistent in the rural areas and in a primitive state in the towns, did not know how to deal with any of these illnesses. A whole host of skin irritations were diagnosed as leprosy, and those afflicted were forced to lead a life outside society. Handicapped people were cared for by their families at home as were the aged. The notion that they should live apart from their relatives was altogether foreign to the medieval mind. Those who did not have anyone to care for them depended on monasteries and convents for a place to stay.

Besides disease, life could also be cut short by warfare. Obviously foreign invaders took their toll, but even more regrettable was the feudal warfare that went on inside the Christian area of Europe. Most people simply thought war to be a natural condition of humanity. Training for it by experimenting with new weapons and strategies was a constant preoccupation just as it is for today's armies. Trying to discover better weapons did not commence in the twentieth century.

No medieval town was secure unless it had walls to protect it. Soldiers patrolled them day and night.

Churchmen could only hope to mitigate war's worst effects. In the 980s the West Frankish bishops agreed on instituting the **Peace of God.** This levied an excommunication on anyone who used force on women, children, peasants, or clerics. Early in the eleventh century the concept was expanded by clergy in Burgundy. They promulgated the **Truce of God,** which prohibited going to battle from Friday morning until Sunday evening. Holy days, of which there were quite a few, were also ruled out for fighting.

Arts and Literature

In the late tenth and eleventh centuries Islamic Spain on one corner of Europe and Constantinople on the other were the major centers of European culture. Both held extensive libraries and eminent scholars that decry any attempt to label these times as dark.

No one group was more active in intellectual pursuits than the Jews living in the cosmopolitan atmosphere of Andalusian towns. New Sephardic communities blossomed while older ones renewed themselves. Hisdai Ibn Shaprut, a scholar of Córdoba, held a high position in the court of Abd ar-Rahman III. With his wealth he endowed a school for religious study. Other Jews served as translators, for they were fluent in both Hebrew and Arabic. There were also poets, spiritual masters, scientists, and doctors among the Jews of Spain, which makes the eleventh century the Golden Age of Hebrew literature.

For most scholars the **Talmud** became, after the Torah, the most important object of their concern. The Talmud was a greater challenge for it was an anthology, filled with every kind of literature, from law to poetry to sermons, expressing the opinions of dozens of rabbis as they commented upon the sacred writings. Children were taught to read from it, and old men had its pages buried with them.

In Christian Europe the arts clustered about the monastic revival. All the arts received an impetus from the monastic revival, which spread throughout the continent setting its imprint wherever it touched in stone, wood, gold, and parchment.

The monastery of Cluny was at the center of artistic achievement. Here some of the more talented monks studied architecture and the arts reviving the cultural traditions of western Europe that were lost after the dissolution of the Roman Empire. Because their research focused on Roman buildings, the adaptations made by the Cluniac architects reflected this earlier style and is known as **Romanesque.** The Romanesque was characterized by round arches placed on huge piers. Tunnel vaults were used to replace the wooden roofs that formerly covered the interior. This development allowed the builders to make their churches larger and taller than any built before this time.

The third abbey church at Cluny, begun in A.D. 1088 while Hugh of Semur ruled as abbot, became the largest building in western Europe and a model for Romanesque monastic architecture. It was 415 feet long, while the nave held five aisles that were in total 118 feet wide. The vaulted roof over the nave was 98 feet high. Such dimensions had never before been attempted in western Europe. The monks constructed the church so large in order to accommodate the great processions and the thousands of pilgrims who visited Cluny throughout the year. One observer described Cluny as "shining on the earth like a second sun." Today only a single transept of this church remains to testify to its former magnificence.

Sculpture was also promoted by the Cluniac monks. The best remaining work, especially the intricate sculptures over the doors of a church, is found at Vézélay. Here, for the first time in the Middle Ages, the art of sculpture was revived.

Painting was still another art form fostered at Cluny. From the delicate illumination of manuscripts to the huge frescoes painted upon the walls and ceilings of the church, monastic artists delighted the eye. Other arts included metalworking in silver and gold, ceramics, weaving, and glassmaking. All were fashioned for the ornate liturgical celebrations that characterized medieval worship.

Cluny also contributed to the development of music. Odo, abbot in A.D. 927, insisted on exact choral recitation of the Psalms. He wrote a treatise on music in which he assigned letters and intervals to the tones of the musical scale. This made it possible for people to sing a tune without having to memorize it. In the next century another monk, Guido of Arezzo, expanded on Odo's work at Cluny in his own monastery and placed notes upon a staff thereby inventing the system of modern musical notation. During Guido's time polyphonic music became popular, in addition to the usual plainsong melodies of monastic choirs.

It may be thought strange that the monastery, which men entered in order to live apart from the world, should become a workshop of the arts. However, for the monks who lived in this age, the beauty of carved stone and pleasant psalmody offered a foretaste of heavenly joy on earth. It was a time when humanity badly needed this kind of encouragement.

In Italy eleventh-century churches retained the early Christian basilica style.

The most accomplished of Christian scholars was Gerbert of Aurillac, later Pope Silvester II, who was both a friend of and an advisor to Otto III. After completing an early education in his native France, Gerbert went off to Catalonia for 2 years to be close to the frontier of Muslim Spain, western Europe's major source of intellectual stimulation. When he returned north of the Pyrenees to Reims, Gerbert brought Arabic numerals and the abacus with him, introducing these inventions to Christian Europe. Gerbert wrote commentaries on arithmetic, astronomy, and music and designed the construction of several types of organs.

Conclusion

The expansion of Western civilization brought a better life to the people who now lived within the borders of Europe. The missionaries offered a religion that freed them from magic and the cruder aspects of nature worship. They also taught the new people of Europe how to read and write, how to build a stone building, how to illuminate a manuscript, and how to sing a psalm.

The reform of the church was well underway by A.D. 1100, an important undertaking since lay control could easily have thwarted its growth and sapped its energy. The independence of Cluny showed in a remarkable way what an ecclesiastical foundation could accomplish when not inhibited by secular control. Cluny's sponsorship of the arts marked a major advance in European culture.

Better agricultural methods promoted increased food production. Although the standard of living for Europe's serfs remained miserably low, it can be hoped, if not proven, that they ate a little better and their houses were built a bit sturdier during this age.

Unfortunately the church's officials did little to change the minds of kings and nobles that they were chosen by God to be a privileged class. Europe's aristocrats, wealthy only because of the accident of birth, remained indifferent to the gap existing between rich and poor. Nor was there progress in lessening the nobles' attraction to violence. The First Crusade, sponsored by the pope himself, promoted Europe's first ideological war, but unfortunately not its last.

CHAPTER 24 REVIEW
WESTERN RECOVERY AND EAST EUROPEAN AWAKENING

Summary
- The Holy Roman Empire was formed in Germany by the three Ottos.
- Church reform began with the foundation of the abbey of Cluny.
- The Investiture Controversy pitted the emperors against the pope.
- Islamic Spain continued as a center of translation and intellectual life.
- The Normans became western Europe's most energetic people, conquering southern Italy and England.
- Byzantium was endangered from Bulgarians and Seljuk Turks.
- Poland, Hungary, Bohemia, and Kievan Russia became kingdoms in the tenth century.

Identify
People: Otto I; Pope Gregory VII; Abd ar-Rahman III; William the Conqueror; Robert Guiscard; Varangians; Olaf Tryggvason; Mieszko I; Emperor Basil II
Places: Lechfeld; Cluny; Canossa; Clontarf; Manzikert; Kiev
Events: founding the Holy Roman Empire; First Crusade; Investiture Controversy

Define

priors	Peace of God	primogeniture	boyars
shire	consecration	two-field system	cardinals
simony	Talmud	moldboard plow	synods
Almoravids	shire	hundreds	reeve
writs	Althing	doge	
scholasticus	moldboard	consecration	
benefice	Romanesque	Truce of God	

Multiple Choice
1. Otto I is known to be the
   (a) King of England.
   (b) King of France.
   (c) first Holy Roman Emperor.
   (d) first King of Italy.

2. The Investiture Controversy refers to an argument over
   (a) placing bishops in their offices.
   (b) placing kings on their thrones.
   (c) electing an emperor.
   (d) electing the pope.

3. In A.D. 1066 Duke William of Normandy successfully invaded
   (a) England.
   (b) Italy.
   (c) France.
   (d) the Netherlands.

4. Idealists believed unity in Europe could be achieved under the leadership of
   (a) the kings of France and England.
   (b) the Holy Roman Emperor and the pope.
   (c) the Kings of France and the Holy Roman Emperor.
   (d) the pope of Rome and the Byzantine Emperor.

5. The battle of Lechfeld meant the end of raids by
   (a) the Magyars.
   (b) the Muslims.
   (c) the Vikings.
   (d) the Seljuks.

6. Clerical celibacy was welcomed by Europe's kings because
   (a) the pope wanted it.
   (b) church offices could be hereditary.
   (c) it provided efficient civil servants.
   (d) clerics could not have children eligible to inherit lands.

7. Cluny's special status was due to
   (a) its location in Saxony.
   (b) freedom from interference of noble patrons.
   (c) its many abbeys scattered through Europe.
   (d) its proximity to the papal court.

8. At an investiture ceremony a new bishop received from his lord
   (a) a book of rules.
   (b) the Bible.
   (c) his ring and staff.
   (d) title to his residence.

9. A synod is
   (a) a form of investiture.
   (b) a meeting of the clergy.
   (c) a meeting of knights.
   (d) the king's council.

10. The end of the Investiture Controversy came with
    (a) the coronation of Otto III.
    (b) the Concordat of Worms.
    (c) the Synod of Reims.
    (d) the Golden Bull of Prague.

11. The great intellectual center of Spain was
    (a) Madrid.
    (b) Toledo.
    (c) Barcelona.
    (d) Córdoba.

12. The Almoravids entered Spain from
    (a) Tunisia.
    (b) Algeria.
    (c) Morocco.
    (d) Ghana.

13. The contest for leadership of France was between
    (a) the Holy Roman Emperor and the King of France.
    (b) the kings of France and the papacy.
    (c) the Capetian dynasty and Dukes of Normandy.
    (d) the Capetian dynasty and the Carolingians.

14. The capital of Norman Sicily was
    (a) Catania.
    (b) Messana.
    (c) Palermo.
    (d) Syracuse.

15. At the Battle of Hastings, the opponent of William the Conqueror was
    (a) Canute.
    (b) Harold, earl of Wessex.
    (c) Edward the Confessor.
    (d) Godwin.

16. A writ is
    (a) a court judgment.
    (b) an administrative decree.
    (c) an eviction notice.
    (d) an audit.

17. The head of Venice was called
    (a) king.
    (b) baron.
    (c) doge.
    (d) count.

18. Manzikert's outcome meant that
    (a) the Byzantines no longer needed help from the west.
    (b) Alexios I Komnenos sent a delegation to the Mongols.
    (c) the Seljuks withdrew to Inner Asia.
    (d) none of the above.

19. Prague became the capital of
    (a) Poland.
    (b) Great Moravia.
    (c) Bohemia.
    (d) Hungary.

20. The first Kievan prince to become a Christian was
    (a) Oleg.
    (b) Rurik.
    (c) Svyatoslav.
    (d) Vladimir.

21. The role of women in Europe was generally one
    (a) of a public life.
    (b) of family life.
    (c) of life in the church.
    (d) confined to the arts.

Essay Questions
1. Describe the tasks of women in Europe during the Middle Ages.
2. Why did Europe never unite into a single state?
3. Discuss the importance of commerce in medieval Europe.
4. What changes in agriculture took place in the period after A.D. 900?
5. What determined the later arrival of civilization in eastern Europe north of the Danube?

Answers

1. c	8. c	15. b
2. a	9. b	16. b
3. a	10. b	17. c
4. b	11. d	18. d
5. a	12. c	19. c
6. d	13. c	20. d
7. b	14. c	21. b

CHAPTER 25

Developments in the Americas

The leadership in the Mexican region of the Americas passed to new people in the period after A.D. 500. Both the Mayans and the people of Teotihuacán faltered as more vigorous people arrived on the scene. In Peru several cultures, noted for their large cities and sophisticated pottery skills, dominate the history of the region.

Disasters in Mexico

About the year A.D. 550, construction of Mayan temple pyramids stopped for a period of about 50 years. Then, after this pause, Mayan civilization revived. Temple construction commenced again in the lowlands, a period of growth that lasted for the next 300 years. Then war among different Mayan cities caused their civilization to self-destruct, in an unbelievable bloodbath that killed up to 80% of the population. The few farmers that remained could no longer hold back the rain forest.

By A.D. 900, the great age of the Mayans was at an end in Guatemala and Honduras. The Mayans continued to live in Yucatán (they still do), but the civilization that they once supported had lost its creative spirit.

Society in Teotihuacán also faltered about this same time. It was believed that at the end of every century, which lasted 52 years in this Indian culture, it was the occasion to tear down old buildings and start with new. About the year A.D. 750 the great city of Teotihuacán was robbed and then burned to the ground. The amount of destruction was greater than any previous time. Wood was placed around the pyramid temples and then set on fire.

Because no records exist from that period, archaeologists presumed that on this occasion invaders were responsible. Some scholars have recently suggested that the people of Teotihuacán did it themselves. Perhaps a natural disaster, such as a prolonged drought, may have occurred causing a terrible famine. People expected that the gods should help them, but when the priests could not get the gods to respond, the men and women of Teotihuacán became angry and burned down their temples with a vengeance never seen before. They abandoned the site forever.

Toltecs Dominate Mexico

If the destruction of Teotihuacán was in fact due to invaders, likely candidates were warlike peoples who spread over Mexico about this time. These were the **Chichimecs.** They slaughtered any Mexican peoples who offered resistance, but if a region surrendered, the Chichimecs were content to have its inhabitants pay tribute. By this time metalworking was introduced to Mexico and employed for ornaments and jewelry, but seldom for weapons.

With the passage of time, some Chichimec tribes, among them the Toltecs, became less fierce. Their first known Toltec leader was a chieftain named Topiltzin, who ruled at the close of the tenth century. In later times many legends were told about him. One myth held that he was partly divine, a reincarnation of the ancient serpent-god Quetzalcóatl. At Tula, his capital, skilled artisans set to work to build a large city for the Toltecs, now so prosperous. By A.D. 970 Tula was the dominant city in the Valley of Mexico, collecting tribute from all the tribes surrounding it.

The carving of a Toltec warrior served as a pillar.

Then something strange happened. Topiltzin decided that everyone must worship Quetzalcóatl, his patron. Many people in Tula resisted; they had no desire to change their beliefs and sacrifice to Quetzalcóatl. His opponents forced Topiltzin to leave Tula. Before he left, according to the story, Topiltzin promised he would return in the rising sun in the east.

The citizens of Tula, in imitation of Tenochtitlán, were intent upon pyramid building. The largest was five stories high. Great stone warriors standing in a line guarded the temple's summit. The same pattern was repeated at other Toltec sites.

Toltec armies marched all over Mexico and Guatemala, conquering the other Indian peoples. About the year A.D. 1000, the Toltecs overran what was left of the Maya population in Yucatán. The Toltecs who settled there joined with Mayan artisans to build a new capital, similar to what they recalled of Tula, at Chichén Itzá. A cooperative effort resulted in the construction of a great temple complex with altars for sacrifices to the Toltec gods. These gods, like all those in Central America, demanded blood of humans to be kept alive themselves.

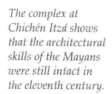

The complex at Chichén Itzá shows that the architectural skills of the Mayans were still intact in the eleventh century.

Chichén Itzá held an astronomical observatory and a sacred well. Priests threw people, many of them children, into this well when the gods were upset. Gold, jewelry, and other objects also went into it, making it possible for modern archaeologists to learn much about the Yucatán way of life.

The constant need for captives to be sacrificed to the Toltec gods meant that few tears were shed when in the mid-twelfth century one more group of Chichimecs overthrew Tula and destroyed it. When Tula collapsed, no strong power was left in central Mexico.

Mississippian Culture in North America

North of the Rio Grande in what is now the United States, the level of culture lagged behind that of Mexico. Two societies did appear, the Adena and Hopewell, both of them noted for their interest in mound building. Here chieftains were buried with grave gifts that came from a considerable distance.

About A.D. 500 the American Indians known as the Mississippians assumed leadership in the valley of the river whose name archaeologists have given them. The Mississippians were farmers of corn and beans, unlike their predecessors who probably did not practice agriculture. They lived in villages or towns of considerable size, the largest near the city of Cahokia, Illinois, where 85 mounds are now counted. The largest, probably in imitation of the constructions in Mexico, was a huge pyramid, 100 feet high.

In the Southwest the American Indians living in what is now New Mexico and Arizona were also corn farmers. Three different cultures developed: Mogollon, Hohokam, and Anasazi. The Hohokam constructed a network of canals to bring water to their fields because where they lived is a very dry area. Some of the waterways, up to 10 feet deep, traveled 30 miles, requiring significant engineering skills. Anasazi people are the predecessors of the Pueblo Indians. They are distinguished by their home construction; about A.D. 1000 they began to build apartments and cliff dwellings.

Events in South America

About the year A.D. 500 the Tiahuanaco culture arose near Lake Titicaca, a large body of water 14,000 feet above sea level in the Andes. The importance of Tiahuanaco came from its new and powerful god whose sanctuary was here. His image, that of a stubby man with a huge headdress, is still to be seen on a temple gateway. From his eyes come tears. This "weeping god" had apparently become the most popular divinity of the Peruvian Indians. The frequent finds of his image show that people worshipped him the length of the Andes, from present-day Ecuador to Chile.

The city of Tiahuanaco contained many stone buildings. Among them were a fortress and houses for the priests who directed the worship to the weeping god. Some of the stones used in the city's buildings weigh up to 100 tons. Masons knew how to fit them together with copper clamps.

The people who lived in Tiahuanaco held their prominence until about the year A.D. 1000. By that time other Peruvian people had appeared on the scene.

Nazca, Chimu, and Moche

The Nazca, living to the north of Tiahuanaco, were expert in making textiles and pottery. On a single pot an artist might use 11 different colors of paint, depicting animals and birds. The Nazca were also fond of drawing large geometrical figures of all kinds on the ground outside their villages. These figures were made by scratching away the dark gravel on the surface so as to reveal the lighter material underneath.

A Nazca drawing can only be seen in its entirety from the sky.

Some scholars believe these figures were astronomical observatories since they line up with certain heavenly bodies. There are also spirals and animal shapes. What is mysterious is that these figures can be seen only from the sky. It was impossible for the Nazca who built the figures to see them at ground level.

Another people made up the Chimu nation of northern Peru. The Chimu built their capital at Chan-Chan, a city of temples, parks, and man-made lagoons. The Chimu developed a way to cast golden objects by first carving the object in wax, shaping a mold over it, and then melting out the wax so that gold could be put in to replace it. This is called the **lost wax method** of making gold objects. Chimu society could be ruthless. Doctors who made a mistake and killed their patients were themselves killed. The doctor's body was then tied together with the patient's body for burial.

The Moche Indians at this time created the first large social organization in Peru. In order to construct canals and maintain them, the chiefs rounded up ordinary people and put them into forced labor crews. Moche warriors carried clubs and shields and wore padded helmets to protect themselves from blows to the head.

In the southern Andes, after A.D. 700, the discovery of how to mix tin with copper gave birth to the first Bronze Age of the Americas. It required another century for smiths to learn how to shape it.

Despite all their building skills, South American Indians never discovered the wheel. Everything that had to be transported was done by humans or on llamas' backs, and these animals can only carry 100 pounds. In Mexico no llamas were present, so that workers there had only themselves for carrying burdens. South American Indians also never developed a writing system. Coinage or any medium of exchange was also absent. This meant that trading had to be done by barter, a difficult way to determine fair exchanges.

On the other hand, South American Indians were expert in goldsmithing and stone work. Some archaeologists believe that no artisans in any other world society ever surpassed them in these areas.

In the rest of South America, away from the civilizing influences of Peru, Indians remained in hunting and gathering tribes. Often they lived quite isolated from one another. In the Amazon rain forest the Indians cultivated manioc, a root that can be eaten only after its poisonous properties are washed out. Many Indians developed a taste for drugs, especially in the Andes, where chewing on coca leaves gave people a defense against the cold. Tobacco juice was also drunk as a narcotic.

Some Indians in the Amazon were head-hunters, a gruesome custom that continued up to the twentieth century. On the other hand, Amazon Indians created a way of life admirably suited to their environment.

Indian villagers of the Amazon still live through hunting and fishing.

Conclusion

The destruction of Teotihuacán and the disappearance of the sophisticated Mayan way of life were setbacks for Mexican civilization. Several centuries were to pass before new energy came into Central America. Peru fared much better with a succession of cultures that brought a high level of satisfaction to thousands of people.

CHAPTER 25 REVIEW
DEVELOPMENTS IN THE AMERICAS

Summary
- A series of disasters, some natural and others the result of war, struck the Mayans and Teotihuacán.
- The Toltecs formed the next major culture of Mexico.
- The Mississippian culture, north of the Rio Grande, assumed leadership in this part of the world.

Identify
People: Toltecs; Topiltzin; Hohokan; Nazca; Mississippians; Anasazi
Places: Guatemala; Cahokia; Honduras; Chichén Itzá; Tula; Tiahuanaco
Events: destruction of Mayan and Teotihuacán civilizations; formation of the Toltec Empire

Define
Chichimecs	lost wax method
Yucatán	Quetzalcóatl

Multiple Choice
1. The end of the Mayan civilization in Guatemala apparently resulted from
   (a) flooding.
   (b) an invasion of Chichimecs.
   (c) the migration of people from Yucatán.
   (d) intercity warfare.

2. A "century" closed in Teotihuacán
   (a) every 100 years.
   (b) every 50 years.
   (c) every 52 years.
   (d) every 500 years.

3. The dominant city of Mexico in the late tenth century was
   (a) Chichén Itzá.
   (b) Teotihuacán.
   (c) Tenochtitlán.
   (d) Tula.

4. The Mississippians were similar to other Indian societies in their concern to
   (a) build pyramids.
   (b) locate their cities on a lake.
   (c) hunt bison.
   (d) use horses to form a cavalry.

5. The weeping god is associated with
   (a) Teotihuacán.
   (b) Cahokia.
   (c) Tiahuanaco.
   (d) Tula.

6. These South American Indians scratched figures on the ground for unknown purposes:
   (a) the Chimu.
   (b) the Nazca.
   (c) the Moche.
   (d) the Hohokam.

Essay Questions
   1. What are possible reasons for the waning of Mayan civilization in the eighth century?
   2. What made trade difficult in the Americas?

Answers
1. d   4. a
2. c   5. c
3. d   6. b

UNIT **5**

CHANGING TRADITIONS:
A.D. **1100–1500**

CHAPTER 26

Crusaders, Turks, and Mongols

Southwest Asia was the scene of major shifts of power during the period of the Late Middle Ages. The Seljuk Turkish world, dominant in the eleventh century, practically fell apart in the twelfth. Its decline was one reason the Crusaders enjoyed an initial success during the First Crusade. With the Seljuks out of the way, the Ottomans replaced them as the major state of Southwest Asia.

Even though the Ottomans seemed to go from victory to victory, a dark cloud gathered on the horizon, the Mongols. For a time it appeared that the Mongols had the potential to doom the Islamic hold on southwestern Asia, a fate the Muslims narrowly escaped thanks to the intervention of Egypt.

Anatolia's fate may well have been decided earlier when urban life and commerce were weakened as a result of environmental factors. The fragile forests of the countryside had become depleted when peasants cut them down for fuel and building material for their homes without any concern for replanting the trees. The resulting erosion of the precious topsoil made farming unproductive for the population. They began an exodus from the region, leaving the land empty. The Seljuks were content to pasture animals rather than raise crops and where once there had been farms, now there were grasslands.

Latin East

The Crusaders' capture of Jerusalem in the last year of the eleventh century opened a short-lived period of Western occupation of Palestine and parts of Syria. The knights chose Godfrey of Bouillon, a Flemish noble to

The entrance to the church of the Holy Sepulchre. The present church dates from Crusader times.

assume the leadership of their state, with the title, Defender of the Holy Sepulcher. After his death a year later, his brother Baldwin followed him as King of Jerusalem. He was chief of the other three crusading states—Tripoli, Antioch, and Edessa—where other Western princes ruled.

The First Crusade was primarily motivated by religious fervor. Nevertheless, many who signed on went east in the hope of obtaining personal wealth and property. Others participated out of a yen for adventure.

In the Crusader lands the Latins introduced French feudalism, a social and economic system that was familiar to them in their homeland. From lands confiscated from the Muslims, the princes handed out fiefs to their vassals. Catholic bishops replaced the Eastern bishops as religious leaders, but on the local level the parish priests held on as long as they mentioned the pope in their prayers.

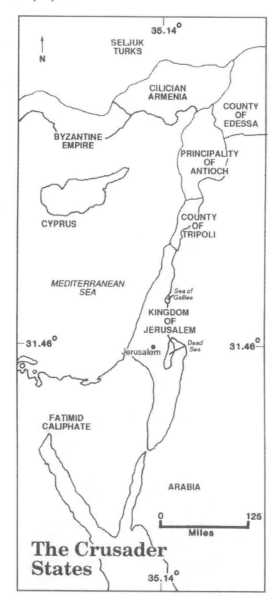

The Crusader States

Baldwin's main problems were men and money. Many knights left Palestine for home after they had secured Jerusalem, taking with them their sergeants. Still the Crusaders continued campaigns that cleared the Lebanese coast from Tyre to Beirut. The knights ordered massive castles constructed to defend the territories they won, their size meant to overwhelm the Muslim peasantry who worked as serfs for their Crusader lords.

The Krak des Chavaliers, now in modern Syria, was the largest castle built by the Crusaders.

The military position of the Crusaders was always precarious, for the number of soldiers never exceeded several thousand. To make up for the lack of manpower, several military orders formed of knights who took monastic vows of poverty, chastity, and obedience to their superior, and in addition a solemn promise to defend the Holy Land. The two most notable were the Templars and the Knights Hospitalers of St. John. Although these military orders were founded to aid the retention of Jerusalem, they became rivals with each other and the kings of Jerusalem. As they quibbled, the power of their enemies grew.

All that the Muslims needed to begin a reconquest was leadership. This they found in Zangi, the beg of Mosul. In A.D. 1144 he overwhelmed the Christian defenders of Edessa. The fall of this principality so shocked the public in Europe that it gave rise to the Second Crusade. The pope entrusted the preaching of the venture to Bernard of Clairvaux, then the most well-known cleric of the West. Bernard enlisted two kings, Louis VII of France and Conrad III of the Roman Empire. The expeditions of the kings were disasters with weather and battles against both Turks and hostile Byzantines taking their toll.

The monarchs counted it a victory when they won Damascus, which actually served as a buffer against a much stronger opponent, Nureddin. Satisfied that they had done enough, they headed back to Europe. Bernard expressed his feeling that their venture was "an abyss so deep that I must call him blessed, if he is not scandalized." Nureddin soon cleared Syria of Crusaders.

Leadership of the Muslims now passed to Salah al-Din (Saladin), a Kurdish warrior in the service of the Egyptian Fatimids. In July 1187 Salah al-Din crushed a party of knights at Hittin, capturing Guy, the king of Jerusalem. In October, Salah al-Din entered Jerusalem.

Once more the news of a disaster in the Holy Land sparked a wave of anger, resulting in the Third Crusade. Its leader was the Roman Emperor, Frederick Barbarossa. After marching through the Balkans and then through southern Anatolia, the emperor collapsed and died from a heart attack. Most of his leaderless army turned back.

In A.D. 1228 Emperor Frederick II regained Jerusalem through diplomacy, rather than fighting, but the truce lasted but 12 years. In A.D. 1291, Acre, the last fortress city of the Crusaders, was lost.

The Lusignan castle of Cyprus became the residence of the exiled kings of Jerusalem.

The Crusader states were little more than an irritant in the context of Southwest Asian history. They did have an effect on the Muslims, who subsequently regarded Western Christians as aggressive and boorish, and on the Byzantines, who were convinced of their treachery. For the West, the Crusades were an exciting adventure, opening a whole new world of ideas and products never before experienced. The Crusader states were the first western European colonies to live abroad.

Mongols

The Muslim world was not aware that events happening in distant eastern Asia would affect them much more than the Crusades had. Their lands were soon to be shattered by an invasion. Almost overnight the Mongols exploded into Southwest Asia.

Before the thirteenth century the Mongols lived to the south and east of Lake Baykal, above the Gobi Desert in Inner Asia. Mongol men and women were, for the most part, nomadic herders. They lived in houses, called **yurts**, which were made of horsehair felt that was stretched over poles. These could be easily carried on their horses.

Mongol young men were taught by their fathers to be expert horsemen. They practiced shooting an arrow while riding both forward and backward,

A Mongol couple stand outside a yurt, their tent home.

as well as leaning below the horse's belly so as not to present a target. They could wheel their horses into formations or break them up in an instant. It was not unknown for an army to travel 80 miles in a single day.

Early in the thirteenth century the Mongols determined to go on campaign. To lead them they chose for khan a chieftain named Temujin. Personal loyalty counted for everything in Mongol society, and Temujin took advantage of that sentiment. His title was Ghengis Khan, in Mongolian this translates into supreme ruler. Ghengis Khan's attention focused on East Asia, but his grandson had reason to expand Mongol concerns farther west. The terrorism of the Assassins was the excuse he needed. He sent his commander Hulagu Khan to put an end to their behavior.

Hulagu brought his Mongol army into eastern Persia and destroyed the Assassin stronghold. Hulagu Khan then turned his army against the Seljuk Turks. In A.D. 1243 the Seljuk sultan confronted the Mongols at Kösedagh, where the Mongols won such a victory that the Seljuk power was forever shattered. Finally the khan's armies advanced on Baghdad. In A.D. 1258 Hulagu Khan occupied the city, robbed it of its wealth, killed the caliph, and practically destroyed everything in it. The Mongol destruction of Baghdad marks the end of the Abbasid Caliphate.

Mongol armies appeared to be invincible, as one by one the cities of Syria and Palestine were looted and then destroyed. They had now defeated all the strong Muslim nations of Southwest Asia. It appeared that all the Islamic heartland was about to be lost.

Only one strong Muslim power remained. This was Mamluk Egypt. Two years after the fall of Baghdad, the Mongols faced an Egyptian army at Ayn Jalut in Palestine. No one thought the Egyptians had much of a chance, but they were proved wrong. The Muslim Egyptian general Al-Din Baybars won the battle, forcing the Mongols to retreat eastward. Baybars was content to allow them to remain in Persia, but freed Syria and Palestine from their hold. A Mongol dynasty continued to govern Persia for the next several centuries.

The Mongols' near conquest of Southwest Asia shook the Muslim leaders of that part of the world. The great cities, the irrigation systems, and the port facilities that once were the pride of the Islamic nations lay devastated.

Why were the Mongols so destructive? The reason seems to have been that they wanted to gain a reputation so terrible that people would surrender rather than offer resistance.

After the Mongols abandoned Syria and Palestine, Christians who were still a majority of the people in the thirteenth century found themselves in trouble. Christians had often sided with the Mongols, hoping that the invaders might rid them of their Muslim rulers. In Baghdad Hulagu Khan, whose first wife was Christian, destroyed the mosques but not the churches. Now that the Mongols were gone, the restored Muslim rulers no longer trusted their Christian subjects and made life harder for them. As a result, many Christian communities converted to Islam, beginning the decline that has reduced the churches of Southwest Asia to minorities.

Formation of the Ottoman State

In Anatolia the Mongol victories over the Seljuk sultan allowed many small principalities to develop. For a time there was no central leadership. In one of these states, however, a chieftain named Osman rallied the Turkish warriors to his side. His soldiers, the **ghazzis**, had only one reason to exist, to fight for their Muslim faith.

Because Osman's state was on the border with the Byzantine Empire in northwestern Turkey, soldiers enlisted here rather than in the interior of the country, which was removed by distance from the Christian world. People flocked from all over Anatolia to Yenishehir, the capital of the Ottoman sultan, who gave his name to the dynasty he founded.

The grave of a Sufi founder in Konya, Turkey is decorated in brilliant blue tiles.

Yenishehir and the other towns of the Ottomans attracted merchants and Muslim scholars as well as soldiers. When compared to what was left of the Byzantine cities, Muslim towns presented quite a contrast. Tradesmen in the Ottoman towns formed **guilds** that promoted social and religious activities. In A.D. 1333 the traveler Ibn Battuta visited Anatolia and described the guilds, "Nowhere in the world will you find men so eager to welcome travelers, so prompt to serve food and to satisfy the wants of others . . . . A stranger is made to feel as if he were meeting the dearest of his own relatives."

In the middle years of the 1300s, the Ottomans pushed out the last Byzantine governors of Anatolia and installed their own leaders. Farms that were once held by Greeks or Armenians were turned over to the **siphais**, the Ottoman cavalrymen. The land remained the property of the Ottoman sultans but was distributed to his soldiers. Siphais could use the land as long as they were enlisted in the Ottoman army.

In A.D. 1354 Sultan Orhan crossed into Europe as a participant in a Byzantine civil war in progress around Constantinople. Several more campaigns in Europe convinced the sultan to make a permanent settlement there. In Southwest Asia, many small states had an opportunity to emerge as the Ottomans concentrated upon Europe.

During the reign of Sultan Murad I, the Ottomans were acknowledged as the leading power of Anatolia and the Balkans. Murad had interests in both. In Anatolia a number of Turkish principalities had to be brought under Ottoman control, a task that had almost concluded, when once again the news went out, "The Mongols are coming."

This time the Mongol leader was Timur the Lame, or Timur Leng. In A.D. 1402 his army was at Ankara, awaiting the Ottoman sultan Bayezid. Battle was joined, the Ottomans were crushed, and Sultan Bayezid was captured. Timur kept the once proud sultan in a cage to display him to his enemies. Timur's forces reached as far as Izmir; then he turned eastward, and the rest of Southwest Asia breathed easier.

After a period of civil war the Ottomans regained Anatolia, although their hold was always threatened by other Turkish leaders who wanted to be free of Ottoman rule. The rulers of Egypt, the Mamluks also watched with interest how far the ambitions of the Ottoman sultans would carry them.

Conclusion

In A.D. 1500 the then-reigning sultan, Bayezid II, could well be satisfied with the accomplishments of his ancestors. Anatolia was now safely Ottoman, and the Greek and Armenian population were resigned to a minority position. The Turkish element in Anatolia was on the increase as more nomadic people poured into the region.

Mamluk Egypt was a rival in Syria and Palestine, but that could be solved later. Persia was still reeling from the Mongols. The future of the Ottomans looked very bright.

CHAPTER 26 REVIEW
CRUSADERS, TURKS, AND MONGOLS

Summary
- The Crusaders established the kingdom of Jerusalem along French feudal lines.
- The Crusader states were too small and weak to survive an attack from Salah al-Din.
- The Mongols from Inner Asia came into Southwest Asia and destroyed Baghdad.
- The Ottomans followed the Seljuks as the dominant power in Anatolia.

Identify
People: Godfrey of Bouillon; Knights of St. John; Nureddin; Salah al-Din; Hulagu Khan; Osman; Baybars; Timur Leng
Places: Edessa; Kösedagh; Ayn Jalut; Yenishehir
Events: establishment of Crusader states; Mongol invasions

Define
ghazzis   yurts   siphais   guilds

Multiple Choice
1. One reason for the demise of Byzantine Anatolia was
    (a) overgrazing of the land.
    (b) depopulation.
    (c) the Crusades.
    (d) the Mongols.

2. The Latin Crusader states included
    (a) Edessa.
    (b) Tripoli.
    (c) Jerusalem.
    (d) all the above.

3. The crusading military orders were monks dedicated to
    (a) works of charity.
    (b) defending the Holy Land.
    (c) negotiating with the Muslims.
    (d) serving pilgrims.

4. The year A.D. 1187 was the occasion for
    (a) the Mongol victory over the Seljuks.
    (b) the Seljuk victory over the Mongols.
    (c) the Latin conquest of Jerusalem.
    (d) the fall of Jerusalem to Salah al-Din.

5. Baybars was the Egyptian general at the
    (a) fall of Jerusalem.
    (b) battle of Ayn Jalut.
    (c) battle of Kösedagh.
    (d) capture of Baghdad.

6. The second wave of Mongols to enter Southwest Asia was led by
    (a) Timur Leng.
    (b) Ghengis Khan.
    (c) Orhan.
    (d) Hulagu Khan.

Essay Questions
 1. Why were the Crusader states unable to hold onto their territories?
 2. Why were the Mongol invasions important for Christians in Southwest Asia?
 3. Discuss the rise of the Ottoman Turks.

Answers
1. a   4. d
2. d   5. b
3. b   6. a

The Late Middle Ages in India and Southeast Asia

Certain patterns emerge during the Late Middle Ages of India that are similar to the flow of events of earlier times. A new series of Muslim invaders appear in Afghanistan. They descend into India and establish an empire; then after several decades, rebellions threaten the power of the central government. This chain of events was almost inevitable because the Muslim rulers rewarded their nobles with tax-free land in return for military service. Strong personalities among the nobility were anxious to shake off the strictures of the central government.

Islam and Hinduism

In the first of the invasions, the Turkish chieftain Muhammad Ghuri led his armies into the Ganges plain, destroying what could not be carried away. Nalanda, the great center of Buddhist learning that housed thousands of monks, went up in flames. The monks scattered to the winds, many of them taking refuge in Nepal and Tibet, thereby confirming the Buddhist faith in those regions.

The collapse of Buddhism is one of the major religious events of eleventh century India. At the time of the conquest, monastic life was already in decline, more concerned with magic than prayer, and the Muslim invasion was just the last straw to push Buddhism over the edge. Thousands of Buddhist communities went over to Islam. Individual conversions were very difficult because such a decision would have meant social ostracism.

On the other hand, Hindus, except for those in the lowest castes, found little attractive about Islam. Brahmans, in fact, were exempt from taxation, giving them no economic incentive to convert. Muslims and Hindus often worked together and dressed alike, but they kept their social lives distinct, and towns held separate Hindu and Muslim quarters.

Within Islam certain distinctions developed that approached the Hindu caste system. Even **sati**, the requirement for a widow to die on her husband's funeral pyre, entered Islam. For many reasons Muslim rulers often found it advantageous to use Hindus in their civil service and armies and difficult not to adopt some aspects of their culture.

Sunrise on the Ganges for Hindus is a special time for bathing and prayer.

The main propagators of Islam were merchants who were **sufis,** members of Muslim brotherhoods. Sufism had many similarities to Hindu bahkti and was attractive because of the close ties it engendered among its members and its charitable activities.

To lessen the impact of Sufism, the brahmans sought to make Hinduism more appealing. Personal devotion, **bahkti,** received even more attention, with groups formed to encourage men, women, people of all castes, and even untouchables to join prayer groups noted for chants, dances, and the use of drugs that were meant to induce the worshipper into an ecstatic state. The focus was on three divinities—Shiva, Krishna, and Kali.

Shiva is shown dancing in a ring of fire.

Islam was especially successful in gaining converts in Bengal. After A.D. 1339 it became a region independent of the Delhi sultanate. Sufi **pirs,** (teachers) were very active in winning over the hearts of Hindus living there. Yet one of the greatest of Hindu teachers, Krishna Caitanya, a revered mystic, taught the worship of Krishna in Bengal during this period. In the fifteenth century Kabir, a Muslim weaver, produced poetry of extreme sensitivity. He stressed the similarities, rather than the differences, between the two communities. All men and women were equal in his view, no matter their caste.

Indian civilization enriched Islam, giving its Muslim conquerors skills in mathematics and astronomy that were later passed on to Europe. Medicine and music were additional gifts. Also note that the game of chess passed from India into the Muslim countries.

Slave Dynasty of Delhi

Muhammad Ghuri made Delhi on the Yamuna River his capital. Because Delhi was located in the center of northern India, Ghuri could survey the Ganges plain from his palace in all directions. He later returned to Afghanistan, leaving a lieutenant in Delhi to carry on.

The rulers who governed from Delhi started their lives as slaves, who were enlisted in the Muslim armies. If they were talented and good fortune came their way, young men taken as slaves quickly rose through the ranks, a select few reaching the sultanate. Assassination of the ruler was not uncommon if an ambitious general was dissatisfied. From A.D. 1236 to 1240, the sultanate was held by a woman, Raziyya. She was the only woman to hold a major public office in India until Indira Gandhi in A.D. 1966.

War was constant between regional Muslim rulers and Hindu Rajputs. Rajput armies consisted of cavalry and corps of war elephants. To provide funds for all their military activities and building programs, the Delhi sultans collected exorbitant taxes from the peasantry. The heaviest burdens fell upon the Hindu **dhimmis,** for they had to pay this poll tax as well as those levied on their crops.

The Delhi sultanate at first did not extend into the Deccan plateau or southern India where a variety of Hindu states managed to ward off the invaders. As a result, the Hindus, Jains, and Christians who lived in this part of India did not have the same experience with Islamic armies as the non-Muslims of the north.

During the reign of Sultan Muhammad Ala-ud-Din from A.D. 1296 to 1316, the Mongols threatened to invade India. The sultan's armies proved strong enough to turn them back in a major triumph. This success encouraged Ala-ud-Din to turn his armies against the Hindu states of the Deccan and southern India. In A.D. 1309, for the first time, Muslim forces reached all the way to the tip of India.

The fourteenth century was not an easy one for the majority of Indians. Raiding, pillaging, and constant warfare caused suffering for much of the population. During one campaign 400,000 men and women met their death. The bitterness of these years etched itself into the consciousness of the Hindu people.

One enterprising sultan tried to institute a novel way to enhance the amount of money in circulation. He issued copper and bronze coins that were the equivalent of the silver ones in circulation. Learning of the opportunity to turn pots and pans into coinage, Indian housewives melted down the family kitchen utensils. The sultan had to retreat, recognizing that his monetary reform was a mistake.

In A.D. 1398 the Delhi sultan faced a major challenge. Timur Leng marched his cavalry into Afghanistan in preparation for a descent into India. Timur's army rolled over all opposition, crushing the sultan's armies.

Hindu priests bathe at dawn to purify themselves.

Few people in world history have had such indifference toward human life. Timur's armies killed tens of thousands of people in India, took other thousands prisoner, and so destroyed Delhi that a chronicler wrote that over the city "not even a bird was left to fly." Indian captives whom Timur took back to his capital designed their captor's magnificent tomb in Samarkand, now in modern Uzbekistan.

Timur put a puppet official in India, but his authority carried little weight. All over India independent rulers sprang up, both Muslim and Hindu depending on who could raise the larger army. One of the most successful was Ahmad Shah in Gujarat. Ahmad Shah made his capital, Ahmadabad, famous for its lively trade with all parts of Asia. He built mosques, hospitals, and schools that still remain as a testament to his concerns. The Slave Dynasty of Delhi continued past A.D. 1500, but by that date it was only a shadow of its former self.

Camel herders of northern India still trade their animals in markets that reach back to the times of the Delhi sultanate.

The Muslim invasions made an indelible mark on Indian history. Mistrust and hatred between conquerors and conquered, between Muslim and Hindu, grew out of the experience of these years.

Sri Lanka and Southeast Asia

From A.D. 1100 to 1500 Tamils from India emigrated to Sri Lanka and established their own kingdom on the island. This meant that two different ethnic groups now had their homes there, and tension between them was never far off.

The countries of Southeast Asia were placed in the middle of their two major neighbors, India and China. The Burmese, Thais, Cambodians, and most Indonesian islanders were caught up in the circle of India. Vietnam, on the other hand, depended on Chinese cultural models while vigorously rejecting the emperor's political control.

The Khmer (Cambodian) kingdom with its capital at Angkor Thom, was one of the region's richer states. The Khmer ruler claimed he was an agent of the Hindu gods and goddesses that provided the people of the country with their bountiful crops.

Much of the country's wealth went to the priestly class that officiated in the temples of the kingdom. Clergy who served in smaller temples paid a sum of money to the priests of the larger, central temples.

Canals covered the countryside and were used for transporting people and goods. Reservoirs caught the rain from the monsoons, for the distribution of water throughout the year into the omnipresent rice paddies.

At the beginning of the twelfth century, the Khmer king, Suryavarman II, commissioned the construction of a religious complex near the capital that was known as Angkor Wat. Its construction was truly monumental, requiring 30 years of labor by thousands of people. The number of buildings at Angkor Wat, today located in modern Cambodia, made it the largest religious shrine in the world. Its central temple once held five gilded towers representing the home of the gods.

Angkor Wat was the largest religious complex ever built in the history of the world.

Originally the Hindu god Vishnu was Angkor Wat's principal deity, but as Buddhism spread in Southeast Asia, monks of that religion added their temples to the complex. Pilgrims of both faiths made Angkor Wat their destination. In the fifteenth century Phnom Penh became the capital, and Angkor Wat, with its many temples, was abandoned to the jungle, its very existence soon forgotten.

The influence of Theravada Buddhism was everywhere evident in Burma, where the kings lavished the wealth of the nation on the construction of temples. The Thais, immigrants in the early twelfth century from China to Southeast Asia, also joined in building large Buddhist monasteries and places of worship.

A modern mosque in Malaysia testifies to the influence of Islam in Southeast Asia.

Java and Sumatra were the preeminent states of Indonesia, equally under the influence of Buddhism. As more Muslim merchants appeared in their ports, Islam obtained a foothold. After a Mongol expedition in the thirteenth century struck both states, traders from Muslim countries renewed their contacts with the islanders. Sufi pirs taught the logic of a single God. To the detriment of both Hinduism and Buddhism, Islam seized the initative in the islands of the Indonesian seas.

Conclusion

India and Southeast Asia had their share of invasion and conflict at this time. Yet whenever there was a peaceful interval, rulers poured their wealth into temples and monasteries, a testament to the human spirit. The Indian Ocean trade continued to expand and with it the Islamic faith.

405

CHAPTER 27 REVIEW
THE LATE MIDDLE AGES IN INDIA AND SOUTHEAST ASIA

Summary
- The Muslims in India practically extinguished Buddhism.
- Islam was in sharp contrast to Hinduism.
- A dynasty of slaves made Delhi the capital of India.
- Constant wars struck the Indian people, especially damaging was the invasion of Timur Leng.
- Sri Lanka received a large migration of Tamils from India.
- The Khmers built the great religious center of Angkor Wat.

Identify
People: Muhammad Ghuri; Raziyya; Ala-ud-Din
Places: Nalanda; Bengal; Delhi; Angkor Wat; Java
Events: establishment of slave dynasty of Delhi; Mongols attack India; Southeast Asian states come under Indian influence

Define
sati   bahkti   sufis   pirs

Multiple Choice
1. One effect of the destruction of Nalanda was
    (a) the establishment of a Muslim school on its foundation.
    (b) the spread of Buddhism to Nepal.
    (c) the growth of Hinduism in southern India.
    (d) the growth of Buddhism in Japan.

2. In India, Muslims
    (a) often adopted Hindu customs.
    (b) had no use for any type of Hindu culture.
    (c) adopted the religious views of the Hindus.
    (d) translated the Qur'an into Sanskrit.

3. Kabir is remembered as a Muslim
    (a) sultan.
    (b) beg.
    (c) poet.
    (d) caliph.

4. In A.D. 1309 for the first time
    (a) Delhi became a capital.
    (b) Muslim forces reached the tip of India.
    (c) Timur Leng appeared in India.
    (d) Hulagu Khan entered India.

5. Timur Leng's tomb is in
    (a) Ghazni.
    (b) Ahmadabad.
    (c) Uzbekistan.
    (d) Delhi.

6. The temple complex at Angkor Wat was first dedicated to
    (a) Shiva.
    (b) Vishnu.
    (c) Kali.
    (d) Buddha.

Essay Questions
    1. How do you explain the growth of Islam in India and Southeast Asia?
    2. Discuss the position of Hindus during the Delhi sultanate.

Answers
1. b   4. b
2. a   5. c
3. c   6. b

East Asia in an Age of Khans and Samurai

Even though China was very large and ten cities held over a million inhabitants in the twelfth century, the Chinese were not able to repel invaders from the north. The Mongols, for so long excluded from China, made a major impact on the country, creating their own, the Yuan, dynasty.

Last Days of Song China

Two events of note appeared in the last days of Song China. One was the effort of Chinese merchants to extend their trading network abroad. This resulted in the creation of a merchant marine, since Chinese traders found their best customers in the islands to the south. The classical Chinese boat, the **junk,** called at Indonesia's island ports for rice, pearls, spices, and ivory.

In the area of scholarship, Ju Xi made a lasting impression by reviving Confucianism in a commentary he wrote. In this work he sought to take what was best in Confucius, Daoism, and Buddhism to draw up a synthesis known as **Neo-Confucianism.**

Ju Xi taught that evil was the result of ignorance. When individuals are born, they have innate ideas that must be drawn out through education. Much of what he said appears very close to Plato's ideas, although Ju Xi never heard of the Greek philospher.

In A.D. 1126 the Jurchen, a tribal people of Manchuria, pierced the Great Wall and descended on Kaifeng, the Song capital. They captured the emperor and 3,000 of his officials. The Jurchen leader proclaimed himself to be the Son of Heaven. His claim was challenged when a Song relative in Hangzhou, a city of South China, announced his intention to carry on the dynasty there. As a result, China had two emperors during the twelfth century.

Khubilai Khan

The Mongols, living to the north of the Chinese, had little use for the sedentary life of their southern neighbors. The Great Wall of China had as its main purpose to keep the Mongols out, but it had fallen into disrepair. This allowed the energetic Mongols to burst into China.

The Chinese considered the Mongols barbarians and their way of life primitive. Mongol cities were no more than tents. Unlike the settled Chinese farmers, the Mongols were constantly on the move. They traveled frequently because of the dry conditions in their homeland, which often meant that the supply of grass available for their herds was quickly exhausted.

Late in the twelfth century at a meeting of the Mongolian tribal chieftains, one of them, Temujin, was chosen to become **Ghengis Khan,** the supreme ruler. Under his leadership the might of the Mongol forces was first felt in northern China. In A.D. 1215, Ghengis Khan's warriors charged into China leaving devastation wherever their armies passed through.

Ghengis Khan commenced a dynasty that carried the Mongols all over Asia and Europe.

The Mongols destroyed everything that could not be carried with them. After northern China was occupied and the Jurchens ousted, Ghengis Khan turned over his command to a general while he went on to other conquests until his death in A.D. 1227.

The final battles fought in North China were completed during the rule of his son, Ögödei Khan. Once Ögödei cleared the north of Chinese armies, he directed his horsemen to invade the Song lands in the south. In A.D. 1264 Ögödei's son, Khubilai, won all of China and announced that he was the new Son of Heaven. The Mongols would have taken the country much sooner had their horses not gotten stuck in the mud so often while fighting in rice paddies.

Khubilai was not a rough warrior who knew nothing of culture. A tutor had educated him in Chinese ways. Khubilai took on the values of a Chinese gentleman but kept the ambitions of a Mongol khan. Not only did he rule China, but after A.D. 1271 he also held the position of Great Khan, the chief of Mongol people wherever they were found.

The emperor built a number of residences in China. One, his summer palace, was located in Shangdu. The emperor also built a palace at Beijing, that the Mongols knew as Dadu. This allowed him to be in close contact with his homeland. Khubilai's palace held a banquet hall with enough places for 6,000 guests.

Khubilai kept hundreds of astrologers nearby to warn him if the heavens were not favorable to a decision. He also had a bodyguard made up of 9,000 soldiers, one third of them on duty at a time. When he went hunting he rode in a litter on the back of 4 elephants. On one New Years' Day, 5,000 elephants marched in the imperial parade.

Khubilai Khan promised good government for China. One of his counselors advised, "The empire was won on horseback, but it cannot be governed on horseback." This taught the khan that he could not depend upon his army for everything.

A number of improvements were made during Khubilai's time. New roads were built throughout the country. Government messengers lived in post houses along these roads, ever ready to pass on messages. The system was so effective that the emperors' commands could swiftly reach all corners of his territories. In addition to the roads, workers started digging new canals, and old waterways were dredged to improve transportation.

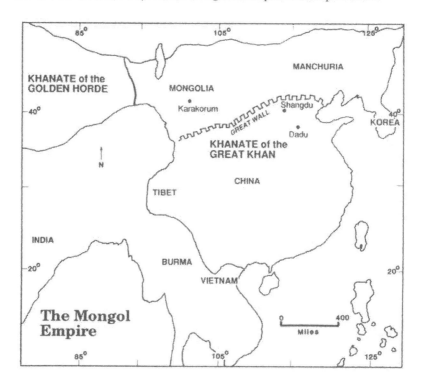

Khubilai needed to staff the civil service but did not really trust his Chinese subjects. Consequently, he frequently employed foreigners who came to Beijing. The most famous of these was a Venetian from Europe, Marco Polo. For 17 years Marco Polo served the Mongol emperor in different capacities. After returning to Europe, he wrote a book about his experiences that first introduced China to Europeans.

Marco Polo left a vivid description of Khubilai's palace at Shangdu:

> When a person leaves this city (of Gavor), he rides for three days until he arrives at the town of Shangdu, built by Khubilai, the Great Khan, who now sits on the throne. Here he lives in a palace of marble and many other rich stones. The palace halls and rooms are covered with gold and are more beautiful than anyone can imagine.
>
> Outside this palace there is a wall so huge that it extends for 15 miles enclosing a park full of rivers and fountains. In it the Great Khan keeps a variety of goats, deer, and other small animals. Their purpose is to provide food for the large cats and falcons that are kept in cages. The park is well watered.

> When the Great Khan decides to take a ride on his horse,
> he may take a leopard along. As soon as he spies an animal,
> he lets the leopard loose and it takes its prey, or he may take it
> back for his caged falcons. This is his way of enjoying himself.

Marco Polo, *Il Milione*, LXIII (Milan: Editoriale Lucchi, 1961), 89–90. Author's translation.

Khubilai was not content with ruling only China. Korea and North Vietnam were his, and South Vietnam, Tibet, Thailand, and Burma were tributaries. He twice sent his navy to attack Japan, but the Mongol attacks failed. It was one of his few disappointments. He died in A.D. 1294 at 80 years of age.

Khubilai had over one hundred children, but only one of these could succeed his father to the throne. He and the other successors of the Great Khan governed China for the next 74 years but were never able to match the illustrious days of Khubilai. Too many fights within the royal household consumed the dynasty's energy. There were no new Mongol conquests.

So long as the khans ruled in Beijing, their Mongol countrymen enjoyed a privileged position. Only the Chinese paid taxes; Mongols did not. Society was divided into four classes: Mongols, foreigners whom the Mongols called "people with colored eyes," the northern Chinese, and finally the southern Chinese who were ranked at the bottom. The Chinese could not carry weapons and were forbidden to learn the Mongol language.

Many Chinese scholars, landowners, and former officials, who once gave the countryside its local government, retired. They went to their homes in the country where they read Confucius and took up writing and painting. New art forms appeared, especially realistic portraits of flowers, horses, and insects. The Chinese novel first appeared as did theater and compositions of music for orchestras.

Chinese aristocrats felt confident that there were not enough Mongols to dominate such a large country for a very long time. They were willing to wait, but not everyone was so patient. Thousands of peasants were starving because floods along the Yellow River reduced their food supply. Small groups of Daoists and Buddhists formed secret societies that planned how they might overthrow the Mongols. One Buddhist group, the **White Lotus Society**, claimed that a savior would appear to drive out their hated rulers. Another sect, the **Red Turbans**, rebelled, but were soon put down.

At last, in A.D. 1368, a Chinese peasant army led by a former Buddhist monk, Zhu Yuanzhang, was successful in overthrowing the Mongols. Zhu Yuanzhang was the first leader of a new Chinese dynasty, the Mings.

China's Brilliant Dynasty, the Ming

The word *ming* means brilliant in Chinese. It was the quality that was meant to characterize the next three centuries of Chinese life.

Zhu Yuanzhang made Nanjing the capital because it was here that he had his first success. The White Lotus Society believed that he was the savior who had been promised to free them from the Mongols. Despite the support he had received from secret societies, the first Ming emperor ruled that they were no longer legal after he came to power. The emperor wanted no more rebellions.

411

In every way Emperor Zhu Yuanzhang tried to put China back together as it was before the Mongol occupation. Confucian scholars returned to the court to urge that harmony could be restored only when everyone obeyed the emperor whom Heaven had chosen to govern China. Examinations were held to determine the best candidates for offices in the government once again. Zhu Yuanzhang was convinced that the Mongol period had been a nightmare, and most of his subjects agreed with him.

A remarkable rebound occurred in China. Once more agriculture and trade flourished throughout the countryside. The most evident sign of Chinese prosperity was the great naval expeditions funded by the Ming emperors from the year A.D. 1403 onward. An enormous fleet of 28,000 soldiers and sailors and hundreds of ships were collected in a southern Chinese port. The fleet had orders to collect tribute from China's neighbors and to let them know that a powerful emperor again governed that country.

A total of seven voyages were undertaken. The Chinese sailed all the way across the Indian Ocean with stops in India, Sri Lanka, and the Arabian peninsula. Some of the ships traveled as far as eastern Africa. These great expeditions were the largest the world had ever seen, yet they brought very little value to the Chinese. It was prestige, not trade, that the Ming emperors wanted. Despite their ability to build huge ships, the Chinese never became a naval power.

In A.D. 1421 in the midst of these sea ventures, the Ming emperor moved the capital back to Beijing. Here he ordered the building of great red walls to enclose his palace and its outbuildings. It received the name, the **Forbidden City.** Moving to Beijing placed the emperor nearer the Great Wall, making it easier for him to take command against the Mongols on the other side of the Wall.

The Ming emperors often worshipped in Beijing's Temple of Heaven.

The great voyages of the Ming now came to an abrupt halt. An imperial edict called off any further expeditions. The reason behind this order is not known. Probably the emperor's advisors felt that the point had been made, for the "barbarian world" had shown the proper respect to the emperor. There was no reason to go on. Another possibility for stopping the expeditions may be that expenses for building the imperial residence in Beijing had cut into the funds for the navy.

After Beijing was again the capital, the Ming rulers sought to be buried in magnificent tombs located nearby. Deep under the ground, great chambers were carved out of the earth to provide a final resting place for the Sons of Heaven. A road lined with animal sculptures led to the tombs. There were 24 of these stone animals: elephants, giraffes, and camels. It was said that at midnight those animals that had been standing lay down and the animals that were sitting all day stood up.

An avenue of animals line the entrance to the tombs of the Ming emperors.

Shoguns of Japan

By the year A.D. 1100 the Japanese rural aristocrats were at each other's throats. Robbers were so many in the forests that it was unsafe to travel. Pirates took to the sea to make their living through plunder. Governors sent out from Heian-Kyo frequently made themselves independent of imperial authorities. Japan was falling into anarchy. Only 10% of the peasants paid taxes to Heian-Kyo. The rest were serfs loyal only to local rural chiefs.

Into this vacuum of leadership stepped a young officer, Minamoto Yoritomo, head of the Minamoto clan. He had extensive lands and followers in the country. In A.D. 1182 Minamoto Yoritomo prevailed upon the emperor to award him the title, **shogun,** which means general. It was to be a permanent title that could be passed on in the Minamoto family. Yoritomo did not want to live in Heian-Kyo, with its beguiling luxury, but made his residence in Kamakura, a town just south of modern Tokyo.

The emperor allowed his shogun to rule the country in whatever way he saw fit. The shogun could make laws, pass judgment on criminals, disperse funds in the treasury, and appoint the emperor's officials. The shogun depended on the landowning class to provide soldiers in wartime, much as the feudal system in Europe. Many similarities exist.

Japanese soldiers, the **samurai,** became a special class of people during the Kamakura Shogunate. The samurai had only one purpose in life, to fight for his lord. The highest virtue for the samurai was loyalty. No suffering or hardship was too much to prove that he could be trusted. He was taught, "When a samurai's stomach is empty, it is a disgrace to feel hungry." Death was preferred to dishonor. In fact, about the only way to redeem oneself in case of some embarrassment was ritual suicide.

The samurai's code of honor was called **bushido.** Unlike European chivalry, bushido had no religious basis. It was a code of behavior that told the samurai how to act toward others of his class, those families that were landowners and had a noble ancestry. There was no great concern that a samurai should help the poor and weak.

The samurai costume was very heavy and ornate. Over his head he wore a helmet, often shaped like an animal. Then came armor for his neck and shoulders. His armor covered his body with little iron strips, which were sewn together with a cord of leather or cloth, thus giving him a great amount of flexibility.

The samurai dressed in a heavily armored costume.

The most precious possession of a samurai was his two-handed sword. When a boy was born into a samurai family, a sword was put next to him. Throughout his years as a child he was taught how to use the sword, how to slash and stab, and where to aim it when fighting an opponent. The sword became an object of religious importance. It had to be purified before it could be used. This devotion to their weapons meant that the Japanese made the best swords in all the world.

In battle the samurai fought on horseback. Before a fight between two warriors, bushido required that a warrior should announce his name, his ancestry, and if he had fought any memorable battles. His opponent was then given time to do the same. Once the contest started, it became very bloody. The victor cut off the head of the loser.

There was a close connection between the samurai and the great landowner, the **daimyo,** for whom he fought. It was the daimyo who assigned the warrior his land and the serfs who were to farm it for him.

Samurai warriors are pictured charging into battle.

Kamakura Shogunate

After Minamoto Yoritomo established a permanent residence, a distance of 300 miles from Heian-Kyo, Kamakura began to prosper. Yoritomo believed he could keep free of the politics that often surrounded the imperial court, as long as Kamakura officials stayed close to home.

In its own way, Kamakura became a second capital because architects and artists were drawn here to work for the shogun. The frequent visits of the daimyo on official business provided patronage for the arts and literature and prosperity for Kamakura's merchants.

Into Japan's self-contained world, a serious threat appeared late in the thirteenth century. In A.D. 1274 a message arrived from Khubilai Khan. He announced that he intended to make Japan part of his empire. When the shogun heard this, he rallied the lords as they had never joined together before. As expected, the Mongol army landed in Kyushu, the island nearest Korea. The samurai charges were more than enough to drive off the Mongols.

The Mongols were not used to defeat. They came again 7 years later, one fleet from Korea with 50,000 soldiers and another from China with 100,000 men. Again the feudal warriors of Japan furiously attacked without worrying about the code of bushido. The Mongols did not fight as individuals anyway. Then as both sides continued to battle, a typhoon struck and destroyed the Mongol fleets. The survivors slipped back to China.

The Japanese credited the victory to their gods. They believed that they had sent divine winds, **kamikaze**, to help them.

The Kamakura Buddha is so large that people can climb inside it.

This victory won, the shoguns of the early fourteenth century grew lax. They were soon jolted by a General Ashikaga who overran Kamakura and arranged that his family should govern Japan. The Ashikaga shoguns moved back to Heian-Kyo. During the 260 years of their rule, Japan entered a new phase of feudalism.

The Ashikaga were content to govern the region about the capital. They let the rest of the country go its own way. As a result, the daimyo became ever more powerful. Ambitious lords wanted to keep their samurai occupied, so what better to do than attack their neighbors? Samurai swords had no chance to get rusty.

Although it might be thought that the constant wars that characterized the fifteenth century were a burden on the economy, such was not the case. Because only the samurai were allowed to fight, battles did not affect anyone other than these soldiers and their lords. Japanese serfs continued to work in the rice paddies, and townspeople built up their trade, now assisted by the increased use of Chinese coinage.

The several hundred daimyo scattered throughout Japan built large palaces for themselves, spent huge sums on entertainment, and when not fighting each other, sought to live very comfortable lives. Even the emperors had enough resources in A.D. 1397 to build the famous Golden Pavilion in Heian-Kyo.

One of the entertainments enjoyed by upper-class Japanese was the **No play.** The No play grew out of songs and dances staged by choruses. The chorus told the story while individual actors played out their parts. The plot was unimportant. There was little scenery but very elaborate costuming. The audience attended to see how skillfully the actors adopted poses, accompanied by drums and flutes in the background.

Japanese traders sought out markets throughout southeastern Asia in the fifteenth century. Some made their homes in Thailand and the Philippines. Home ports were improved to handle increased trade. When Japanese trading expeditions were rebuffed, they easily turned to piracy, for Chinese cities along the coast had little protection against Japanese raids.

Feudal manners changed a bit in the period of the late 1400s. The daimyo began arming peasants to increase the size of their armies. Another change occurred in the position of women. Before A.D. 1400, women were often involved in the political life of their husbands, but in the stress of never-ending wars, they lost the position they once held. Because all resources went toward building up armies, women's rights to own property in their own name and for their own purposes came to an end. Freedom for individuals, for both women and men, declined in this age of feudal anarchy.

A Korean Buddha gives his blessing to the world.

Korea and Vietnam

In A.D. 1218 Ghengis Khan's armies marched into Korea, adding one more nation to the vast territories belonging to the Mongol Empire. For the next century and a half, the Koreans were forced to be the Mongols' unwilling subjects. In the mid-fourteenth century the collapse of the Mongols allowed the rise of the Yi dynasty in A.D. 1392.

With their capital at Seoul, the Yi monarchs, as their predecessors, continued to adapt Chinese culture to their own environment. Models of administration, Confucian ethics, and the examination system for public office were a part of Korean government. The arts of Korea, however, remained very much their own, especially the styles of pottery.

Printing developed extensively during Yi times, using movable metal type to reproduce an alphabet that reproduced the sounds of Korean spoken speech.

Two dynasties appeared in Vietnam during the period from A.D. 1100. The first, the Li, was centered in the Red River Valley, where constant attention was required to maintain the irrigation system. The second was the Tran dynasty, commencing in A.D. 1225.

Three times the Mongols occupied Hanoi and as many times had to withdraw. The Mongols were then content to receive tribute. Once the Mongols in China fell from power, the Ming emperors decided it was in their interest to conquer Vietnam, so once again in A.D. 1406 the Vietnamese were forced to accept Chinese officials and troops in their midst.

The leader of the resistance was Le Loi, and by A.D. 1427 he could claim victory. The Chinese withdrew, on a promise of tribute. In Hanoi, Le Loi set up a rule that lasted until the latter eighteenth century. Le Loi pointed out to the Chinese, "We have our own mountains and rivers, and our own customs and traditions." In fact, Chinese cultural patterns remained welcome in Vietnam even when the Chinese themselves were not.

Conclusion

East Asian accomplishments appear impressive in this age when Mongol invaders seemed to be everywhere a threat or a fact of life. In the midst of the coming and going of dynasties and invaders, the people of East Asia developed a way of life flexible enough to bear the day's burdens while awaiting tomorrow's surprises.

CHAPTER 28 REVIEW
EAST ASIA IN AN AGE OF KHANS AND SAMURAI

Summary
- During the last days of Song China, merchants took to the sea.
- Ju Xi taught Neo-Confucianism.
- The Mongols successfully invaded China in the early thirteenth century.
- Khubilai Khan became the leading Mongol ruler of China.
- The Ming dynasty followed the Mongols as China's rulers.
- Major naval expeditions were dispatched by the Mings into the Indian Ocean.
- Japan entered a period of history in which the shoguns were masters of the country.
- Japanese soldiers, the samurai, lived in a society similar to European knights.

Identify
People: Ju Xi; Jurchen; Ghengis Khan; Khubilai Khan; Marco Polo; Zhu Yuanshang; Minamoto Yoritomo; Ashikaga; Le Loi
Places: Hangzhou; Beijing; Nanjing; Kamakura; Seoul; Hanoi
Events: Mongol dynasty established at Beijing; Ming naval expeditions; shoguns rule Japan

Define

Neo-Confucianism	samurai
Forbidden City	No play
kamikaze	daimyo
junk	Ghengis Khan
bushido	White Lotus Society
shoguns	Red Turbans

Multiple Choice
1. Khubilai Khan was the most impressive
   (a) clock maker of Song times.
   (b) Mongol emperor of China.
   (c) Chinese emperor of Mongolia.
   (d) son of Ghengis Khan.

2. This man's book made Europeans aware of China:
   (a) Matteo Ricci.
   (b) William Penchant.
   (c) Marco Polo.
   (d) Ferdinand Magellan.

3. During the Ming dynasty
   (a) the Mongols controlled China.
   (b) Confucian scholars returned to their position.
   (c) the Manchus were in control of China.
   (d) the first contact between Japan and China occurred.

4. Ming emperors sent out a fleet into
   (a) the Pacific Ocean.
   (b) the Atlantic Ocean.
   (c) the Arctic Sea.
   (d) the Indian Ocean.

5. The Forbidden City is found in
   (a) Nanjing.
   (b) Hangzhou.
   (c) Beijing.
   (d) Kamakura.

6. Yoritomo Minamoto is remembered for having
   (a) directed the Great Reform.
   (b) replaced the emperor in A.D. 794.
   (c) established a new dynasty.
   (d) founded the Shogunate.

7. A samurai was
   (a) a prime minister.
   (b) a great landowner.
   (c) a warrior.
   (d) a Shinto priest.

8. After the Shogunate was established, a second capital grew up at
   (a) Edo.
   (b) Tokyo.
   (c) Kamakura.
   (d) Heian-Kyo.

9. In the late thirteenth century these invaders were defeated by the Japanese:
   (a) the Manchus.
   (b) the Mongols.
   (c) the Chinese.
   (d) the Koreans.

10. Bushido was
    (a) the Japanese capital.
    (b) the residence of the shoguns.
    (c) a code of honor among the samurai.
    (d) a Japanese sword.

11. Women in Japan lost status in the fifteenth century because of emphasis on
    (a) war.
    (b) landowning.
    (c) literacy.
    (d) government positions.

12. The Tran dynasty appeared in the thirteenth century
    (a) in Korea.
    (b) in Cambodia.
    (c) in Vietnam.
    (d) in Burma.

Essay Questions
1. Why did Marco Polo's book enjoy such popularity in Europe?
2. What was the role of the Mongols in China and Japan?
3. Compare feudalism in Japan with that of Europe.
4. What effect did the Ming expeditions have on the Indian Ocean nations?
5. Discuss the relations between China, Korea, and Vietnam.

Answers

1. b	5. c	9. b
2. c	6. d	10. c
3. b	7. c	11. a
4. d	8. c	12. c

African Empires

A theme of this chapter concentrates on the interaction between Muslims and Africans. Not since the days of the Romans was outside contact with North Africa so frequent as when Arab travelers penetrated deep into the African interior. Mamluk Egypt straddled the worlds of southwestern Asia and North Africa, bound to them by a common faith in Islam. In both the sahel and the forest kingdoms of Guinea, impressive kingdoms arose based on the ever-expanding Sahara trade routes.

Mamluk Egypt

The victory of Al-Din Baybars over the Mongols at Ayn Jalut in A.D. 1260 saved the Muslim world from catastrophe. His dynasty is known in Egyptian history as **Mamluk**, the word for slave. The reason for a slave dynasty was the same as in India in the Delhi sultanate. Young men, taken as slaves, were brought into the country and then rose through the ranks until they became military commanders. Following the law of the survival of the fittest, one finally attained the sultanate itself.

The Mamluk dynasty began in A.D. 1249 and lasted until 1517. Most of the Mamluks were men born and captured in the Black Sea region, Turks not yet converts to Islam or Circassians, a Caucasian tribal people. Many never bothered to learn Arabic, and their Muslim faith was only nominal. They held power because they were ruthless and were quick to silence opposition, yet the average tenure of a sultan was 6 years. Few mixed with the natives for whom they held contempt, believing the Egyptians fit only to pay taxes.

In order to collect these revenues, the Mamluks assigned estates to their fellow soldiers who were to police the inhabitants living on them. When required, in return for their privileges, they had to report with a number of soldiers commensurate to the size of their fiefdoms. Mamluk officers were uninterested in the outside world, causing Egypt's ports along the Nile to decay. Nomadic Bedouin tribes, free of central control, fell back into plundering to support themselves. Fresh contingents of slaves replenished the ranks of the Mamluks.

After his victory, Baybars invited Ahmed Abu-Qasim, a relative of the last ruling caliph of Baghdad, to set up his residence in Cairo. Abu-Qasim's presence confirmed the legitimacy of the Mamluks' claim that Cairo was now the leading Islamic state, the heir of Baghdad. The caliphs became little more than puppets in the hands of the Mamluks.

Egypt was riddled with corruption during these years because the foreigners who governed it cared for nothing but power and pleasure. Despite its decline, Mamluk Egypt remained strong enough to hold on to much of Syria and Palestine and, when the Ottoman star began its rise, to monitor its progress.

African Life Among the Blacks

When authors write about Africa, they often speak of **tribes.** The word *tribe* can have many meanings. Usually it refers to a group of people who speak a common language, look upon themselves as related through kinship, and hold common religious beliefs and a shared history. Some African tribes were no more than a few hundred people, others numbered in the millions and formed great kingdoms.

Within each tribe there was a chief and, in larger ones, a king. Usually the king was very important for he was responsible for the welfare of his subjects, acting as the commander of the army, chief priest, head judge, and lawmaker. Often rigid rules determined whom the king could marry and what ceremonies he had to perform. His household numbered dozens of people, and his residence was the most spacious in the capital. Special clothes and symbols were associated with him. The chief or king had a council of elders who advised him and acted on his behalf.

Like the Chinese, African people had a great respect for ancestors. Also, like the Chinese, they believed in a large number of gods and spirits that had to be kept contented lest they do harm. A living family had a responsibility both to the dead and to future generations. There was little crime in African societies, for parents and relatives kept close watch over the education of children. A family was rich if it had many friends and many children.

In some tribal societies the man came to live with his bride's parents; in others the woman came to live at her husband's house. Usually a man had to bring a gift to his bride's family because it was losing a helper. This might be a piece of land or several cattle.

An African village at the side of the desert may often be built of reeds.

423

In 90% of African societies, polygamy was usual. This arrangement assured that every woman always had someone to look after her in time of sickness or old age. Widows were cared for by a brother, nephew, or son.

One wife was always the principal one. Wives who were taken later had a separate house and their own gardens and animals. Some kings had harems of several hundred wives, a sign of their wealth and importance.

Every tribe had secret societies that provided a variety of functions. One was to educate children in the tribes' traditions and customs. Societies also had special festivals where songs and dances, accompanied by drums, filled the night hours. The masks that the dancers wore became a special kind of African art. Some were meant to be funny; others were meant to be frightening.

Most African people expressed themselves in dance, music, and storytelling. For some people dancing would go on for hours with a whole community caught up in a festive mood. For others the less vigorous entertainment of storytelling was quite enough.

Mali

Despite the destruction of the Ghanian Empire in the eleventh century, the city itself was reoccupied until the thirteenth. At that time Mali became the strongest state of West Africa, creating a new empire that took over a territory much larger than Ghana had ever ruled. Mali was the second of the sahel kingdoms.

The people who founded Mali were the Malinke, a people related to the Ghanians for both spoke a common language. Its first great ruler, Sundiata, governed Mali from A.D. 1230 to 1255.

At this time the caravan trade was in revival, with Muslim merchants making more frequent calls in the sahel markets. Often Islam seemed to be attractive to the blacks, and Sundiata considered conversion. There was, however, much to be said for traditional African religion for it held that the king enjoyed divine power. It allowed him to live a privileged life, often secluded from the eyes of ordinary people, because of his special status.

On the other hand, by converting to Islam certain advantages were present. Islam promoted a unified state. By becoming a Muslim, an African ruler gained access to a world religion that supplied writers, civil servants, and scholars to staff his court. Sundiata made that choice. He and all his successors were Muslims who carried the title **mansa,** which means emperor.

Mali, like Ghana, grew wealthy because it controlled a large territory, including the gold-producing mines of western Africa. Its extent reached all the way to the Atlantic Ocean. The Mali capital at Niani grew to be a city of 6,000 households. Its king captained a military force formed of cavalry armed with bow and arrow and lances.

Without doubt the most famous of Mali's emperors was Mansa Musa, who began his rule in Mali in A.D. 1312. For Mansa Musa it was a serious matter to keep strictly all the rules that are demanded of Muslims. He was also anxious to reward those scholars who kept him aware of what he must do to please God. Despite the difficulties it would involve, Mansa Musa determined to make the pilgrimage to Mecca.

In A.D. 1324 Mansa Musa and his court arrived in Cairo. The people of Cairo could hardly believe their eyes. One account claimed that there were 15,000 people in his party, 500 of them slaves carrying bags of gold.

In the first known map of Africa, the Catalan Atlas, illuminators pictured Mansa Musa on his throne.

The Mamluk sultan of Cairo welcomed him to his city, but an argument erupted about which one should bow before the other. After the disagreement was settled, the two exchanged gifts, and Mansa Musa was given a palace to live in while he rested in Cairo. Over the next several months the Mali king and his followers gave away so much of their gold, or used it to buy so many Egyptian goods, that it took years for Cairo's prices to come down.

On his return from pilgrimage, Mansa Musa brought with him dozens of Qur'anic scholars who sought to purify the Islamic religion as practiced in Mali. This was difficult because many people combined Islam with their traditional beliefs.

Timbuktu, a city on the Niger River in Mali's kingdom, became a major center of Muslim scholarship after A.D. 1300. Students came from all parts of the Muslim world to study in the libraries and schools of the city. The Timbuktu population rose to 50,000, as merchants and artisans joined the scholars.

The fame of Mansa Musa and the fabled wealth of his kingdom inspired Europeans to try to reach Mali and open trade with it. The first known map of Africa, drawn in A.D. 1375, shows Mansa Musa sitting on a throne, with the title, "Lord of the Negroes."

Kanem-Bornu and Songhai

Other states appeared in the sahel during this time period. Located at the end of Saharan trade routes, villages became towns and chieftains became sultans. All were Muslims whose authority was enforced by a cavalry of warriors. Horses to supply their armies were now a major import from North Africa.

One of these sultanates was found in Kanem-Bornu, a region near Lake Chad, deep in the African interior. Its warriors, covered with chain armor, were a frightening sight to its neighbors. They were quite willing to pay tribute to keep them away.

Another was the Songhai kingdom with its capital at Gao on the Niger. The Arab traveler El Bekri describes mealtime in Gao:

> When the king is seated, the drum is beaten and the young women begin dancing letting their thick hair swing down. No one does any business in the town until the king has finished his meal. Then the leftovers are thrown into the Niger and those present utter cries and exclamations, which announce to the people that the king has finished eating.

After A.D. 1465 Timbuktu was within the Songhai Empire so that the Gao monarchs became the city's patrons. They were anxious to continue the earlier building program in the city with the result that more mosques and public buildings graced the city. The Songhai ruler also outfitted several warships to police the Niger River, creating the first African navy.

Forest Kingdoms of Guinea

To the south of the sahel lay Guinea, the forest area of western Africa. Here the climate was so humid and the rains so frequent that the large trees, filled with chattering monkeys and brightly plumed birds, shaded the ground all day long. The poor soil of the rain forest made the growing of crops difficult even after the trees were cut down.

Because the cavalry of the kingdoms to the north was useless in the rain forest, the people who lived here enjoyed greater security and protection than those living on the flat land of the sahel. By the thirteenth century, at the very edge of the rain forest, several towns appeared with markets for the exchange of forest products. Towns such as Katsina, Kano, and Maiduguri became centers of trade, forming states that grew wealthy from marketing ivory, salt, and especially gold dust. Cloth made in Morocco was in great demand for these products.

The African nobles of the forest regions preferred living in towns. Here kings had their residences with the elite who served them living nearby. Ordinary people built their communities at a distance from the royal towns.

The Yoruba were the most creative of the forest peoples. In their walled royal towns, artists learned to sculpt heads of their rulers. There was a long tradition of sculpture in this region, but no one was ever so skilled as the artists of Ife, the Yoruba capital.

The Yorubas cast their portraits in bronze. Some show a king with his symbols of power, a crown and scepter. The heads are true to life, showing the scars that were put on the faces to follow Yoruba fashion.

Other arts included wood carvings of human figures and animals. Some artists did not want to duplicate nature as much as they wanted to emphasize certain characteristics of their subjects. African wood carvings, especially of masks, became a major influence on twentieth century European art.

A woman, if a queen mother, played a major role in politics.

Ethiopia

The Ethiopian kingdom was East Africa's wealthiest nation in the twelfth century. At Lalibala, a site named for the king who was its patron, architects carved ten Christian churches out of the red volcanic rock.

A pit was dug into the ground. Then patient sculptors went to work, first to fashion the church exterior and afterward to hollow out the interior. The roof, covered by crosses, was at ground level. Inside the church the walls were painted with frescos in vivid colors, telling the stories of the Bible and of Ethiopian saints. The patron saint of Ethiopia, Takla Haymanot, was then active in missionary activity, spreading Christianity to neighboring peoples.

A change in dynasty late in the thirteenth century brought to power a king who claimed that he was the direct descendant of King Solomon of Jerusalem and the Queen of Sheba. This dynasty, called Solomonid, remained on the throne of Ethiopia until the twentieth century.

In the 1300s the truce between the Christian Nubians and Muslim Egyptians collapsed. Muslims overran Nubia extinguishing the Christian states and approached the Ethiopian northern border. The Ethiopians also had problems from the Somali people to the south. For the next two centuries Christian Ethiopia was under siege.

In the fourteenth century a number of Europeans reached Ethiopia, encouraged to believe that its king was the mythical Prester John. For centuries the story of a Christian African monarch circulated through western Europe. In Rome and the royal courts of Europe, it was believed that a

Christian alliance with this king, or his descendants, might well put pressure on the Muslim countries that lay between them. Ethiopian embassies visited Venice, Rome, and Portugal during the fifteenth century, but none solved the logistical problem of a joint attack upon the Muslims.

The rock churches of Lalibala remain one of Ethiopian architects' outstanding achievements.

East Africa and the Indian Ocean Trade

At the same time that Tuareg traders were starting the first markets in western Africa, people on the coast of eastern Africa continued their contact with the lively trading world of the Indian Ocean. Instead of camel caravans bringing merchants, the towns of East Africa had long depended upon ships arriving in their harbors with goods from as far away as China and the islands of Indonesia.

Some of the traders came to stay—Shi'ite Muslims from Oman, a southern Arab region, and later Persians from the region of Shiraz. Scholars believe that the Persians founded the city of Mogadishu on the Somali coast.

The blacks who traded with these foreigners spoke Bantu. They had, after many centuries of moving, traveled all the way from western Africa to occupy the regions of modern-day Kenya, Tanzania, and Mozambique. Some were herders of cattle; others were farmers. The farmers eagerly adopted the food plants introduced from Southeast Asia: bananas, coconuts, rice, and yams.

The trade between the Bantu and Indian Ocean traders was in ivory, gold, palm oil, rhinoceros horn, and tortoise shell. Iron ore, too, was important. Kilwa Island, now off the coast of modern-day Tanzania, grew to be East Africa's busiest port. The sultan who ruled Kilwa built himself a coral stone palace of over one hundred rooms. He also minted copper coins, the first money of sub-Saharan Africa. Little by little the Indian

Ocean traders—Muslim Arabs and Persians—converted large numbers of the Bantu people to Islam. A common language, **Swahili**, which mixed Bantu and Arabic, was spoken up and down the coast from Mogadishu to Sofala. Swahili was a written language, using the Arabic alphabet.

The Indian Ocean trade was so brisk that after A.D. 1200 a string of 30 cities lined the eastern African coast. Minarets of mosques and palace domes dotted town skylines.

South Africa

The continued emigration of Bantu-speaking peoples southward was the major event of South Africa prior to A.D. 1500. The Mbuti, Khoi Khoi, and San, hunters who once roamed the highlands of eastern Africa, were pushed into the desert or deep into the rain forest where their descendants remain to this day.

The Bantu knew how to make iron weapons, hoes, and axes, which gave them a distinct advantage over hunters who had not learned metalworking. The **slash-and-burn** method of Bantu farming required frequent moves since the soil quickly wore out. Bantu herders were, at the same time, always in search of new and better pastures for their cattle.

Some Bantu peoples formed kingdoms in central or southern Africa. One was the Bakongo whose territories were along the Atlantic coast of the Zaire River. The Bakongo kingdom dated from the fourteenth century and held more than 2,000,000 people. Its capital, Mbanzakongo, was a large and thriving city where ironsmiths were famous for the variety of instruments that they fashioned.

Another Bantu kingdom grew up at Great Zimbabwe. A modern African nation has taken its name from the stone city that is now found within its borders. Great Zimbabwe was the capital of a Bantu kingdom for four centuries, from the eleventh through the fifteenth century. The people of Zimbabwe used granite stone without mortar to create a complex of buildings that included public ceremonial structures and a great solid tower.

The walls of Great Zimbabwe kept the settlement safe from outsiders.

Conclusion

Mamluk Egypt, after its contribution to the Islamic peoples in saving them from the Mongols, sank back into a torpor. Its government, the creation of slaves, did not fit it for leadership. The sahel kingdoms and those of Guinea were remarkable for their introduction of urban life into Africa's interior and western coastal regions. East African prosperity came from the profits gathered in the growth of Indian Ocean trade.

CHAPTER 29 REVIEW
AFRICAN EMPIRES

Summary
- The Mamluk dynasty made Egypt the dominant power of North Africa.
- The caliphs now lived in Cairo.
- Among the blacks of Africa, a wide variety of political and social customs existed.
- Mali replaced Ghana as the center of commercial life in West Africa.
- Timbuktu became a city of Muslim scholars.
- Forest kingdoms appeared in Guinea.
- Ethiopia and the cities of the East African coast prospered from traders of the Indian Ocean.
- Great Zimbabwe emerged as the capital of a southern African kingdom.

Identify
People: Ad-Din Baybars; Ahmed Abu-Qasim; Malinke; Sundiata; Mansa Musa; Yoruba; Edo
Places: Timbuktu; Ife; Lalibala; Nubia; Kilwa Island; Gao; Great Zimbabwe; Bakongo
Events: establishment of Mamluk sultans in Egypt; confirmation of societal values of black Africans

Define
Mamluk dynasty   Swahili   mansa   tribes   slash-and-burn

Multiple Choice
1. Mamluk Egypt's rulers were made legitimate because
   (a) they were born outside Egypt.
   (b) they were brought to Egypt as slaves.
   (c) they had the strongest army in northern Africa.
   (d) the caliphs in Cairo confirmed their status.

2. Sundiata was the first great ruler of
   (a) Ghana.
   (b) Kanem-Bornu.
   (c) Mali.
   (d) Songhai.

3. The most important woman in most black African societies was
   (a) the oldest sister of the king.
   (b) the youngest sister of the king.
   (c) the queen mother.
   (d) the wife of the ruler.

4. The center of learning in the Mali kingdom was
   (a) Zimbabwe.
   (b) Ife.
   (c) Timbuktu.
   (d) Khartoum.

5. The most important king of Mali was
   (a) Sundiata.
   (b) Mansa Musa.
   (c) Lalibala.
   (d) Sekou Touré.

6. The best African art was produced by
   (a) the Yoruba.
   (b) the Ibo.
   (c) the Edo.
   (d) the Axumites.

7. Rock-cut churches are to be found in Ethiopia at
   (a) Great Zimbabwe.
   (b) Timbuktu.
   (c) Lalibala.
   (d) the Sudd.

8. The Bantu people in East Africa spoke a common language:
   (a) Urdu.
   (b) Swahili.
   (c) Arabic.
   (d) Kilwa.

9. Zimbabwe's construction in this material made it different from other African capitals
   (a) wood.
   (b) stone.
   (c) brick.
   (d) plaster.

10. Secret societies were important in Africa because
    (a) they educated children into their tribe's traditions.
    (b) they formed dance groups.
    (c) they sponsored drum contests.
    (d) they gave political support to the kings.

Essay Questions
   1. Why were the sahel empires important for Africa?
   2. Discuss the government of Mamluk Egypt.
   3. What prompted the Portuguese to begin their voyages of discovery?

Answers
1. d   6. a
2. c   7. c
3. c   8. b
4. c   9. b
5. b   10. a

CHAPTER 30

Europe in the High Middle Ages

In all great world civilizations, with the only exception being ancient Egypt, the city was at the center of creative accomplishment. Bringing large numbers of people together into a confined space may not always be physically comfortable, but it does facilitate the exchange of ideas and inventions. The High Middle Ages was such a time. When Europeans could feel secure enough to congregate in towns, to construct public buildings and cathedrals, and to govern themselves in political and economic affairs, European civilization was deeply enriched.

Revival of Towns

Before the eleventh century, European society was overwhelmingly rural. Towns in the west, outside of Muslim Spain, were hardly deserving of the name. After A.D. 1000 European security improved after the Viking and Magyar invasions ended. As a result of improved farming techniques, the draining of marshes, and the clearing of forests, the population rose dramatically. Between A.D. 1100 and 1300 it is estimated that the English people increased from 1,500,000 to 4,500,000 while the number of French and Germans doubled, from about 4,000,000 to 8,000,000.

These new people had to be fed, clothed, and housed. In the countryside, especially near the villages that were fast becoming towns, subsistence farming was transformed into cash crops that provided food and raw materials for the growing urban market. Townspeople in the Middle Ages were always only a small proportion of the total population. Nevertheless, their influence was far greater than their numbers. It was among the townspeople that new ideas and products were likely to appear.

The nucleus of a town was formed by the businessmen of the Middle Ages. In those areas of Europe where a highly dense population was coupled to a strong demand for manufactured products, town life grew fastest. Those conditions were met in Flanders, northern Italy, and certain German regions.

A number of factors determined Europe's growing economy. One was the ease by which goods could be moved by water. The many rivers of Europe became highways on which products could be transported at little cost. Even bulky products could be floated downstream on rafts and sold at reasonable prices. A port at the mouth of a river, such as Marseille, experienced enormous growth in the thirteenth century. Wherever overland transportation for long distances had to be used, only luxury goods destined for purchase by wealthy people proved worth the effort.

Another element contributing to the rise of western European prosperity was the independent spirit of its merchants. They were willing to risk their capital for the sake of profit. By contrast, tradespeople in other parts of the world tended to be cautious and conservative. They could only trust relatives.

An upsurge in mining during the twelfth century also affected economic expansion. Iron, copper, and lead supplied the raw materials for the pots and pans, arms and harnesses that the merchants offered for sale.

Increased demand for coinage and jewelry spurred a search for silver and gold. Until the thirteenth century western Europe's gold supply came from West Africa across the Sahara, but the amount was inadequate and the delivery was uncertain. At the close of the thirteenth century, as a result of new discoveries and the opening of more mines, gold coins were again struck by the governments of European kingdoms.

Various laws, both civil and ecclesiastical, prohibited loaning money at interest. This was considered to be **usury**, which was forbidden by a number of Biblical texts. In an effort to remain nominally faithful to the prohibition, Christians in need of credit found subterfuges such as borrowing from Jews who were exempt from the prohibition. Legal scholars debated questions concerning value, price, and money, but church authorities held firm, forbidding a lender to regain anything but the principal of a loan.

Cities of the twelfth century were originally located on property belonging to the king, the church, or one of the nobles. In most western European towns it was the bishop who was the lord, for except in southern France and Italy, nobles preferred living in their castles in the countryside.

Italian merchants used their wealth to put up colorful churches as exemplified in this church of Florence.

Town councils, made up of wealthy citizens, sought from the kings charters that would exactly define their rights and obligations. Even though these charters were favorable to episcopal landowners at first, very quickly the kings recognized that it was in their interest to be generous to the townspeople who provided a significant proportion of their revenue. A natural alliance was soon formed between towns and kings.

There were many bitter arguments over the contents of these charters because the bishops did not want to lose control of the towns. The merchants' councils, known as **communes,** usually won the contest with the bishops. This allowed them to collect taxes, to raise a militia, and to build town halls and walls to symbolize their freedom from feudal ties.

Inside the towns, narrow streets wound among the houses and led to the central square where the church and public buildings were located. These structures were completely unheated and quite uncomfortable during the long European winters. Removed a short distance from the public square, private houses crowded together with their upper stories jutting precariously over the streets.

Sanitation was woefully inadequate. Public latrines caused terrible odors and often flooded into the streets. The city water supply was dirty and polluted, dependent on cisterns and wells.

The medieval town was not a pleasant place in which to live, but it was better than life in a rural village. This was certainly true for runaway serfs who, if they remained undetected for a year and a day, were adjudged by law to be free. For peasants bound to the land and laboring throughout the year in hard seasonal work, life in a town seemed to offer golden opportunities.

Compared to the countryside, towns were very exciting places. There was a never-ending pageant of traffic along the streets. Besides shopkeepers and their customers, entertainers with trained animals, acrobats, and musical groups survived on donations given by their audiences. Merchants from foreign parts added to the interest and were especially numerous during the great fairs that moved around western Europe. The fairs in the Champagne area of northeastern France, which lay astride the trade routes between Italy and Flanders, drew thousands of people to buy and sell and to enjoy a holiday. Here the textiles of the north were eagerly exchanged for products of the Mediterranean, such as olive oil and wine.

Townspeople were concerned about cleanliness. Both private and public baths were common. In A.D. 1268 Paris had 32 bathhouses. Men and women shared booths that were very similar to a hot tub. People could order lunch while bathing, which was regarded as a pleasant social experience. It was only a century later that public bathing declined as the bathhouses became the haunt of prostitutes and, falling afoul of the law, were closed.

The most important institutions within the medieval town were the **guilds.** These were organizations of merchants who specialized in the buying and selling of a particular product. The guilds' origins lay in the traditions and customs of pre-urban times when traveling merchants worked out business agreements among themselves.

These merchant guilds were very powerful organizations for they determined their own membership and supervised the production and distribution of guild products. They set prices and established the quantity of goods to be produced. Merchant guild members kept a monopoly on the ownership of tools and the places of work for their employees.

Artisans also sought, less successfully, to protect their interests by forming guilds, but they were no match for the political and economic power held by merchant guilds. They were able, however, to legislate internal matters. For example, the tanners' guild could determine how many apprentices should be allowed to take training and the length of time demanded before graduating to a higher position.

Economic Life

An agricultural boom began in Europe about A.D. 1150 and continued for the next 150 years. The increased productivity from farming allowed many serfs to improve their position. Some accumulated enough cash to pay off their contracts. They became free peasant farmers, able to sell their produce in whatever market offered the highest price.

New techniques for growing crops contributed to an increase in the amount of food produced. The heavy-wheeled plow, tipped with iron, made digging into the hard clay soils of northern Europe easier. Use of the harrow became more common to level out the field before planting. The application of fertilizer was better understood. Cereal crops, so important to the diet of people living north of the Alps, were augmented by two further introductions from Spain: sorghum and hard wheat. The latter made a better kind of bread and became the staple ingredient for spaghetti and macaroni.

The vineyards that still line the banks of the Rhine River were first cultivated on terraces constructed in the High Middle Ages. The fine grapes they produced made wine as popular a beverage as beer among Germans of the Rhineland.

The use of mechanical energy also broadened. Water mills were already well known, but they became much more efficient by building weirs, especially on French rivers. Where rivers were lacking, inventive farmers used windmills to do their work. The mills had many uses. They ground grain, olives, and grapes; stamped metal; and produced paper. A series of hammers attached to the gears of the mill replaced human feet in the process of fulling, cleaning, and thickening wool. Villagers used mills so much that they became a place to meet friends for conversation. Nevertheless, gathering at the mill was never as popular as gathering at the village tavern.

Medieval engineers, many of them monks attached to the monastery of Cîteaux, learned how to bring water in pipes from springs and wells over long distances. They also constructed systems to drain away refuse water from kitchens and lavatories.

Mining of coal first took place in the southern Netherlands in the early thirteenth century. Early coal mines were shallow pits, but later miners learned how to sink shafts underground, and by A.D. 1300 the English were exporting coal to the continent. Other mining activities extracted silver, copper, and tin ores.

The Germans were particularly skilled at mining. Sometimes a whole town contained only miners. The kings of Europe, recognizing the economic importance of German miners, granted them exemptions from certain taxes and military service and allowed them to set up their own courts.

Another occupation of the High Middle Ages was stone quarrying. France held the best limestone, and quarries were found all over the country, some directly under the city of Paris. Iron-making was also important because the armor and weapons of medieval knights were made of iron. Housewives and farmers needed kitchen utensils and tools that only blacksmiths could make.

In rural areas loggers were found in great numbers because wood was the standard construction material for housing and furniture, and huge amounts were consumed for fuel. Wood was also used in building forts, ships, barrels, and bridges. Regions of the great forests of France and Germany adjacent to towns fell beneath the ax, and the price of lumber rose with the increasing demand. There were thousands of furnaces in the medieval forests turning wood into charcoal.

Intellectual Life and the Birth of the University

The High Middle Ages of Europe was a time of great intellectual achievement. An influx of manuscripts from the Muslim countries brought the knowledge of classical Greece and the Arab world to the West.

From the fifth to the eleventh centuries, St. Augustine's thought dominated Western Christian thought. Early in the twelfth century Peter Abélard arose to challenge Augustine's views. Abélard, caustic and difficult as a person, was a man to be reckoned with, an intellectual marvel. As a teacher he had few peers. The instruction he gave in Paris gained him the affection and loyalty of dozens of disciples. For them he wrote a number of works, including *Sic et Non* (Yes and No), a work in which he brought together passages from a wide variety of earlier authors on a broad scope of topics.

Abélard believed that a question should be proposed; then the proponents and opponents should be lined up on both sides of the issue so that the best arguments became evident. His methodology is known as **Scholasticism.** It served as the basis for higher education over the next several centuries.

Abélard was convinced that the **universal,** that which is common to all things having the same nature, had no real existence. Contrary to those who followed Plato's idea of **forms,** he argued that universals, or concepts, exist only in the mind. They are abstractions. The actual substance, which has real existence as an individual thing, exists outside the mind.

The philosophical dialogue that began with Abélard broadened as more works translated into Latin from Arabic and Greek were studied in the West. Frenchmen moved to Toledo and other Spanish towns where they collected the manuscripts of Ptolemy, Euclid, and the mathematician Muhammad al-Khwarizmi, which they rendered into Latin, initiating a leap forward in Europe's knowledge of cosmology, geometry, and mathematics.

Spain also had its own scholars, among them Ibn Rushd (Averroes to the Latins) and the Jewish scholar Moses ben Maimon (Maimonides). Ibn Rushd, capitalizing on the great interest in Aristotle among Muslim scholars, elaborated so extensively on the Greek philosopher that he enjoyed the title The Commentator. Maimonides undertook the examination of Hebrew scriptures with the tools provided by Aristotle. His book, *The Guide for the Perplexed,* was meant to point out a path for those who sought a synthesis between faith and reason, and his *Mishneh Torah* (Repetition of the Law) codified the 613 commandments that he found in the Bible and Talmud.

This revival of learning resulted in the founding of medieval Europe's most important creation, the university. Cathedral schools had provided clerical training for many centuries, but the universities offered a broad curriculum and attracted a wider spectrum of students.

The university in all its dimensions first appeared at Bologna in Italy. Here Roman law was favored by young men who hoped to find a career in the service of princes. Knowledge of the Code of Justinian, the framework of Roman law, was avidly pursued. The kings of the time appreciated the Code's centralizing thrust.

A university lecture could stir up lively debate among students.

Paris had the foremost university north of the Alps. In A.D. 1200 King Philip Augustus gave it a charter, exempting those who studied there from the jurisdiction of municipal authorities. Later, Pope Innocent III decreed that it should have a school of theology. Four university **nations** were to be found at Paris, corresponding to the larger ethnic groups represented: French, Norman, Picard, and German-English. The faculties were also four in number: arts, law, medicine, and theology. Universities appeared in England at Oxford and Cambridge, in northern Italy at Padua, and in Spain at Salamanca.

University nations were organized under rectors whose task was to ensure the well-being of the members. They lived in **colleges,** homes for the students that a wealthy benefactor endowed. The college collected fees for their services, and any surplus was used to quench the thirst of the nation's officers.

Students in southern European universities exercised a great deal more authority than modern students. They could levy fines on professors who left town without permission or skipped a difficult chapter in a text. At the end of their course of study, an examination, if successfully passed, admitted the candidates into the guild of **masters.** They were then able to find employment as university teachers, doctors, lawyers, or clerics.

The new student arriving at the university for the first time began his education in the faculty of arts. Here he attended lectures given in Latin on the **trivium.** These were grammar, rhetoric, and dialectic, all dealing with the use of words. He also studied the **quadrivium:** arithmetic, geometry, astronomy, and music, subjects based on the use of numbers. After students had reached a certain competency in these fields, they proceeded to the study of law, theology, or medicine that prepared them for their careers. Only men attended the university because women were not found in these occupations.

The discovery of the natural philosophy of the ancient Greeks revolutionized the world of medieval thought. Previously, only Aristotle's *Logic* was known in the West thanks to an earlier translation. For the first time in Western history, scholars took the physical world seriously, just as Aristotle had done. Their search into causation changed the vision of medieval scholars, preparing the way for the discoveries of science and technology that subsequently occurred in European history.

Albert the Great was the first Scholastic to recognize how Aristotle's works were revolutionary to the medieval understanding of reality. A Dominican friar who taught at Paris, he made available a paraphrase of all Aristotle's works to his students.

One of Albert's students was a young Dominican friar, Thomas Aquinas, who had come to Paris from southern Italy. More than anyone else from among Albert's disciples, Thomas expanded and eventually surpassed the work of his master. In A.D. 1252 he himself became a teacher at Paris, lecturing on philosophy and theology and writing texts for his students. The number of his written works is incredible, filling 18 large volumes.

Thomas Aquinas was the most accomplished teacher at Paris during the High Middle Ages.

The greatest contributions of Aquinas were the *Summa Theologica* (Summary of Theology) and the *Summa Contra Gentiles* (Summary Against the Gentiles). These works constituted an orderly and encyclopedic presentation of Christian thought on God, man, and the universe. Aquinas took Aristotle's ideas and used them to illuminate Christian revelation.

Thomas was not alone in promoting a new approach to reality. His system was one among many. One colleague was Bonaventure, a Franciscan whose theology sought to combine Aristotle with traditional Platonism. Another was Robert Grosseteste, chancellor of Oxford, who argued that experimentation was the surest way to reach truth. He put forth the notion that mathematics should be the basis for explaining scientific phenomena.

Nicholas Oresme also taught at Paris and made the revolutionary claim that the earth, rotating on an axis, was a celestial body that along with the planets revolves around the sun. Although he was correct, Oresme had no proof for his theories, and his work was discounted.

Roger Bacon thought along the same lines as Grosseteste. He asserted that only the examination of evidence produced truth. Bacon was the first to use the term *experimental science*, arguing that it is superior to other types of epistemological processes. Thanks to medieval educators, a division was made between the natural world and the divine, an insight that nature was the product of the creator and not to be identified with him.

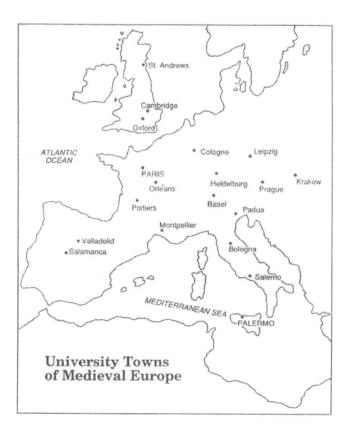

**University Towns
of Medieval Europe**

Cathedrals

Just as the university was the greatest achievement of the European medieval mind, the Gothic cathedral was the climax of its artistic creativity. All over Europe these churches are still to be found, testaments to the devotion of medieval Christians.

The cathedrals were built not only as places of worship but also as civic monuments, mountains of stone meant to enhance the importance of the towns and the people that constructed them. The ground plan was still based upon the Roman basilica, but now the nave and aisles were cut by a transept, creating the figure of a Latin cross. The areas covered were immense: at Paris, 63,000 square feet; at Chartres, 65,000 square feet; and at Cologne, the largest in northern Europe, 90,000 square feet. The west portal, the entrance, was elaborately decorated. Over the doors the **rose window** caught the light from the setting sun. The facade was flanked with towers to enhance its dignity, although some cathedrals never received their spires. **Flying buttresses** ingeniously supported the walls.

In the interior, the roof with its pointed arches looked like the inner hull of an inverted ship. Its mass was supported by ribbed vaults whose columns carried the weight of the roof to the ground. Bright tapestries covered the walls. The nave might have a marble or iron grill to separate the place of the clergy from that of the people. Here were found choir stalls for the **canons,** clergy attached to the cathedral, who, like the monks, recited the Divine Office of psalms and prayers throughout the day.

Notre Dame of Paris became one of the most famous of Gothic cathedrals.

Nearly all the great Gothic cathedrals were begun in the 50-year period of the middle years of the twelfth century, from A.D. 1125 to 1175. Their construction was an act of faith, for none who began the work would ever see the cathedral finished.

Stained glass making was one of the most accomplished arts of the Middle Ages. The windows of the Gothic cathedrals became jeweled presentations of the life of Christ and the saints. To color the glass, powdered iron and copper oxide were mixed with the glass. Artisans with incredible skill fired and molded the glass and then placed it within strips of lead to complete the composition.

The spires of Cologne's cathedral pierce the sky.

The Papacy Ascendant

In A.D. 1123, the year following the conclusion of the investiture controversy, Pope Calixtus II summoned the first general council to be held in the West. It met at the Lateran Palace, the residence of the popes in Rome. Calixtus's goal was to separate the clergy into a class apart, governed by bishops who would be responsible only to the pope. Enforced celibacy was to be the distinguishing mark of the Latin clergy. For the future, Calixtus ruled that clerical marriage was to be considered invalid. In this way he struck a major blow against the powerful bonds of kinship and inheritance that were so troublesome in the context of clerical appointment.

The medieval papacy reached its height during the pontificate of Innocent III, who was elected pope in A.D. 1198 when he was only 37 years old. Innocent firmly believed that he must lead all European Christendom because his rule embraced spiritual and eternal affairs, while secular rulers were only concerned with less important temporal matters.

Innocent III feared no European rule. He excommunicated the French king, Philip Augustus, for divorcing his wife and placed England under **interdict,** a decree banning all religious sacraments, when King John rejected his appointee for Canterbury. Innocent's promotion of the crusades gave impetus to the Spanish reconquest as well as to the misfired Fourth Crusade. His staff, which made up the Roman Curia, was recognized as the most efficient in all Europe.

One of the reasons for Innocent's success was the foundation of several new religious orders in his time. A group of French monks dissatisfied with Cluny, which they believed had become too wealthy and too bureaucratic for its own good, left to form a new community. They located at Cîteaux where they intended to follow Benedict's rule with much more simplicity and fidelity.

In A.D. 1112 Cîteaux received a novice, Bernard, destined to become the twelfth century's outstanding churchman. His talents were so many and his influence so widespread that few men in history have dominated their age to an equal extent. From his monastery at Clairvaux, where he was abbot, Bernard monitored the activities of popes and kings, advised and counseled them, settled their disputes, or urged them to action.

By mid-century the Cistercians had 300 houses throughout Europe. The simplicity of the order's way of life stood in contrast to Cluny. No gold or silver ornaments were permitted, and contact with the outside world was kept to a minimum. Discipline was monitored through yearly meetings of representatives of the order. The Cistercians admitted older men, widowers, or illiterate peasants, who were known as **conversi,** whom the monasteries came to depend upon as shepherds and farm laborers. A comparable order of women formed a female branch of the Cistercian order.

This age also produced an extraordinary woman, Hildegard of Bingen. As abbess she governed the Benedictine house at Rupertsberg after A.D. 1147. Hildegard was a visionary who also composed music and spiritual works of deep insight.

After Bernard's death in A.D. 1153, Christendom had to wait a half century for someone of equal stature to appear. This was Francis of Assisi, born Pietro Bernardone, the son of a wealthy Italian merchant. As a young man Francis followed the usual lifestyle of young aristocrats, but one day he happened to stop at a ruined church to pray. There he believed he heard the image on the cross speak to him, asking that he see to it that the church was repaired.

Francis went into town and sold all his family's property to raise money to give it to the priest to reconstruct the church. His father was furious and hauled him before the local bishop. Here Francis solemnly renounced the right to inherit his family's wealth and, taking off his clothes, left the room naked. He took up the life of a beggar, preaching and carrying a broom to sweep out neglected churches.

Nature for Francis was one great marvel of God's goodness. When no one else would listen to his sermons, he talked to birds and other animals. His charismatic personality attracted a following, and eventually the **Friars Minor,** the name he gave to his group, received the approval of Pope Innocent III.

Assisi today is quite a contrast to the simplicity of the Franciscan order's early days.

A contemporary of Francis, the Spaniard Dominic de Guzman, founded the Order of Preachers, which became known as the Dominicans. The Dominicans became the great scholars of the day and the principal judges of the **Inquisition,** the court established to seek out Christian heretics. Other religious orders founded at this time were the Augustinian Canons, the Carmelites, and the Servites. All worked among the growing urban populations of western Europe, rejecting the monastic model, which religious men and women previously followed.

Political Events in the British Isles

In A.D. 1154 after a period of civil war, the direct line of William the Conqueror ended and a new dynasty, the Angevin or Plantagenet, came to the throne in England. Its first representative was Henry II, whose mother was a daughter of Henry I and whose father was the Count of Anjou, a region of central France.

Henry II was highly ambitious. Not content with the Angevin inheritance in England where crown lands amounted to about 25% of the country, he married Eleanor of Aquitaine, formerly queen of Louis VII. This increased his French holdings, and more than doubled the lands under his sovereignty. In England, Henry initiated a series of actions against the great barons who, because of the anarchic conditions during the violent times preceding his accession, were restive under central rule.

Henry was determined that the church of England should support his goals. In A.D. 1162 he named his chancellor, Thomas Becket, to the archbishopric of Canterbury, expecting that their friendship would guarantee close cooperation between church and state. Within 2 years, however, they were at odds. At a meeting in Clarendon, Henry revoked many church privileges despite Becket's refusal to agree to these changes. Becket left for exile in France, while Henry sought to persuade the archbishop's supporters of his errors. The pope, unreservedly on Becket's side, threatened to place England under interdict, unless Becket was restored. Henry had to back down. Becket returned and excommunicated those churchmen who had upheld Henry at Clarendon.

The outraged king complained, "Shall a man who has eaten my bread insult the king and not one of my laggard servants do me justice for such an injury?" Taking him at his word, four of Henry's knights went to Canterbury cathedral and on December 29, 1170, struck down the archbishop with their swords.

All Europe regarded Thomas a martyr. Within 3 years he was declared a saint, and believers thought his tomb in Canterbury's cathedral began working miracles. Driven by popular opinion, Henry did penance by going to Canterbury, walking the last few miles barefoot. There the monks scourged him for his crime, but Henry's conviction that his church policy was a correct one allowed him to return to it several years later.

Henry's attention now turned to Irish affairs. Squabbles over the Irish high kingship created an opportunity for the Normans to intervene. Moreover, due to complaints reaching Rome, the pope encouraged the English to occupy the country. A Norman knight, Richard de Clare, known as Strongbow, began the suppression of Ireland. Having finished campaigning in France, Henry landed at Waterford in A.D. 1171 to prevent Strongbow from establishing an independent position on the island.

Strongbow and his Norman companions had no choice but to accept Henry's demands and acknowledge him lord of Ireland. Norman adventurers from England and Wales passed over into the island where they claimed Irish land and built castles to hold onto it. This drew Ireland into a reluctant relationship with England that lasts to our own time.

The last few years of Henry's rule were made difficult because his wife and sons conspired against him, each to ensure that the succession should be arranged to suit their own interests. The victor was Richard, a strong, vigorous man whose real interest was war rather than administration. He spent little time in England but went off on the Third Crusade, earning him the title of Lion-Heart. His brother John ruled in his absence and upon his death succeeded him as king.

John could not be trusted. He was unpopular to the degree that his brother Richard was a hero. When Pope Innocent III placed England under interdict, he released John's subjects from obedience to him, reasoning that a sinful king should not be obeyed. He encouraged other sovereigns to consider an invasion of England. Philip Augustus, the king of France, gathered an army so frightening to John that he not only made peace with

Norman monks set up an abbey at Jerpoint in Ireland's County Kilkenny.

Innocent but placed England in vassalage to the pope, thus sparing the kingdom from foreign attack, but not from further difficulties.

In June 1215 John's nobles met with him at Runnymeade and demanded that he sign the **Magna Carta.** This was a document that gave English barons and church members a great deal of autonomy while limiting John's powers. Even though Magna Carta was neither revolutionary nor democratic, it had a significant impact on later history when rights advanced to the nobility at that time were extended to the general population.

Magna Carta placed the king under the law, not above it. Its articles were later broadly interpreted to contain a prohibition on taxation without consent, a requirement that the government pay for the taking of property, and a guarantee of trial by one's peers. John later sought to repudiate Magna Carta, but he died within the year, leaving the kingdom to Henry III, still a minor at the time of his coronation.

It is important to those who are the heirs of the English tradition that **common law,** not the Code of Justinian, provided the legal framework within which society functioned. It was called common because it was applied universally throughout the kingdom. Having risen out of Anglo-Saxon practice, it gave to English law qualities that made it distinct from Roman law, which was based on royal absolutism.

Kingdoms of Continental Europe

A growing national consciousness appeared in Scandinavia's three countries in the High Middle Ages. Along with this consciousness a class spirit developed among the nobility who adopted the feudal customs of their southern neighbors as well as their penchant for military adventures. The Danish king Waldemar the Great, who began his rule in A.D. 1157, expanded his territories eastward and established a new capital at Copenhagen. In the thirteenth century the Danes sent expeditions into the eastern Baltic, to Estonia, where they founded the city of Reval (now Tallinn).

While the Danes dominated the Baltic, King Haakon IV of Norway conquered Iceland, but at home he so favored German immigrants that Norway's commercial wealth fell into their hands rather than into those of local tradespeople.

In Sweden, population growth encouraged colonists to move eastward, making their home in southern Finland. At this time many Finns, along with the Lapps, a people linguistically akin to them, were reindeer herders.

To the south of Scandinavia, France was still a geographical rather than a political entity as the twelfth century opened. The early Capetian kings living in Paris had little control over the nobles who were their nominal vassals. Holding a strong fortress made a nobleman immune to royal threats.

Nation-building began when Louis VI, the Fat, ruler of France from A.D. 1108 to 1137, slowly whittled away at baronial territories and privileges. He was fortunate to have Suger, abbot of the royal monastery of St. Denis, in his service. Suger was anxious to have Paris look like a royal capital, so he sponsored an extensive building program at the royal abbey of St. Denis. There he built the first Gothic church in France.

After Louis VI's death, his son Louis VII began a long reign that extended to A.D. 1180. He was a hard-working monarch who wisely retained Suger as his principal advisor. His rule was interrupted by a call to the Crusades. Suger warned Louis that he was needed at home, but he ignored the abbot's warning.

Louis took his wife, Eleanor of Aquitaine, with him and was gone for the next 2.5 years in the Second Crusade. He had no success and returned a defeated man. To add to his problems, it was obvious that the queen had lost interest in him. Back in France, it was discovered the royal couple were cousins; hence, their marriage was annulled. Eleanor was now free to marry Henry, Duke of Normandy, soon to become Henry II, king of England. Therefore, Louis lost Aquitaine, which fell into the pocket of Henry II and made him a more powerful ruler in France than Louis.

Louis' son, Philip II, was but 15 when his father died. Philip grew up to be crafty and unscrupulous, but those qualities were no hindrance to his plans to centralize France. He, too, took the cross but returned to Paris after a short, fruitless stay abroad.

Philip concentrated on enhancing the royal bureaucracy. He created an official known as the **bailie** in the north and **seneschal** in the south to represent the king in providing royal justice and in collecting revenue. Philip spent most of his time in residence at Paris where he undertook a rebuilding of the Louvre, the royal palace. He paved the streets, established markets, and erected hospitals. His interests extended to the progress made on Notre Dame and the university. History calls him Philip Augustus, like the Caesar who held the same title. He received it for the same reasons: just as Caesar Augustus inaugurated the Roman Empire, Philip was the founder of the French monarchy's rise to power.

The religious enthusiasm that sponsored cathedral-building in Philip's day also produced a religious movement whose members believed that piety should turn in an opposite direction. It first appeared in Languedoc among certain inhabitants called **Cathari,** or pure ones, who lived around the town of Albi. Here a dualistic theology was advocated. It argued that all material things were bad, that the world was dominated by the Evil Spirit, and that the true believer must free the soul from matter by strict asceticism.

Strange as it may seem, Cathar doctrine became popular among both nobility and common people because it offered a simple answer to the complexities of this world. Catholic bishops' efforts to expunge it were remarkably unsuccessful as the Cathari rejected any compromise with the institutional church.

Philip Augustus sat back to watch while northern barons, claiming that they were seeking to restore orthodoxy, moved into the south to war against those considered heretics. Battles were fought with extreme cruelty, and many civilians lost their lives. After a decade of bloodshed, victory went to the Catholic knights.

Several years afterward a special court, the Inquisition, was founded to deal with any future heresies. Fear and violence, not persuasion, now were used to enforce orthodoxy. The Inquisitors heard cases of suspected heretics even if the charge was made by an anonymous accuser. There was no protection against self-incrimination.

Although such a procedure is altogether repugnant to modern sensibilities, public heretics in the Middle Ages were considered dangerous people, carrying a kind of spiritually communicable disease. If they were allowed to spread false doctrine, the whole Christian community could be infected. On these grounds severe public penances were levied on those found guilty. The worst offenders, those who had a prior conviction and then returned to their heresy, might be sentenced to death by burning at the stake.

It was Louis IX, grandson of Philip, who brought the French monarchy to its height during his reign from A.D. 1226 to 1270. Louis became an ideal monarch, much like Charlemagne, but also a saint, something beyond the grasp of his predecessor.

Louis's example offered a new outlook to the class of knights. Some of the roughness of soldiering was smoothed over, and courtesy replaced boorishness. This new spirit is known as **chivalry**. It turned the warrior from delighting in massacre to protecting the poor and defenseless. It was reflected in the literature of the times. **Troubadours,** wandering poets, sang of the knight in love, willing to serve his lady no matter the cost. The troubadours transported their audiences into a make-believe world of fairies, magicians, and dragons and confirmed chivalric ideals.

The High Middle Ages were a time of fear for the Jews of France. The aggressive spirit of Christians at war with Islam spilled over into attacks on them. All manner of charges were levied at their alleged crimes. Although educated Christians could make a distinction between Islam and Judaism, the masses of people did not. They resented the strong communal spirit of the Jews, which was regarded as sinister, and their perseverance in Judaism was seen as an affront to the Christian religion.

City authorities required Jews to locate in certain sections of towns where they lived in self-contained neighborhoods. There they had little contact with the Christians who had turned so hostile.

European monarchs as well as Pope Innocent III legislated in the spirit of the times, placing restrictions on Jewish housing and forcing Jews to wear a special kind of hat and other clothes to identify them as nonbelievers. In some towns a yellow patch became the sign of one's Jewishness. King Louis IX of France, so respected by his Christian subjects, ordered copies of the Talmud seized and burned. In Paris 24 carts of Hebrew literature were hurled into the flames.

In Spain the twelfth century saw a decline in the strength of the Muslim Almoravids, a group of warriors called in from Morocco to buttress the rulers of al-Andalus. As the Christian population grew, their armies became more formidable, but so did those of their opponents.

New invaders, the **Almohads,** charged out of Morocco into Spain. The Almohads belonged to a radical Islamic sect and, like the Almoravids when they first entered the country, were motivated by fervent religious devotion.

Spain held two major Christian kingdoms. One was Aragon, whose monarchs were soon to rival those of Castile as Christian champions. They annexed the region of Barcelona giving them a major port on the Mediterranean. Castile's armies dominated the **Reconquest,** penetrating deep into Muslim lands below Toledo. With papal aid, Alfonso VIII of Castile commenced a series of attacks on the Muslims that culminated in A.D. 1212 at the battle of Las Navas de Tolosa. This victory guaranteed the eclipse of Almohad power in Spain and opened a vast empty territory for Christian settlement. Here large estates were carved out for cattle ranches and sheep pastures owned by the crown, the church, or the nobility.

Fredericks of the Holy Roman Empire

The close of the investiture controversy did not bring peace to the Holy Roman Empire. Partisans who supported the emperors continued to fight with those who favored the church's interests. Townspeople clashed with bishops and nobles hoping to ally themselves with royal power, but the emperors held back. They needed the nobility, who made up their armies, to continue an activist policy south of the Alps. Germany fell into near anarchy until in A.D. 1152 Frederick Barbarossa of the Hohenstaufen family won out.

Frederick, with his handsome red beard, hence Barbarossa, was a charismatic figure. His regal bearing showed him to be convinced of his fitness for the imperial office. He was generous to his friends and merciless toward his enemies, very much in the tradition of Charlemagne and Otto I.

Frederick was not satisfied with effective control over Germany. If he was Roman emperor, then he must also govern Italy. Frederick laid plans to unite the Norman kingdom of Sicily to the Holy Roman Empire. This was a project vigorously resisted by the pope because papal territory would then be completely surrounded by Hohenstaufen lands. Frederick, however, was resourceful enough to arrange a wedding in A.D. 1186 between his son and heir, the future Henry VI, and Constance, daughter of Roger II of Sicily. A quarrel between Frederick and the pope over the marriage was suspended on the news that Jerusalem had fallen back into Muslim hands. Frederick, faithful to his role as protector of Christendom, took the cross and embarked on the Third Crusade. He died on the way after a heart attack and fall from his horse in Cilician Armenia before reaching Jerusalem.

Barbarossa's son, Henry VI, inherited all of Italy except for Venice and the Papal States. The popes, as they feared, were at his mercy. He wanted to build an empire in the Mediterranean but, in the midst of preparations, Henry suddenly died leaving his 3-year-old child, Frederick, a ward of the pope. The regency of the young Frederick II was marked by renewed turbulence in Germany. When he was old enough to be crowned emperor, Frederick promised the pope that he would vacate Sicily soon afterward, but his heart was on the island, not in Germany, and he kept his residence in Palermo.

Frederick's preference for Sicily can be readily understood. Here the foundation for strong monarchical rule was carefully laid by his grandfather, Roger II. For almost 50 years Roger ruled with an iron hand. He forbade his knights to engage in private warfare, ordered all court cases brought to the royal court in Palermo, and established a strong financial base through rigorous taxation and royal monopolies on the sale of salt and lumber.

Because of his many-sided personality, Frederick II was known as the wonder of the world. He was interested in science and wrote a treatise on birds that became a standard work on the subject. He was also a student of philosophy and political science. To facilitate learning, Frederick chartered a university at Naples to train those who would enter his bureaucracy.

Frederick replaced feudal obligations by a regular system of taxation. Simony in church affairs and bribery for gaining civil office were made serious offenses, and the well-trained Sicilian bureaucracy became a model for other European states. After Frederick's death, however, a long interregnum gave evidence that the Hohenstaufen star was in decline. The popes would have their victory.

In the north of Italy the Lombard towns and Venice continued to lead the rest of Europe in commerce and banking because of their early success in these fields. Population increased as both peasants and nobility poured into the cities from rural Italy. Although nominally under the empire, the Lombard towns were sufficiently powerful to ignore or even make war against their sovereign.

Artists have decorated the entrance to St. Mark's cathedral in Venice with a mosaic of the church.

Venice was in the same position vis-à-vis its Byzantine ruler. Town councils controlled the government relegating both bishops and nobles to a secondary position. The communes determined taxation, minted coinage, set up their own courts, and recruited an army. Venice spoke of itself as the Republic of St. Mark, which was so named for its patron saint.

Eastern Europe Between Germans and Mongols

The twelfth century found the Polish people beset by many serious problems. Central to all of these was the weakness of the monarchy and the strength of the high nobility, the magnates, and the numerous smaller aristocrats, the **szlachta**. Both groups considered it in their interest to keep the monarchs impotent so that their own power and wealth could be enhanced.

King Boleslaw III played into the nobility's hands when at his death his will divided the kingdom into five principalities. His eldest son was assigned Kraków, where he held the title of Grand Duke, and was to supervise the activities of the other Polish princes. Such cooperation proved an illusion. Instead of harmony, civil strife plagued the country for the remainder of the twelfth century.

A street in Warsaw today recalls little of the first settlement in the twelfth century. All of the buildings in this picture are restorations constructed after World War II.

At the northeast corner of Poland, adjacent to the area of Polish Mazovia, lived a people known as the Prussians. They were both farmers and herdsmen, but what most distinguished them was their fierce resistance to outsiders. When Konrad, Polish duke of Mazovia, tried to incorporate their lands and convert them to Christianity, they forced out his soldiers. Frustrated by their intransigence, Konrad invited the military order of the **Teutonic Knights** to come to his assistance.

The Knights were a German religious order which, like other crusading orders, was founded to garrison the Holy Land. After the Christians were pushed from Palestine, the Knights first moved to Venice and then to Hungary where their welcome after several years' stay turned sour. The invitation to war against the Prussians gave them a rare opportunity to rekindle the crusading spirit in their ranks.

The Knights kept whatever lands they occupied for themselves, so that over a period of 50 years the Prussians were so worn down that they ceased to exist as a people. While the country might still be known as Prussia, and the people who lived there Prussians, the name now referred to German colonists. Unwittingly, Konrad of Mazovia had allowed a strong German state to be created by the Knights, powerful enough to block Polish access to the Baltic for centuries to come.

Bohemia in the twelfth century was marked by the success of Prague's princes in extending their autonomy within the Holy Roman Empire. Czech agricultural production, mining, and trade grew with Bohemia's increased political importance. German settlers were also welcomed into the kingdom and given privileged status as an enticement to settle underpopulated areas of the nation. They governed themselves under German, rather than Bohemian, law. The Germans were expert miners who knew how to reach the silver and gold ores that lay buried in the Sudeten Mountains.

In the twelfth century Hungary's monarchy was troubled by dynastic problems similar to those that afflicted Poland. Nevertheless, political instability did not hamper continued Magyar expansion. Transylvania, to the east of Hungary proper, received more immigrants. Szekels, close kin to the Magyars as well as Germans, called Saxons, were present in large numbers. The Saxons established seven towns in the southeastern part of the province. Here they elected their own leaders and enjoyed an autonomous position.

Hungarian kings also led expeditions to the south, wresting Dalmatia from Venice and overthrowing the king of Croatia. In A.D. 1102 they annexed these Slavic lands. A Hungarian governor was appointed, and the administration of Croatia and Dalmatia was placed under Magyar officials. The Croatians were joined to the Hungarian crown for the next 800 years.

When the twelfth century opened, the Russian lands were suffering from civil wars waged by princes seeking to extend their territories. The Russian people also had to contend with attacks launched by the Polovtsi tribes that occupied the steppe lands of Ukraine. The situation improved in A.D. 1113 when the inhabitants of Kiev invited the best of the Russian princes, Vladimir Monomakh, to govern their city. Vladimir was an able ruler, a patron of learning, and a friend of the poor. In his *Testament* he could rightfully claim, "I did not allow the mighty to distress the poor peasant or the destitute widow."

After the death of Monomakh, the Russian princes returned to fighting among themselves. Economic prosperity declined as a result of these conflicts, and the Polovtsi closed the river route to Constantinople.

Late in the twelfth century, the Russian prince of Suzdal captured Kiev and moved the capital to his city. Afterward Vladimir, far to the northeast, became the leading Russian town as Kiev went up in flames because of a Polovtsi attack.

Meanwhile, deep inside Inner Asia, the Mongols planned an assault on Russia. Warned of their peril, the Polovtsi came to terms with the Russians, and a joint Polovtsi-Russian army marched to meet the invaders at the Kalka River. There the Mongols inflicted a serious defeat upon them. After this victory the Mongols returned home, but in A.D. 1237 they came into Russia a second time under the leadership of Batu Khan.

The Mongol forces of Batu Khan were so destructive that almost all Slavic people living east of the Dnieper were either killed or forced to flee. Only two Russian cities were left intact: Novgorod and Pskov. The armies of Batu Khan, having finished with Russia, poured into Poland slaughtering the hapless populace, burning and looting the towns.

An artist has pictured Mongols besieging a European city. They carry the head of a prisoner on a spear.

The Mongols' farthest advance reached Legnica in Silesia where Prince Henry II attempted a stand. He was killed in the battle, and his army crushed, but Batu Khan took his warriors out of Poland, moving them south to Hungary. King Bela IV raised an army to meet them, but it was defeated, and the king fled to a Dalmatian island. The invaders then spread out over the country. According to one estimate, a million people, half the Magyar population, were either killed or taken captive. When the Mongols left, Bela returned to his prostrate kingdom.

After the Mongols occupied a region, they were anxious to restore the economy so as to collect tribute from the conquered people. They were good administrators and hard-headed businessmen, with trading interests extending from China to western Europe. Using the Volga, the Dnieper, and the Don as commercial arteries to the south, furs, slaves, and forest products reached both Constantinople and Baghdad with profits for all. The trip of the Venetian Marco Polo to China could not have been made except for the security from the Black Sea to Beijing provided by the Mongols.

Although Poland did not experience Mongol settlement, it was left reeling from the losses suffered as a result of the invasion. Large areas were so depopulated that the surviving landowners recruited German farmers and townsmen to come to Poland. These immigrants were allowed to keep their own laws and local administration as in Bohemia. New towns rose on Polish soil, but the inhabitants were foreigners, especially in Silesia, which received the bulk of the newcomers. Jews, too, now poured into Poland seeking security from persecution in western Europe.

Both Germans and Jews found employment facilitating the Polish salt trade. This commodity was used for the preservation of cabbage and herring, two items essential to the diet of people living in the Baltic area. In addition to salt, quantities of grain and wood were also exported to western Europe.

Because these shipments were in bulk and meant for a distant market, those who profited most tended to be the intermediaries, not the peasants.

North of Poland a variety of peoples lived along the eastern shore of the Baltic Sea. Estonians were in the far north, Livs and Cours were in the central area, and Lithuanians lived in the south. They were distinguished from one another by ethnic and linguistic boundaries. All except the Estonians spoke a Baltic language of Indo-European origin. The Estonians, close relatives of the Finns, spoke a Uralic-Altaic tongue.

Baltic society was highly structured. Among the Lithuanians a formidable warrior class dominated all other elements. The people lived in villages where only a few specialists such as iron- and harness-makers plied their trade. Everyone else was engaged in herding and farming.

Byzantium

The Byzantine state in the eleventh and twelfth centuries was much affected by the Latin West because crusading armies marched across its territories twice during this period. Yet face-to-face contact did not improve relations between the people of the West and East because the Byzantines considered the Franks in their midst barbaric, while the Westerners thought the Greeks weak and capricious. The devout Byzantines especially resented the treatment meted out to Eastern clergy who were forced to accept Latin bishops as their superiors wherever Crusaders held sway.

A monastary on the island of Amorgos hugs a place between the mountains and the sea.

The most serious event to trouble Byzantine and Latin relations was the **Fourth Crusade,** which occurred early in the thirteenth century. Promoted by Pope Innocent III to regain Jerusalem, knights recruited in northern France appeared in Venice seeking the Republic's aid to transport them to the East.

The Venetians signed a treaty promising to outfit a fleet for over 30,000 men. When it was time for the Crusade to embark, however, only one third that number had arrived. Money to pay the Venetians was eaten up by delays. The doge, Enrico Dandolo, saw but one way for the Crusaders to discharge their debts. He enlisted them in an attack upon Zara, a town on the Adriatic that once had been under Venetian control.

At this point Alexios, son of the deposed Emperor Isaac Angelos, joined the expedition and promised to aid the Crusaders if they helped him regain Constantinople's throne for his father. The leaders of the Crusade apparently regarded his proposal a stroke of good fortune. In June 1203 the fleet arrived off Constantinople only to discover that Alexios had deceived them. The Crusaders then decided to take Constantinople by force. After several weeks of preparation, the Latins occupied the city, and Alexios and his father were installed as legitimate sovereigns.

Before the Latin attack, no enemy had ever breached Constantinople's walls. The western soldiers entered the city by charging the sea wall.

The local population hated the rulers imposed on them. In the following year the father died, the son was overthrown, and the Latins felt that they had no choice but to assume the direct rule of the city. Immense destruction swept Constantinople during the first few days of occupation as Western soldiers looted the capital of treasures amassed over eight centuries.

The Latin conquest was to prove short-lived, from A.D. 1204 to 1261. Its only immediate effect was to further weaken the Byzantines before the Turkish challenge of the fourteenth century. Its long-range result was to convince the Greeks that Western Christians were never to be trusted.

Conclusion

During the High Middle Ages civilization made significant advances in the West. Town life and the centralization of government promoted change for the better in political and economic spheres. For the first time since Roman days, townspeople north of the Alps were in sufficient numbers to form a middle class. They proved themselves as they enrolled in universities and directed their energies into the building of cathedrals. Wealth could now be amassed through trade or practicing a profession as well as by landowning. Both the king's bureaucrats and the church's officials were better trained and more efficient in their service to state and church, the two major institutions of the High Middle Ages.

In the East, Mongols and Latin Crusaders disrupted the traditional patterns of life. Their presence was an alien one, recognized as such by the natives who sought to be rid of them as soon as they had the strength. The Greeks disposed of the Latins rather quickly. It took a longer time for the Russian peoples to break the Mongol hold, but the energy required for this struggle seems to have sapped much of their strength. Universities and cathedrals in the East were much slower to develop. Only in recent times has the gap between the western and eastern nations of Europe narrowed.

CHAPTER 30 REVIEW
EUROPE IN THE HIGH MIDDLE AGES

Summary
- Town life revived in Europe after the twelfth century.
- A contest went on between townspeople and the lords who owned the land.
- Merchant and artisan guilds organized the sale and manufacture of products.
- New techniques and crops advanced agriculture.
- Intellectual life became organized in the universities.
- The Gothic cathedral became the high point of medieval architecture.
- The popes of the Middle Ages argued for their right to judge the consciences of Europe's rulers.
- New religious orders appeared in the church.
- Kings, queens, and emperors fought each other over land and prestige.
- Mongols struck the Russian lands and eastern Europe in the thirteenth century causing great loss of life and property.
- The Fourth Crusade occupied Constantinople rather than the Holy Land.

Identify
People: Peter Abélard; Ibn Rushd; Moses ben Maimon; Innocent III; Thomas Becket; Thomas Aquinas; Cathari; Bernard of Clairvaux; Hildegard of Bingen; Francis of Assisi; Eleanor of Aquitaine
Places: Toledo; Cîteaux; Waterford; Venice; Prussia; Prague; Croatia; Transylvania
Events: revival of towns; improved agriculture; founding of universities; building of cathedrals

Define

usury	universals	interdict
commune	*Summa Theologica*	Friars Minor
guild	Magna Carta	troubadours
szlachta	Fourth Crusade	Teutonic Knights
Inquisition	universities	masters
rose window	colleges	trivium
canons	common law	quadrivium
conversi	seneschal	Cathari
Spanish Reconquest	bailie	chivalry
Scholasticism	flying buttress	

Multiple Choice
1. Towns revived in Europe after A.D. 1100 because
   (a) councils invited people to move into towns.
   (b) there was greater production of food.
   (c) people wanted to get away from life in castles.
   (d) none of the above.

2. A serf could be freed if not found
   (a) for a year and a day.
   (b) for 5 years.
   (c) for 6 months.
   (d) for 3 months.

3. In the thirteenth century European kings made commerce more easy
   (a) by building roads.
   (b) by building canals.
   (c) by establishing a navy.
   (d) by minting gold coins.

4. Merchants in the Middle Ages formed trade organizations called
   (a) companies.
   (b) corporations.
   (c) chambers of commerce.
   (d) guilds.

5. An apprentice was someone
   (a) learning a trade.
   (b) finished with school.
   (c) looking for a job.
   (d) serving on a court.

6. The Fourth Crusade saw the Latin conquest of
   (a) Constantinople.
   (b) Jerusalem.
   (c) Rome.
   (d) Baghdad.

7. In the thirteenth century these people moved into eastern Europe:
   (a) Seljuk Turks.
   (b) Arabs.
   (c) Mongols.
   (d) Iranians.

8. Peter Abélard's book is known as
   (a) *Summary of Theology.*
   (b) *The Divine Comedy.*
   (c) *Canterbury Tales.*
   (d) *Yes and No.*

9. The most important medieval scholar and churchman was
   (a) Peter Abélard.
   (b) Plato.
   (c) Aristotle.
   (d) Thomas Aquinas.

10. A Romanesque church will always have
    (a) pointed arches.
    (b) rounded arches.
    (c) flying buttresses.
    (d) many windows.

11. Many cathedrals were built in Europe, such as in Paris and Cologne, using this architectural style:
    (a) Gothic.
    (b) German.
    (c) Roman.
    (d) Romanesque.

12. Magna Carta was a famous document in England which
    (a) set up the Parliament.
    (b) limited the powers of the king.
    (c) established the University of Cambridge.
    (d) made England a republic.

13. Common law, rather than Justinian's Code, operated in
    (a) England.
    (b) France.
    (c) Venice.
    (d) Normandy.

Essay Questions
1. Discuss the importance of town life in medieval Europe.
2. Explain the origin of the university and its structure.
3. Discuss the importance of Magna Carta.
4. What were the results of the Fourth Crusade?

Answers

1. b	6. a	11. a
2. a	7. c	12. b
3. d	8. d	13. a
4. d	9. d	
5. a	10. b	

CHAPTER 31

Europe's Late Middle Ages and the Early Renaissance

About the year A.D. 1250 medieval western Europe reached the height of its achievement. Bustling towns and prosperous farms covered the landscape, and both urban and rural populations enjoyed a standard of living higher than any since Roman times. The church was well administered, for the friars had pumped new vigor into it. Monarchs were stronger than their predecessors, and royal justice extended over a greater number of people than ever before.

Unfortunately, when a predominantly rural society such as that in Europe reaches a certain peak, a downward trend develops. Agricultural prosperity moves in cycles, like nature itself, generous one year and stingy the next. Toward the close of the thirteenth century, serious problems began to appear, and the condition of Europe's people worsened.

Weather and Disease

Records that make it possible to trace weather conditions during this era show that Europe's climate turned colder as the year A.D. 1300 approached. All over northern Europe heavy rains and early frosts wreaked havoc on medieval farmers' efforts to produce food. City people shared in the suffering when the markets went bare.

This climatic change was only the beginning of trouble. The advent of a terrible disease was even more devastating. This was the **Black Death,** the plague that struck Europe beginning in A.D. 1348. It swept over the continent leaving a trail of misery.

Nothing so terrible had afflicted Europeans since Justinian's time. It is estimated that fully one third of the population was carried off by this dreaded disease. Whole towns and villages succumbed to its ravages, and corpses were stacked in piles with no one to bury them.

The disease was caused by a bacillus carried by fleas that lived in the fur of a particular kind of black rat. When Italian ships visited infested Southwest Asian ports, rats carrying the lethal fleas clambered aboard the vessels. Unknowingly the ships returned home with the rodents hidden below deck, and when the ships docked, the rats scurried ashore. Therefore, the Italian trading cities of Genoa, Venice, and Pisa were the first to be affected. Then the disease spread to other Mediterranean and Atlantic ports. The rats moved inland and the people there became infected and carriers themselves if the disease lodged in their lungs.

Because no one knew what caused disease in the Middle Ages, the wildest kind of excuses were put forward to explain the plague. Bad air was blamed, some thought Satan was behind it, while others believed that God was demonstrating his displeasure with humankind. Death by plague was terrible because it struck so suddenly. Boils appeared in a person's armpits and groin; then vomiting commenced accompanied by high fever. Within hours the victim was usually dead.

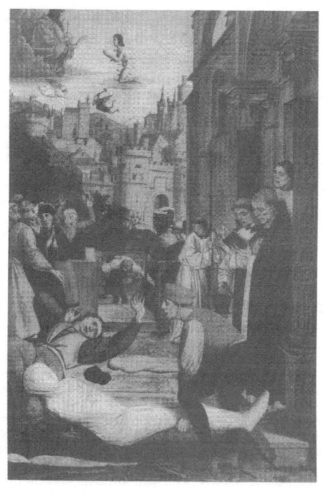

Churchmen in this painting offer prayers for the victims of the plague.

The physical effects of the pestilence were coupled with strange psychological behavior. Some people reacted by living without restraint. Others plunged into such ascetical practices as marching in flagellant processions from town to town. Many individuals sank into despair, having lost so many friends and relatives.

For several decades the economic life of western Europe was thrown back into a situation mirroring the fifth century period of invasions. Even when the worst of the plague abated, it burst out again at intervals through the rest of the century. The slacking of its virulence apparently came as a result of a rapid decline of black rats when a large increase of brown rats overwhelmed their food supply.

Warfare and Its Consequences

Endemic violence became more prevalent in the late thirteenth and early fourteenth centuries. European noblemen believed that their proper role was to be warriors, and they spent most of their time preparing for or engaged in combat.

The nobles claimed to follow a code of chivalry that made them champions of distressed maidens and poor orphans. However, it was the members of their own class that caused the distress and violence that made the orphans in the first place.

Causes of conflict might develop from any real or imagined injustice or slight. Violence rather than compromise was often the way to settle arguments over property, concerns about a wife's dowry, or the disposition of the estate of a deceased baron. During the long winter months of northern Europe, when there was little to occupy them, the nobles became restless. When spring arrived, it was time for military adventure, a welcome change from their enforced idleness.

Infantrymen and artillerymen were recruited from the lower classes. Noblemen did not find that kind of military profession appealing. Because fighting on horseback had always been an aristocrat's proper role in battle, the knights resisted the change in weaponry. They wanted to be considered important even when they were not.

The disruption caused by famine, disease, and war translated into social conflict toward the end of the fourteenth century. The agricultural workers of France and England who bore much of the burden attendant upon the waging of the Hundred Years' War rose up in desperation against their landowners. For a brief moment they were successful. Then the nobility crushed them with extreme cruelty, as an example for any in the future who might want to challenge the established order.

Hundred Years' War

In the fourteenth century a conflict broke out between the kings of England and France, known as the **Hundred Years' War** because it lasted so long. At dispute was who should be king of France. The English royal house, coming from Normandy, had legitimate claims to the French crown.

In A.D. 1428 a remarkable woman, Joan of Arc, played a role during this war. She was only a young French peasant girl when she believed that she heard the voices of several saints encouraging her to do battle with the English.

The heir to the French throne, Charles, had never been crowned and seemed somewhat indifferent regarding his future. Charles had a court, but because Reims, the traditional site for the coronation for French kings lay deep behind English lines, he was afraid to risk coronation. Joan arrived at

461

his court dressed in armor. Although Charles was in disguise, she picked him out of the crowd and told her story of the voices. She assured Charles that God wanted him to be crowned and that he should give her an army.

Joan so impressed Charles that she got her soldiers, and with them she won a major battle before the city of Orléans. With Charles and his vassals, Joan drove through to Reims. There he was crowned Charles VII. Eventually Joan's good fortune was reversed. The English captured her, put her on trial as a witch, and then sentenced her to execution. She was burned at the stake. Later the decision made by the judges was overruled, but it was too late to help Joan.

In A.D. 1453 the French and English at last agreed to peace. Although the English had won most of the battles in the Hundred Years' War, they lacked the people and wealth to stay in France.

One effect of the conflict was a technological improvement of weaponry. The long bow, which the English acquired from the Welsh, could readily pierce the armor of the French knights so that once more the infantryman came to be Europe's most efficient warrior.

A Renaissance army combined cannon and pikes, a kind of long spear.

Artillery was effectively used for the first time at the battle of Crécy in A.D. 1346. Europeans discovered how gunpowder could be used to project a lead ball out of a container at great speed. Early cannons were notoriously inaccurate, but the noise they made when fired coupled with the remarkable distance the cannonballs traveled made generals anxious to put them into their arsenals.

British Isles

The rise of Parliament marked England's history in the Late Middle Ages. In A.D. 1265 Simon de Montfort, leader of the barons in opposition to the king, summoned four knights from every shire and two townsmen from every borough to discuss affairs in the country. Thirty years later, during the reign of Edward I, Parliament and the king were frequently in consultation. England was well on its way to representative government, for Parliament brought Englishmen from all over the realm to discuss issues, advise the monarch, and to give their consent to his projects.

King Edward I of England meets with King Alexander I of Scotland before Parliament. Its members sit on sacks of wool.

Then came the Hundred Years' War and living conditions became more difficult, not only because of the war but also because of the outbreak of the Black Death. If that was not enough, in A.D. 1381 the Peasants' Revolt underscored the misery of the farm laborers. Although defeated, the peasants put a scare into the barons and the king. On a brighter note, Geoffery Chaucer, a government official, commenced his engaging *Canterbury Tales* at this time. Both in Scotland and Ireland, Norman barons shared power with the royal houses, while the Celtic population provided the farm laborers.

In the late fifteenth century two rival families of England attempted to place one of their own members on the throne. The resulting conflict is called the **War of the Roses.** The House of York, which had a white rose as its family emblem, fought on one side, while its opponent, the House of Lancaster, had a red rose for its symbol.

In A.D. 1485, victory went to the red rose when Henry Tudor defeated a Yorkist army and was crowned king of England. His dynasty, the Tudors, was to rule for over a century, producing some of the most colorful rulers in English history.

Ferdinand and Isabella

The progress of the Christian kingdoms in Spain to complete the **Reconquest** finished in A.D. 1492. In that year Granada, the last Muslim stronghold, fell to King Ferdinand and Queen Isabella.

Before that event occurred, the Iberian peninsula was divided into several different kingdoms. The two most prominent were Castile in the center of the peninsula and Aragon in the far northeast. When Isabella, heiress to Castile's throne, married Ferdinand, son of the king of Aragon, the two agreed that they must have a strong national monarchy. They reduced the authority of the nobles, revised town charters, and changed Spanish law so as to centralize power in their hands.

Ferdinand and Isabella then turned to investigating the religious lives of their subjects. Already some Jews and Muslims had converted to Christianity. Some were sincere, but a large number had become Catholic only to avoid persecution and secretly continued to hold on to their former religious beliefs.

Seville's cathedral is southern Europe's largest.

To find out who they were, the monarchs established a court of **Inquisition.** The Spanish Inquisition's task was to make sure that there was no sliding back into Jewish or Muslim beliefs. Individuals found guilty of doing this had their property taken away. If convicted a second time, they could be burned at the stake. No one knows the exact number of people who died, but the estimate is in the hundreds.

France

The strongest king of France in the Late Middle Ages was Philip the Fair, who began his reign in A.D. 1285. Philip was consumed by ambition to mold France into a single nation loyal above all to its king. He was also intent upon gaining control of the church in his lands no matter the cost.

Philip the Fair was so angered at Pope Boniface VIII, when he forbade the king's taxation of the French clergy to pursue a war against England, that he sent an armed force to seize the pontiff. Boniface was taken while in his palace at Anagni and held prisoner until the citizens of the town freed him. He died a few weeks later in October 1303. For the first time in medieval history, a pope had been publically humiliated by a secular monarch. The power of the church's leaders was crushed by the cold steel of the French king's soldiers.

The French king was not content with his victory. His ambition went much further. He so dominated the cardinals called to elect a new pope that they elected his choice, the Archbishop of Bordeaux. Selecting the name Clement V, the pope asked that he be crowned at Lyon rather than at Rome. Then, on the excuse that his health was too poor to make the trip to Italy, Clement broke the 1,200-year-old tradition that the head of Catholicism should live there. He took up residence at Avignon, a papal estate on the Rhône River, which placed him in close proximity to Philip.

The popes lived in this palace at Avignon, France, during the Babylonian captivity.

Clement was so much the creature of the king that he congratulated him on his attempted deposition of Boniface VIII and raised no objections to the king's suppression of the Knights Templars. The Templars, no longer in the Holy Land, were still active in gathering funds for their return and had become very wealthy. By suppressing them on charges of immorality, the king lined his pockets, although officially their properties went to the Knights of St. John.

After Clement's papacy, six other popes followed him at Avignon, where a great papal palace was built. The city became a center of ecclesiastical administrators and curial officials. Church courts were kept busy hearing cases brought from all over Europe, and Avignon was the busiest center of legal activity on the continent. Because diplomats, missionaries, and office-seekers streamed back and forth from Avignon, the revenues brought to church officials were very impressive. The Western church had never been so centralized.

In A.D. 1378 Pope Gregory XI returned to Rome for a visit and died while there. The attempt of the French kings to dominate the church reached an end.

Holy Roman Empire

The conflict between the popes and the emperors concluded with a victory for the popes. The Hohenstaufen dynasty gave way in A.D. 1273 to the house of Habsburg. At the time no one could have predicted the Habsburg's longevity. While it did not always provide the emperors, there was always a Habsburg in the wings for the next 700 years.

Despite the fact that the emperors were not able to coerce the German princes to follow them, except for those times when it was in their interest to do so, there was always a lively contest and no lack of candidates when a vacancy occurred. Since the office was elective, maneuvering was the order of the day. In A.D. 1356 Emperor Charles IV issued a **Golden Bull,** setting down a permanent electoral system. Seven electors, three bishops, and four princes were to form the committee to chose the candidate.

Merchants of the empire discovered a way to better their financial situation at this time. They formed a federation of cities, the **Hanseatic League,** to control the lucrative Baltic trade. For over a century its merchants prospered, until internal dissension and competition from stronger national monarchies sapped its vitality.

Events in Eastern Europe

Society in eastern Europe north of the Danube River continued to be divided sharply between nobility and peasants. The peasants of eastern Europe were nearly all serfs, tied to the land and forced to work on the estates of the landowners.

Both the Polish and Hungarian kings were more concerned with keeping good relations with the nobles and clergy than with trying to help the peasants. The nobles and clergy supplied their armies so the kings believed they had no choice.

In A.D. 1386 Poland and Lithuania's nobles accepted a single dynasty, the Jagiellonian, to bolster their position in eastern Europe. Kraków, the capital, became Poland's leading city and the home of a university.

It is obvious that the threat of Ottoman conquest should have brought forth a common response from the Balkan peoples if they hoped to remain independent. This did not happen. The Turks met them one at a time. The Serbians and Ottomans clashed at Kosovo Polje on June 15, 1389. Here at the most famous battle ever fought on Serbian soil, the Ottoman armies crushed the forces of Prince Lazar. But the Turks paid dearly for their victory. Sultan Murad I was killed. Nevertheless, Serbia became a vassal of the Turks, and its prince had to send troops to join the Ottomans.

Bulgaria, first defeated by the Serbs, was also a divided nation when the Turks appeared. Sofia was occupied first and then Turnovo, and all resistance was over by the beginning of the fifteenth century. North of the Danube an area called the Principalities of Moldavia and Wallachia were next to experience a Turkish invasion. The people here were Romanian and for centuries had suffered from isolation. Hardly had Romanian national life begun than the Turks were at the gate.

The Romanian princes had to pay tribute and furnish troops to the Turks in order to avoid occupation. One of the Romanian chiefs resisted the Turks and would not cooperate. His name was Vlad the Impaler, and his cruelty knew no bounds. People spoke of him as the devil. (The word *devil* in Romanian is *dracul*.) He became the legendary figure of literature, Count Dracula.

Fall of Constantinople

In the latter part of the thirteenth century, a Byzantine general effected the reconquest of Constantinople from the Latins. It was hardly a reconquest in the military sense because the Latin defenders were so few and the Venetian fleet was at sea. When the Byzantine army came within sight of the city, they simply occupied it. The Emperor Baldwin II and the Catholic patriarch left for the West, and the Latin empire came to an inglorious end.

The emperor who moved into the regained city was Michael VIII Paleologos. The dynasty he founded lasted as long as Constantinople remained in Christian hands.

In the fourteenth century, despite its many problems and shrinking size, civil war erupted within the Byzantine state. The worst conflict was between John V Paleologos and the former chief minister of his father, John Kantacuzenos. John V won the contest only to discover that the Ottoman Turks had taken advantage of the weakened empire to set up a permanent base in Europe at Gallipoli.

By A.D. 1400 the Ottoman Turks were in control of large parts of the Balkans, cutting off Constantinople from the West. The only access to the Byzantine capital was by sea. The future of the Byzantine state looked very bleak. However, 2 years later the Mongol victory over the Ottomans delayed the conquest of Constantinople for half a century. Then once more a strong ruler, Mehmed II, ascended the Ottoman throne. He had his heart set on capturing the Byzantine capital.

In April 1453 Mehmed ordered a bombardment against the walls of Constantinople. These fortifications were built to withstand lances and arrows, not the great stones hurled by the cannon available to the Turkish forces. After 2 months, the great city fell. The last emperor, Constantine XI, died in the final battle.

Mehmed II received the name Conqueror for his victory over the Byzantine Empire. After his soldiers had mopped up any remaining opposition, he entered the city to pray at the great Church of the Holy Wisdom,

Mehmed II built this fortress, Rumeli Hisar, to cut off the passage of ships to the population of Constantinople.

which was then converted into a mosque. Three years later he took Athens and those parts of Greece still outside Turkish control. His plan was to extend Ottoman territories deep inside Europe, but he died before he reached this goal.

Mehmed followed Islamic precedent in allowing the Christians and Jews of his empire to govern themselves in internal affairs with their religious leaders for chiefs. The **cizye,** the poll tax required of non-Muslims, became a major part of Ottoman revenues. In addition, Christians had a further obligation, the child tax. About every 4 years, the Ottoman army visited the Balkan villages and took the most promising boys away from their homes. They were placed in camps, educated to be Muslims, and trained to serve as the sultan's soldiers or civil officials. These young men formed a special army unit, the **Janissaries.** Girls, too, might be taken for the sultan and his officials' harems.

Moscow and the Russian Lands

In the thirteenth century, the Mongols dominated the Russian lands, organized into a nation known as the Golden Horde. Because they preferred living on the steppes of Ukraine, the native Russian princes collected taxes for them in the forest areas. As agents of the Khan of the Golden Horde, they obtained a document of appointment from him known as the **yarlyk.**

The tragedy of the Mongol occupation was that it cut Russia off from the rest of European culture, and the Russian lands stagnated. There was little opportunity for progress or development. Moreover, the princes kept the usual Slavic custom of dividing their estates among all their sons, a system known as **appanage.** Although each son got some territory in this way, none received enough, and each generation saw the principalities become smaller.

Novgorod was the leading Russian city of the time. Its site on the Volkhov River just after it leaves Lake Ilmen made it a thriving commercial center. A great bridge crossed the Volkhov to connect the two parts of the town, the one inhabited by workers, the other by merchants. A popular assembly of men, the **veche,** gathered whenever the great bell that hung in the public square was rung.

The prince of Novgorod did not hold much power. He was severely limited by sharing authority with the mayor of the town, so that his role was primarily a military one.

To the southeast of Novgorod lay the town of Moscow; in the late thirteenth century it was still recovering from the Mongol attack. When Prince Alexander Nevsky of Novgorod apportioned the Russian lands among his sons, he gave Moscow and a few villages to his youngest son, Daniel. Beginning with this small principality, Daniel and his successors expanded

Novgorod's major buildings were granaries meant to resemble churches.

his territory to include the length of the Moskva River. Daniel's son, Iuri, won the title of Grand Prince from the Khan of the Golden Horde. This put him in charge of collecting the khan's tribute from the other Russian cities.

Early in the fourteenth century Metropolitan Peter, head of the Russian church, came to Moscow and, with the cooperation of the Grand Prince Ivan Kalita, commissioned the cathedral of the Dormition in the Moscow Kremlin. Henceforward, the heads of the church made Moscow their residence.

Prince Dimitry inherited the leadership of the country at a time when the Muscovites were pressed both by the Lithuanians and by other Russian princes. Nevertheless he refused to deliver the tribute to the khan. Khan Mamai, determined to punish Dimitry, gathered a large army for an attack upon Moscow. He met the Russian armies at Kulikovo Pole adjacent to the Don River in September 1380 before the khan's Lithuanian allies arrived. A battle took place with immense slaughter on both sides. The victory went to Dimitry who added Donskoy to his name to recall his triumph.

The fall of Constantinople to the Turks was especially difficult for the Russian people. It meant that they were cut off from their spiritual homeland, the Byzantine Orthodox church, and its head, the patriarch of Constantinople. The Russians were now the only Orthodox Christian nation in the world that did not have Muslims for their rulers.

Red Square was always the heart of Moscow.

In A.D. 1462 Ivan the Great commenced his rule in Moscow. He encouraged his subjects to think of him in terms of continuing the line of Byzantine emperors. To support his claim, he married Zoe Palaeologina, the niece of the last emperor. Zoe had lived in Italian exile and, when she went to Moscow, brought Italian architects with her to enhance the Kremlin.

A prophecy existed to give Ivan encouragement:

> The Church of Old Rome fell for its heresy. The gates of the Second Rome, Constantinople, were hewn down by the axes of the infidel Turks, but the church of Moscow, the New Rome, shines brighter than ever over the whole universe . . . . Two Romes have fallen, but the third stands fast. A fourth there cannot be.

Ivan proved to be a great warrior. His goal was to bring the other Russian principalities under Moscow's sovereignty. One by one they fell to him, even Novgorod, which for so long had been the dominant city of northern Russia.

Origins of the Renaissance

There are certain times in every world society when a burst of energy occurs. New ideas, new inventions, or a deep spiritual insight will start people thinking in a different way. This is what occurred in Europe during the period of history known as the Renaissance.

Renaissance is the French word for rebirth. What was reborn in the fourteenth century was a fascination for imitating the classical world of ancient Greece and Rome. Renaissance people wanted to break with the Middle Ages, to chart a new direction. Authors agreed that the medieval Christian view of life was not adequate. It needed to be supplemented with the values of classical civilization.

Renaissance men and women disliked medieval religious forms, for they saw them putting limitations on individual expression. It was during the Renaissance that the Middle Ages got the name Dark Ages, and the cathedrals of northern Europe became known as Gothic, the product of barbaric Germans.

It was actually only a small group of European men and women who were caught up in the spirit of the Renaissance. Francesco Petrarch holds claim to the title Father of the Renaissance, for his essays gave the Renaissance its direction. He and his compatriots promoted finding the good life in pursuing the arts, literature, and good conversation with friends.

It should be no surprise to learn that the Renaissance began with its center in Italy, in the city of Florence. In the fourteenth century, Florence was already the most prosperous city of the peninsula. From Florence the Renaissance moved to other Italian cities, to Milan, Venice, and Rome.

The famous Medici family of Florence contributed to the city's prominence. Generations of the family had become wealthy through trade and banking, and they used much of their wealth to patronize the arts and to further public works in their town.

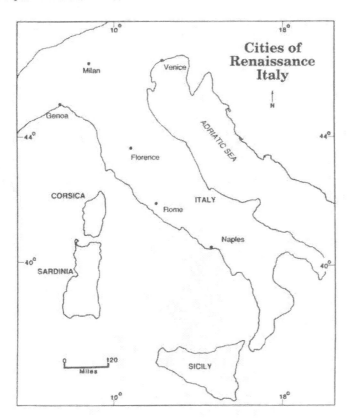

Humanism

Fifteenth century Italian scholars examined the lives of the heros and heroines who lived during the periods of Greek and Roman glory. Out of this search for values came **humanism,** the philosophy of the Renaissance.

True humanists were recognized by a love for collecting manuscripts and books. By A.D. 1450, librarians were familiar with almost all Latin manuscripts that remained from the ancient world. The search then began for Greek and Hebrew works.

The search for Greek texts came at just the right time. The Byzantine Empire in the fifteenth century was little more than the city of Constantinople, and its intellectuals saw no future in the East. They began moving to western Europe and brought their libraries with them. Wealthy Italians welcomed the Greeks with open arms and gave them jobs tutoring their children.

One of the lasting effects of the Renaissance was a concern for public education. Literature, history, art, and music are a part of the school curriculum as a result of what Renaissance scholars believed everyone should know.

The philosophy taught in the universities of the time was **nominalism.** Nominalism, already hinted at by Abélard, asserted that reality was found only in the individual object and its qualities. The **universal,** so important to followers of Aristotle's philosophy, was judged to be but a name or a term without any existence. The major proponent of nominalism was William of Ockham, a Franciscan who had a long career as teacher, writer, and political activist.

Ockham argued that Aristotle created universals without need. The link between God and the individual object was direct and immediate. Since Ockham was such an empiricist, he further argued that faith was based only on probabilities and was not subject to proof. Obviously, this was destructive of church authority, and Ockham was no favorite of the popes.

Nominalism gave greater freedom to enquiry, but there were few great scientists in the fourteenth century. Some progress was made in medicine at Padua, but for the most part, the inability of medical doctors to cope with the challenge of the Black Death had destroyed much of their credibility.

Leonardo de Medici was so popular in Renaissance Florence he received the name, "the Magnificient."

Nominalism contributed to the era's stress upon the individual person. Medieval writers had concentrated on the importance of the community. Renaissance authors, on the other hand, proposed that what mattered was individual excellence, as had been the case in Periclean Athens. They argued that the community was simply a group of individuals. A just society would appear only when each individual made a contribution.

Arts and Artists of Italy

The citizens of Florence were very anxious to have a cathedral to mirror their city's greatness. Architects drew up plans for a large church with an octagonal dome. Then construction commenced, but the work went very slowly. A century passed from the start of the project to the time when builders were ready to put on the cathedral roof. No one was then found, however, who could figure out how to do it. The distance the dome had to span was too great.

Then Filippo Brunelleschi stepped forward with his solution. Brunelleschi had gone to Rome to study the dome of the Pantheon. From it he learned the techniques to put its dome on the cathedral. Since A.D. 1436 it has towered over Florence, a monument to Brunelleschi's skills and the city he served so well.

The great dome of the cathedral of Florence dominates the city's skyline.

At the end of the fifteenth century, Florence became the home of the all-around genius, Leonardo da Vinci. Leonardo's interest covered all the arts, for he was a painter, sculptor, and inventor. As he moved from town to town, Leonardo left many of his paintings unfinished. While in Milan he painted his best known mural, *The Last Supper*. After returning to Florence, he completed the *Mona Lisa*, one of the world's most famous portraits.

A contemporary, Giorgio Vasari, assessed the painting with enthusiasm:

> What a wonderful thing it is to see how art imitates nature, because in it all features are pictured in great detail. A moist luster is in the eyes just as in life, surrounded by the slightest touch of reds and hairs that can only be depicted with the

greatest precision. The lids are perfectly natural and the hairs appear on the skin, where sometimes they are thick, other times scarce, in a way that could not be more natural.

The nose holds all the delicate reddish colors in its nostrils that are there in actual life. The mouth with its opening and red lips and cheeks seem to be living flesh, not color. Looking at her throat it is possible to imagine that it has a beating pulse. When they look at the skill portrayed in this work, the most accomplished artists must despair if they would imitate it.

Giorgio Vasari, *Le vite de' più eccellenti Pittori, Scultori e Architetti.* Naples, Fransesco Rossi-Romano Editore, 1859, p. 253. Author's translation.

Leonardo da Vinci worked on his portrait of the Mona Lisa from 1503 to 1506.

At the very time that the Florentines were consumed in art, a wave of religious enthusiasm swept through the town. The inspiration came from a Dominican friar, Girolamo Savonarola, whose fiery sermons filled Florentine men and women with a terrible fear of hell. Men and women threw their books, fine clothes, and jewelry into great bonfires.

After a few years of success, his supporters abandoned Savonarola. City authorities arrested him, put him on trial, and ordered him hanged. His body was then burned. Savonarola's attempt to make Florence a city of saints died with him. His life reflects how quickly in Renaissance times a hero might become a criminal.

Two other great Italian artists of the fifteenth century Renaissance were Fillipo Lippi and Sandro Botticelli. Lippi painted frescos in several cathedrals and a variety of canvasses of biblical scenes. Sandro Botticelli, a pensioner of the Medici, studied for years in Florence and became a prolific painter. He drew on the stories of ancient Greece and Rome. Some art critics believe his *Birth of Venus* is one of the greatest masterpieces of the entire Renaissance period.

Not all fifteenth century painting was confined to Italy. In distant Flanders, then part of the Netherlands, Jan Van Eyck invented a new way of painting. He used oil for the colored pigment rather than egg tempera. Van Eyck demonstrated his talents in portraits of Flemish merchants and bankers who had so much in common with the upper class in Italian cities.

The painters of the Renaissance revolutionized art. Not only did they use oil and choose to do portraits of living people rather than saints, but they also attempted to make painting more realistic. By making distant figures smaller and with the careful use of shading, they made viewers a part of the painting. It was Renaissance artists who introduced perspective to painting.

Florence also produced, in the person of Dante Aligheri, the last medieval poet and the first of the Renaissance. His *Divine Comedy* reflects his artistry in approaching the highest standards of poetry. The *Divine Comedy* was so praised that the Florentine dialect became the common Italian vernacular.

Printing

It might be argued that the most significant event to occur in the Renaissance was not in the arts, but rather in technology, with the invention of printing. No other invention of the fifteenth century did so much to increase knowledge and spread information.

European printers took the same steps as the Chinese in the development of their craft. They first carved and inked manuscript illustrations and then moved to captions and a whole page of text. About A.D. 1446 Johannes Gutenberg settled in Mainz in Germany where he formed a partnership to promote his invention using molds to produce movable metal type on a printing press. Gutenberg's Bible is the oldest printed book of Europe.

The discovery of printing in Europe brought about an explosion of information. A class of people, especially in cities, was ready and eager for the books that began to pour off the presses. In other societies, literacy was confined to upper class men and women and merchants, but the simplicity of the Latin alphabet made reading easy for a broad range of western Europeans.

As presses became more efficient, the price of books dropped. Hand-copied manuscripts were extremely expensive and often contained errors. Printed books, on the other hand, were cheap and had few mistakes. By A.D. 1500, there were dozens of printing presses throughout western Europe.

Daily Life in Renaissance Times

The homes of the upper class in Italy and France were quite well furnished and comfortable. Chairs, sofas, and tables were designed with great care. The houses had glass windows or at least wooden shutters to allow light and air to come inside. Carpets, often brought to Europe from Southwest Asia, covered the floor.

At meal time people sat down to a table where china replaced the crude dishes of the past. Knives and spoons were handy for eating. The fork, recently invented, became popular at Renaissance dinners.

People dressed more elegantly than ever before, with both men and women favoring bright colors. Dresses came in brocade, velvet, and silk. Men wore jackets and hose, fancy hats, and fur capes.

Women in the families of the upper class married when they were about 14 years of age to men who were twice as old. Some girls received very good educations, such as the Este sisters, Beatrice and Isabella, of Milan and Mantua. They could compose letters in Latin just as easily as their husbands. Unfortunately, most women, despite their training, were not allowed to be independent. Every woman had to depend on what a father, brother, or husband thought was correct. While upper-class men were allowed to come and go as they pleased, women were confined to the house.

Renaissance men and women dressed in colorful clothes to be fashionable.

Women in rural Europe enjoyed more freedom, but they, too, were considered too weak and emotional to be trusted. The law permitted husbands to beat their wives, and a woman could do nothing about it. A French woman author, Christine de Pisan, published a book, *The City of Women*, which argued that there was as much talent in a community of women as in one composed of men. However, her voice was a solitary one.

It is one of the contradictions of the Renaissance that in an age that considered itself more enlightened than any other, there was a great concern over witches and the influence they had over human activities. Because of this fear, hundreds of people suffered humiliation, torture, and even death.

It is hard to know what made the pursuit of witches so popular. In the Middle Ages, there had been a few episodes when popular imagination caused people to seek out someone they thought caused a flood, an

Duchess Isabella d'Este brought artists, humanists, and musicians to her court at Mantua.

animal to be sick, or a well to dry up. In Renaissance times there was a universal scare with all parts of society affected, a phenomenon lasting until A.D. 1750.

Usually the accused were old women, many of them eccentric in one manner or other. In some ways the search for witches and sorcerers was an effort to be rid of social outcasts. The more outrageous the charge, the more people were likely to be swept by this mass hysteria. Authors wrote books on how to identify witches and described signs that appeared on their bodies. When tortured, many accused of **witchcraft** confessed to actions that never occurred.

Great Western Schism

Complaints over the papal residence in Avignon rose on all sides, especially from outside France in the latter part of the fourteenth century. Therefore, the cardinals who met in Rome to choose a successor to Pope Gregory found themselves surrounded by an angry mob of Roman citizens who let it be known that they wanted an Italian candidate for the office. The cardinals capitulated, electing the Italian archbishop of Bari, who chose to be called Urban VI.

The new pope showed nothing but contempt for his cardinal electors, insulting and humiliating them. The result was an exodus of the French majority for Naples. There they declared the first election invalid because of coercion and proceeded to elect one of their own, Robert of Geneva, as pope. He took the name of Clement VII. With two rival popes, all of western Europe was forced to choose between them. France and its political allies tended to support Clement VII, while the enemies of France acknowledged Urban VI as pope.

The **Great Schism** was now a fact. The problems of a divided church meant that there were two colleges of cardinals, two curias, and two offices for collecting papal taxes. To find a way out of this confusion, the faculty at the University of Paris, led by Chancellor John Gerson, suggested a council of the Church, an assembly of all the bishops, to sort out the facts. The Conciliar Movement, as it came to be called, argued that a council had supreme ecclesiastical authority surpassing that of the popes.

It was no easy task to get a universal council to meet, so the first step was taken by France in A.D. 1398 at a national council. This assembly withdrew its support from the Avignon pope and threatened to create a national church under the king. This possibility moved the situation closer to solution as no one in western Europe then believed that the answer to a church with two heads was to create churches with a dozen national heads.

In A.D. 1408 the cardinals of both popes issued a call for a council to meet at Pisa the following year. At Pisa over 500 bishops and abbots met and deposed both of the reigning popes when they refused to resign. They chose another candidate, but since the incumbents in Rome and Avignon remained, the Pisan pope meant that the church now had three heads. The situation was resolved only some years later with the resignation of the claimants and the election of a compromise candidate. Obviously the church's inability to find an answer to its divided leadership offered national monarchs an opportunity to gain control over the church in their countries.

The popes in the latter fifteenth century seemed more interested in their role as Italian princes and patrons of the arts than as leaders of the Catholic church. They vied with Florentine officials to take the lead in beautifying their cities. This period marked the construction of the Sistine Chapel and the inauguration of its famous choir.

European Exploration and Colonization

In the fifteenth century the expansion of Europeans and their culture into other continents, indeed into all other parts of the world, commenced. Before this time Europeans were seldom in contact with other world societies. Few people, mostly Crusaders or Italian merchants, went abroad, and only a handful of foreigners visited Europe.

Curiosity, sparked by the Renaissance fascination with things distant, made the study of geography extremely popular. Better maps appeared with more accurate plotting of mountains, rivers, and seas.

During the Early Renaissance navigational aids, long used by the Chinese and Arabs, finally entered Europe. The compass and the **astrolabe,** a device to measure latitude by taking a reading on the sun or other celestial body, were improved and became more common.

The construction of sturdier ships was also of major importance. Western Europe had tall trees that could be used to make masts sufficiently high to support the weight of heavier and more numerous sails. Obviously a mast made of two logs would not hold up in stormy Atlantic weather. The fact that timber grew tall in the West helped the shipmakers design the kind of crafts needed for ocean travel. In addition they discovered the right combination of sail, lateen and square, which could best take advantage of the wind.

The astrolabe could tell sailors their latitude at sea, but not their longitude.

The Portuguese opened the era of discovery. Their first interest was in Africa. From there came gold and ivory. His appointment as governor to Ceuta, a small enclave off the Moroccan coast, whetted the interest of Prince Henry, third son of the Portuguese king, for further African exploration and conquest. Henry promoted a school at Sagres for geographers whose charge was to chart the African coast. History knows him as Henry the Navigator.

Henry thought that eventually Africa south of the Sahara could be reached and that Portugal could take over the trade of the Muslim Arabs and Berbers. The rumor of a Christian empire in Africa, ruled by a "Prester John," abetted his plans.

Prince Henry's dream of exploration had to contend with the fear that a sea of fire lay to the south of the Sahara. It was not easy to convince either crews or captains to sail along the forbidding Mauritanian coast. Nevertheless, in A.D. 1446 they reached the Senegal River, and gold dust and slaves were brought back to Portugal. The Portuguese ships continued southward and by A.D. 1473 Diogo Cão crossed the equator. Nine years later the Portuguese built their first large port on the western African coast, calling it St. George of Mina.

The next major expedition was led by Bartholomeu Dias. Around Namibia he was blown out to sea and when he sighted land once more the coast was leading northward. Personally convinced that he had rounded Africa at the Cape of Storms he was not able to persuade his crew to go on, so he had to turn back.

It remained for Vasco da Gama to do what Dias had hoped to accomplish, to sail around Africa and reach India. In A.D. 1498 his ship, guided by an Indian pilot, landed in Calicut in southern India. Da Gama did not receive a great welcome since local merchants feared Portuguese competition. Nevertheless, he secured a cargo of pepper and cinnamon and sailed back to an enthusiastic welcome in Lisbon. The trade of the Indian Ocean was soon to become a Portuguese monopoly.

The Portuguese intended to make the Indian Ocean and the East African ports their own, placing garrisons ashore to protect their interests. Muslim traders, who for centuries controlled the markets between East Africa, India, and the Spice Islands, were pushed aside. The gold from the Zambezi River region became a Portuguese monopoly.

Prince Henry the Navigator of Portugal sponsored the first European explorations of Africa.

In West Africa, Catholic missionaries baptized the king and queen of Bakongo. Young men from the kingdom were sent back to Portugal for an education. They returned home with a different set of values, many of them unwelcome in the African environment.

Christopher Columbus

The greatest of fifteenth century discoveries was accomplished by Christopher Columbus when he discovered the Americas on behalf of the Spanish monarchs. It is true that the Vikings had already reached North America, a region they called **Vinland** before him, but nothing had come of their find. Thus Columbus rightly holds the title of the first European discoverer of America.

Columbus, like all knowledgeable people of his day, knew the world was round. He also believed it to be much smaller than it really is. Columbus was convinced that a voyage westward would bring him to China or Japan, an idea that he never abandoned, for there was no thought of a land mass between Europe and the Orient.

Columbus was known as an able seaman and navigator, but no one who had enough money wanted to risk outfitting ships to prove he was right. After years of arguing his case, he at last convinced the proper sovereign, Isabella of Castile, to put up the funds to equip three vessels.

On August 3, 1492, he sailed out of the Palos harbor. In order to keep his crews from mutiny, he kept two logs: one to chart what he believed was his true position and another to show them that they were not really that far from Spain. However, by October 10 he had to agree to turn back if land was not sighted within a day. Twenty-four hours was all that was needed, because the small San Salvador island in the Bahamas appeared on the horizon. On October 12 Columbus landed to take possession of it in the name of the Spanish sovereigns.

Columbus thought he had reached an island off the Japanese coast. Later, when he touched Cuba, he presumed he had found Japan itself and was greatly disappointed not to discover an imperial capital. Instead he met only the peaceful Arawak Indians who had only trinkets to offer him. Before sailing back to Spain, Columbus built a fort from the wood of the *Santa Maria*, which had sunk, and left a settlement of forty men on the island of Hispaniola, modern Haiti.

He reached Lisbon the following March and made his way to Castile to report on his momentous journey. There he told his listeners that he had discovered some islands off the Asian coast that were very rich and whose inhabitants were anxious to become Christian.

Christopher Columbus was one of the greatest seamen of the Age of Discovery.

Ferdinand and Isabella agreed to send him back and petitioned the pope to draw a line between Columbus's discoveries and those of the Portuguese. This was to secure for themselves a clear title to those finds. Pope Alexander VI, a Spaniard himself, was happy to oblige.

Three more times Columbus sailed westward, and each time he believed himself to be closer to China. He refused to admit he had made a much more important discovery. The Spaniards who expected to see him return with gold and silks began to ignore him, for they were disappointed with such meager results. Columbus died in A.D. 1506 a rejected man.

His discoveries proved to be the most momentous event of the fifteenth century, but it would take a long time for this to be recognized. He opened up a new world for Europeans, thanks to his expert seamanship and courage.

Conclusion

By the close of the fourteenth century, Europeans could be pleased that they had survived. Famine, war, and pestilence had not broken their spirit. Even though the church was still in crisis when the last generation of the century was alive, few doubted that a solution would eventually be found. The growing menace of the Ottoman Turks was on the horizon but as yet was troublesome only to the areas of southeastern Europe that had always seemed a far and distant land to the West. Constantinople stood on the Bosporus as a bastion of Christendom against Islam.

When the fifteenth century ended, Europe was in a much different situation. The lives of most people were back to normal, and the Renaissance offered European culture a new way to look at the world. The Ottoman menace, far from dissipating, was greater than ever for Western Christians because Constantinople was now in Turkish hands. Nevertheless, the news of discoveries in Africa, Asia, and now a new world not yet given the name America, excited the European imagination and overshadowed everything else. After 1500 the Atlantic states of Europe, for the first time in history, assumed the leadership of the world.

CHAPTER 31 REVIEW
EUROPE'S LATE MIDDLE AGES AND THE EARLY RENAISSANCE

Summary
- Weather and the Black Death took a heavy toll on Europeans in the four-teenth century.
- The Hundred Years' War consumed much of the wealth of England and France.
- Social unrest plagued much of western Europe because of peasant hard-ship.
- The popes lived at Avignon for most of the fourteenth century.
- Ottoman Turks captured Constantinople and the Balkans.
- Precedence in Russia passed to the princes of Moscow.
- The Renaissance revived interest in the Latin and Greek classics.
- In Italy artists excelled in architecture, painting, and sculpture.
- The invention of printing marked a major step forward for disseminating information.
- The age of European discovery commenced during the Renaissance.

Identify
People: Joan of Arc; Mehmed the Conqueror; Medici; Ferdinand and Isabella; The Golden Horde; Filippo Brunelleschi; Philip the Fair; Francesco Petrarch; Johannes Gutenberg; Leonardo da Vinci; Vasco da Gama

Places: Crécy; Kosovo Polje; Avignon; Gallipoli; Kraków; Milan; St. George of Mina; San Salvador

Events: weather, war, and disease struck hard at Europe in the fourteenth century; Ottoman Turks took Constantinople and the Balkans; the Renaissance began in Italy and printing in Germany; the age of European discovery began

Define

Black Death	Hanseatic League	nominalism
Hundred Years' War	Parliament	witchcraft
humanism	Great Western Schism	Golden Bull of 1356
War of the Roses	Spanish Inquisition	veche
cizye	yarlyk	universal
Janissaries	appanage	astrolabe
Vinland		

Multiple Choice
1. In the fourteenth century Europe's colder weather meant
    (a) the outbreak of the Black Death.
    (b) a shorter growing season.
    (c) a lack of fuel.
    (d) fewer ships on the Mediterranean.

2. The Black Death is thought to have been
    (a) pneumonia.
    (b) tuberculosis.
    (c) smallpox.
    (d) bubonic plague.

3. Joan of Arc's greatest victory was at
   (a) Orléans.
   (b) Paris.
   (c) Crécy.
   (d) Amiens.

4. For 70 years the popes lived in
   (a) Venice.
   (b) Avignon.
   (c) Lyon.
   (d) Marseille.

5. This country had the largest number of Jews and Muslims in the Middle Ages:
   (a) Poland.
   (b) Russia.
   (c) Croatia.
   (d) Spain.

6. The Renaissance was interested in
   (a) imitating the classical world of Greece and Rome.
   (b) imitating the Middle Ages.
   (c) building Gothic cathedrals.
   (d) all the above.

7. He has been given the title Father of the Renaissance:
   (a) Giotto.
   (b) Shakespeare.
   (c) Petrarch.
   (d) Galileo.

8. The Florentine family closely associated with the Renaissance was
   (a) the Andriotti.
   (b) the Clementi.
   (c) the Augustiani.
   (d) the Medici.

9. The philosophy of Renaissance times was
   (a) Humanism.
   (b) Scholasticism.
   (c) Platonism.
   (d) Cartesianism.

10. One aspect of the Renaissance was a stress on
    (a) philosophy.
    (b) individualism.
    (c) theology.
    (d) science.

11. Perspective in painting involves putting objects
    (a) in three dimensions.
    (b) in two dimensions.
    (c) on a flat surface.
    (d) on a round surface.

12. One of the most important inventions to come out of the Renaissance developed in Mainz:
    (a) surgery.
    (b) the telescope.
    (c) the compass.
    (d) printing.

13. Christine de Pisan's *The City of Women* argued
    (a) men should marry older women.
    (b) men and women have equal talent.
    (c) women are more talented than men.
    (d) women should be elected to political office.

14. An irrational fear that arose in Renaissance times was concerned with
    (a) poisoned water.
    (b) witches.
    (c) tobacco.
    (d) poisoned food.

15. A long war fought between the kings of France and England in the fifteenth century was
    (a) the War of the Roses.
    (b) the Norman conquest.
    (c) the Peninsular War.
    (d) the Hundred Years' War.

16. Henry, a prince of Portugal, was called The Navigator because
    (a) he promoted expeditions to explore the African coast.
    (b) he was first to sail across the equator.
    (c) he was the navigator of Columbus.
    (d) he sailed around Africa.

17. The first European to reach the tip of southern Africa was
    (a) Columbus.
    (b) da Gama.
    (c) Dias.
    (d) Vespucci.

18. The queen who financed Columbus was
    (a) Eleanor.
    (b) Elizabeth.
    (c) Isabella.
    (d) Mary.

Essay Questions
1. How did the Black Death begin and what were its consequences?
2. Why would the fourteenth century be one of social unrest?
3. What was the effect of the Avignon papacy and the Great Western Schism upon the church?
4. What could the emperors in Constantinople have done to save their city?
5. What is the connection between the Renaissance and the Age of Discovery?
6. How do you assess Christopher Columbus's voyages?

Answers

1. b	7. c	13. b
2. d	8. d	14. b
3. a	9. a	15. d
4. b	10. b	16. a
5. d	11. a	17. c
6. a	12. d	18. c

Aztecs and Incas

About the year A.D. 1200 the Aztecs made their appearance in the Valley of Mexico. They were another group of Chichimec Indians who had been wandering about northern Mexico for many centuries. There was nothing to hint in earlier times that they were one day going to be the most powerful Indian nation of Central America.

Early Aztec History

Their language, **Nahuatl,** and their religion distinguished them from other Chichimecs. They carried about their most important god, whose image was made of wood, in a bundle. His name was a very long one: **Huitzilopochtli,** which literally means the left-handed hummingbird.

When the Aztecs appeared in the Valley of Mexico, the Toltecs allowed them to settle on some of their land. But the Aztecs proved to be bad neighbors. Huitzilopochtli, like all the Central American gods, needed human victims, and the Aztecs killed a Toltec princess. This made their hosts so angry that they drove the Aztecs into the marshlands bordering Lake Texcoco.

According to a myth, while searching for a place to settle, the Aztecs received a message from their god. Huitzilopochtli told the Aztecs that they should build their town wherever they found an eagle on a cactus holding a snake in its beak. They found such a sign on an island in Lake Texcoco. This legend explains why the Mexican flag has a picture of an eagle holding a snake and perched on a cactus.

Building Tenochtitlán

The Aztecs named their island city Tenochtitlán after its foundation about A.D. 1325. It quickly grew in size and importance. To increase food production, the Aztecs planted crops on floating islands known as **chinampas.** (They really did not float. Willow trees and ropes anchored them to the ground.)

The island location of Tenochtitlán proved to be ideal. It gave the Aztecs protection in that historic period from raids of other warlike Indians stronger than themselves. At the same time it allowed the Aztecs to use the lake to surprise and attack other towns when they wanted to capture people or property.

Aztec pressure caused the towns about Lake Texcoco to ally themselves with Tenochtitlán in order to survive. Tribute and captives poured into the Aztec capital, which now could afford to build several temple-pyramids to its gods.

Chinampas were an extremely efficient way to grow food.

By A.D. 1500 Tenochtitlán may well have held 200,000 people, making it the largest city of the Americas and one of the largest in the world. It was the equal of any town found in Europe and was certainly neater, for the Aztecs sought to keep their city clean. The homes of both rich and poor lined the city's many canals and roads. The houses resembled apartments built around courtyards. Everywhere there were gardens, for the Aztecs liked to keep flowers all about them. Two great markets brought merchants from all over Mexico to exchange goods.

The temple-pyramids were not as large as those built at Teotihuacán, but they were still very impressive. Unfortunately these temple-pyramids were places of death for tens of thousands of people. Huitzilopochtli demanded the hearts of captives and even of Aztec people themselves. Priests opened the chests of victims while they were still alive and offered the beating hearts to the gods.

An illustrated manuscript shows an Aztec sacrifice.

Aztec society was obsessed with linking human sacrifice to their religious views, an inheritance of the Indian societies that preceded them. Much of the brilliance of their civilization was marred by a religion that ended the lives of so many innocent people.

Every Aztec man was a warrior, for the army was constantly on campaign against other nations to get the captives the gods required. The warrior was promised a glorious afterlife if he died in battle. The soldiers fought with spears, bows and arrows, and an especially wicked weapon, a club with razor-sharp pieces of flint or obsidian on its edges.

The government of the Aztecs depended on the absolute will of the emperor. A council of Aztec nobility selected him from among the men of the royal family. His dress and conduct emphasized his importance. Second in command was a male official with the interesting title Snake Woman.

Although the Aztecs conquered a large part of central Mexico, they made no effort to unify their empire. They had no policy beyond the constant need to find victims for their gods.

North of the Rio Grande

By A.D. 1200 the Anasazi cliff constructions ended and were abandoned 100 years later. Because no evidence of violence is present, archaeologists suggest that a prolonged and devastating drought forced people to find new homes. Another possibility blames the Anasazi emigration on the appearance of new American Indian tribes entering the Southwest, the Apache and Navajo. These people had a tradition of fighting with a reinforced bow superior to any weapon of the Anasazi. When the Apache and Navajo took up herding and agriculture, their population increased considerably, making them into strong and powerful nations.

In the Mississippi culture, once so flourishing at Cahokia, a similar picture of decline appeared. Soon after A.D. 1500 the people of Cahokia left their city for unknown reasons.

Inca Empire of South America

The Incas had a myth about their origin that said that the Sun, the supreme deity, gave birth to four brothers and four sisters. They came out of a cave at a time when the first people in the world appeared. The brothers fought one another until only one, Manco Capac, remained. He married one of his sisters and began the Inca dynasty that was destined to rule over all the Andes' people.

The Incas, in fact, were only one small group of South American Indians like many others who lived on the western side of the Andes. Their capital was at Cuzco in southern Peru, located in a fertile valley surrounded by a plateau.

Pachacuti, the ninth ruler of the dynasty was the true founder of Inca greatness, for he organized the army that, in A.D. 1438, conquered the western coast of South America. His conquests mark the beginning of recorded history in South America.

Pachacuti's armies, with llamas carrying their supplies, marched from Cuzco south to Lake Titicaca and north to what is now Colombia. Often Pachacuti successfully convinced other Indian peoples to submit to Inca rule without war.

Since the Incas had no writing, they developed professional memorizers, who had a responsibility to recall the great deeds of the Inca rulers. They used a device known as a **quipu** to help them remember. A quipu consisted of one large string and many small ones. These same quipus also were used for counting. Knots on the strings represented numbers. The accounts told by the Inca memorizers were later written down by Spanish chroniclers after the conquest of Peru.

To consolidate his state, Pachacuti required all official business to be conducted in Quechua, the Inca language. He also ordered everyone to worship Viracocha, the god of the Incas. In addition, the emperor relocated rebellious people, moving them out of their homeland to foreign places, a method of control that has often been a favorite of rulers throughout world history.

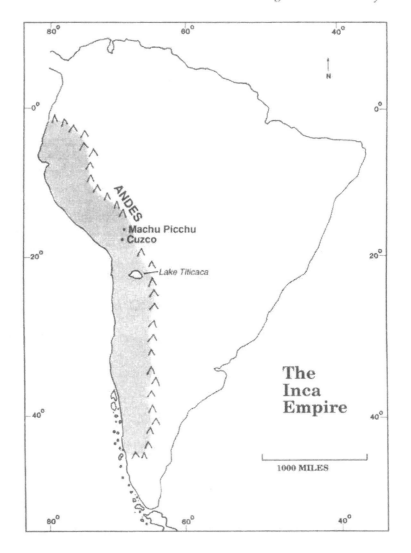

The civilization called Inca is named for its leader, the Inca or the emperor. The Incas called their land Tawantinsuyu, the country of the four quarters, for they viewed their lands as seen from Cuzco.

Society Among the Incas

Inca society was divided between those who were born Inca and those Indians who were not. Within the Inca society a major difference separated the nobility and ordinary people.

At the very peak of society was the Inca and his family. Since he was considered the descendant of the Sun, he had absolute rule over his people. In fact, he claimed that all men were his sons and that all women were his daughters. Although he had many wives, there was a chief wife who was the queen or the **coya.** She was considered the daughter of the moon and had a special position in directing women's affairs. She ruled at times when the Inca was on campaign with the army. In addition, in normal times the coya was in charge one month of the year, usually in September.

The Inca nobility, called Big Ears by the Spaniards, because they wore such large gold and silver earplugs, enjoyed a life of leisure. They did not have to work, but lived from rents on their estates. Their sons were given a formal education for 4 years at Cuzco. Then they enlisted in the army. After their military service, some were called upon to serve as governors of provinces.

Ordinary people among the Incas belonged to groups related by kinship. At their head a local chief directed the activities of the group in farming and working on government projects. These included building roads, repairing temples, or the worst job of all, working in the gold and copper mines. The village chiefs had to draft men for these jobs.

The Inca also required a certain amount of cloth from his subjects. This task fell to the women. It was noted by the first Spaniards in Peru that women were always busy spinning thread while walking or sitting at home.

Inca women were masters of weaving. No other civilization produced textiles of the quality made in Peru. Either cotton or wool from the llama or alpaca was the raw material. The fibers were cleaned and spun together onto a stick or spindle that had a stone hanging from it so it could easily twirl. Women then wove the thread sitting at a loom. The Inca loom had two wooden bars. To keep the right amount of tension on the vertical threads of the loom, a strap attached to the back of the weaver was tightened or loosened.

Indian women in Peru enjoyed a favorable position in society since women were considered the daughters of the Inca. They owned land in their own names and had rights to water and to pasture for their animals. Boys and girls sought out their own mates and in a ceremony supervised by an Inca governor were paired off for marriage. If a boy did not have a girl, the governor found one for him. At the marriage the couple joined hands and exchanged a gift of sandals.

A young couple may have been delighted when their first child was born. Yet the Andes' tradition held that children should not be shown too much affection. The women gave their babies cold baths, which were thought to make them strong. When the children were 2 or 3 years old, their hair was cut, and they were finally given a name.

Some girls became **alcallas,** a distinct class of women in Inca society. The most beautiful of Indian girls, when 9 or 10 years old, were taken from their families and placed in a special school. They were taught by older alcallas how to behave. After several years of training, some were brought to Cuzco to become wives of the Inca, while others were married into noble families. The rest of the alcallas, those who did not marry, stayed on as teachers in the provincial schools.

Most young men and women in Inca society were farmers. Men broke the ground using a foot plow, an instrument somewhat like a spade with a bar for the foot to push the blade into the ground. Women followed with a hoe to prepare the ground for seed.

Andes Indians had a special way to end a drought. They believed that lack of rain was caused by the gods who were offended for one reason or another. They tied black llamas or dogs to a stake with food placed just out of reach. The hungry animals howled and cried, and the noise was supposed to bother the gods so much that to quiet them they would make it rain.

The Incas had a remarkable social security system. When a person became ill or too old to work, he or she received rations of food from government warehouses. The Spaniards of the sixteenth century were amazed to find no beggars in Inca society, for no similar system provided for the elderly poor in Europe.

Engineering

There was a state planning office whose job was to assign projects to farmers for their government service. Mountains needed to be terraced for farming, and canals had to be built to carry water to the land. Indians who were not Incas bore most of this burden and hated it. Inca supervisors punished laborers harshly, if they were slackers. Yet the death penalty was rarely used, for only the Inca or a provincial governor had the right to order it. Forced labor battalions disliked their tasks because all their work benefitted only the emperor and the government. Few rewards came to the laborers themselves.

The greatest accomplishment of Inca planners was the great road system they developed, in some ways comparable to that of the Romans. These roads were built for the army to move swiftly from one part of the empire to another. Many of the roads required solving daunting engineering problems. Suspension bridges had to be built over ravines and swift Andes' rivers. Stairways had to be chipped out of the rock in order to cross mountains. Because the Incas did not have wheeled vehicles, the roads did not have to be very wide.

Along the Inca roads there were inns for the weary traveler to rest and get something to eat. Government messengers also kept their rooms here. Couriers left Cuzco with memorized messages from the emperor and passed them on to other runners stationed at the inns. A message could be transported as far as 140 miles in a day, the fastest land communication system dependent on humans ever invented.

Inca builders were especially skilled stoneworkers. They liked to shape irregular stones of huge proportions to fit against one another. Using no mortar, they structured the stones so carefully that even in earthquake-prone Peru, many Inca buildings and walls still stand. The builders made Cuzco a city of many palaces, temples, and plazas. Cuzco's Temple of the Sun was actually covered with gold. Machu Picchu, the great fortress of the army located on an Andes' mountain summit, provides the best example of Inca stone construction.

Inca engineers were adept at moving huge stones.

By A.D. 1500 the Inca empire extended from Colombia to central Chile, containing more than 100 nations and possibly totaling up to 12,000,000 people.

Conclusion

The Indian civilizations of the Americas show both brilliance and darkness. The Indians excelled as farmers. They domesticated about 50% of the world's present food plants. The cities of Mexico and Peru testify to the skills of architects, sculptors, and painters. Women in these societies produced textiles of such beauty that they have seldom been equaled. Jewelers made gold, silver, jade, and copper decorations that still shine with special luster.

Yet in some ways Aztec and Inca isolation from the rest of the world kept the Indian civilizations from innovation. They never received the stimuli of new ideas and technologies that other world societies enjoyed. In the sixteenth century stone tools were still in use everywhere, writing was known but to a few elite, the wheel and shipbuilding were disregarded. The American Indians were not prepared in any way for the events of the sixteenth century when European discoverers entered their world.

Chapter 32 Review
Aztecs and Incas

Summary
- The Aztecs were part of the nomadic Chichimecs.
- They built their capital at Tenochtitlán on an island.
- The Anasazi abandoned their cliff dwellings because of drought.
- The Incas created a large empire in Peru.
- Inca society was highly stratified.
- The greatest material accomplishment of the Incas was in stone working and road building.

Identify
People: Apache; Navajo; Pachacuti
Places: Lake Texcoco; Tenochtitlán; Cuzco
Events: creation of Aztec empire in the Valley of Mexico; beginning of the Inca Empire in Peru

Define

Nahuatl	Huitzilopochtli	quipu
coya	alcallas	chinampas

Multiple Choice
1. The government of the Aztecs was based on
   (a) democracy.
   (b) oligarchy.
   (c) a republic.
   (d) an emperor.

2. A chinampa is used for
   (a) digging roots.
   (b) pruning trees.
   (c) combing hair.
   (d) growing crops.

3. South American Indians were handicapped because
   (a) they did not know about the wheel.
   (b) they were not able to domesticate horses.
   (c) their coinage was only in copper.
   (d) all the above.

4. The Inca capital was at
   (a) Cuzco.
   (b) Machu Picchu.
   (c) Tiahuanaco.
   (d) Tenochtitlán.

5. Inca society gave equality to
   (a) rich and poor.
   (b) Indians and Spaniards.
   (c) men and women.
   (d) servants and masters.

6. The origin of the Inca empire is credited to
   (a) Inca Topa.
   (b) Inca Pachacuti.
   (c) Moctezuma.
   (d) Francisco Pizzaro.

Essay Questions
1. Discuss the rise of the Aztecs in creating an empire.
2. What were the positive and negative features of the Aztec Empire?
3. Discuss the role of women in the Inca society.

Answers
1. d   4. a
2. d   5. c
3. d   6. b

Index

Abbasid Caliphs, 262–264
Abelard, 437
Achaemenids, 112–113
Acropolis, 157
Africa, 227–235, 300–307,
    422–433
  East, trade, 428–429
  North, roman influence,
    233
  South, 429–430
Agriculture:
  Byzantine, 313–314
  Hittites, 45
  Indus Valley, 71
  medieval Europe, 370–371
  revolution, 20–22
Akhenaten, religious
    reform, 61–62
Akkadians, 41–42, 45
Alexander the Great,
    177–184
Almohads, 448
Alphabet, 110
Americas:
  development, 380–390
  hunters, 95
  Indian civilizations,
    238–249
  people, first, 95–97
Amorites, 41–42
Anasazi, 382–383, 489
Anatolia, 43, 113–115
Ancient World, Mediter-
    ranean regions, 83–94
Angkor Wat, 404–405
Animal herding, 22–24
Anti-Semitism, 447
Aqueducts, 210
Aquinas, Thomas, 439
Arab conquests, 258–259
Arabian Peninsula, 253–254
Arameans, 109–110
Aristotle, 168–169
ar-Rahman, Abd, 340–342
Artillery, 462–463
Artisans, 39
Aryans, 72–73
  political life, 120
Ashoka, 129–130
Asia:
  East, 408–421
    traditions, 277–299
  Southeast, late middle
    ages, 400–407
  Southwest:
    empires, 101–119
    Islamic influence,
      253–269

Assisi, 442–443
Assyrians, 101–102
Athens, 157
Attila the Hun, 220–221
Augustan Age, 203–205
Aurelius, Marcus, 213–214
Aurock, 22
Australopithecus anamensis, 3
Axum, 235, 304
Aztecs, 487–495

Babylonians, 102–103
Balkans, struggle over,
    312–313
Bantu, 234, 429–430
Barbarian kingdoms, 321
Becket, Thomas, 444
Bedouin, 253–254
Behistun Rock, 112
Berbers, 301–303, 358
Bhagavad Gita, 122
Bible, Hebrew, 104–105
Black Death, 459–461, 472
Blood types, 95
Bow and arrow, 10
Brahman religion, 120–122
Bronze age, 25, 83–84
  Crete, 86
Buddha, 125–127
Buddhism, 131–132,
    284–285
  China, 146–147
  collapse of, 400
  Japan, introduction to,
    290–291
Burin, 9
Burma, 295
Byblos, 45
Byzantine Empire, 308–317,
    453–454
  church, 316–317
  culture, slavs, 342–344
  daily times, 313–316
  first crusade, 362–365
  –Persian Conflict, 258

Caesar, Julius, 197–198
Caligula, 205
Canaanites, 45, 103, 109–110
Canon, 105
Canterbury, 442, 444
Carolingian minuscule, 331
Carthage, 231
Castes, 123–124
Catal Huyuk, 18–20
Cathar doctrine, 446–447
Cathedrals, 440–441
Catholics, 346

Celts, 198–199
Charlemagne, age of,
    328–350
  cultural progress, 331
  empire, 330
  farmers, 337–339
  merchants, 337–339
Chaucer, Geoffery, 463
Chavin civilization,
    245–247
Chimu, 383–384
China, 76–78, 137–153
  bronze, 138
  Buddhism, 146–147
  Confucius, 140–141
  geography, 75–76
  Great Reform, 291–292
  Great Wall, 143
  Han periods, 144–148
  influences on Japan, 289
  middle kingdom, 79–80
  Ming dynasty, 411–413
  prehistoric, 75–82
  Qin dynasty, 142–14
  religion, 78
  Shang dynasty, 137–139
  silk, 138–139
  Song dynasty, 285–289,
    408
  Sui dynasty, 277–278
  Tangs, Golden Age,
    278–285
  writing, 79, 138
  Zhou period, 139–140
Christians, 207–208
Church of the Holy
    Wisdom, 311–312
Church Reformation,
    355–358
Circus Maximus, 209
Claudius, 205
Cleopatra, 232
Cluny, 355–356
Code of Justinian, 309–310,
    437
Colonization, 478–481
Columbus, Christopher,
    480–481
Concordat of Worms, 357
Confucius, 140–141, 283
Constantine, 216–218
Constantinople, 308–311,
    363–366
  fall of, 467–468
Copper, 91
Coptic Church, 232, 304
Corn, domestication, 96
Crete, 84–88

Cro-Magnons, 9–13
  art, 12
  inventions, 11–12
  language, 10–11
  race, 10–11
  tools, 9–10
Crusades, 362–365, 391–394,
    444, 446, 454
Cuneiform, 34, 37
Cycladic origins, 83–84

Daoism, 141–142, 146
daVinci, Leonardo, 473–474
Deccan plateau, 67
deGama, Vasco, 479
Delhi, Slave dynasty,
    402–403
Denmark, 361, 445–446
Dias, Bartholomeu, 479
Diffusion, 21
Diocletian, 215
Domestication, animals,
    22–24
Dravidians, 72
Druids, 199

Edict of Milan, 216
Egypt, 51–66
  ancient, classes, 55
  arts, 59
  decline, 62–63
  earliest, 52–54
  exodus of Jews, 106–107
  Hellenistic, 230–231
  invasions, 60, 227–228
  Mamluk, 422–423
  middle kingdom, 59–60
  Muslims, 300–301
  new kingdom, 60
  old kingdom, 54–56
  religion, 56–58, 61–62
  Roman influence, 231–232
Einkorn, 20
Elamites, 41
Elba, 45
England, 319–321
  Parliament, rise of,
    463–464
Eridu, 35
Ethiopia, 301, 304–305,
    427–428
Etruscans, 187–188
Europe:
  early middle ages, 308–327
  early renaissance,
    459–486
  eastern, 365–367, 450–453
    awakening, 351–379

late middle ages, 466–470
high middle ages, 433–458
   economics, 436–437
   intellectual achievements, 437–439
   kingdoms, 445–448
late middle ages, 459–486
   disease, 459–461
   warfare, 461
   weather, 459–461
medieval:
   art, 372–374
   literature, 372–374
   society, 368–370
   work, 370–372
   towns, revival of, 433–435
   western recovery, 351–379
Exploration, 478–481

Farming, invention of, 20–22
Ferdinand and Isabella, 464
Fertile Crescent, 17, 33–50
Feudal Order, 336–339
Finland, 446
Fire, 11–12
Flying buttresses, 440
France:
   late middle ages, 465–466
   Merovingian, 321–322
Franks, 331–332
Fredericks, Roman Empire, 448–449

Ganges River, 67, 127
Geography:
   China, 75–76
   India, 67–68
Germans, and Eastern Europe, 450–453
Ghana, 301–303
Gilgamesh, 41
Grand Canal, China, 278
Great Reform, China, 291–292
Great Schism, 477–478
Greece:
   ancient, 154–155
   architecture, 163–164
   arts, 165–166
   athletics, 171–172
   philosophers, 166–169
   religion, 170–171
   science, 169–170
   theater, 164–165
Athens, 157
civilization, 154–176
colonization, 156–157

democracy, 157–159
Dorian invasion, 155
invasion by Persians, 160–162
Peloponnesian War, 162–163
renaissance, 155–156
Sparta, 159–160
Gregory, 319, 323, 356–357
Guilds, 39–40, 435
Guinea, Forest Kingdoms, 426
Gupta Empire, 131–132
Gutenberg Bible, 475

Habsburgs, 466
Hammurabi, 42
Han periods, 144–148
Harappa, 69–71
Hatshepsut, 60–61
Hatti, 43
Hebrews, 104–108
   exodus from Egypt, 106–107
   monarchy, 107–108
   See also: Jews
Hellenistic World, 180–182
   Egypt, 230–231
Henry II, 443–445
Hieroglyphics, 51
Hinayana, 131
Hinduism, 120–122, 132, 271, 400–402
Hittites, 43–45
Hohokam, 382–383
Homer, 155–156
Homo erectus, 3–7
Homo sapiens, 7–9
Homosexuality, medieval Europe, 368
Humanism, 471–423
Humans, first, 3–16
Hundred Years' War, 461–463
Hungarians, 345, 365–366
Huns, 220–221, 270
Hurrians, 44–45
Hyksos period, 60

Iberian Peninsula, peoples, 358
Ice age, 6–7
Ideograms, 37
Immortals, 112
Incas, 487–495
   engineering, 492–493
   society, 491–492
India:
   castes, 123–124
   classical age, 120–136
   early middle ages, 270–276

geography, 67–68
invasions, 127, 130
Jains, 124–125
late middle ages, 400–407
migrations, 270
Muslim invasions, 272–274
South, 130
Indo-European Migrations, 88–89
Indus Valley, 67–73
   economy, 71–72
   people, 68–69
Ireland, 318–319, 361
Islam, 255–258
   India, 400–402
Israel, ancient, 108
Italian peninsula, 186
Italy:
   ancient, 185
   arts, 473–475
   economic development, 361–362
   papacy, 322–323
   peoples, 186–188
   renaissance, 471

Jains, 124–125
Japan, 149–150
   Buddhism, introduction of, 290–291
   Chinese influences, 289
   Heian, 292–294
   Kamakura Shogunate, 415–417
   Shoguns, 413–417
Jericho, 18–20
Jesus of Nazareth, 206–207
Jewelry:
   cro-magnons, 11
   Sumerian, 39
Jews, 104–109
   age of Charlemagne, 339
   exodus from Egypt, 106–107
   medieval Europe, 373
   and Romans, 194–195
Joan of Arc, 461–462
Justinian, 309–312

Kamakura Shogunate, 415–417
Kanem-Bornu, 425–426
Kethubim, 105
Khan, Gengis, 395, 409, 417
Khan, Khubilai, 408–411
Khazars, 344
Khmers, 295, 404
Kish, 35
Korea, 149, 294, 417–418
Kush, 228–229

Lagash, 35
Laozi, 141–142
Legalists, 142
Li Dynasty, 417–418
Linear A, 87
Linear B, 88
Lugal, 35

Macedonia, rise of, 177–178
Magna Carta, 445
Magyars, 345, 365–366
Mahayana, 131
Maimonides, 437
Malaria, 234
Mali, 424–425
Mamluk Egypt, 422–423
Mathematics, Sumerians, 38
Mauryan Empire, 127–128
Mayans, 240, 242–245, 380
   calendar, 245
   religion, 244
   writing, 244–245
Mazdaism, 113
Mecca, 254
Mediterranean:
   regions, ancient world, 83–94
   triad, 83–84
Megalith, 25–26, 89
Meng Ko, 141–142
Merovingian France, 321–322
Mesopotamia:
   city-states, 34–35
   civilizations, 33–34
   invaders, 41–42
Metal working, 25
Mexico:
   development, 96
   disasters, 380
   Olmec civilization, 238–240
   Toltec domination, 381–382
Ming dynasty, 411–413
Minoan civilization, 85–88
Mississippians, 382–383
Mittani, 44–45
Moche, 383–84
Mogollon, 382–383
Mohenjo-Daro, 69–71
Monasteries, 318–319
Monasticism, western, 323
Money, 434
Mongols, 394–396, 408–411, 417–418
   Eastern Europe, 450–453
   empire, 410
   Russia, 468–469
Mortar and pestle, 18
Moscow, 468–470

Index

Mud volcanos, 71
Muhammad, 255–258
Musa, Mansa, 425
Muslims, Egypt, 300–301
Mycenaeans, 90–91

Natufians, 17–18
Navigation, 478–479
Nazca, 383–384
Neandertals, 7–8
Nebi'im, 105
Neolithic age, 17–30
    towns, 17–20
Nero, 205–206
Nicene Creed, 218
Nile Valley, 51
Nominalism, 472
Normans, 359–361
Northmen, 332–333
Norway, 361, 446
Notre Dame, 441

Obsidian, 19
Odovacer, 221–222
Olmec civilization, 238–240
Olympics, 171–172
Oracle bones, 78
Orthodox churches, 346
Ostrogoths, 217
Otto, 352–354
Ottoman State, formation, 396–397

Pakistan, 69
Paleolithic Age, 3–7
Pantheon, 209–210
Papacy, 322–323, 442–443
Patricians, 189–191
Pax Romana, 208–209, 212–213
Peloponnesian War, 162–163
Peloponnesus, 89–90
Persians, 111–113
    culture, 112–113
    Greek invasion, 160–162
    invasion of India, 127
Peru, 245–247
Pharaoh, 54–58
Phoenicians, 109–110
Pictograms, 37
Pit houses, 95
Plato, 167–168, 437
Plow, 38, 41
Poles, 365, 450–453, 466
Pottery, 24
Ptolemy, 230
Pyramids, 57–58

Qin Dynasty, 142–144
Qur'an, 255–257, 261–262, 272

Reformation, 355–358
Renaissance:
    daily life, 475–477
    origins of, 470–471
    printing, 475
Roman:
    buildings, 209–211
    early, 188–189
    Empire, 203–226, 466
        Fredericks, 448–450
        German Nation, 351–354
    entertainment, 211–212
    expansion, 191–193
    influence on Egypt, 231–232
    influence on North Africa, 233
    religion, 195–196
    Republic, 195–202
        economic problems, 196–198
        formation, 189
        political problems, 196–198
    society, 190–191
Rosetta Stone, 51
Rushd, Ibn, 437

Saint Augustine, 437
Salt trade, 302–303
Samaritans, 108–109
Samurai, 413–414
Sanskrit, 72
Scholasticism, 437
Serf, 336
Sericulture, 77
Shamans, China, 78
Shang dynasty, 79–80, 137–139
Shi'ites, 258–259, 264, 428
Shintoism, 289
Shoguns, 413–417
Siddartha, 125–127
Silk, 77
Silk Road, 145, 148, 314
Slash and burn, 20, 429
Slave dynasty, 402–403
Slavs, 342–344
Smelting, 25
Socrates, 167
Solomonid dynasty, 427
Song dynasty, 285–289, 408
    cultural life, 288–289

economic activity, 287–288
Song of Roland, 329
Songhai, 425–426
South America, 97
    events, 383
Spain:
    Ferdinand and Isabella, 464
    Islamic, 340–342
    peoples, 358
Spanish Inquisition, 443, 447, 464
Sparta, 159–160
Sri Lanka, 67, 133, 404–405
Stone age:
    new, 17–30
        agricultural revolution, 20–22
        technology, 24–25
    old, 3–13
Stonehenge, 26
Sufism, 401
Sui dynasty, 277–278
Sumerians, 34–42
    culture, 40–41
    economics, 38–40
    language, 37
    religion, 35–36
    renaissance, 42
Sunnites, 258–259
Sweden, 446
Syrian peoples, 45, 103

Tangs, Golden Age, 278–285
    architecture, 281–282
    arts, 282–282
    astronomy, 283–284
    inventions, 283–284
    literature, 282–283
    religion, 284–285
Tantrism, 271
Technology, stone age, new, 24–25
Tenochtitlan, 487–489
Teotihuacan, 241–242
Teutonic Knights, 450–451
Theodora, 309–312
Theodosius, 218–219
Tiberius, 205
Tigris-Euphrates Valley, 34
    Assyrians, 101–102
Toltecs, 381–382
Tools, 7
Torah, 105
Tower of Babel, 36
Tran dynasty, 417–418

Triumvirate, 197
Turks, 264–266, 396–397, 422
Tutankhamen, 62

Ugarit, 45
Umayyad Caliphate, 259–262, 358
University, 438
Upanishads, 122–123
Ur, 35
Uruk, 35

Vassals, 336
Vietnam, 150, 294, 417–418
Viking Raiders, 333–335
Visigoths, 217, 219–220, 312

War of the Roses, 464
Wheels, development of, 38
White Lotus Society, 411
William the Conqueror, 360–361, 443
Wine trade, 83–84
Witchcraft, 461–462, 476–477
Women:
    African empires, 423–424
    Byzantine, 315–316
    Incan, 491–492
    Islamic, 262
    late middle ages, 476–477
    medieval Europe, 368–369
    Song dynasty, 286
Writing, development of, 37

Xia dynasty, 77–78
Xunzi, 142

Yahweh, 105–106
Yangshao, 76
Yangtze River, 75
Yellow River, 75
Yi dynasty, 417
Yoga, 271
Yoruba, 426
Yu the Great, 77–78

Zen, 291
Zhou period, 139–140
Ziggurat, 36

Made in the USA
Lexington, KY
09 May 2016